FOCUS: MUSIC
NORTHEAST BRAZIL

CW01021402

Focus: Music of Northeast Brazil examines the historical and contemporary manifestations of the music of Brazil, a country with a musical landscape that is layered with complexity and diversity. Based on the author's field research during the past twenty years, the book describes and analyzes the social and historical contexts and contemporary musical practices of Afro-Brazilian religion, selected Carnival traditions, Bahia's black cultural renaissance, the traditions of rural migrants, and currents in new popular music.

- Part I, *Understanding Music in Brazil,* presents important issues and topics that encompass all of Brazil, and provides a general survey of Brazil's diverse musical landscape.
- Part II, *Creating Music in Brazil,* presents historical trajectories and contemporary examples of Afro-Brazilian traditions, Carnival music, and northeastern popular music.
- Part III, *Focusing In,* presents two case studies that explore the ground-level activities of contemporary musicians in northeast Brazil and the ways in which they move between local, national, and international realms.

The accompanying CD offers vivid musical examples that are discussed in the text, with special attention given to the ways in which folk and popular music from the rich northeastern region has been used to construct complex dimensions of race in articulating Brazilian regional and national identities.

Larry Crook is Professor of Music and Co-Director of the Center for World Arts at the University of Florida.

The Focus on World Music Series is designed specifically for area courses in world music and ethnomusicology. Written by the top ethnomusicologists in their field, the Focus books balance sound pedagogy with exemplary scholarship. Each book provides a telescopic view of the musics and cultures addressed, giving the reader a general introduction on the music and culture of the area and then zooming in on different musical styles with in-depth case studies.

Visit the companion website for this new edition:

www.routledge.com/textbooks/focusonworldmusic

This website includes further resources for both instructors and students.

FOCUS ON WORLD MUSIC

Series Editor: Michael B. Bakan

Focus: Music of European Nationalism
Second Edition
Philip V. Bohlman

Focus: Music of South Africa
Second Edition
Carol A. Muller

Focus: Gamelan Music of Indonesia
Second Edition
Henry Spiller

Focus: Music of Northeast Brazil
Second Edition
Larry Crook

FOCUS:
MUSIC OF
NORTHEAST BRAZIL

Second Edition

Larry Crook

University of Florida

Routledge
Taylor & Francis Group

NEW YORK AND LONDON

First edition published 2005 by ABC-CLIO, Inc.
This edition published 2009
by Routledge
270 Madison Ave, New York, NY 10016

Simultaneously published in the UK
by Routledge
2 Park Square, Milton Park, Abingdon, Oxon OX14 4RN

Routledge is an imprint of the Taylor & Francis Group, an informa business

Typeset in Minion by
Swales & Willis Ltd, Exeter, Devon
Printed and bound in the United States of America on acid-free paper by
Sheridan Books, Inc

Library of Congress Cataloging in Publication Data
Crook, Larry.
Focus: Music of northeast Brazil/Larry Crook. – 2nd ed.
    p. cm. – (Focus on world music)
    Previous ed.: Santa Barbara, CA: ABC-CLIO, c2005, under title: Brazilian music.
    Includes bibliographical references, discography and index.
    1. Popular music–Brazil–History and criticism.   2. Popular music–Brazil,
Northeast–History and criticism.   I. Crook, Larry. Brazilian music.   II. Title.
    III. Title: Music of northeast Brazil.
    ML3487.B7C76 2008
    780.981'3--dc22   2008025193

ISBN10: 0–415–96066–5 (hbk)
ISBN10: 0–415–96065–7 (pbk)
ISBN10: 0–203–88652–6 (ebk)

ISBN13: 978–0–415–96066–3 (hbk)
ISBN13: 978–0–415–96065–6 (pbk)
ISBN13: 978–0–203–88652–6 (ebk)

Contents

Figures

Musical Examples

Musical Examples on Compact Disc

For additional information on each track, see the Appendix, pp. 243–58.

Series Foreword

The past decade has witnessed extraordinary growth in the areas of ethnomusicology and world music publishing. With the publication of both the ten-volume *Garland Encyclopedia of World Music* and the second edition of the *New Grove Dictionary of Music and Musicians* (2001), we now have access to general reference resources that ethnomusicologists and world music enthusiasts of even just a few years ago could only have dreamed of. University and other academic presses—Chicago, Oxford, Cambridge, Illinois, Temple, Wesleyan, Indiana, California, Routledge—have produced excellent ethnomusicological monographs, edited volumes, and smaller-scale reference works in ever-increasing numbers, many accompanied by CDs, DVDs, and other media that bring the musics described vividly to life. A host of new introductory-level textbooks for freshman/sophomore-level world music survey courses have come out too, along with new editions of long-established textbooks catering to that market. New instructional resources for teaching these same kinds of introductory survey courses have been created in addition, the Oxford Global Music Series perhaps most notable among them. Furthermore the Internet has of course revolutionized everything, with thousands upon thousands of web-based resources—from superb scholarly and educational resources such as Smithsonian Global Sound (www.smithsonianglobalsound.org) and *Grove Music Online* to the wild frontiers of YouTube and myriad commercial online music providers—all now available from your desktop at the click of a mouse.

Yet for all of this profuse and diverse publishing activity, there remains a conspicuous gap in the literature. We still lack a solid corpus of high-quality textbooks designed specifically for area courses in world music, ethnomusicology, and interdisciplinary programs with a strong music component. The need for such texts is greatest where courses for upper-division undergraduate and entry-level graduate students are taught, but it extends to courses at the freshman and sophomore levels as well, especially those enrolling music majors and other students who are serious and motivated.

What has been needed for such courses are books that balance sound pedagogy with exemplary scholarship, and that are substantive in content yet readily accessible to specialist and non-specialist readers alike. These books would be written in a lively and engaging style by leading ethnomusicologists and educators, bringing wide inter-disciplinary scope and relevance to the contemporary concerns of their readership. They would, moreover, provide a telescopic view of the musics and cultures they addressed, zooming in from broad-based surveys of expansive music-culture areas and topics toward compelling, in-depth case studies of specific musicultural traditions and their myriad transformations in the modern world.

This is precisely what Routledge's *Focus on World Music* series delivers, with books that are authoritative, accessible, pedagogically strong, richly illustrated, and accompanied by a compelling compact disc of musical examples linked integrally to the text. I am delighted to be part of the team that has brought this exciting and important series to fruition. I hope you enjoy reading these books as much as I have!

Michael B. Bakan
The Florida State University
Series Editor

Preface

The young Brazilians that I met while in college at the University of Texas in Austin in the early 1970s were from many different states in Brazil—some from Rio de Janeiro, others from São Paulo, a few from Rio Grande do Sul, and others from somewhere they described as the Northeast. The northeasterners spoke of their region of Brazil in particularly nostalgic terms that evoked bittersweet images of a dry interior, architecture from a colonial past, and a strong African presence. This was the area of the country, they said, where one could find the real Brazil. From that point on, I was intrigued with the Northeast region of Brazil.

By the time that I decided to undertake research for my dissertation in 1987, I had researched many aspects of Brazilian music and was drawn once again to the Northeast. I lived in the state of Pernambuco for eighteen months and traveled around the interior of the Northeast learning about the music of the fife-and-drum groups called bandas de pífanos. It was during this time that I befriended João do Pife, an amazing flute player from Caruaru, Pernambuco. Together with my wife, Sylvia, and young daughter, Vanessa, I became closely linked to João and his family. More than anyone else, João introduced me to the world of the Northeast and the life of common musicians in Brazil. He became one of the best friends I have ever had. Looking back on our friendship and our many hours together talking and playing music, I realize that it was João who gave me the greatest appreciation and love for Brazilian culture from the Northeast.

Why a Book Focusing on the Music of Northeastern Brazil?

Writing a book on Brazilian music presents many challenges. Brazil is a country with approximately 175 million inhabitants and—like the United States—has a musical landscape that is layered with complexity and diversity. An attempt to cover all of Brazil's musical activity evenly would result in a rather superficial survey; to appreciate Brazilian society, its people, and its music, we must delve deeper. This book emphasizes musical traditions of Brazil that I know best, from my own personal interactions with Brazilian musicians. The centrality of the Northeast and its musical traditions in the social imagination of the modern Brazilian nation is a recurring theme in the book. Like so many Brazilians have done in the past, we can discover in the musical traditions associated with the Northeast the musical heartbeat that has helped create and sustain the modern, ever-changing Brazilian nation. In the Northeast are the roots of many of the patterns of social, cultural, and racial interaction that have come to characterize Brazilian society. Chief among these has been the notion that the racial and cultural mixture of the country's African, European, and indigenous peoples is at the core of Brazilian identity. In Brazil's long history, music and racial identification have been continuously linked. In fact, music is one of the prime cultural markers informing notions of racial identity and heritage in Brazil. *Music of Northeast Brazil* investigates the many ways in which Brazilians have used music as a powerful tool in crafting their identities. To appreciate modern Brazilian society, its diverse musical culture, and the special role of northeastern traditions in the country, we must delve deep into this vast and complex land.

Music of Northeast Brazil was written to be accessible to a wide range of readers and can be used in interdisciplinary area studies courses (upper-division undergraduate and entry-level graduate) as well as in more specialized courses focusing specifically on music. The telescoping nature of the three-part structure of the book—moving from an overview of Brazil, its music, and broad topics to increasingly focused explorations of specific musical traditions with selected in-depth case studies—provides the broad contexts and concrete examples in which to think about and understand local and global realities of Brazilian music. Each chapter includes boxed inserts that serve to amplify specific topics and events without interrupting the readability of the text. In addition, timelines are provided to help students conceptualize the materials presented within a historical framework.

Organization

This book is divided into seven chapters, which are grouped into three parts. Part I "Understanding Music in Brazil" (Chapters 1 and 2) is broad in scope, presents important issues and topics that encompass all of Brazil, and provides a general survey of Brazil's diverse musical landscape. Chapter 1 discusses the history of Brazil as a country divided into two complementary domains and conceptual realms: a modern and industrialized South and an old and rural Northeast. Focusing on the historical importance of the Northeast, I explore how the conceptualization of racial mixture in Brazil led to a complex, hybrid culture in the country. Appreciating the complexities of racial identification in Brazil is fundamental to an understanding of how music has been used to both support and contest the idea that Brazil is a racially egalitarian society. Chapter 2 surveys many of Brazil's musical styles and describes some the country's most important and unique musical instruments. As an example of a uniquely Brazilian instrument, I describe the *pandeiro* (Brazilian tambourine) and its importance in Brazilian music.

Part II "Creating Music in Brazil" (Chapters 3, 4, 5) presents historical trajectories and contemporary examples of Afro-Brazilian traditions, Carnival music from Recife, and northeastern popular music. Each of these chapters links music making to issues of racial identification, racial mixture, and national identity. Chapter 3 delves into Afro-Brazilian traditions of the Candomblé religion and its impact on the development of Carnival music from the cities of Salvador da Bahia and Recife, Pernambuco. Chapter 4 traces the history of frevo, a Brazilian Carnival music founded on the notion of the racial and cultural mixture between Europeans and Africans. Chapter 5 deals with popular music rooted in the rural traditions of the northeastern backlands and analyzes the importance of this music in articulating a regional component of Brazilian national identity.

Part III "Focusing In: Intimate Portraits and the Reinvention of Brazilian Music" (Chapters 6 and 7) explores the ground-level activities of contemporary musicians in Northeast Brazil and the ways in which they move between local, national, and international realms. Chapter 6 presents case studies of two musical traditions typically associated with rural interior regions of the Northeast: *bandas de pífanos* (fife and drum bands) and *cantoria de viola* (improvised sung poetry accompanied by the guitar-like *viola*). Chapter 7 explores contemporary urban popular music from the cities of Salvador and Recife. Since the 1970s in Salvador, musicians have developed a dynamic new Carnival music that questions the idea that Brazil is a racial democracy. Highlighting transnational African identities for the black community of Salvador, the musicians and their music became part of the world music scene in the 1990s. In Recife, an eclectic popular music style called *mangue beat* grew out of the re-examination of local musical traditions in the context of global pop influences. Recife's musicians remixed venerable local traditions while simultaneously engaging with national and global contexts of musical production.

Supplements

The accompanying CD features selections exemplifying much of the music described in the text. Most of the tracks on the CD come from recordings that I made in Brazil from 1987 to 2006. Others are from commercially released recordings in Brazil. Information about the recordings, the contexts in which the recordings were made, the performers who played on them, and transcriptions and translations of the lyrics are provided in the Appendix. A website for the book was created to assist student and teacher with discussion topics, reading and listening guides, and links to additional text, audio, and video resources. The book's companion website can be found at **www.routledge.com/text books/focusonworldmusic**.

Changes to the Second Edition

Michael Bakan first asked me to participate in the *World Music Series* published by ABC-CLIO. The second edition, now titled *Music of Northeast Brazil* is part of the *Focus on World Music Series* with Routledge. It includes all material from the first edition, updated with new information to reflect recent developments and to correct errors from the first edition. I have reworked the book into the telescoping model of the series by broadening the scope of the first two chapters and shifting the order of the subsequent chapters. I added an extended discussion of the Brazilian tambourine titled "The Brazilian Pandeiro Then and Now" in Chapter 2, which is accompanied by an additional sound example (track 3) on the accompanying CD. The addition of timelines for each chapter and the companion website make the book more accessible and user-friendly for student and teacher.

Acknowledgments

The writing of this book would not have been possible without the help of a great many people and the support of several institutions. I conducted the bulk of the research for the manuscript during two extended trips to Brazil. The first was an eighteen-month field research trip from January 1987 to June 1988, with funding from a Fulbright-Hayes Fellowship grant, while I was a pursuing a PhD in ethnomusicology at the University of Texas. The second was an eight-month trip from August 2000 to April 2001, with a sabbatical award from the University of Florida. In addition, I have made numerous shorter trips to Brazil with the assistance of research funding from the University of Florida's Office of Research and Graduate Education, Fine Arts Scholarship Enhancement Fund, and the Center for Latin American Studies. I gratefully acknowledge all of this support.

I owe my academic mentor and longtime friend, Gerard Béhague, an enormous debt of gratitude for sparking my initial interests in both musical scholarship and Brazilian music. It was through his patient guidance and friendship that I came to dedicate my professional career to the study of Brazilian music. I will forever be thankful. I am also indebted to three of my other teachers at the University of Texas: Greg Urban, Steven Feld, and Stephen Slawek. To all three, I say thank you for guiding me through my studies and helping me grow intellectually.

My travels in Brazil and my understanding of its culture have been facilitated by many colleagues, friends, and teachers. Thank you Anthony Seeger, Ralph Waddey, José Jorge de Carvalho, and John Murphy for providing me with valuable personal contacts in Brazil. Thank you Charles Perrone, Randal Johnson, and Welson Tremura for conversations, musical collaborations, and valuable insights into Brazilian music and culture. Thank you to my many friends and collaborators in Brazil, who have given enormous help to me and to my family and whose ideas and experiences animate the pages of this book: Alexandrino and Edleuza Rocha, Bernardo Aguiar, Marcos Suzano, Scott Feiner, Jorginho do Pandeiro, Celsinho Silva, Oscar Bolão, João do Pife (João Alfredo da Silva), Nilza da Silva, Biu do Pife (Severino Pedro da Silva), Tavares da Gaita (José Tavares da Silva), Carlos Malta, Luiz Guimarães, Hugo Martins, Sérgio Gusmão, José Menezes, Adelson Pereira da Silva, Duda, Edmilson Ferreira, Antônio Lisboa, Jorge Martins, Kleber Magrão, Guga Santos, Spok (Inaldo Cavalcanti), Mamão (Luciano Ricardo Maciel da Silva), Dona Elda (Elda Ivo Viana de Lira) and Shacon (Shacon Viana) of Nação Porto Rico do Oriente, Siba (Sérgio Veloso), Tote Gira (Antonio Santos), Jelon Vieira, Lula de Oiyá, José Amaro Santos da Silva, Antônio do Nascimento, Carlos Sandroni, Renato Phaelante, Zé da Flauta, Severino Alfredo dos Santos, Neguinho do Samba (Antonio Luís Alves de Souza), João Prosidono de Oliveira, José Arruda de

Oliveira, Marivaldo do Ilê, Antônio Carlos dos Santos, Jefferson Bacelar, João Jorge Santos Rodrigues, Marco César, and Valéria Moraes. There are many others as well.

Michael Bakan has been insightful, diligent, and timely as series editor for both first and second editions of the book. Thank you, Michael. I am grateful to Alicia Merritt at ABC-CLIO, who provided expertise and patience in shepherding this project through the publication of the first edition. For the second edition I wish to acknowledge the help of Denny Tek and the editorial expertise of Constance Ditzel at Routledge.

I wish to thank my parents, Norman and Ruby Crook, and my brother, David Crook, for a lifetime of unconditional love and support. Finally, my greatest thanks and deepest gratitude are reserved for Sylvia, Vanessa, and Alexander, who have been with me daily as I planned, researched, wrote, and prepared the second edition of this book.

PART **I**

Understanding Music in Brazil

"Understanding Music in Brazil" investigates broad historical, cultural, and social contexts in which the diversity of music in Brazil can be located and understood. The Northeast region of Brazil comes into focus as central to understanding contemporary cultural patterns that characterize Brazil and its music. In Chapter 1, the history of Brazilian thoughts on race, on miscegenation, and on the interplay of music and racial identity are examined in relation to the development of Brazil in the nineteenth century as a modern nation divided into two conceptual realms: an old and traditional Northeast and young and progressive South. Chapter 2 builds on the notions that diversity and hybridity are key characteristics of Brazilian culture and presents a survey of musical instruments and traditions of music from throughout Brazil while highlighting the important role that music from the Northeast has played in creating the image of the modern nation of Brazil. Special attention is given to the importance of Carnival as a context for music making and to the uniquely Brazilian percussion instrument, the *pandeiro*.

CHAPTER 1

Brazil: A Country Divided

Three Carnival Scenes from Recife, Pernambuco

Scene 1: Maracatu de Baque Virado

At first, I could only hear them. Then I felt the unrelenting, driving pulse swirl around and slowly engulf me. Before long, above the crowd, I could make out a royal banner swaying like a sailboat on the sea; billowing and twirling behind it was a huge parasol in vivid colors. The entire crowd was moving in unison, like synchronized waves rolling onto a beach or ripples emanating from a rock thrown into the center of a pond. Raw energy was palpable as the music gradually took possession of the entire street. Large drums were beaten in a simple yet bewildering pattern. Then the sounds seemed to get even closer. All of a sudden, my perception of the music shifted entirely. Like tuning into a radio station, the signal became clear. "Oh, I get it!" I thought to myself. Dancing, drumming, and singing all converged into one hard-driving groove. A young man, swept by in a current of revelers, shouted, "Ma-ra-ca-tu" (Mah-rock-ah-too).

The banner of the group boldly proclaimed "Nação Porto Rico do Oriente" (Nation of the Rich Port of the East). Under the spinning parasol was a regal couple who looked to me to be Africans in royal European attire—an ebony black king and a queen of this Porto Rico nation elaborately dressed in Louis XV costumes. There were also princes and princesses, dukes and duchesses, ambassadors, court ladies carrying small black dolls, Roman centurions, matronly black women dressed in flowing white skirts, slaves, drummers, and singers. As the entourage took uncontested control of the area, the musicians commanded everyone's attention. Black drummers playing large, double-headed bass drums with thick skins dominated the scene with a military-like presence. Their bodies—arms, legs, torsos, and hips—moved in choreographed precision as they beat their drums with such intensity that I thought the skins would surely break. The

Figure 1.1 King and queen of the maracatu Nação Porto Rico do Oriente during Recife's Carnival, 2001 (photo by Larry Crook).

threat of danger flowed from the aggressiveness of their drumming. Close by was another row of performers, who tossed large, beaded gourds from side to side while one huge iron bell was being struck hard enough to dent an automobile fender. Suddenly, the entire row of drummers halted and then pounded out an intricately synchronized pattern in unison. Another stop and a singer's voice bellowed out above the crowd: "Nagô, Nagô! Our queen has been crowned; our king has come from Africa!" *Track 1* on the accompanying compact disc (CD) offers an example of a *maracatu* (a Carnival group from Recife, Pernambuco).

Scene 2: Bloco Carnavalesco

I pushed my way along the outskirts of the crowd, freeing myself as I ducked around a corner. I soon became aware of a sweet, lyric melody in a minor key; it floated above the elaborately decorated wooden sign that read "Bloco da Saudade" (Group of Longing). Everyone in the crowd seemed to know the words to the song, and they sang along with the strolling musicians playing guitars, mandolins, banjos, flutes, clarinets, tambourines, and other instruments. In front of the instrumentalists, a chorus of woman dressed in finely embroidered matching outfits, with looks of longing in their eyes, raised their hands high above their heads and sang "Alegre Bando."

Partial lyrics from "Alegre Bando" ("Happy Band"), a marcha de bloco by Edgard Moraes

Abram alas, queridos foliões
Que vai passar o alegre bando,
Trazendo mil recordações,
Deixando o povo com prazer cantando
A canção que faz lembrar
Passados carnavais das fantasias tradicionais

English translation:

Open the wings, dear Carnival revelers
Because the lively group is passing by
Bringing thousands of memories
Leaving people joyful as they sing
The song that makes them remember
Past Carnivals of traditional costumes

Both the lilting melody and these lyrics calmed the sea of humanity filling the street as everyone young and old sang of the glories of past Carnivals and the memories of departed friends and family members.

Partial lyrics from "A Dor de uma Saudade" ("The Pain of Longing"), a marcha de bloco by Edgard Moraes

The pain of longing
Forever lives in my heart
Remembering someone who departed
Leaving a memory
Never more . . .
The good times that I witnessed in other Carnivals
Have to come back[1]

Most of the string and wind instrumentalists performed the melody with the singers while a few others strummed simple chords on their guitars. Between the singing of verses, instruments played the sweet melodies together, in unison. The group looked and acted like an extended family that was coming together for its annual reunion. The olive-colored skin and facial features of the people made me think that their ancestors had once lived in southern Europe; perhaps they were Mediterranean in origin. In front of me, members of the older generation were instructing the children to behave and to join them in singing songs. Young couples with babies in their arms danced gracefully down the street just ahead. There were also teenage girls and boys, who grouped themselves together and moved off to the side to sing and dance. The whole experience seemed like a dream to me. Track 2 ("Alegre Bando") on the CD suggests the feel of this music.

Scene 3: Caboclinho

I heard the wooden clacking of yet another group that was approaching with a fast-paced rhythm of light drumming and the melody of a high-pitched flute or whistle of some sort. Within a couple of minutes, the street was filled with two lines of quickly moving dancers costumed like tropical forest Indians in thousands of yellow, blue, green, and red feathers. The dancers carried short bows and arrows, which they played like percussion instruments: "clack-clack-clack-clack." Almost all members of this group were dark-skinned and appeared to be in their teens or early twenties. The men, as well as some of the women, were bare-chested. The dancing was intricate, and the dancers moved quickly in the crowded area, creating a dance space out of the narrow street. Pairs of male and female dancers performed short choreographed vignettes in front of the entire group, eliciting whoops and hollers from the onlookers. A banner identified the group as a *caboclinho*

Figure 1.2 Members of a Bloco das Flores in Recife's Carnival, 2001 (photo by Larry Crook).

(little Indian group). Some of the members wore extremely elaborate headpieces that were 3 to 4 feet tall and equally as wide and rose high above the crowd. An Indian chief and his queen were there, as well as Indian princesses, a shamanic medicine man, and many warriors.

At last came the musicians. They were also dressed in costumes depicting tropical forest Indians from the Amazon, with headpieces, wrist and ankle bands, and short skirts all made of colorful feathers and natural fibers. Their instruments were simple: a flute, a small drum, and metal shakers. The flutist blew into the end of his instrument, which looked home-made and had only four finger holes. He played short, repeating melodies, and the other musicians followed after him as if he were the Pied Piper of Hamelin. The small drum had two skins that were tuned very tightly. Across the top skin were stretched two strings, which produced a buzzing sound when the skin was struck: "buzz-da-duh, buzz-da-duh, buzz-da-duh." Finally came the metal shakers. They looked like medieval weapons of torture and featured a circle of short tubes with a geometric arrangement of sharp metal cones on both ends. The percussionist whirled around as he played them in non-stop fashion. His playing reminded me of a fitness workout: arms in full motion, deep knee bends, leg kicks in perfect timing to the music.

Figure 1.3
Caboclinho dancer performing in Recife's Carnival, 2001 (photo by Larry Crook).

Locating Brazil and Its Diverse Musical Culture

The three Carnival scenes I have just described provide glimpses into the diverse nature of music within Brazil. I encountered these and many other musical traditions in 2001 while participating in that year's Carnival in the city of Recife, in Northeast Brazil. In this book we will explore Brazil's complex musical landscape and locate patterns of social and cultural interactions among its people that have come to characterize Brazilian society. As we investigate the important role music has played in the ways Brazilians think about racial identity and miscegenation (racial mixture), we will consider the enduring national narrative dividing the country into two contrasting yet complementary realms: a traditional Northeast and a modernized South. Beginning with broad topics and contexts and then moving to increasingly focused explorations of specific musical traditions featuring intimate profiles of contemporary musicians, we will think about local and global realities of Brazilian music. Throughout the book, our emphasis will be on Northeastern music and its role as the creative heartbeat that continues to pump life-giving blood to the Brazilian nation as it helps sustain its people. In this chapter, I will explain my own involvement with Brazil and its music and then explore how the ideas on racial mixture in Brazil have led to a complex, hybrid culture in the country.

I first became interested in Brazilian music in the 1970s while I was an undergraduate music student at the University of Texas at Austin. Austin was a thriving music town, known widely in those days for its progressive country music scene and its world-famous Armadillo World Headquarters. Live music seemed to be everywhere, and the local community supported a diversity of musical scenes, including classical, rock, blues, jazz, and a variety of Latino styles. I played drums and percussion in several Austin jazz and rock groups and often collaborated with Latin musicians in the area. At the university, I met a number of Brazilian students who wanted to form a Brazilian batucada percussion group to play samba for an upcoming Brazilian-style Carnival party. Using some old marching band drums and a few Brazilian instruments, we rehearsed a handful of the basic rhythmic patterns and learned some of the well-known Brazilian songs. Among these were marches such as "Cidade Maravilhosa"; others were sambas such as "Festa pra um Rei Negro." Ours was not a highly "professional" music group. In fact, most of the members were students studying for careers in business and other profitable professions. I was the only music major among the group. My new Brazilian friends were interested in showing me how to play the samba, and as I struggled to learn the patterns, I remember that one of them said something like, "You just have to have fun with it, play with it." The music was infectious, and I was immediately hooked. That is when I first became a "Brazil nut."

Eventually I found myself living in Recife, a large city in the state of Pernambuco, located at the very tip of northeastern Brazil, where the South American continent extends the farthest east into the Atlantic Ocean. Carnival is Brazil's largest public festival, and participating in four days and nights of non-stop music and dance is an experience like no other. However, there is not just one Brazilian Carnival; Brazil is a land of many Carnivals, with towns and cities throughout the country holding distinct yearly celebrations. The most celebrated Carnival in the country comes from the city of Rio de Janeiro in southern Brazil. Scenes of Rio's elaborate parades—full of scantily clad dancing women (and some near-nude men dressed as women), hundreds of musicians, and ornate floats—are broadcast to televisions throughout the world each year. The three scenes I described from the less-known Carnival of Recife do not offer the same kind of images that television broadcasts export out of the country as Brazilian Carnival. Our perceptions of Brazilian Carnival, Brazilian musical culture, and Brazil itself have been shaped, in large part, by the broadcast, recording, print, and electronic media that circulate internationally.

If we grew up in North America, we might imagine an Amazonian rainforest with strange insects, animals, and tropical plants when we think of Brazil. There might be a Brazilian Indian in a dugout canoe negotiating his way through an exotic river, with man-eating piranhas swimming alongside. Perhaps we will recall documentaries on television depicting the ceremonial songs and dances of indigenous peoples living in the Amazon. Some of us might have heard of bossa nova and remember the song "The Girl from Ipanema," a lyrical fantasy about a beautiful tall and tan girl walking down the Ipanema beach in Rio de Janeiro. Travelogue films of Brazil typically feature images of palm trees, beaches, and tanned bodies, with a soundtrack of bossa nova quietly playing in the background. Those of us with long memories may think of the Brazilian singer Carmen Miranda and her "tutti-frutti" hat, made internationally famous by Hollywood movies in the 1940s. Singing and acting on the silver screen, Miranda was invariably depicted as a hot-blooded Latin American temptress inviting viewers to go the "South American way"; she conquered the United States like no other Latin American entertainer ever has.[2] If we were watching Cable News Network (CNN) on a February evening a while back, we might have witnessed the glittery spectacle of the samba parades in downtown Rio de Janeiro. Hundreds of drummers and dancers lined the parade venue as elaborate floats came close behind, transporting dozens of other musicians and costumed revelers. Watching Carnival from Rio de Janeiro on our own televisions, we may have been swept up in the bacchanalian exuberance of the predominantly dark-skinned people propelled by the fast and furious samba rhythms. These are a few of the images and sounds of Brazil and its musical culture that have been dispatched, like postcards, throughout the world. However, there is much more to Brazil and its culture than these images might suggest. The musical and cultural diversity of Latin America's largest nation is astounding, and describing the many musical traditions of Brazil could fill dozens of books.

Brazil's musical culture has something for everyone. The country's best-known music and musicians come from the cosmopolitan urban environs of the South, especially from the city of Rio de Janeiro. Brazil's famous Rock in Rio Festival, for instance, drew over 1 million fans for its inaugural seven-day program of megaconcerts in 1985, featuring home-grown Brazilian rock bands as well as international acts. Sepultura, a Brazilian heavy-metal band from Minas Gerais (now based out of Phoenix, Arizona), has an avid following of fans throughout the world. Without any doubt, Brazil's most celebrated music is the samba. Since the 1930s, the samba has been synonymous with Brazilian music and with the country's national identity across the globe. In Brazil, the term *samba* designates a set of related folk and popular music styles found throughout the country, but it was the urban samba as developed in Rio de Janeiro that was popularized nationally in the 1930s and then exported around the world in the 1940s. Two decades later, the cool and intimate sounds of bossa nova emerged among the upper-middle-class artist–intellectuals of Rio de Janeiro's affluent beachfront neighborhoods. Bossa nova's bohemian musicians had an affinity for both samba and jazz, and their music quickly became an international fad, especially among North American and European audiences. In the realm of art music, one of the world's greatest composers of the twentieth-century was Heitor Villa-Lobos, a native of Rio de Janeiro. International travels and concerts featuring his music cemented the exalted position of Villa-Lobos alongside the most prominent European and American composers and made him *the* Brazilian composer of the twentieth century.

These musicians and musical styles mentioned thus far come from the urban areas of southern Brazil and reflect, in different ways, the cosmopolitan and international images of the country that have been spread around the world. Less known internationally are the musical styles and cultural traditions from the Northeast region of the country, where

Figure 1.4 Map of Brazil showing its major states and cities.

Brazil's earliest colonial activities first flourished more than 400 years ago. It is this "other Brazil"—the Brazil of the Northeast, with the major colonial urban centers of Salvador da Bahia and Recife, Pernambuco, on the tropical Atlantic coast and a vast rural region in the interior known as the *sertão*—that today's Brazilians perceive as the wellspring of their country's "authentic" national character and the home of its "purest" traditional culture and music. The Northeast is where the Portuguese New World experiment in the tropics first began and where the unique set of Brazilian social habits developed. It was also in the hot tropical climate of the Northeast that the Portuguese initially intermixed with Africans and Amerindians (indigenous peoples of the Americas) to produce the first "Brazilians" and to forge Brazil's characteristic hybrid culture. This view of the Northeast as the "old" and traditional area of the country, as an area culturally distinct from the modern and cosmopolitan South, is a rather recent development in the way Brazilians understand their country. The conceptualization of the country as two complementary halves, one "modern" (the South) and the other "traditional" (the Northeast), began to take shape during Brazil's transition from a colonial society to an independent modern nation in the nineteenth century. In the twentieth century, the Northeast region increasingly came to represent the country's rich folkloric past in the context of Brazil's overarching nationalist enterprise that required the creation of a national consensus culture to link the entire country. Music was an extremely important component of this enterprise, and Brazilian musicians consistently turned to the cultural traditions of the Northeast in their quest to create "authentic" Brazilian musical styles for the nation.

Brazil is an immense nation with a population estimated at 175 million and a territory of more than 3 million square miles (roughly half the landmass of the South American continent). In both size and population, it is the largest nation in South America. Many people are surprised to learn that Portuguese (the official language of Brazil) is as common in South America as Spanish. Within Brazil's national borders, there are dramatic contrasts in the physical landscape:

- Lush tropical rainforests in the enormous Amazonian basin
- Arid, drought-prone scrubland in the sertão of the Northeast interior
- Grassy prairies in the far south
- Floodplains and swamplands in the *pantanal* of the central west
- The huge waterfalls of Iguaçu where Brazil, Paraguay, and Argentina come together
- A coastline stretching thousands of miles along the Atlantic Ocean.

Although there are vast hinterlands that are sparsely populated, Brazil also has some of the world's most congested urban areas. Its largest cities are found in the southern half of the country. They are enormous. The city of São Paulo is South America's leading financial and industrial center and has an estimated population of around 18 million inhabitants. Rio de Janeiro is Brazil's entertainment capital and boasts a population of close to 10 million within its metropolitan area. These cities are thousands of miles and worlds away from the Amazonian rainforests. Brazil is populated primarily by the descendants of Europeans (Portuguese), Africans (from West and Central Africa), and native Amerindians from the lowlands of South America. Europeans and Africans first inhabited this part of the world in the 1500s. Miscegenation (the mixture of the races) and cultural interaction among these three populations led to a complex mix of peoples and cultures in Brazil's colonial period. Immigration since the mid-1800s has made today's Brazil an even more complex, multiracial, and pluriethnic society, with large minority communities of Italian, Japanese, Slavic, Arabic, and Jewish peoples. Racial and cultural mixture among these peoples is one of the defining characteristics of Brazilian society.

In contemporary Brazil, one can observe the complex nature of racial mixture by walking down the street of almost any city or town. Every conceivable variation of skin color and physical features seems to be present. Carnival season is a time when the racial heritage of the country and its hybrid cultural traditions are displayed constantly. Urban Carnival groups such as those described in the beginning scenes of this chapter often depict African, Amerindian, and European heritage not only through visual means such as costuming but also through musical styles and the use of specific musical instruments. For instance, the association of feathered headdresses and flutes with Amerindian culture is a widespread stereotype in Brazil. During Carnival in Brazilian cities, it is often black and mixed-race Brazilians, not Amerindians, who play flutes and wear headdresses evoking Amerindian heritage. Similarly, black Carnival groups incorporate elements of historical European costuming in their presentations, as with the maracatu in Recife. There, although the Louis XV-inspired royal vestments are part of the visual presentation of the group, the style of the participatory drumming, singing, and dancing is closely associated with African heritage. Brazilian cultural heritage, like racial identification in the country, is mixed, complex, and diverse. Nowhere is this situation more evident than in the Brazilian Northeast.

Chronology of Selected Events in Brazilian History and Culture

1500	Pedro Alvares Cabral lands on the coast of Northeast Brazil
1549	Salvador da Bahia designated as capital of Brazil
1580–1640	Portugal and Brazil under Spanish rule
1624–1654	Dutch take control of Northeast Brazil
1666	First written description of the coronation of a "black king" (Rei de Angola) in Brazil
1695	Death of Zumbi, last leader of the Palmares in northeastern Brazil
1763	Capital of Brazil transferred from Salvador da Bahia to Rio de Janeiro
1808	Portuguese royal family and court transferred to Rio de Janeiro; Royal Press and Royal Library founded
1822	Brazilian declaration of independence from Portugal and the establishment of the Brazilian Empire with coronation of Pedro I
1831	Establishment of the National Guard Bands
1844	First Carnival masquerade ball held in Brazil (Rio de Janeiro)
1888	Lei Aúria ("Golden Law") passed by the Brazilian parliament and signed by Princess Isabela, establishes the total abolition of slavery
1889	Proclamation of the Republic of Brazil
1896–97	Rebellion in Canudos, Bahia

1902	First sound recordings made in Brazil (Rio de Janeiro)
1905	African-inspired Carnival practices banned in Bahia
1916	Release of "Pelo Telefone," generally acknowledged as the first samba in Brazil to be recorded
1922	Semana de Arte Moderna (Week of Modern Art) held in São Paulo energizing the modernist movement in Brazil; Pixinguinha and Os Oito Batutas perform in Paris
1928	Deixa Falar (Let Them Speak), the first escola de samba (samba school) is organized in the Estácio neighborhood of Rio de Janeiro
1933	*Casa Grande e Senzala* (The Masters and the Slaves) by Gilberto Freyre is published
1937	Coup d'etat installs Getúlio Vargas as dictator and establishes the Estado Novo
1946	Recording of "Baião" by Luiz Gonzaga and Humberto Texeira released by Quatro Ases e um Coringa
1960	Brasília inaugurated as the new capital and Federal District of Brazil
1964	Military coup in Brazil
1974	Ilê Aiyê, Bahia's first bloco afro founded
1988	Brazil celebrates the centenary of the abolition of slavery

Dividing a Nation and Marginalizing a Region

Over the course of the eighteenth century, political and economic power in the Brazilian colony shifted from the northeastern coastal area to the southern and south-central regions of the country. During the following century, Brazil progressed from a colony to an empire to a republic. From the nineteenth century on, Brazilians increasingly conceptualized their country as one divided into northeastern and southern regions, each area endowed with distinct attributes and characteristics. The notion of the indelible differences between the South (as culturally progressive, industrialized, and modern) and the Northeast (as culturally conservative, rural, and traditional) was an important part of the way in which Brazil emerged as a modern nation. In the South, Rio de Janeiro became both the political and the cultural center of the country, whereas São Paulo developed into the industrial engine that drove the country's economy. Casting their collective gaze northward, southern Brazilians viewed their northeastern cousins as representatives of an old social order whose backward lifestyles and cultural patterns anchored Brazil to its agrarian past and its colonial slave era. Seeking to modernize, Brazil's new urban middle and upper classes looked increasingly to Europe to provide models for the political, economic, and cultural development of the country. In the realm of culture, this modern enterprise included the adoption of European concert music and opera as well as salon dance genres such as the polka, waltz, and mazurka and many other cosmopolitan forms of leisure entertainment.

Woven into the conceptualization of national progress, which took hold firmly during the late nineteenth century, were theories of European racial and cultural superiority.

State-supported European immigration into southern Brazil in the nineteenth and early twentieth centuries served to "whiten" the South's population and highlight its racial and cultural distinctiveness from the Northeast, where African and mixed *caboclo* (European and Amerindian) bloodlines were generally assumed to prevail. In reality, Rio de Janeiro had become one of Brazil's primary entry ports for the slave trade during the eighteenth century. Additionally, the coffee boom in the South and the abolition of slavery in the late nineteenth century resulted in massive internal migrations of blacks and people of mixed races from the Northeast to the South. By the end of the nineteenth century, Rio de Janeiro had the largest urban concentration of blacks in the country. In São Paulo, the official state subsidy of foreign immigration (largely European) led to the de facto exclusion of blacks in the labor force in favor of white European immigrants.

At the same time that the white European immigrants were flooding the Brazilian labor force, music and other cultural practices from the Northeast were increasingly viewed as the source of Brazilian national essence in the early twentieth century. In effect, the Northeast became the ideological font for Brazilian culture, representing the traditional side of the nation, whereas the South became an ideological zone of technological innovation, progress, and modernization. The problematic and contradictory relationship that was established between the Northeast and the South reflected the intersection of the geographic and temporal dimensions that created the modern nation of Brazil. The conceptual tension between the old (traditional) and modern (progressive) spheres of the nation was thus mapped onto the geography of the country as two complementary halves (Northeast and South).

The Brazilian Northeast is typically defined as an area comprising eight or nine of Brazil's twenty-six states and some 20 percent of the country's population. In size and population, the region is larger than most other Latin American countries. The Northeast has been romanticized in literature, songs, and films and analyzed in numerous scholarly works. As Brazil emerged as a modern nation in the late nineteenth and early twentieth centuries, the northeastern region came to symbolize the society's colonial past and its most direct link to non-European cultural heritage. The coastal strip of the Northeast (especially the areas in and around the port city of Salvador da Bahia) was frequently depicted as the most "African" part of the country because of the tenacious survival of "exotic" African cultural practices in the region. Indeed, the city of Salvador is sometimes called Brazil's "Black Rome." It was there that African-based cultural retention was believed to be strongest. The search for African cultural survivals from the country's premodern past occupied the attention of many Brazilian folklorists, anthropologists, and musicologists. Not surprisingly, when the samba from Rio de Janeiro was elevated to the status of Brazil's "national rhythm" in the 1930s, the African roots of the music and dance became part of a national narrative. This narrative relates that the primitive impulses of the music and dance initially flourished in coastal northeastern culture during the colonial period; in the nineteenth century, black migrants from Bahia carried the samba to the South, especially into the urban environment of Rio de Janeiro. During the 1930s, all sectors of Brazilian society adopted and magically transformed it into the country's national music and dance. With roots in African heritage, the samba was championed as a national symbol of the country's racial and cultural mixture between Africans and Europeans.

In contrast to the view of the urban coastal Northeast as the country's most Africanized area, the dry sertão region of the northeastern interior provided modern Brazil with a powerful image of the country's agrarian past, where the miscegenation of Amerindian and Portuguese peoples had produced a mixed-race peasant population and culture. By the end of the nineteenth century, southern Brazilians viewed the northeastern sertão as a national "problem area," believing that geographic and climatic conditions had combined with racial and cultural heritage to retard its development and leave it centuries behind modern civilization. A series of severe droughts in the late nineteenth century led the federal government to define the eight-state Northeast region as a "drought polygon." During the Great Drought between 1877 and 1880, an estimated 250,000 people died and an equal number of poor caboclo peasants migrated out of the region. Newspaper accounts of the situation in the Northeast fed the growing curiosity of the urban middle and upper classes regarding the strange culture and folkways of the area. Press stories—mainly from southern newspapers in Rio de Janeiro and São Paulo—and popular literature created the image of the Northeast as a wild and uncivilized land where *cangaceiros* (bandits), *coronéis* (political strongmen), and fanatical religious leaders fought one another for physical and spiritual control of the backlands and their population.

Inventing the Sertão: Rebellion in the Backlands

The episode that crystallized popular national opinion regarding the backwardness of the Northeast was a messianic movement led by the Catholic mystic Antônio Conselheiro in the last decades of the nineteenth century. By the 1890s, Conselheiro had attracted some 15,000 to 25,000 followers to a settlement named Canudos deep in the backlands of Bahia. His followers—largely poor and landless caboclo peasants—were drawn to his ascetic image and his populist Christian message that the weak would inherit the earth. Local upper-class landowners in the area saw the sociorelgious movement as a threat to their rule (including their entitlement to cheap peasant labor) and urged state and federal forces to take action against Conselheiro and his community of followers in Canudos. Rumors and press reports describing Canudos as a hotbed of revolutionary sentiment prompted the government to send in the military to eradicate the Canudos "problem." It was rumored that Conselheiro was advocating an overthrow of the recently established Brazilian Republic and supported a return to monarchical rule in Brazil. A series of bloody assaults by the Brazilian army resulted in thousands of deaths among both Conselheiro's peasant followers and the government forces. At the time of this episode, one of Brazil's most celebrated writers, Euclides da Cunha (1866–1909), began his career as a newspaper reporter and was sent from São Paulo to cover the fighting at Canudos. Da Cunha's newpaper articles and later his widely read book *Os Sertões* (*Rebellion in the Backlands*, originally published in 1902) gave many southern Brazilians (and northeastern urban coastal dwellers) their first in-depth glimpse of the caboclo culture of the northeastern sertão. In *Os Sertões*, da Cunha provided his readers with an exotic image of the country's collective primordial past, rooted in the agrarian peasant culture of the Northeast. He described the typical northeastern caboclo as an adaptable, tenacious, and independent person and identified backland existence as the core of Brazilian national life and key to Brazil's national identity. His work confronted the public's notion of Brazilian progress and modernity (based on urban expansion, industrialization, and adherence to the latest European fashions) with a contrasting view of the traditional roots of their country embodied in the northeastern sertão and its inhabitants. In da Cunha's view, if the South represented the present and future of the country, the Northeast represented its past. The phenomenal success of *Os Sertoes* helped create an image of the Northeast as a region separated in both time and space from the "civilized" South. It also helped solidify the Northeast as the location where the roots of the modern Brazilian nation would be found.[3]

Writer Ariano Suassuna is an intellectual champion of the notion that the sertão and its music should be regarded as the most authentic source for Brazilian cultural identity. He noted (my translation):

> The music of the *sertão* developed around rhythms that are guarded by tradition. External influences have not penetrated the area since its pastoral period, and it [the music] has remained a collective archaic survival, maintained heroically by the common people. The music of that region is the result of the fusion of Iberian music with the primitive melodies of the Indians, whose *mameluco* descendents [the offsprings of Amerindian and European parentage] comprise almost the entire population of the *sertão*.[4]

As articulated by this writer, the musical traditions of the sertão represented archaic elements of Brazilian culture preserved in their pristine state since the early times of the colonial period. This notion was more than merely an elitist perception that located the northeastern interior as a cultural preserve for the agrarian, folkloric past of the country rooted in European and Amerindian mixture. It was also a powerful idea that resonated at all levels of society throughout Brazil and served as a cultural counterpoint to the strong sense of African and European mixture based in the coastal Northeast. Soon after the samba from Rio de Janeiro was adopted as Brazil's de facto official music and the nation's cultural symbol of African and European blending, Luiz Gonzaga, an aspiring musician from the sertão, popularized northeastern country-style music from his homeland to national audiences through radio broadcasts and recordings in the 1940s and 1950s. Gonzaga and his northeastern music, known as *baião,* provided a regional style of popular music that evoked authentic rural Brazilian caboclo culture for the nation and served as a counterbalance to the urban samba from Rio de Janeiro. Although the samba symbolized the country's African and European cultural mixture, Gonzaga's baião symbolized the country's Amerindian and Portuguese synthesis. The samba and the baião worked in tandem to establish the symbolic cultural reference points for the modern nation of Brazil. In both cases, the idea of miscegenation (racial and cultural) played a vital role in the popularity and marketing of these forms of music among the Brazilian public.

The Roots of a Miscegenated Society: Amerindian, African, and European Heritage in Brazil

Brazil is perhaps the most miscegenated society in the world. Extensive interracial mixing, social relations, and cultural hybridity among peoples of European, African, and Amerindian heritage characterized both the initial process of colonization under Portuguese rule and the later development of Brazil as an independent modern nation. Social imagination regarding racial and cultural mixing has also been a powerful force in defining Brazil's national character. The initial patterns of social interaction and economic relations among the races were established during the slave era in colonial times, particularly in the Northeast territory of the country. The enormous influence of African civilizations on Brazil (especially from the Congo–Angola and Yoruba–Fon areas of Central and West Africa) is often attributed to the Portuguese colonizers' easy acceptance of cultural practices transmitted by the Africans they enslaved.[5] The historical interaction of the Portuguese with peoples from the African continent well before they colonized Brazil prepared them for a multiracial society in the tropics.

Prior to the accidental landing in eastern South America of the Portuguese explorer Pedro Alves Cabral (in April 1500), the territory now known as Brazil was populated by an estimated 2.4 million Amerindians of various groups who spoke numerous indigenous languages and maintained rich cultural heritages. The first Amerindians to interact with the Portuguese, French, and Dutch strangers were the Tupi-speaking peoples who inhabited the coastal areas. Their encounters were friendly at first but rapidly turned hostile as the Portuguese began exploiting the natural resources of the land for European commerce and employing church and crown to achieve economic, political, and religious objectives in the colony. At first, the Northeast coastal area was exploited for hardwood extraction; then, it was developed as one of the world's leading regions for the production of sugarcane. In time, Brazilian territory would also provide European markets with tobacco, cotton, coffee, and precious metals. Many native communities were destroyed, and their inhabitants fled to the interior to get away from European influence. Enslavement, forced relocations, systematic genocide, and European diseases for which they had developed no immunities combined to reduce the native people in Brazilian lands to a little over an estimated 1 million by the early 1800s. Today, only some 100,000 native Brazilians remain.

When native Amerindian populations refused to submit to Portugal's authority and proved unreliable as labor sources, the Portuguese turned quickly to Africa. Between roughly 1550 and 1810, over 5 million Africans, primarily from Central and West Africa, were forcibly enslaved and transported to Brazilian territories. The largest ports of entry into Brazil were Salvador da Bahia and Recife in the Northeast and Rio de Janeiro in the South. In contrast to the rapid decline of the native inhabitants, Portuguese and African populations grew steadily through migration (voluntary and forced) and biological reproduction (also both voluntary and forced). Voluntary migrations from Portugal and its colonial Atlantic islands of Madeira and the Azores began in the sixteenth century and expanded in the seventeenth and eighteenth centuries as a result of the establishment of the thriving sugarcane industry in coastal Northeast Brazil and the reports of gold strikes in the interior regions of the country. Portuguese migrants to this faraway land were often poor males approximately twenty to thirty years of age. They went to Brazil alone, without women and without their families. The sexual relations of Portuguese colonial men with Amerindian and African women (frequently violent and coerced) helped produce a large population of mixed-race inhabitants throughout the Brazilian colony. One result of this was the complex and fluid system of racial identification in Brazil, as evidenced by the proliferation of terms for mixed-race progeny. The most common terms used for identifying peoples of mixed racial heritage include *mulatto* (European and African), caboclo and *mameluco* (European and Amerindian), and *cafuzo* (Amerindian and African). These and dozens of other popular classifications (*mestiço, moreno, chulo, pardo*, and so on) describe hair types, skin pigmentations, and other physical attributes of multirace identity in Brazil. The complexity of racial identification is evident in this nuanced attention to skin color and other aspects of physical appearance. Equally important, however, are the cultural and economic factors that combined with physical attributes to produce a complex system of classifications that linked racial identity to hierarchies of social standing in Brazil.

A hierarchical system of social stratification, in which color and other racial markers correlated with social classification, first developed as an integral component of Brazil's slave-based colonial society. In this system, wealthy landowners (almost entirely of white Portuguese descent) held exclusive rights to economic, political, and social power in the colony. The lower strata of colonial society—free and enslaved blacks, mixed-race individuals, and poor whites—became accustomed to a paternalistic system of relations marked by their submission and deference toward the white ruling class. With the stroke of a pen, Princess Isabela signed the Golden Law in 1888 that abolished slavery in Brazil. However, the social hierarchy of race relations that had been established during the slave era did not vanish when the ink from her pen had dried. Indeed, the newly freed black population entered a complex multiracial society in which the hierarchical system of social stratification continued to be linked closely to racial identification. As racial inequality continued, Brazil's multiracial complexity led to a fundamentally different approach to race and racial identification than that of the system that developed in the United States. As indicated previously, from early colonial times onwards, Brazilian society included a large percentage of mixed-race individuals. In the United States, a rigidly imposed Anglo-American value system dominated and led to strict patterns of segregation and the vilification of miscegenation. This, in turn, led to the conceptualization of the United States as a fundamentally biracial (black and white) society. Indigenous populations were not even considered part of the national society. Members of the minute population of mixed-race progeny in the United States were considered social outcasts and were categorized by extremely pejorative terms such as "half-breed," "bastard," and "mongrel." In contrast, race mixing and intercultural hybridity were core components of Brazilian colonial society from its very beginning. In the colony, Portuguese authorities promoted race mixing as a means to increase the population of the territories and to assimilate Africans into colonial society. In Brazil, it was possible for a mulatto born on a sugar plantation of an enslaved mother and a white father to learn a useful trade, gain freedom, and rise to a higher stratum of colonial society. This situation led Brazilians to adopt a more nuanced understanding of racial identification and further distinguished the tropical South American society from the biracial pattern that emerged in the United States. Additionally, a certain flexibility emerged in which socioeconomic position and social status partially determined an individual's racial identification. For instance, a light-skinned mulatto man of means could rise substantially in terms of his social standing. Marking his elevated status, he would be referred to as white, whereas a man of lower social standing but a similar skin tone would be considered a mulatto. The fluid system of racial identification that evolved in the colonial society partially explains why the dominant intellectual theories of race and race relations that developed in modern Brazil have tended to downplay the importance of race itself in regard to social and economic inequality. Making race an "invisible" factor in regard to inequality helped foster the notion that Brazilian society was a racial democracy.

Creating and Contesting Brazil's Racial Democracy

Gilberto Freyre, one of Brazil's most influential social thinkers of the twentieth century, championed the idea that the long history of Portuguese interaction with Africa and African peoples had led Brazil's Portuguese colonizers to be more tolerant of racial differences and cultural diversity than were other European colonizers. A northeasterner from the state of Pernambuco, Freyre proposed that mixture itself (racial, cultural, and psychological) was the defining element of Brazil. Prior to Freyre, most theories of race and race relations in Brazil had been based largely on the assumption that there were inferior and superior races of people in the world. Adopting racial Darwinism, some Brazilian intellectuals believed that "inferior" African races posed a threat to Brazil's advancement into the modern age. One solution they proposed to deal with this so-called problem was to attract European immigration into the country in order to whiten the gene pool of Brazil's population. The Brazilian theory of "whitening," as it came to be known, was supposedly an enlightened variation of European scientific racism and was widely accepted among the elite in Brazil in the early years of the twentieth century. In this view, miscegenation between whites and blacks was a pragmatic way by which natural selection would eventually eliminate inferior African racial traits among Brazil's multiracial population. The attempt to Europeanize the population was nested within a general set of ideas that linked Europe to the modern world and Africa to a premodern status. Liberal Brazilian elites also envisioned the process of whitening as a way to overcome the negative legacy of colonial slavery in their country. Freyre had a radically different view and questioned the evolutionary premise of inferior and superior races of people. Coming from the northeastern state of Pernambuco, he himself was a descendant of local slaveholding sugarcane patriarchs of the coastal zone. He had grown up among the vestiges of a plantation society and amid the radical changes of Brazilian society at the turn of the twentieth century. After studying in the United States, Freyre began pondering the historical circumstances that had led to the unique tropical Brazilian civilization and its fluid system of racial classification and intimate relations among the races.

In the 1930s, Freyre advanced the notion that Brazil was, at its core, a mixed (caboclo and mulatto) society in which the Amerindian, African, and European contributions were equally valuable and culturally based racial differences should be celebrated and not bred out of the population. In his most influential book, *The Masters and the Slaves* (originally published in Portuguese as *Casa Grande e Senzala* in 1933), Freyre successfully argued that Brazil's multicultural and multiracial nature was, in fact, the country's greatest national asset. With its nostalgic view of the rise and decline of the sugar plantation society of the coastal area of the Brazilian Northeast, the book paints the picture of a society constructed around intimate relations (cultural, sexual, and psychological) between enslaved blacks and their white masters. Freyre was primarily interested in affirming the value of African contributions to Brazilian society, and his celebration of cultural (rather than biologically determined) racial difference was a positive advancement in Brazilian intellectual thought on race. For Freyre, Brazil itself was a New World "Luso-tropical" civilization founded on the positive elements of racial and cultural miscegenation. Countering Anglo-Saxon theories of Latin American inferiority linked to biologically rooted notions of racial difference (nineteenth-century scientific racism), he celebrated the culturally based origins of racial difference as a positive feature of Brazil's national development.[6] It was from this mixed racial and cultural heritage that the racially harmonious Brazilian society would take its rightful and unique place among the modern nations of the world. Freyre's work was the first scholarly examination of the relation between miscegenation and the Brazilian national character from a positive viewpoint. His theory provided the intellectual basis for imagining an inclusive Brazilian community for the modern nation. At the same time, however, Freyre's influential works paved the way for masking the racial inequalities that were also part of Brazilian society. His ideas and the masking of racial inequality were politically convenient for engendering a sense of national belonging among all sectors of Brazil's diverse population. The key was creating and sustaining an emerging myth that defined modern Brazil as a racial democracy. This view held that although there might be disparities between the poor and rich sectors in terms of equal access to the society's economic, political, and educational resources, such inequalities were class-based and had no direct correlation to race in Brazil. Elite Brazilians (whites) saw their society as a tropical alternative to the stark segregation and institutionalized racism of the United States. This contrast with the overt racism of the United States was a powerful tool for fostering the idea that all segments of the population in Brazil, regardless of racial identification, had a stake in the national enterprise.

The idea that Brazil is a harmonious racial democracy has been deeply ingrained in the national psyche. Even today, many Brazilians consider questioning the veracity of the belief as tantamount to being unpatriotic. However, this notion of a racial democracy was contested by Brazilian and foreign social scientists beginning in the 1960s, as they engaged in research that showed social and economic opportunity did, in fact, correlate directly with skin color in the country. That is, they found that the darker one's skin, the fewer the available opportunities in areas such as employment, education, and political leadership. Contemporary analyses of racial discrimination and a rising racial consciousness among black intellectuals in the 1970s also helped to debunk the racial democracy myth. The emergence of a black civil rights movement in Brazil—beginning in the late 1960s—countered official versions of harmonious race relations in the country with contested visions of a Brazilian society in which deeply seated racial discriminations had persisted even after slavery was officially ended. The conflict between these two views of Brazil's race relations came to a head in 1988 during the 100-year anniversary of Princess Isabela's signing of the Golden Law abolishing slavery. Many cultural and political groups defining themselves as black responded to the country's official celebrations with protest marches and critical discussions concerning abolition's true meaning for Brazil's black population.[7]

Once again, the Northeast would play a key role in defining racial issues in the country. Afro-Brazilian music and dance groups in Salvador da Bahia were among the most important organizations participating in those protest events in the late 1980s. The use of the music of cultural groups in mobilizing large segments of the population underscores the significance of music and culture in Brazil, which goes well beyond the aesthetic realm.

Although the elite theories of harmonious race relations have been rightfully challenged, they continue to resonate with the Brazilian population and still function as key components of Brazil's national identity. In a country where the multiracial population is the majority, the socially defined physical markers of racial identification are fluid. The color line is a movable index, and racial identities are complex, mixed, relational, and multiple. In this context, the cultural components of race have been crucial in constructing racial identities and in defining strategic positions in Brazilian society. Among cultural practices in Brazil, none has been more fundamental in these arenas than music.

Linking Music, Racial Identification, and the Aesthetics of Participation

Brazil's northeastern coastal strip extending northward from Bahia through Pernambuco and all the way to Maranhão—especially the area around the port city of Salvador da Bahia and its environs—has long been considered Brazil's most African region. This is not surprising given the fact that the two largest cities of the area, Salvador da Bahia and Recife, were the country's primary ports of entry for enslaved Africans before slavers turned their attention southward to Rio de Janeiro. Pernambuco was a prosperous area of early Portuguese settlement and featured the twin cities of Olinda and Recife, which emerged within some 10 miles of each other. Bahia's port city of Salvador controlled an extended Mediterranean-like bay area known as the Recôncavo, which quickly became the wealthiest and most densely populated region of the Brazilian colony. The Portuguese also designated Salvador da Bahia as the first administrative and political center of the colony. European-style erudite music in these two centers of activity was patronized by the Roman Catholic Church and the Portuguese ruling class but included the participation of blacks and mulattoes as well. Local chapelmasters composed and organized music for the church and gave instruction in European music to blacks and mulattoes as early as 1600. On large sugar plantations, orchestras and choruses of slave musicians sang and played European music. Lower-class Portuguese and Africans and the emerging mulatto population also performed all manner of European and African vernacular musical traditions. Like patterns of miscegenation among the races, the musical situation of the colonial Northeast featured extensive cultural mixing and artistic fusions of traditions.

The emergence of the idea of uniquely Afro-Brazilian styles of music making was also related to early colonial activity in the Northeast. In that colonial environment, musical practices created the social and aesthetic space for Brazilian populations to form, nurture, and mobilize their collective identities and to maintain a social memory of their African cultural heritage. The growing mixed-race population in the area drew substantially from African expressive culture in creating new Brazilian forms of music and dance. Additionally, the African influence was so pervasive in the northeastern coast area that many of the Portuguese colonial slaveowners and poor white settlers themselves became highly Africanized through their cultural adoptions. Because of this widespread cultural influence, African heritage was maintained not only within communities of Afro-Brazilians but also in the lifestyles that developed among the general population.

This situation added to the complexity of racial identification in the country. As a result, Brazilian intellectuals in the early twentieth century became preoccupied with assessing the African cultural contributions to modern Brazilian society. Much of their scholarship was concerned with sorting out the varying degrees of African cultural survival (retention), culture loss (acculturation), and cultural blending (syncretism) in Brazil. Some scholars emphasized the retention and tenacity of African traits in Afro-Brazilian culture; others saw the breakdown of African traits in contexts of cultural contact and modernization. The search for Africanisms (and the concepts of retention, syncretism, and acculturation) was symptomatic of elitist postcolonial thought itself, which privileged the social and cultural assimilation of subordinate groups to dominant segments of Brazilian society. This pattern of elite scholarship is also common throughout Latin America.[8]

Intellectual discussions often relegated Afro-Brazilian cultural practices, especially music and dance, to the subordinate realm of folklore, reserving the more elevated category of fine art to certain elite, European-derived musical traditions. In Brazil, as elsewhere in Latin America, this ideology reflected the Eurocentric biases of the intellectual elite and was unequivocally backed by the hierarchical (unequal) power relations that existed within Brazil's multiracial society. Soon after slavery was abolished in the country, Afro-Brazilian cultural practices, including music, were relegated to a museum-like ideological location, safely distanced from the economic and social realities of the country's black population, which continued to be the poorest segment of society. This marginalization also served to confine Afro-Brazilian musical culture to an idealized and frozen kind of African heritage. Conceptualized as folklore, Afro-Brazilian musical traditions were implicitly devalued within an unquestioned and European-derived hierarchy of the fine arts.

The fact that Afro-Brazilian music was implicitly placed within the quaint category of folklore does not mean that it did not serve as an important source of inspiration for the development of high art forms among Brazil's elite composers working in European-based traditions. To the contrary, Brazilian art music composers in the first half of the twentieth century drew substantially on Afro-Brazilian source material in crafting nationalist compositions to musically represent their country. Considering the northeastern coastal region (especially the states of Bahia and Pernambuco) as the country's main preserve of Afro-Brazilian culture, many Brazilian composers went on trips to the Northeast to collect Afro-Brazilian music in its "pure" and "authentic" state. For instance, Brazilian nationalist composer Camargo Guarnieri traveled to Bahia to attend the Afro-Brazilian Congress of 1937 and stayed in the area to observe and collect Afro-Brazilian source material for his future compositions. Asked what he thought of Bahia by a reporter for the newspaper *Estado da Bahia,* the respected composer responded (my translation):

> Listen, I came here as a representative of the [São Paulo] Department of Culture . . . to study the music of the candomblé religion, the popular music of Bahia. I encountered things that disoriented me completely. I never thought I would encounter a samba in a triple meter, however I encountered a case that really surprised me. Ah, the folkloric richness. I am enchanted with the folklore of Bahia. I already have more than 100 musical themes, of samba, of capoeira Angola, of candomblé. The pity is that I have to leave here in a few days and return to the South. But my wish is to remain here.[9]

In this interview, Guarnieri mentioned three of the most important musical traditions from Bahia that symbolized African heritage for him and for other Brazilians: the samba, *capoeira de Angola* (a music and dance game believed to have come from Angola that was practiced by slaves in Bahia), and Candomblé (the best-known and most orthodox of Brazil's African-based religions). The description of the southern composer's disorientation at encountering a samba in triple meter (a rhythmic organization of three beats) highlights the fact that Afro-Brazilian music often presented conceptual problems for Brazilian composers. Although it is clear that he was aesthetically drawn to these "folkloric" forms of Afro-Brazilian music, it is also clear that Guarneiri, highly trained in European art music, did not fully understand the seemingly mysterious properties that animated this music.

Guarneiri's disorientation may have been similar to some of my own experiences as I encountered maracatu drumming, and in this context, it is worth reprising a portion of my description of the maracatu scene that opened this chapter: "Raw energy was palpable as the music gradually took possession of the entire street. Large drums were beaten in a simple yet bewildering pattern. Then the sounds seemed to get even closer. All of a sudden, my perception of the music shifted entirely. Like tuning into a radio station, the signal became clear. 'Oh, I get it!' I thought to myself. Dancing, drumming, and singing all converged into one hard-driving groove." Once I had linked into the hard-driving groove of the drumming, everything seemed to fall into place. The music was simultaneously simple and complex; it demanded participation from all those who could feel it. This kind of interaction among participants in musical events has been widely noted for many styles of African music. Afro-Brazilian music carries on this tradition. To really "get it," one must be deeply engaged in a kind of interplay of competency with the more skilled "performers," who provide the security of a solid musical base. This inspires widespread participation and creates the environment for social bonding. In reality, everyone is a potential performer at such events. A well-played samba or a maracatu inspires Brazilians because of this participatory quality and forges bonds of identity among those competent in the aesthetic rules of the game.

The Afro-Brazilian music of the northeastern coastal areas was crucial in establishing a baseline for assessing the authenticity of the Afro-Brazilian musical style in the country. Perhaps no musical tradition in Brazil is considered more genuinely African than that associated with the Afro-Brazilian religion known as Candomblé. This religion and its music provides what José Jorge de Carvalho called the dominant "matrix" of Afro-Brazilian identity in Brazil.[10] Racial identity within Candomblé is not based on biologically or geographically determined concepts but rather on the aesthetics of participation achieved through dancing, singing, and drumming. The music that accompanies the religious rituals of Candomblé features a distinctively West African style of drumming and vocal texture without any additional melodic instruments. It is a powerful music that demands direct participation from the members of the religion. African-based religious music and dance also provide important reference points for Afro-Brazilian identity in the larger context of Brazilian society. Popular musicians and composers in Brazil frequently draw from Afro-Brazilian religious practices for musical and spiritual inspiration; understanding the basic nature of Afro-Brazilian religious music lays the aesthetic foundation for understanding much about Afro-Brazilian music in general. The same style of participation through music and dance that engenders a powerful feeling of African identity within Candomblé is also found in many other forms of Afro-Brazilian music and dance, such as the maracatu of Recife's Carnival. This is one of the most powerful qualities of Afro-Brazilian music.

A Musical Example of Intercultural Mixing in Colonial Brazil: Charamelas and Processional Music

Opportunities for intercultural mixing among Amerindian, Portuguese, and African populations were present from the outset of Brazil's colonial society. This was particularly true of the coastal settlements, where ceremonial and processional music was an integral component of public life during the colonial period. Most public festivities in colonial Brazil—civic as well as religious—were organized under the auspices and direction of the Catholic Church and included the participation of military and civic ensembles reflecting a wide range of influences. These public occasions were important social events in community life and served as an effective means of linking religious and political authority and establishing public control. They also presented opportunities for cultivating intercultural connections among different racial segments of the population. The development of hybrid musical practices was a vital part of this intercultural process.

Music for public festivities was typically placed under the control of the local chapelmaster—the musical director of the local cathedral and the most important musician in most communities. A chapelmaster's duties included selecting, rehearsing, conducting, performing, and even composing music for the various religious services held throughout the liturgical year of the Catholic Church. In addition, the chapelmaster was involved in the musical instruction and training of many lay musicians in his area. Music instruction was given to the African, European, and mixed-race populations of the coastal settlements, which in turn generated the vocal and instrumental resources for establishing local choirs and orchestras with the ability to perform European polyphonic music. Though the style and repertoire was European, the musicians were often racially mixed. For outdoor public occasions requiring music, the chapelmaster contracted additional community musicians as needed. In some communities, the chapelmaster held a virtual monopoly on musical activity within his jurisdiction.[11] By 1611, there were enough music activities in Pernambuco to produce the four separate musical ensembles that were observed accompanying a procession.[12]

In contrast to the tightly controlled repertory and style of the liturgical music used for religious services within the church, the style of music permitted for the outdoor festivities appears to have been far less restricted. Military bands and civic musicians contributed music to community festivities.[13] Outdoor celebrations thus provided a musical and social environment in which European instrumental and vocal styles commingled with African and, to a lesser extent, Amerindian musical heritage. This context gave community musicians (especially blacks and mulattoes) increased opportunities for freelance employment and stimulated the development of a hybrid popular culture of music making in Brazil's urban areas. Blacks and mulattoes dominated in this area of musical activity.

Colonial archives from churches, convents, and religious brotherhoods in Rio de Janeiro, Bahia, and Pernambuco make frequent mention of expenses paid to "black," "Negro," and "African" musicians who performed for processions and other community-wide festivals. Describing the colonial situation in Pernambuco, Brazilian musicologist and Catholic priest Jaime C. Diniz noted (my translation):

> In old times, our religious festivals were not put on without the incorporation of "Negro chamaleiros" dressed in colorful garments [who performed] in the churchyard and in the processions. They contributed enormously to the brilliant display of the celebrations of those times. Bell ringing, fireworks, and charamelas engulfed the expressive ambiance [causing] all of the people in the area to realize that there was going to be a feast, a great feast, and a wonderful feast. No feast was given in Pernambuco during the colonial times without the charamelas of our black musicians. And with what pride they demonstrated their artistic skills![14]

Diniz went on to say that in colonial times in Pernambuco, band musicians and charamela players were almost always blacks. In his detailed archival research in Pernambuco, he uncovered numerous documents from churches, convents, and religious brotherhoods, dating from the seventeenth through the early nineteenth century, that listed expenses for the "pretos charameleiros" (black charamela players) to play in various celebrations. What exactly was the charamela to which so many documents refer?

Charamela was the Portuguese generic designation for double-reeded woodwind instruments similar to the present-day oboe. The term also sometimes referred to single-reed clarinets. In Spain and Spanish America, similar instruments were called *chirimia*. In English-speaking territories, this type of instrument was referred to as a shawm. Charamela also referred to the groups of musicians who played the instruments of the same name in consort with flutes, trumpets, trombones, and a variety of drums. The initial model for the Brazilian charamela groups, like the instruments themselves, came from Europe. In Spain, Portugal, and Europe's northern countries, similar ensembles were important components of court, religious, military, and civic life. European military units frequently included fifes, drums, shawms, trumpets, large side drums, and timpani. Closely related were the European town bands known as *altas* that were popular on the continent from the fourteenth through sixteenth centuries. Similar to the bands used for military purposes, these civic town ensembles included loud outdoor instruments such as shawms, trumpets, sackbuts (trombone-like instruments), and a variety of drums. Throughout Europe, town councils and local aristocrats had these loud alta bands perform for municipal and court functions. Independent musicians formed freelance groups to play for events sponsored by civic organizations and confraternities. Like the jazz musicians of later centuries, these instrumentalists often doubled on two or more wind instruments, could read and perform from sheet music, and also learned to improvise melodies. The alta band tradition was imported to Brazil by Portuguese colonists in the form of the charamela groups.

In Brazil, the musical repertoire and instrumental techniques of the independent charamela groups were learned from local chapelmasters and from black charamela musicians who participated in military ensembles. No sheet music has survived, and documented evidence regarding the actual sound of the Brazilian charamela ensembles is sketchy. All we have are pictures and descriptions of such groups. However, it is likely that the charamela ensembles operated in a manner similar to the European alta tradition. They probably mixed written and oral traditions of music making, and at least some of the musicians would have been capable of improvising. Among the instrumentalists mentioned in the receipt books of churches from the seventeenth through early nineteenth centuries in Pernambuco were those who played shawms, flutes, trumpet, timpani, and side drums. The charamela musical ensembles were composed of whites and mulattoes as well as free and enslaved blacks and thus functioned as a point of contact between European and African musical heritage. The high percentage of black musicians among their ranks suggests that the charamela groups possibly mixed elements of African musical style into the European repertoire. The probability of such intercultural mixing is made more likely given the fact that such charamela groups occasionally accompanied the processions in which black kings and queens were symbolically crowned in Brazilian colonial times. Describing the role of the charamela groups in colonial Recife, Diniz noted (my translation): "The musical groups called 'charamelas' were never absent from the [religious] festivities of the Senhora do Rosário, and also, most likely, embellished the coronation of the King and Queen of the Angolas or of the Creoles. The charamelas were the specialty of the blacks, either enslaved or not. The tradition [of charamelas] derives directly from Portuguese culture, implanted into the Brazilian Northeast a long time ago."[15]

The celebrations to crown black kings and queens were the forerunners of Recife's Carnival groups that are now called maracatu. It is worth noting the description of a black procession that took place in Recife in 1666 (my translation): "After some four hundred men and one hundred women attended mass, they elected a king and a queen, they marched through the streets singing and reciting verses that they themselves improvised, preceded by atabaques, trumpets, and tambourines."[16] From this description, it is unclear if the improvised singing—probably African in both style and substance—was directly accompanied by the music of the instrumental group of trumpets and drums or if the two existed as separate musical components of the procession. Though not mentioned directly in the description, the instrumental group was possibly one of the black charamelas of the area. As social peers, the instrumental musicians and the singers probably engaged in some form of musical mixing of European and African elements.

The first direct mention of a charamela group being paid for playing at the feasts of the Brotherhood of Nossa Senhora do Rosário dos Pretos in Recife comes from 1709.[17] In addition to using the European wind, brass, and percussion instruments of the charamela ensembles, the public festivities of the brotherhood also mixed African instruments such as the marimba with Portuguese guitars. The inclusion of charamelas and other mixed ensembles with African and European instruments in the festivities surrounding the crowning of symbolic African kings and queens as well as in Catholic Church processions indicates the fluid and hybrid nature of public celebration during colonial times in Pernambuco. Such intercultural mingling was also common in Salvador da Bahia and Rio de Janeiro.

In both Rio de Janeiro and Salvador, free black and mulatto musicians who earned most of their living as barbers also formed their own independent ensembles of wind, string, and percussion instruments to play for public occasions.[18] Under their own leadership, members of these itinerant popular music formations were carving out social, economic, and artistic space for the blending of African and European music. These freelance urban musical ensembles contrasted with the colonial orchestras in rural Brazil, which featured black musicians but were under the control of European music directors. The freelance black and mulatto charamela and barber musicians had more creative freedom to mix European and African musical elements. Throughout colonial Brazil, public celebrations and urban street life provided contexts for the development of hybrid musical practices blending European and African traditions and helped stimulate an emerging popular culture in which musicians found increasing opportunities. In addition, military and militia units, cutting across racial groups, made an important contribution to the development of Brazil's popular musical culture and played a key role in the establishment of a literate instrumental musical tradition in the nineteenth century.

The mixing of African and European traditions in the charamelas in colonial Brazil reflected the larger process of intercultural miscegenation that characterized Brazilian society from its earliest days. In almost all other realms of music making throughout Brazil's long history, this pattern has continued.

.

CHAPTER 2

Brazilian Music in Focus:
A History of Hybridity

Cannibalizing the World

Brazilian musicians have a knack for blurring the boundaries of the musical traditions of their country and mixing one tradition with another. Music and musicians from rural and urban areas of Brazil freely interact with each other, regional traditions are embedded in national forms of music, and musicians often serve as cultural mediators linking the interests of different sectors of Brazilian society. Further complicating the musical landscape is the fact that Brazilian musicians of all social ranks and racial identifications demonstrate a keen ability to mix their local, regional, and national traditions with non-Brazilian musical influences. All of this mixing in the music of Brazil is part of the more general characteristic of hybridity noted for Brazilian society in Chapter 1. Intellectuals first championed racial mixture as the defining national characteristic of the country in the early twentieth century, and the idea of cultural hybridity permeated the realm of artistic production as well. For instance, an important branch of the Brazilian vanguard modernist movement of the 1920s espoused the notion that visual artists, writers, and composers should selectively cannibalize both Brazilian and non-Brazilian cultural sources in order to produce genuine Brazilian art forms. It was in the act of cannibalizing, not in the search for an exotic Brazilian cultural essence, that these artists defined themselves as Brazilian; the act of freely devouring and digesting multiple sources—foreign and domestic—became one of the defining characteristics of their artistic production.

Emerging in the southern cities of São Paulo and Rio de Janeiro, the elite artists who followed this "cannibilist manifesto" were particularly interested in the urban popular culture of their country, where racial and cultural mixture was unavoidable. The metaphor of cannibalism works well for understanding the creative impulses and ideologies that animated Brazilian artists as they created artwork reflecting the urban realities in their society. The idea of cannibalism also works well in understanding relationships and interactions between local musical practices and broader contexts of reality in Brazil, in rural as well as urban areas. In surveying the rich Brazilian musical landscape, we find many instances where the consumption and digestion of local and non-local sources lead musicians to create new musical forms. In some cases, they consciously mix their local musical practices with those of national or international contexts. In other instances, this digestive hybridity happens, perhaps less consciously, when musicians confront the changing nature of their world, in which multiple influences have become integral parts of their local reality. Throughout Brazil's history, musicians have dealt with these situations by creating hybrid music to define their time and place as Brazilians.

In addition to mixing and adapting various instruments, genres, and repertoires from "outside" music, Brazilians are adept at reinterpreting old styles of local musical traditions to fulfill emerging needs. Such creative artistic work intersects with important social, cultural, and economic issues in Brazil. Many forms of live musical interaction among small groups of participants (folk music) serve as resources for Brazil's music industry, which spreads its products (popular music) through the media of mass communications. In a similar manner, mediated forms of cultural expression (whether in staged concert settings or in the various media of mass communication) are part of the everyday experiences of local musicians, audiences, and cultural practitioners throughout the country. The more elite forms of musical production (art music) also cross-pollinate with the mass and vernacular music traditions in the country. It is the interplay of these forms of music that makes Brazilian musical culture complex and interesting. In this chapter, I will investigate major traditions of Brazilian music that reveal the interplay of local, national, and international circuits of cultural activity and flows of information. This investigation will highlight the important role that music from the Northeast has played in creating the image of the modern nation of Brazil. After a brief consideration of Brazil's principal musical instruments, including the ubiquitous pandeiro, I will discuss the significance of Brazilian Carnival and the contributions that northeastern popular music has made in defining Brazilian musical culture.

Musical Instruments of Brazil

The majority of the instruments of Brazil's vast musical culture can be traced to the country's Amerindian, European, or African heritages. Anthropologists, historians, and musicologists have frequently attempted to search for the precise origins of particular instruments. Through archaeological finds, oral testimony, and written records, we can learn much about such origins. However, for most Brazilians, esoteric knowledge about the origins of specific instruments is of little importance or relevance. What is more relevant and revealing is that certain types of musical instruments have come to symbolize Brazil's tripartite racial heritage. In the broadest terms, Amerindian, African, and Portuguese heritage in Brazil is symbolized through the flute, the drum, and the guitar, respectively.

Prior to their encounters with Europeans and Africans, indigenous groups in Brazil predominantly used flutes, clarinet- and oboe-like reed instruments, gourd shakers, shell rattles, wood drums with animal-skin membranes, and other rhythmic instruments in their music. Based in general historical accuracy, the association of flutes with the country's indigenous populations has become a cultural trope in Brazilian society, especially among the majority non-indigenous population. In urban Carnival parades, invented "Indian tribes" are frequently represented with musicians playing flutes of some sort. Recall the scenes of the caboclinho Carnival group from Recife that I described in Chapter 1. The flute that was played in that caboclinho is not derived from any specific indigenous group that one could locate on a map of Brazil. Rather, it is the general idea of Indians playing flutes that animates popular imagination regarding indigenous contributions to Brazilian musical culture. In Recife's Carnival, caboclinho groups portray the bravery and nobility of indigenous struggles against the Portuguese invaders, and the flute is an essential marker of indigenous identity. Throughout the sertão region of Northeast Brazil, where an extensive racial and cultural mixing of Amerindian populations and Portuguese settlers took place, one of the most common musical ensembles among the poor caboclo population features side-blown flutes made from a local cane known as *taquara* or *taboca* (indigenous terms for local species of bamboo). The mixed-race caboclo musicians who make and play these flutes associate the instruments with vaguely defined indigenous origins and tell many variations of the story of how the "savage" Indians from an earlier era showed their caboclo ancestors how to make the flutes using fire and cane. These stories reinforce local imagery about flutes and Indians and create a historical narrative of an intercultural collaboration that took place

Figure 2.1 A flute (gaita) played by a caboclinho musician during Recife's Carnival, 2001 (photo by Larry Crook).

in the Brazilian sertão. Extended to the idea of the nation, the stories also illuminate popular conceptions regarding indigenous contributions to Brazilian culture in general.

If rustic flutes evoke a sense of indigenous heritage for Brazilians in rural and urban areas, drums and drumming summon the most powerful African-related imagery throughout the country. In addition to a variety of drum types that are traceable to specific African origins, African performance aesthetics and techniques have transformed many European-style drums into the domain of Afro-Brazilian musical expression. For instance, many of the double-headed drums used in the large samba groups in Rio de Janeiro are adaptations of military band instruments introduced into Brazil by the Portuguese and other Europeans. However, the stick/hand techniques and syncopated samba rhythms played on these drums are unmistakably African in inspiration and style.

The drum types most closely associated with African heritage are the single-headed, conga-like instruments called *atabaque*. These are wooden drums with animal skins and are used in both Afro-Brazilian religious and secular music. In the orthodox Afro-Brazilian religious setting of Candomblé, a family of three atabaque drums is most common. In this context, the lead drummer assumes the role of master drummer and plays improvisatory variations of set patterns that are coordinated with danced embodiments of African deities. In both style and detail, this drumming engenders a deep African sensibility within Brazil. In the more syncretic popular religions of Brazil that mix elements of Candomblé, Catholicism, and indigenous religion, the presence of the atabaque drums provides a strong link to Afro-Brazilian aesthetics. Atabaque drums are also used in many secular forms of Afro-Brazilian music, such as the *samba de roda* (circle samba) and the *capoeira* from Bahia. In recent years, black carnival groups in Bahia

Figure 2.2 Three atabaque drums from Bahia: from right to left, the rum, rumpi, and lê (photo by Larry Crook).

known as *blocos afro* (Afroblocs) have incorporated a new drum known as the *timbal,* which uses a thin nylon membrane and is reminiscent of both the atabaque and the internationally popular West African *jembe* drum. The timbal effectively links two important domains of African symbolism in Brazil: (1) a local Afro-Brazilian heritage (atabaque), and (2) international African drum culture.

No instrumental type is more closely associated with Portuguese heritage in Brazil than the guitar. Plucked stringed instruments of the guitar family were carried to Brazil by the Portuguese and were then spread throughout the country. During Brazilian colonial days, a forerunner of the modern guitar known as the *viola* was a favored instrument among upper and lower classes. In the Portuguese ruling class, the viola provided accompaniment for serenading and for romantic and sentimental Brazilian songs. In rural areas, home-made folk varieties of the viola were used to accompany songs and dances of Portuguese folk origins. In modern Brazil, the viola has become the most characteristic instrument of Portuguese folk heritage, now largely associated with the rural life of the country. In contrast, the modern six-string guitar (known as the *violão* in Brazil) exemplifies the country's urban popular and elite musical traditions. Brazilian guitarists are known the world over for their virtuosic playing, which incorporates both international classical guitar techniques and improvisatory playing styles developed in Brazil. In addition, Brazil's most important composer, Heitor Villa-Lobos, celebrated the guitar as the quintessential Brazilian musical instrument and wrote many pieces for classical guitar repertoire. Villa-Lobos was also a guitar player and drew directly from the urban popular traditions of his home city of Rio de Janeiro.

Figure 2.3 Brazilian guitarist Marco Pereira (photo by Roberto Cifarelli (Phocusagency).

Figure 2.4 Three Brazilian guitars: from left to right, violão de sete cordas, viola, and cavaquinho (photo by Sylvia Crook).

A Brazilian Musical Instrument Primer

Brazilian Stringed Instruments

The violão (six-stringed guitar) is used in a wide variety of folk, popular, and classical styles that emphasize strumming (*rasqueado*) and finger-picking (*ponteado*) techniques. The violão is used as a basic accompaniment instrument for many types of samba and is also the essential instrument on which bossa nova is played. In *choro* ensembles, an intimate style of Brazilian chamber music, both the six-stringed guitar and the seven-stringed guitar (*violão de sete cordas*) are featured prominently. During the twentieth century, the art of guitar playing in Brazil cut across art, folk, and popular contexts. Brazil's most illustrious art music composer, Villa-Lobos, was also a guitarist. Some of the world's most accomplished guitarists come from Brazil and have established successful international careers. Chief among them are Sérgio and Odair Assad, Marco Pereira, João Bosco, João Gilberto, Baden Powell, and Turíbio Santos.

The *viola* (ten-stringed guitar) is related to the Spanish *vihuela* and has been present in Brazil since the sixteenth century. The Portuguese *viola de mão* (viola of the hand) is the ancestor of the Brazilian viola and dates from the thirteenth century. Today, the viola is used as a folk instrument throughout the country. It accompanies singer-bards in the Northeast (*cantoria de viola*), a regional samba style in Bahia (*samba de viola*), and the country music of south-central Brazil known as *música caipira* (country music). One variety is the *viola dinâmica* (dynamic viola), an instrument related to the North American Dobro with metal resonating cones fitted inside a wooden body.

The *cavaquinho* (small four-string guitar) is a steel-stringed relative of the ukulele that derives from an older Portuguese instrument known as the *machete*. In Brazil, the cavaquinho functions primarily as a strummed, rhythmic–harmonic accompaniment to samba and many other styles of folk and popular music. A few outstanding Brazilian musicians have explored the virtuosic possibilities of the cavaquinho, including Waldir Azevedo and Nelson Cavaquinho.

The *bandolim* (eight-string Brazilian mandolin) is used as a solo melodic instrument in choro music and in the *frevo de bloco* (a style of carnival music from Recife, Pernambuco). Played with a plectrum, the instrument first became popular in the early part of the twentieth century. Among Brazil's best bandolim players are Jacob do Bandolim, Joel Nascimento, and Hamilton de Holanda.

The *rabeca* (folk violin) is found throughout Brazil and is used as a solo instrument in small ensembles. In Northeast Brazil, the rabeca accompanies the *cavalo-marinho* (sea horse), a musical dance-drama performed by sugarcane workers; it also is used in the dance music known as *forró*. In the 1990s, the rabeca was revived and transformed by popular musicians from Pernambuco, most notably by the group Mestre Ambrósio, led by rabeca player Sérgio Veloso.

The *berimbau* (one-stringed bow with a gourd resonator) is the most popular Brazilian stringed instrument of African heritage. Based on models from Central and southern Africa, the berimbau is the primary accompaniment for the capoeira, the martial arts/dance game that deleveped in Bahia during the slave era. Since the 1970s, Brazilian virtuoso percussionists Airto Moreira and Naná Vasconcelos have popularized the berimbau internationally

Woodwind, Brass, and Other Aerophone Instruments

The *pífano* (cane fife) is found throughout the northeastern interior region of Brazil. Pífanos are open-holed flutes and probably derived from a confluence of Amerindian, Iberian, and African heritage. They are used in small ensembles called *bandas de pífanos,* which combine two flutes and two or three drums and cymbals or triangle. Carlos Malta and his band Pife Muderno (Modern Pífano) are a contemporary banda de pífano group of jazz and classical musicians from Rio de Janeiro.

Trumpets, saxophones, clarinets, tubas, and keyed flutes (modern band instru-ments) were introduced into Brazil via the spread of European-style military and civic bands during the nineteenth century. Ensembles featuring these and other band instruments are social and musical institutions in the life of small and large towns throughout Brazil. The band tradition also laid the foundation for the Carnival music of frevo in Recife. Bands were used in the recordings of many early forms of popular music at the turn of the twentieth century in Rio de Janeiro.

The *accordion* is one of the most important instruments in Brazil. It was incorporated into the folk traditions of the common classes throughout the country beginning in the mid-nineteenth century. It became closely associated with folk music from the northeastern sertão when it was popularized nationally by Luiz Gonzaga, who established a standard "northeastern trio" with an accordion, a triangle, and a bass drum called the *zabumba*.

Percussion Instruments

The *agogô* (double metal bell) is derived from West and Central African musical cultures and is used in samba and many other forms of Brazilian music. In the Afro-Brazilian Candomblé religion, its role is to provide a syncopated rhythm that holds the polyrhythmic patterns together.

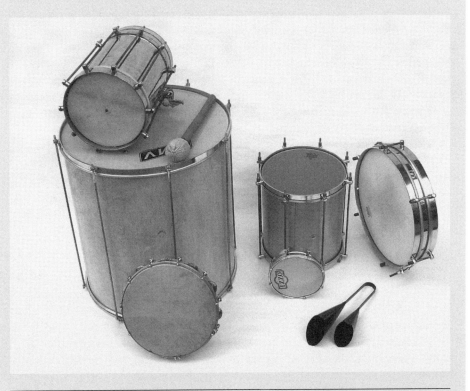

Figure 2.5 Drums and percussion of the samba school clockwise from bottom left: pandeiro, surdo, cuíca, repinique, tarol, agogô, and tamborim (photo by Sylvia Crook).

Atabaque (single-skinned, conical drum) is the most common name for conga-like drums with animal skins in Brazil. Derived from West and Central African models, atabaques are used in Afro-Brazilian religious traditions and secular forms of music and dance. They come in three sizes: *rum* (large), *rumpi* (medium), and *lê* (small).

The *tarol* (double-headed snare drum) is a thin snare drum used in musical ensembles throughout Brazil, including in the large percussion ensembles of the samba schools featured during Carnival in Rio de Janeiro. Various forms of the tarol are also found in the Carnival traditions from Recife, Pernambuco, and from Salvador da Bahia. They are also part of the bandas de pífanos in the Northeast interior.

The *cuíca* (single-headed friction drum) is one of Brazil's most unusual drums. It derives from Central Africa and has a thin bamboo stick attached to the center of the skin. The sound results when the stick is rubbed, producing a kind of whining sound. The cuíca is used extensively in samba.

The *pandeiro* (single-headed frame drum with metal jingles) is the Brazilian tambourine, played with virtuosic techniques involving the thumb, fingers, and palm of the hand. It is Brazil's most versatile percussion instrument and is used in many types of ensembles in the country.

The *repinique* (small double-headed drum) is a lead drum used in the samba schools in Rio de Janeiro and in the blocos afro of Salvador da Bahia. It is typically played with a combination of stick and hand.

The *surdo* (deep double-headed bass drum) comes in various sizes and is used in a variety of musical styles, including the samba schools and the blocos afro. It is typically played with a soft mallet and open hand.

The *tamborim* (small single-headed drum) is a small frame drum that is an essential component of the samba schools and is played with one stick.

The *zabumba* (double-headed bass drum) is most commonly used in the northeastern accordion music (forró) and in the banda de pífanos ensembles. It is played with a soft mallet on one skin and a thin stick on the other.

The Brazilian Pandeiro: Then and Now

The pandeiro is a relatively simple and inexpensive instrument. You can purchase a cheap one for under ten dollars; professional pandeiros can cost as much as three hundred dollars. Essentially a tambourine, pandeiros are used in diverse contexts in Brazil, from highly localized face-to-face performance traditions to the mediated contexts of the mass culture industry. During the early twentieth century, the pandeiro entered the nascent popular music industry of Brazil via recordings of genres including the samba, which would be championed as Brazil's national music. As a result, the pandeiro became the country's defacto national percussion instrument. There are several reasons why the pandeiro, rather than any number of other Brazilian percussion instruments, assumed this nationalized role. The first is the pandeiro's musical versatility as a percussive

Figure 2.6 The Brazilian pandeiro (photo by Vanessa Crook).

rhythmic instrument. Bass, mid-range, and treble tones as well as a wide range of timbres can be extracted from the instrument acoustically. Like the American drumset, the pandeiro is able to synthesize the individual rhythmic patterns of several percussion parts.

As Marcos Suzano—one of Brazil's top pandeiro players—puts it, "the pandeiro is a very generous instrument, it synthesizes an entire *batucada*."[1] Indeed, pandeiro players adapt and rework drum beats and percussion parts from diverse musical styles and set them onto the pandeiro. This synthetic process is a core aesthetic of pandeiro playing and is related to the broader context of Brazilian hybridity. Unlike the drumset, the pandeiro is small and portable making it much easier to carry from gig to gig. Indeed, Brazilian pandeiro players sometimes call the instrument a "*bateria no bolso*" (drumset in a bag).

Throughout Brazil's history, pandeiro players themselves have served important roles as synthesizers of Brazil's musical traditions as they introduced performance techniques from diverse traditions into the popular music of the country. They also served as intercultural mediators creating bonds across class, race, and educational lines. Recent trends in pandeiro playing link global and local flows of intercultural creation with emerging technologies. In the early twenty-first century, the aesthetics of intercultural mediation continue to animate new artistic production on the pandeiro.

A second reason that the pandeiro became the defacto national percussion instrument is that it was never associated exclusively with one segment of the Brazilian population. In colonial Brazil, blacks and whites, rich and poor, males and females, young and old, played the pandeiro. However, this pervasiveness rendered the pandeiro somewhat commonplace and unremarkable. Its status was neither exotic nor elite, and musically, it held a subservient position as an accompaniment to voice, string, and wind instruments. In fact, until the 1990s, pandeiro players were rarely, if ever, featured as soloists or leaders of musical ensembles. While instruments such as the piano, violin, and the flute—and eventually the guitar—were consecrated as worthy of elevated artistic status; or instruments such as the atabaque and berimbau became indices of authentic African heritage, the pandeiro remained a kind of free-floating instrument that moved fluidly across performance traditions that were themselves hybrid cultural expressions generated by ongoing encounters of distinct sectors of Brazilian society. Never really conceptualized as anchored specifically in Afro-Brazilian, Euro-Brazilian, or Indigenous-Brazilian tradition, pandeiro players became intercultural mediators with their instruments.

Historical records of pandeiro-like instruments prior to the nineteenth century in Brazil are rather sketchy. Portuguese settlers and missionaries probably introduced round-frame drums called pandeiros and square frame drums called *adufes* into Brazil early in the sixteenth century. During Brazil's colonial and imperial periods, such instruments accompanied music and dance traditions of the privileged and marginalized populations throughout the country. They served as rhythmic accompaniment to string and wind instruments in indoor settings and to wind and brass instruments in outdoor public spaces where processing and collective dancing occurred. As early as 1666, black Brazilian musicians were observed mixing the pandeiro with both European and African derived instruments in the processions known as Rei de Congo and Rei de Angola.[2]

Today, pandeiros accompany a wide variety of dramatic dances and devotional traditions throughout Brazil. One such tradition, the *pastoril*, is a Christmas enactment in which young girls perform songs and dances in honor of the baby Jesus as they accompany themselves with pandeiros. A related tradition known as the *folia de reis* (company of kings) particularly popular in southeastern Brazil, re-enacts the journey of the Three Kings to Bethelem accompanied by the viola, the pandeiro, and the caixa.[3] Other important danced traditions such as the *congada*—maintained largely among Afro-Brazilian communities—include the ubiquitous use of pandeiros as well.

While the pandeiro was common in colonial cultural practices combining European Catholicism with Afro-Brazilian heritage, it was never part of the official music culture of the Church nor was it consecrated within Afro-Brazilian religious traditions such as Candomblé. Hence, the techniques and repertoires that pandeiro players developed were not controlled by formal instruction nor restricted by religious orthodoxy. Rather, pandeiro playing was a fluid art form that was transmitted freely from one performance tradition to another.

During the late nineteenth and early twentieth centuries, pandeiro players became active agents in the hybrid artistic activities that characterized urban areas in Brazil. Carnival was an important context for the development of new musical styles. In Rio's Carnival, the pandeiro accompanied the lyric songs of the *ranchos carnavalescos* as well as the more percussive *batuques* and sambas of the *blocos* and *escolas de samba*. In the Northeast, it was similarly used in the Carnival blocos of middle-class Italian immigrants as well as in the frevo of the pedestrian frevo clubs of urban laborers.

At the same time, pandeiro players became essential members of the rhythm sections in newly forming popular ensembles whose repertoires included genres such as maxixe, marcha, samba, frevo, coco, and embolada. While pandeiro players were important in the development of Brazil's popular musical styles, the pandeiro itself was never the focus of serious interest among nationalist-oriented artists and intellectuals, nor was it heralded as Brazil's "national instrument." Rather, the pandeiro was largely taken for granted as a part of the Brazilian national musical landscape that was full of hybrid fusions. Under the dictatorial rule of Getúlio Vargas in the 1930s and 1940s, the Brazilian government promoted racial and cultural fusion as a cornerstone of Brazil's national identity. Establishing cultural links with marginalized sectors of society was an important avenue for creating national culture. Pandeiro players provided one such avenue in the musical realm and served as social and aesthetic mediators. A short biographical sketch of an important pandeiro player from the early part of the twentieth century provides an illustration of the ways that distinct sectors of the society interacted.

João da Baiana (1887–1974)

Born in Rio de Janeiro in 1887—a year before the abolition of slavery—João Machado Gomes grew up near Praça Onze, in a neighborhood populated largely by black migrants from Bahia. His grandparents were ex-slaves and operated a neighborhood store in which Afro-Brazilian religious objects were sold. His mother, Tia Perciliana, was an *ialorixá* priestess in Candomblé religion; his father was a Freemason. By most accounts, the family was quite influential in Rio's Afro-Bahian community and was well connected to members of the city's white elite sector including local governmental officials. João's family sponsored community gatherings where Afro-Brazilian traditions such as Candomblé, samba de roda, and batuque were held.

João's urban environment was marked by intercultural mixings of the cultural traditions of diverse segments of the population. For instance, in addition to participating in Candomblé and in the vernacular performance culture of the Afro-Brazilian community in Rio de Janeiro, several of João's older brothers also played guitar, cavaquinho, and violin. Like other local musicians, João and his brothers were involved in the city's emerging popular culture, in *chorões,* and in Carnival. It was likely in the context of Carnival rancho groups in Rio that João first took up the pandeiro. These were hybrid socio-cultural organizations that mixed Euro- and Afro-Brazilian traditions. By the age of eight, João was participating in both ranchos and sambas. In an interview conducted in 1966 for the Museum of Sound and Image in Rio, João stated (my translation): "This was more or less when I was eight years old [1895] and was a . . . [member] of the Dois de Ouro and Pedra do Sal . . . I dedicated myself to the pandeiro because I loved rhythm. Whenever there was a samba de roda, I was the one who could play pandeiro the best."[4]

As a teenager, João collaborated with other influential black musicians of his era including Pixinguinha and Donga to help craft the emerging *carioca samba.* João moved among elite and popular social sectors of the city and established strategic alliances to mitigate the effects of racial confrontations. From the same 1966 interview João also stated that (my translation):

The police persecuted us. [One day] I was going to play pandeiro at the Festa da Penha and the police took my instrument from me. [. . .] There was a party in the Morro da Graça, at senator Pinheiro Machado's house and I didn't show up. So, Pinheiro Machado asked "Where is the pandeiro player?" [. . .] Pinheiro Machado thought it absurd and sent a message that I should speak with him at the Senate house. And so I went . . . and he asked me why I didn't come to his house and I responded that . . . the police had taken my pandeiro at the Festa da Penha. He wanted to know if I had been fighting and then where could he have another pandeiro made for me. I told him that the only place was at Oscar's store, the Cavaquinho de Ouro, on Carioca Street. Pinheiro took a piece of paper and wrote a note instructing Oscar to make me a pandeiro with the following inscription: To João da Baiana, with my admiration—Pinheiro Machado.[5]

João da Baiana's description of this incident supports Hermano Vianna's broader analysis of the interclass connections that were integral to formation of Brazilian samba in the early twentieth century.[6] Thus, alongside the state sanctioned repression of Afro-Brazilian cultural manifestations, important elites such as senator Machado also cultivated relationships with members of the black community. The importance of the pandeiro itself at an elite social event hosted by a senator points up the fluid movement of the instrument across racial and class lines.

Marcos Suzano and Bernardo Aguiar

In contemporary Brazil, pandeiro performance styles continue to evolve as they draw from local and foreign influences. The 1990s witnessed the emergence of a new technique of pandeiro playing among a young generation of contemporary musicians in Rio de Janeiro who have developed virtuosic techniques and exploited electro-acoustic manipulations on the instrument as they incorporate rhythmic grooves from rock, funk, hip-hop, and numerous regional Brazilian styles into their playing. The leader of this new pandeiro revolution is Marcos Suzano, a musician who has turned the pandeiro world around.[7]

Born in Rio de Janeiro in 1964, Suzano's biography illustrates the flows of local and foreign cultural influences on Brazilian music so characteristic of the late twentieth century. Growing up on Rio's South side, in Cobacabana in the 1970s and 1980s, he listened heavily to American and British rock, especially the groups Led Zeppelin, Ten Years After, and King Crimson. His favorite drummers are John Bonham, Sly Dunbar, Bill Bruford, Stewart Copeland, Al Foster, and Numazawa Takashi. While idolizing such international icons, his first live experience in percussion came when he was around 14. Reflecting on the influence of local-based batucada samba percussion in a 1997 interview, he maintained (my translation):

I lived in Copabana and there was this batucada named O Caracol do Copacabana located on the street República do Perú, . . . my brothers and I went almost every day to attend the batucada. Later, I got to know a group of teens on the street and we put together some money to buy instruments: surdo, repinique, and cuíca. Pandeiro was the last one we bought. We drummed together . . . there were 20 or 30 of us that got together to drink beer and pass the hat to buy more instruments. This lasted until I was about 18, 20 years old.[8]

In his twenties, Suzano became interested in the local choro and *samba de raiz* (roots samba) scene in Rio de Janeiro and began concentrating on the pandeiro. He cites Jorginho do Pandeiro of the famous Epoca de Ouro choro group and his son Celsinho as his primary inspirations on pandeiro. In July 2006 Suzano told me he liked the pandeiro because:

the pandeiro can synthesize the samba, can synthesize the batucada, possibly also, because it was the last instrument [we acquired] in the samba school when I began to play. When I saw Jorginho on television playing with Clementina de Jesus, and listening to records of Clara Nunes, Paulinho da Viola, Jorginho playing, Celsinho, the sound of the pandeiro was illuminated for me. It was the most beautiful pandeiro sound, it is the most beautiful samba rhythm, choro rhythm. I had never heard anything like it.[9]

At this time he was beginning to study and work on the way that the pandeiro was played. Brazilian samba and choro playing on the pandeiro typically involves a sequence of four strokes with the right hand beginning with the thumb on the beat: thumb, fingers, palm, fingers, while the left hand holds the instrument relatively flat and stationary. As the strokes are played, the right hand rocks forward for strokes on the fingers and backward for those on the thumb/palm. The thumb, playing near the rim of the skin, produces a low-pitched open stroke reminiscent of the bass drum (surdo) in a samba ensemble while the fingers and palm produce a higher pitched and muffled sound that emphasizes the metal jingles of the pandeiro.

Suzano's fundamental innovation to pandeiro playing in Brazil came when he decided to invert the typical sequence described in Example 2.1 and instead lead with his fingers. Suzano discovered that he could produce a low bass-drum sound with his fingers as well as his thumb when he tuned the pandeiro's skin to a low pitch. In addition, he stressed a back and forth movement in the left hand to provide more power to his right-hand strokes. These innovations allowed him to adapt rhythms from North American rock, funk, hip-hop, and other styles that featured back-beat accents. Pandeiro players typically play accented beats by slapping the skin with a forward motion of the hand. When playing in the traditional pandeiro technique, this naturally places slaps on the syncopated off beats when the fingers strike the skin. By inverting the sequence and

Example 2.1 Basic sequence of a samba on the pandeiro. Letters under the notes indicate the following: T—open bass sound with the thumb; F—muffled sound with the fingers; P—muffled sound with the palm.

leading with the fingers, Suzano was able to slap the accented backbeats so common in American popular music. In the 1990s Suzano created a number of innovative grooves on the pandeiro that were subsequently copied by many Brazilian pandeiro players. One of Suzano's influential grooves was his adaptation of funk, derived from the interplay of snare drum and bass drum on a drumset.

In 1991, Suzano also began working with different ways to amplify the sound of the pandeiro. While performing with the group Aquarela Carioca, Suzano experimented with different microphones, microphone placement, mixers, and electronic effects. Suzano settled on the Shure 98H condenser microphone, which he clips on the rim of the underside of the pandeiro and then runs the signal through an effects processor and several electronic pedals before sending the signal to an amplifier and speakers. His pandeiro is tuned low and the sound is EQed to over-emphasize the bass range of the instrument. This became the Suzano sound heard on influential recordings such as *Olho de Peixe* (Lenine and Suzano, 1993), *Sambatown* (Suzano, 1999) and *Carlos Malta e Pife Muderno* (1999).

In addition to becoming an influential pandeiro performer and recording artist, Marcos Suzano also trained a number of younger musicians through his pandeiro workshops. His early workshops given in the Rio de Janeiro area led to the creation of an all-pandeiro group called Pandemonium featuring his students. One of Suzano's star students is Bernardo Aguiar.

Like Suzano, Aguiar began playing percussion in a local Escola de Samba from Rio's southern zone. He first heard Suzano's Pandemonium group when he was fourteen (1997) and then took one of Suzano's pandeiro workshops. According to Aguiar,

> He used to give courses, usually with eight lessons, for a lot of people. This really disseminated the [Suzano style of] pandeiro. This is something that dis-seminated it a lot. Suzano is intelligent; he invented that technique, innovated it. He invented that technique of grabbing the pandeiro and playing funk. Drumset in a bag! The pandeiro is a drumset in a bag. He picked [the pandeiro] up, studied it, tuned it, and didn't play beginning on the bottom [thumb]; he began on top [fingers]. And nobody had done that [singing the Suzano pandeiro funk beat]. Everybody always began on the bottom.[10]

With the group Pandemonium, Aguiar participated in Percpan 2000 (Panorama of World Percussion) in Salvador da Bahia. Under Suzano's tutelage, Aguiar began performing with some of the best players in Rio and by the age of seventeen was

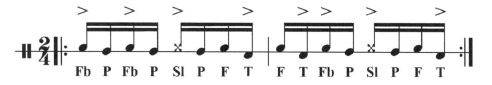

Example 2.2 Marcos Suzano's funk pattern with back beat accents. Fb (open bass sound with the fingers), F (muffled treble sound with the fingers), P (muffled treble sound with the palm), Sl (accented slap with the flat hand), T (open bass sound with the thumb).

Figure 2.7
Marcos Suzano at his apartment in Rio de Janeiro playing pandeiro in front of his computer, signal processors, and other electronic devices he uses when performing or recording (photo by Larry Crook).

substituting for his teacher. Aguiar has played and recorded widely with musicians and musical groups including Rodrigo Lessa, Eduardo Neves, Nelson Sargento, Carlos Malta e Pife Muderno, Altamiro Carrilho, Katia B. and O Rappa.

To gain an appreciation for the art of pandeiro playing, listen to *Track 3* of the compact disc. This is a recording I made of Bernardo Aguiar performing one morning in the park at the Palácio do Catete in Rio de Janeiro. At the beginning of the track Aguiar demonstrates the technique of changing the pitch of the open bass sound on the pandeiro by pressing the thumb of his left hand into the skin. At about 1:04 (one minute and four seconds) into the recording he begins playing the melody to the well-known Brazilian song from the Northeast, "Asa Branca" in this manner. Next, he shows the versatility of the instrument with a variety of slaps, finger rolls, flams, and bass tones. Finally, at about 2:00 (two-minute mark), Aguiar uses the pandeiro to evoke the sound of an entire samba percussion group. In Aguiar's hands, the pandeiro is truly a *bateria no bolso*. We will now

Figure 2.8
Bernardo Aguiar
playing pandeiro
in Rio de Janeiro,
2006 (photo by
Larry Crook).

shift our attention to the yearly context in which an entire samba percussion group made up of multiple pandeiro players and many other instruments plays: Carnival.

Brazilian Carnival and the Samba

Occurring in the hottest days of summer, Carnival—a nationwide, collective party for Brazilians—is Brazil's largest public festival and is celebrated throughout the country. Its closest parallel in the United States is the Mardi Gras of New Orleans. Imagine if Mardi Gras were celebrated simultaneously throughout the United States around the Fourth of July, with all the major U.S. cities having official parades featuring musical and dance groups that had rehearsed for months. Carnival also has something of the "party till you drop" attitude that surrounds New Year's Eve celebrations. Multiply that idea about tenfold and you start to understand the importance of Carnival in Brazil.

Carnival occurs over the four days before Ash Wednesday (a Catholic holy day that begins the forty-day period of Lent preceding Easter). It usually falls within the month of February, when Brazilian summer vacation is in full swing. The period between New Year's and Carnival is full of preparation and celebration. Although the Carnival proper takes place within an intense period of non-stop activity from Saturday through Tuesday, many warm-up parades, public performances, rehearsals, and private balls occur in the weeks and months leading up to this event. This is Carnival season, and by the time the four days of Carnival arrive, people across the country have worked themselves into a fevered pitch.

Since the 1930s, the samba has become synonymous with Carnival in Brazil. Carnival samba is a highly percussive variety of samba, featuring a large drum and percussion ensemble, singing, and rhythmic strumming on Brazil's ukulele-like cavaquinho. For Brazilians, only one thing can compare with samba's popularity—soccer—and in Brazil, the land of soccer, many comparisons are made between the skillful footwork of a soccer star and the quick steps of a samba dancer. Samba drumming is also part of Brazilian soccer matches. Whenever the Brazilian national soccer team plays a match, there is a group of samba drummers in the stands providing Carnival-style samba to energize the team and the Brazilian fans. The undisputed center of soccer, samba, and Carnival in Brazil is Rio de Janeiro, the "Marvelous City."

Rio's Carnival celebration is an internationally famous event dominated by the extensive media coverage of the city's Afro-Brazilian Carnival organizations known as samba schools (escolas de samba). To outsiders, this public festival and the samba schools seem to be about the country's African heritage. To Brazilians, however, Carnival is a ritual that highlights Brazil's unique cultural and racial mixture in addition to the special place that has been reserved for African heritage in the country. The designation of Rio's Carnival groups as samba schools derives from the fact that the very first samba group (Deixa Falar) was founded across the street from an elementary school. Samba schools in Rio de Janeiro first emerged in the late 1920s among poor people from the city's slums, where the majority of the inhabitants were blacks and mulattoes. Many were migrants from Bahia in the Northeast or were the sons and daughters of earlier migrants from that area of the country. In hillside slum communities, the percussion-driven samba style took shape and became the primary moving force behind Rio de Janeiro's Carnival. Today, a large samba school's drum and percussion section, known as a bateria, might include 300 musicians under the direction of a drum master (mestre de bateria) who controls the entire ensemble with an iron fist and demands split-second precision. Playing with incredible speed and accuracy, the various sections of the bateria perform tightly coordinated interlocking rhythmic patterns, which are layered on top of the rock-solid foundation of the surdos, the low-pitched bass drums. Experiencing one of these large percussion ensembles in full force is a breathtaking and awe-inspiring experience. A samba school drum section has a rhythmic groove as strong as any African American marching band drum-line from the southern United States—but with much more energy. Each samba school develops specific cadences and unique signature patterns based on highly syncopated rhythms that fall into four-, eight-, and sixteen-beat units. There is also a playfulness and a characteristic "swing" to samba that defies musical notation and falls somewhere between a feeling of three and four subdivisions of the anchor beats provided by the bass drums. All Brazilians recognize this quality when they hear it in a performance: this is the samba. In addition to the large percussion bateria, samba schools have lead singers who are responsible for controlling hundreds or even thousands of voices (everyone in a samba school seems to be a singer) singing in perfect coordination with the drumming. To the singing and drumming, the small cavaquinho guitar adds harmonic and rhythmic support. Together, this is the driving force that propels a samba school parade.

Mounting the parade of a large samba school in Rio's Carnival can involve tens of thousands of people: musicians, dancers, composers, costume designers, costume makers, float designers, and hosts of other workers. In addition to the musicians, the group has numerous sections called wings, each with coordinated costuming. Of particular importance is the *ala de baianas* (wing of Bahian women). This section of a samba school highlights the historical link of these organizations and of samba itself with Afro-Bahian culture. This wing features matronly black women costumed in flowing dresses and turbans reminiscent of the dresses and accessories worn by women practitioners of the Afro-Brazilian Candomblé religion from Bahia. Candomblé priestesses from that area were important figures in Rio de Janeiro's cultural environment at the turn of the twentieth century.

Every year, a samba school chooses a theme (*enredo*), which must be expressed through the group's costuming, music, song poetry, and dance during the official parade. After the theme is determined, local samba composers write songs based on that theme and submit them to the officials of the samba school for review. During open rehearsals and public competitions in which the general membership of the samba school is allowed to voice its opinions, a winning samba song is chosen for that year's parade. After months of rehearsals, the samba school participants offer a well-choreographed and theatrical presentation of the enredo in front of official judges, who will score them on a variety of elements, including rhythm, harmony, dance, costuming, and overall coordination. Each year, the official competition of Rio's top samba schools is broadcast throughout Brazil on national television.

The initial structure and format of the samba schools from Rio de Janeiro developed during the 1930s and 1940s and then spread to other large cities in Brazil, becoming a national tradition of Carnival. Also during that time, the samba from Rio de Janeiro developed into a recorded popular music and attained unprecedented commercial success within Brazil's national music industry. A basic distinction was established between the samba styles of the hillside slums (including the sambas of the samba schools), where the poor black population resided, and urban commercial sambas produced by Brazil's nascent music industry, which catered to middle-class national tastes. Songwriters in Rio developed the commercialized and slower-paced s*amba-canção* (samba song); it became a mainstay of the popular recording and broadcast industry and was sung by star vocalists such as Francisco Alves and even Carmen Miranda. Other hybrid forms of samba also emerged, mixing rich Afro-Brazilian percussion with guitars and other European instruments. It was this musical mix of African and European aesthetics that made the samba an appropriate national symbol of Brazilian unification.

Prior to the rise of the samba and the samba schools in Rio de Janeiro, the city's Carnival featured parades with marching bands, middle-class revelers singing lyrical songs set to slow march rhythms and accompanied by string and wind instruments, and lower-class groups with percussive-based Afro-Brazilian music and dance expressions.[11] Similar Carnival music traditions were also found in Brazil's other major cities in the nineteenth and early twentieth centuries. A brief look at the historical roots of Brazilian Carnival in the nineteenth century will show how these pre-samba traditions reflected the racial and cultural diversity of the nation.

Carnival in Nineteenth-Century Brazil

Though officially linked to the pre-Lenten period of the Catholic calendar, Brazil's yearly Carnival celebration has been influenced by a variety of non-Christian traditions inherited from both Europe and Africa. Various African masked processions linked to secular and religious occasions and Portuguese traditions of public revelry have been part of public life in Brazilian communities since colonial days. However, the modern Carnival began to take shape only in the mid-nineteenth century, when European-influenced masked balls and outdoor parades were started during Carnival time in Rio de Janeiro, Recife, and Salvador.

In the first decades of the nineteenth century, middle- and upper-class Brazilians increasingly voiced their opposition to the disorderly conduct among the lower classes that occurred each year during the days before Ash Wednesday. They directed their scorn primarily at an old tradition of rowdiness inherited from the Portuguese, known as the *entrudo* (Shrovetide). Somewhat akin to the prankster activities that occur around Halloween in the United States, the entrudo in Brazilian cities was dominated by bands of revelers who threw dirty water, flour, and various vile substances at each other and at passersby they happened to encounter on the streets. A rather unregulated free-for-all, the entrudo was often cited as the cause of the violent encounters in Brazil's burgeoning cities during Carnival season. Beginning in the 1820s, elites waged a widespread campaign against this disorderly public practice. Legislators passed prohibitions, police cracked down on street rowdiness, and newspapers voiced opposition to the "barbaric" practice of the entrudo. For nineteenth-century Brazilian leaders and intellectuals, the entrudo was a prime example of archaic social practices inherited from the Portuguese that were unfit for the civilized modern nation they so desperately wanted Brazil to become. Interest in proscribing the entrudo occurred within the context of the broader national project of constructing a modern nation in the nineteenth century.

Increased export trade (primarily coffee grown in south-central Brazil) stimulated the country's commercial activity, which was largely in the hands of Europeans, North Americans, and a few Brazilians closely allied with the foreign business community. This important group of modernizers established roads and constructed railways connecting Brazil's large coastal cities to interior regions.[12] In tandem with the economic and political transformation of Brazil, new middle- and upper-class urban groups sought to cast off the yoke of cultural heritage from both Portugal—a country seen as backward in relation to the more advanced European nations—and Africa—a continent equated with barbarity. These attitudes stimulated the development of modern Carnival diversions among cosmopolitan urban groups, based on European models.

Beginning in the 1840s, first in Rio de Janeiro (in 1840) and quickly thereafter in Recife and Salvador, European-style masquerade balls became a popular diversion for the elite classes during Carnival season; these balls were patterned on similar events held in Paris and Venice. Recife's first masquerade ball occurred in 1845 in a large private home. Two years later, such balls were organized as commercial events, with entrance fees charged, at the city's Teatro Público and Teatro do Apollo.[13] The desire of Recife's elite to establish cosmopolitan cultural values in common with their counterparts in the nation's imperial capital, Rio de Janeiro (Brazil was an empire with a constitutional monarchy in this period), was revealed in an announcement published in the city's main newspaper, the *Diário de Pernambuco,* on February 8, 1848 (my translation):

> In 1844, at the São Pedro de Alcântara Theater of the Court in Rio de Janeiro, the first Masquerade Ball during Carnival took place. . . . Pernambuco, whose capital [Recife] rivals that of the Court of the [Brazilian] Empire in luxury and cultured refinement, should not be the victim of the prejudices of the eighteenth century. It is with confidence in the civilized and genteel nature of the inhabitants of this, the second capital of the Empire, that the first public Masquerade Ball [in Recife], under the following conditions will be religiously held.[14]

The "civilized and genteel nature" of Recife's elite inhabitants who participated in the masquerade balls reflected the prevailing Eurocentric cultural attitudes of mid-nineteenth-century Brazil. Indeed, it was through the adoption of the cultural practices of modern Europe that Brazilian elites could see themselves as participants in the modern world order of the nineteenth century. For the masquerade balls, dance companies and singers from France and Italy were regularly hired to instruct members of the local elite in the latest European dances. Brazilian string orchestras and military bands provided the musical entertainment at the events, offering a mixture of light classical music and the popular social dance music of the day. Both types of musical ensembles derived from European musical culture. One ball that took place at the Teatro de Santo Antonio in Recife during the Carnival of 1873 was advertised in the *Diário de Pernambuco* (my translation):

> Carnavalesque Revelry with a Grand Masquerade Ball—As of this moment, the regular clientele are advised that the stage has been enlarged to accommodate a grand room with plenty of space for the revelers to party in comfort. . . . The band, directed by the skillful and learned professor of music Guimarães Peixoto, will perform some newly chosen *quadrilhas, valsas, polkas, schottisches,* etc. The celebrated dance professor, Mr. Batista, will direct the grand ballroom as the dance-master.[15]

The inclusion of military bands in these exclusive indoor occasions reveals that the Brazilian elite associated the band tradition with modern European cultural trends and expected band musicians to possess the technical ability to perform the most up-to-date European musical styles. The formal training of Brazilian bandmasters and developments in wind and brass instruments provided the musical literacy and technical resources for bands to perform written music.

In addition to the indoor masquerade balls held at theaters and hotels during the night-time hours, elites also organized outdoor parades during the days of Carnival. Urban social clubs were formed with the explicit purpose of promoting and organizing Carnival activities for their members. These clubs took to the streets during the daylight hours with marching bands and groups of masked revelers. Whereas the string orchestras of the elite shared the stage with the military bands for the indoor events, only the bands performed in the street during Carnival. At other times of the year, marching bands also played for community-wide civic and religious processions. Membership in bands cut across class and race lines in Brazilian communities. The wide range of civic and religious activities and the broad base of their memberships made bands important emblems of unity and pride for their communities. Some vernacular and elite forms of music making were associated with distinct sectors of Brazil's population, but the band tradition cut through such layers. The musical repertoires of the bands also reflected the intercultural nature of the groups and the diverse contexts in which they performed. Hence, while maintaining a core repertoire of military marches and patriotic hymns, these ensembles also performed the international social dances of the day as desired by their cosmopolitan audiences—waltzes, polkas, schottisches, mazurkas, and tangos. In the second half of the nineteenth century, new hybrid genres and styles of music developed in the repertoires of these bands.

Brazilian military and civic bands became creative laboratories where composers, arrangers, performing musicians, and dancers coalesced to develop unique Brazilian forms of music and dance that blended local, regional, and international elements. In the dance halls of Rio de Janeiro, this artistic and social hybridity led to Brazil's first nationalized popular dance music, the *maxixe*, which combined elements of Afro-Brazilian rhythmic syncopation with European designs of harmony and structure. The maxixe was an early form of popular music and would greatly influence the development of the commercial samba. In Recife, European band music mixed with Afro-Brazilian dance forms during outdoor Carnival parading. Parading involved heated rivalries among the marching bands and their racially diverse followers. In this intercultural context, the highly syncopated style of band music known as the frevo was created, becoming a musical symbol of racial and cultural mixture in the urban Northeast. By the turn of the twentieth century, marching bands were an integral part of Carnival parades in Recife, Salvador, and Rio de Janeiro, and they provided a mixed repertoire for Carnival celebrations. Though drawn from European heritage, bands in Brazil reflected patterns of racial and cultural interaction. Before the advent of samba, Carnival in Brazil also featured parading groups with guitars, light woodwind instruments, and lyrical singing.

European String and Wind Bands in Carnival

At the end of the nineteenth century, many urban middle-class participants began forming their own groups to march in Carnival. These groups were often based on extended family and neighborhood affiliations and included men and women singing European-style songs, accompanied primarily by string and wind instruments. These parading groups drew substantially from processions and patronal festivals associated with the country's Catholic heritage. In Rio de Janeiro, Carnival groups called ranchos (wanderers) tapped these traditions and featured the singing of lyrical melodies over slow march rhythms. The musical style was light, based on string and wind instruments, and European in style and structure. In Recife, similar groups of paraders were called *blocos carnavalescos* (Carnival blocs).

The blocos drew heavily on a tradition of folk Catholicism that was popular during the Christmas season and was known as the *pastoril*, involving young girls dressed as shepherdesses who sang songs in unison and danced in honor of the birth of Christ. The blocos carnavalescos carried some of the music and style of the pastoril into Carnival celebrations; the groups were formed primarily among middle-class Portuguese and Italian immigrant families and provided a safe and protected environment in which their "respectable" young girls and women could participate in Recife's rowdy public carnival. Female relatives, especially teenage girls, formed the singing groups, and men of all ages specialized in string bands that provided the accompaniment in groups called *pau e corda* (wood and string). The instruments of these woodwind and string bands, developed mainly from southern European musical traditions, included the flute, clarinet, mandolin, cavaquinho, guitar, violin, and tambourine (the pandeiro). Many of the young men who participated in the pau e corda bands also sang sentimental and romantic songs, which they used for serenading. The overall sound of these string and wind ensembles was well suited to accompany singing, and neither the instrumental nor the vocal group overpowered the other.

These groups and their music symbolized a respectable European presence within the more raucous nature of Carnival. The bloco carnavalesco from Recife that was described in Chapter 1 is a modern descendant of these early twentieth-century groups. In Recife, a tradition of singing Carnival marches to the accompaniment of the pau e corda ensembles now infuses a nostalgic element in the city's celebration. In Rio de Janeiro, similar nostalgic feelings are part of the repertoire of the *marchas de rancho*.

In the past, this light style of Carnival march music contrasted with the louder and more aggressive styles of marching band music. It also contrasted with another type of music and dance in the Brazilian Carnival before the advent of samba—activities that highlighted the Afro-Brazilian heritage of Brazil's black people, who took to the streets singing and dancing with percussion-based music.

Shadows of Africa: Black Carnival Traditions in Brazil

Anyone who attends present-day Carnival in Salvador, Bahia, is sure to be struck by the Afro-Brazilian drumming and dancing that seem to permeate every square inch of the city. On each corner are young black musicians playing a style of music known generically as *samba-reggae*. This particular drumming style is a relatively recent development, but it reflects the undercurrents and roots of a deep Afro-Brazilian presence in the area. These roots are highlighted by Carnival groups called blocos afro, or Afroblocs, which feature large percussion ensembles and vocal groups in costuming that celebrates an African heritage and contemporary black cultural awareness. The two most established Afroblocs are the groups Olodum and Ilê Aiyê. Both of these organizations chose their names to reflect the strong presence of West African Yoruba heritage in Bahia. In Salvador's contemporary Carnival, one will also find many groups from an older Afro-Brazilian tradition known as the *afoxé*, which features the songs and rhythms of Afro-Brazilian religion during the Carnival parades. The Afro-Brazilian heritage has a strong presence as well in Recife's Carnival (though not in as ubiquitous a manner as in Salvador), expressed primarily in the maracatu nations, such as the one I described in Chapter 1. The roots of these groups lie in the colonial institution of the "king of the Congo," in which blacks were allowed to crown symbolic kings and queens of their African "nations" and organize processions with African-style music and dance accompaniment. The maracatu nations, which trace their origins to this heritage and to the local Afro-Brazilian religious houses, are now permanent fixtures in Recife's Carnival. The long history of Afro-Brazilian participation in the Carnivals of the northeastern cities of Recife and Salvador goes back to the late nineteenth century.

Soon after the abolition of slavery in the late 1800s, processions celebrating African heritage entered the annual Carnival celebrations of Brazil's major cities. In both Recife and Salvador, the parading of black carnival groups highlighting "African" themes heralded the initial flourishing of African consciousness within the newly established Republic of Brazil. In Bahia, the new black parading groups included large, well-organized associations of uniformed members; small, spontaneous groups of revelers singing and dancing to samba-related music; and Afro-Brazilian religious communities whose members performed Candomblé music in the groups known as afoxés. In Recife, the maracatu nations provided a parallel African presence in that city's Carnival. The early flourishing of these urban Afro-Brazilian groups in the 1890s was followed by a nationwide crackdown. The Eurocentric, dominant sectors of Brazilian society called for state intervention to prohibit "barbarous" African practices and curtail the "Africanization" of their country's Carnival. But these traditions were never completely stamped out, and Afro-Brazilian communities maintained their cultural expressions as a means of resistance to the dominant values of a Eurocentric society. The Afro-Brazilian communities also made accommodations to European aesthetics and values, including participation in virtually all forms of Carnival music in Brazil. Although marching band parades and string and wind bands in Carnival derived from European heritage, black and mulatto musicians played foundational roles in the evolution of these traditions throughout the twentieth century. In Rio de Janeiro, the growth of the samba schools in the 1930s and 1940s brought vernacular Afro-Brazilian musical aesthetics to national attention and influenced the development of commercial samba. However, the groups that symbolized the deepest layer of African heritage for the country and its Carnival remained in the northeastern cities. In Recife, this deep African heritage was expressed in the maracatu; in Salvador, it was represented in the afoxé. These forms remained important yet marginalized traditions of the Carnivals of their respective cities until a renaissance of African heritage and black cultural awareness occurred in the 1970s. The main stage from which this re-Africanization was launched was the Carnival of Salvador, Bahia.

During the 1970s and 1980s, a rebirth of black musical activity emerged in Salvador's Carnival. A combination of social, political, economic, and cultural factors propelled the re-Africanization of the Carnival and the creation of the Afro bloc Carnival groups, among them Ilê Aiyê and Olodum. These groups reinterpreted Afro-Brazilian traditions such as samba and afoxé and mixed them with contemporary African, African American, and Afro-Caribbean popular music styles. Salvador's bloco afro groups garnered national and international media attention and became part of the world music scene when Paul Simon traveled to Brazil and recorded the Olodum group for his song "The Obvious Child" (1990). This intersection of Carnival and international popular music exemplifies the continued hybridity of Brazil's musical traditions.

The Interplay of Folk and Popular Music in Brazil

The interaction of rural and urban music making and the mixing of local, regional, and national traditions with non-Brazilian music characterize both folk and popular music in Brazil. Even the most local music of the rural areas of the country interacts with national and international trends in music. In the twentieth century, cultural and musical interchanges became more intense as the means of mass communication expanded and internal migrations of the Brazilian population increased. The general pattern of urbanization from the mid-nineteenth century onwards saw rural populations from the interior regions of the country flood into the cities. This development was particularly important for the migration of peoples from the Northeast to the urban environments of the South, which included Afro-Brazilians from the coastal areas of Bahia as well as the mixed-race caboclo populations from the interior sertão. The evolution of Brazil's national popular music in the city of Rio de Janeiro was greatly impacted by this dual movement of peoples and cultural traditions. Early forms of the samba and choro were strongly influenced by black migrants from Bahia, who impacted the musical life of Rio de Janeiro. Equally important were waves of migrations and cultural influences from the sertão. These latter influences paved the way for the development of the country's most important regional form of popular music: the baião. As with the emergence of country music in the United States, the development of the baião reflected nostalgic values of the country's agrarian past. Radio broadcasts and sound recordings circulated national and regional forms of popular entertainment throughout Brazil, in rural and urban areas alike.[16] The development of Carnival music as a mass form of entertainment involved not only the spread of samba as the country's primary national popular music but also the emergence of regional forms of Carnival music, such as the frevo of Recife, that were recorded and broadcast on radio. The circulation of these and other forms of popular music in the second half of the twentieth century was characterized by the increasing influence of regional music on national and international arenas. To explore the regional and cultural associations that inform Brazilians' perceptions of popular music in their country, I will now survey some important folk traditions in Brazil.

Country Roots and Brazilian Popular Music

The country-dance music of the northeastern caboclo population centers around a variety of "Brazilianized" European dance forms (for example, the polka, schottische, and quadrille) as well as uniquely Brazilian forms (such as the baião and forró). Small dance ensembles featuring the accordion, the zabumba bass drum, and the triangle are commonly used to provide the music for occasions in which social dancing occurs. Accordion groups are kept particularly busy during the month of June, when Brazilian winter festivals celebrate three important Catholic saints. Rural communities and urban neighborhoods decorate streets with multicolored flags, build bonfires, and construct temporary structures for social dancing and square-dance competitions. It was largely from these traditions that Luiz Gonzaga popularized northeastern music in the 1940s and 1950s in Rio de Janeiro (Chapter 5).

In that process, Gonzaga also drew on another important instrumental tradition of the sertão—the fife-and-drum groups known as the bandas de pífanos. These ensembles are the preferred musical accompaniment for a range of secular and religious festivities of the caboclo population. The sound of a banda de pífanos evokes strong feelings of religiosity among the caboclo, who use these groups in many rituals of folk Catholicism (Chapter 6). The groups also play for social dancing and share part of their repertoire with the accordion-based bands of the area. Though the principal model for the fife-and-drum groups derives from Portuguese heritage, the symbolic association of the cane flutes with indigenous heritage is also strong. This combination of Portuguese and Amerindian heritage makes the bandas de pífanos important symbols of the mixed caboclo culture for national audiences. Brazilian popular music stars Gilberto Gil and Caetano Veloso referenced the tradition in the 1970s. In the 1990s, flute and saxophone artist Carlos Malta, from Rio de Janeiro, created the first national banda de pífanos group with his band Carlos Malta & Pife Muderno (Modern Fife).

Música sertaneja (Brazilian country music associated with rural musical traditions from the states of São Paulo and Minas Gerais) has exerted considerable influence on Brazilian popular music. Since the mid-1940s, música sertaneja has been one of the most widespread popular musics in Brazil and has a huge following among working-class populations throughout the country, especially among migrant workers in São Paulo.[17] Música sertaneja is rooted in Portuguese musical traditions that were carried on and re-worked in rural southeastern Brazil during colonial times. Stylistic traits that show enduring Portuguese musical influence include: the extensive use of stringed instruments; the use of arched melodies sung and played in parallel thirds and sixths; employment of simple tonality; and the use stanza-refrain and strophic forms with texts organized into quatrains (four-line stanzas) and décimas (ten-line stanzas). In the early twentieth century, the *moda-de-viola, toadas* and other rural genres were brought into the city and recorded. This music, which was marketed initially as *música caipira* and later as música sertaneja, was characterized by *dupla* (paired voices) singing in parallel thirds and sixths (typical of Portuguese folk traditions in southeast Brazil) with the accompaniment of two *violas caipira* (violas from the Caipira lands). Early recordings from the 1920s and 1930s were faithful to the tradition rural genres and attracted interest among both rural and urban working-class audiences. A major figure in the early dissemination of this music was Cornélio Pires, a musical impresario who organized caravans of viola players and singers in the 1920s and is credited as the first person to bring "authentic" rural caipira musicians into the recording studio. In the 1940s and 1950s, *duplas caipiras* such as Torres e Florêncio and Tonico e Tinoco scored hit songs and served to define the broad stylistic elements of the music along traditional lines: singing in parallel thirds and sixths, use of rural caipira dialect with a nasalized singing style, accompaniment by guitar and viola caipira, and lyrics that realistically depicted rural life in the Southeast. Beginning in the 1960s, the name música sertaneja took hold as a less pejorative designation for this music, which was commercialized and transformed with elaborate musical arrangements, singing without heavy caipira accents, and with more nostalgic lyrics. In the 1970s and 1980s, a young generation of rock-influenced musicians took música sertaneja into a pop era with a new level of technical sophistication and production aesthetics with performances featuring "synthesizers, full orchestras, choruses and all sorts of other resources."[18]

Processional traditions associated with popular Catholicism and musical dance dramas (dramatic dances) are also an important part of the cultural life of many rural areas, especially along the coast of the northeastern states and in southeastern Brazil. Originally introduced by Jesuit priests in colonial times to convert the non-Christian Amerindian and African populations, these dances evolved into numerous forms—from simple presentations to elaborate, all-night rituals. Particularly noteworthy is the *bumba-meu-boi*, a folk drama involving the character of a bull that presents a theme of death and resurrection and is accompanied by several different types of regional instrumental ensembles.[19] Closely related is the cavalo-marinho, a folk drama that is particularly strong in the sugarcane-growing areas around the city of Recife. The ensembles that perform for the cavalo-marinho utilize the rabeca folk violin as the lead instrument and perform lively and syncopated dances. Since the mid 1990s, the rabeca has been an important instrumental symbol of the cultural revival movement of urban popular musicians in Recife. This movement seeks to re-establish cultural ties with northeastern roots.

Finally, a singer–poet tradition inherited from medieval Iberian minstrelsy is maintained in the Northeast under the name of *cantoria* (Chapter 6). One of the richest forms of improvised poetry in Latin America, cantoria features song duels between singer–poets who accompany themselves on the viola guitar. Social and political criticism forms the core of the thematic content of the poetry. Cantoria is considered a cultural treasure of the Northeast, and singing competitions and festivals of cantoria now take place in all of Brazil, especially in the southern city of São Paulo. Many popular musicians draw inspiration from this and related poetic-song traditions of the Northeast. In the early years of the twentieth century, guitarists and poets from the Northeast went to Rio de Janeiro and carried poetic and musical influences into the city's musical atmosphere. Particularly influential was the guitarist João Pernambuco.

Afro-Brazilian Roots of Brazilian Popular Music

The orthodox Afro-Brazilian religious music of Candomblé in Bahia is a model for Afro-Brazilian musical practices in the country. The distinctly West African qualities of Candomblé music include:

- "Family" of drums, a metal bell, and/or a shaker, which together perform syncopated rhythmic schemes based on multiple patterns
- Vocal organization that emphasizes call-and-response singing with a leader and chorus and frequent off-beat placement of notes
- Scales of five and six pitches per octave.

The importance of drumming and its integration with dancing is fundamental to Afro-Brazilian religious and secular forms of music. Many older Afro-Brazilian folk dances are traced to the Congo-Angola region of Bantu Africa. These dances are typically performed in a circle, and many include a choreographic movement known as *umbigada* (navel touch). Originally, only singing and percussion accompanied most of these dances. One early circle dance was the batuque. Although the specific dance became extinct, the term *batuque* and its cognates lived on as generic designations for Afro-Brazilian secular dances with powerful percussion accompaniment. For instance, in the urban environs of Rio de Janeiro, *batucada* became a cover term for the percussive dance music of the large baterias (percussion sections) of the samba schools.

The word *samba* itself likely derives from the Quimbundo word *semba*, meaning navel touch. In Brazil, *samba* became a generic term for all sorts of Afro-Brazilian secular dances, and it exists (or did in the past) in a variety of folk forms throughout the country, especially in Bahia. Common characteristics of the samba include duple meter, syncopated rhythms emphasizing a playful ambiguity between duple and triple division of the pulse, and call-and-response singing. The addition of stringed instruments such as the guitar and the cavaquinho to percussion instruments such as the pandeiro, agogô, and atabaque, as well as the practice of singing in parallel thirds, occurred as African and Portuguese peoples and cultural practices intermingled. The samba de roda (still common in Bahia) is a round dance involving small ensembles with such instruments as the atabaque, pandeiro, agogô, cavaquinho, and viola. The Bahian samba de viola, as its name indicates, highlights the role of the viola. In Rio de Janeiro, the *samba de morro* (samba of hillside shantytowns) and the *partido alto* (a type of samba brought to Rio from Bahia) developed early in the twentieth century and had close ties to rural folk sambas. Accompanied by percussion instruments and the cavaquinho, they were important influences on the development of samba schools in the city.

In the Northeast, a widespread form of music, dance, and poetry closely related to the samba is the *côco* (coconut). With many regional variants, the côco as a danced form involves a circle of participants who dance, sing, clap, and play percussion instruments. A lead singer improvises the main verses while a chorus responds with set refrains. One non-danced variant, the *côco de embolada* (tongue twister côco), emphasizes the rapid-fire delivery of comic poetry utilizing double entendre. Côcos are usually accompanied by percussion instruments such as the *ganzá* (metal shaker), pandeiro, and zabumba. The côco has served as an inspiration for several generations of popular musicians in Brazil, including, most recently, the mangue beat generation of Recife musicians represented by Chico Science & Nação Zumbi (Chapter 7).

As mentioned earlier, Carnival celebrations in Brazil have been important contexts for the development of Afro-Brazilian styles of dance and music. In addition to the impact of the Rio de Janeiro Carnival on the development of samba, the Carnival traditions of Recife and Salvador have been particularly fertile grounds for musical styles of national impact. In Recife, the maracatu has become a symbol of Afro-Brazil. Popular musicians from the 1930s to the present have referenced the maracatu as a foundational source of Afro-Brazilian identity. In Salvador da Bahia, the afoxé was part of a major renaissance of Afro-Bahian culture in the 1970s and 1980s, when many new politicized groups were formed. Brazilian popular music star Gilberto Gil marched with the afoxé group Filhos de Gandhi and adapted afoxé music in his own repertoire. His close association with this group helped revitalize the tradition and is a good example of the contemporary interplay of folk and popular music in Brazil.

Another closely related Bahian Carnival tradition, the bloco afro, or Afro bloc, emerged in the 1970s and flourished in the national popular music scenes of the 1980s and 1990s.[20] Professional music ensembles attached to the bloco afro Carnival groups (most notably from Ilê Aiyê, Muzenza, Ara Ketu, and Olodum) incorporated the highly percussive style of the samba played by the larger Carnival associations. Subsequent local adaptations of Caribbean rhythms led to the creation of a distinctive style of hybrid samba called samba-reggae in the 1980s, which was adopted by the Brazilian music industry under the marketing term *axé music*. This musical movement was thrust into the international world music scene when local Bahian groups collaborated with Paul Simon and Michael Jackson in the 1990s.

National Popular Music and the Emergence of Samba

The idea of a unifying music in Brazil is typically dated to the late eighteenth century but specific forms of music only became truly national and popular among most sectors of Brazilian society in the twentieth century. The roots of Brazil's national popular music lie in the eighteenth century. From the early 1700s, two genres, the *lundu* and the *moda*, competed to become the first Brazilian musical forms and symbolically referenced African and European heritage in the country, respectively. The former was both a dance music related to the Afro-Brazilian batuque round dances and a humorous, rhythmically accentuated song type. The popularized lundu was the first manifestation of Afro-Brazilian culture accepted in white society. *Moda* is a generic term for Portuguese song or melody. Found in both Portugal and then Brazil, the term refers to many different song types. Evidence indicates modas were performed at a wedding reception at the viceroy's palace in Bahia in 1729. The *modinha* (little moda) is a sentimental, Brazilianized form of the moda. Both the modinha and the lundu were first popularized by the Brazilian poet–performer Domingos Caldas Barbosa (1738–1800), who was active in the Portuguese court in Lisbon. Barbosa's Brazilian song types were described as vulgar, shocking, and the result of unrestrained sensual love associated with the tropics. From the colonial capital of Rio de Janeiro, the modinha and lundu spread across the nation via sheet music and oral transmission. Among trained composers, the modinha was stylized into an art song. Simultaneously, a more popular song form emerged as a sentimental ballad. Around 1870, modinhas began appearing in serenades and other public settings. In the 1910s and 1920s, Catulo da Paixão Cearense (1866–1946) revitalized the modinha in Rio de Janeiro; he brought stylized rural variants and song forms mainly from the Northeast to Rio's "polite" society.

Interactions between black and white musicians in urban areas also created new musical styles in the second half of the nineteenth century, especially after the abolition of slavery in 1888. The fusion of musical styles and genres had already given rise to new forms among military bands, dance bands, and piano composition with identifiable national traits, especially in several characteristic rhythmic syncopations derived from Afro-Brazilian heritage. A blending of the European polka, the Cuban habanera, the Andalusian tango, and the Brazilian lundu led to the creation of the Brazilian tango, which then led to the first recognized Brazilian dance genre, the maxixe. This form, born in the dance halls of Rio around 1875, was performed widely in the city's theaters and was even exported to Europe.

The instrumental (and occasionally vocal) music known as choro first developed in the last decades of the nineteenth century among serenading musicians in Rio de Janeiro with small ensembles featuring the flute, cavaquinho, and guitar. Choro musicians played European dances at parties and various social occasions. Later developments in choro saw the addition of new instruments (pandeiro, the seven-string guitar or violão de sete cordas), and the rise of professional choro groups in the 1930s called *conjuntos regionais* that served as studio musicians to accompany recording artists.[21] The annual Carnival celebration also became an important context for music making after the 1890s; the polka, march, maxixe, and tango were the preferred dances in the street or in elite clubs before the urban Carnival samba emerged. Marching bands also performed these mixed repertoires for Carnival celebrations.

Samba is the mainstay of modern popular music in Brazil. Since its appearance in the 1910s in published and recorded format, the samba has gone through several stages and has branched into many related forms. It may be performed by singer–guitarists, small ensembles of varying instrumentation, large percussion ensembles (samba schools), or ballroom and jazz orchestras. Songs began to be officially registered as samba in the late 1910s. The spread of the phonograph (the first national recordings date to 1902) and the growth of radio in the 1920s and 1930s aided the ascent of samba as a national form of popular entertainment. National Radio (founded in 1936) helped establish the samba on a nationwide scale. Most samba composers of humble origins were associated with the neighborhood-centered samba schools of Rio's hillside slums. These associations not only provided an important context for the development of Carnival but also gave rise to a number of composers and hybrid styles of samba. These were quickly incorporated into Brazil's popular music industry.

In the formative years of the 1930s, new urban samba in Rio placed an emphasis on melodic and harmonic elements and minimized the rich heritage of Afro-Brazilian drumming traditions. Commercial samba was thus distinct from samba de morro, or hillside slum samba, where the battery of Afro-Brazilian percussion instruments and dance were the focus of music making and Carnival revelry. By the 1930s, the slower-paced samba-canção had become the country's preferred form of sentimental urban musical expression. In the 1940s, the North American big-band sound had an impact on the ballroom samba. Middle-class taste favored crooners of samba-canção. It was not until the early 1970s that the percussive elements of the Carnival samba entered mainstream popular music, and many of Brazil's major musical stars included that sound in their repertoires.

MPB and Diversification of Brazilian Popular Music in the Late Twentieth Century

By the 1970s, the term *MPB* (*música popular brasileira* (popular Brazilian music)) had come into use to refer to the mainstream popular music that was deemed both national in scope and inherently Brazilian. MPB was distinguished from regionalist sounds of (especially) the Northeast, Brazilian rock, and the increasingly important country music of South Brazil known as música sertaneja. For some, the term *MPB* is also used, albeit less rigorously, to denote Brazilian popular music in general from 1900 to the present. A particularly significant factor in the development of MPB was the *Tropicália* movement led by musicians Gilberto Gil and Caetano Veloso from Salvador da Bahia in the late 1960s. The two Bahian musicians successfully spanned regional and national affiliations and audiences and became two of Brazil's most enduring musical artists.

During the 1970s, other sounds of the Northeast also gained renewed prominence on a national scale. The incorporation of northeastern elements in recent urban popular music echoes earlier fads in regional music. The Northeast has exerted considerable influence on Brazil's popular music emanating from Rio de Janeiro, a topic that will be covered in subsequent chapters. In the 1940s, the key new development in the urban popular music was the baião, dance music (and a song form) based on traditional musics of the interior of the Northeast. In the 1946 prototype recording of the song "Baião" (Gonzaga-Teixeira), Luiz Gonzaga established the typical group: vocalist–accordionist, triangle player, and zabumba drummer. The repertory of such ensembles also includes the dance rhythms *xaxado*, *xote* (Brazilianized schottische), and *arrasta-pé* and the more contemporary hybrid called forró. Between 1946 and 1956, this music became a national fad. In the 1950s, dance halls known as forrós, featuring these regional styles, appeared in Rio de Janeiro, São Paulo, and other cities following mass migrations of north-easterners in search of work. In addition to Gonzaga, Jackson do Pandeiro helped popularize northeastern sounds with adaptations of the rapid-fire côco and mixes of baião with urban samba. During the 1970s, electric instrumentation via rock influence became common in northeastern popular music, with mixtures of forró and rock yielding short-lived marketing terms such as *forrock*. Young composers and performers explored and expanded the traditional music of their region, especially the heritages of cantoria and forró. Singer–songwriters Geraldo Azevedo, Zé Ramalho, and Alceu Valença and singers Elba Ramalho and Raimundo Fagner all mixed northeastern elements into their repertoires. Other popular northeastern musicians, such as Nando Cordel, Jorge de Altinho, and Alcimar Monteiro, focused more directly on popularizing and modernizing forró dance music for new audiences. Also, beginning in the 1990s, a forró revivalist movement among university students, appropriately dubbed *forró universitário*, infused new energy into this northeastern dance music. Most recently, Gilberto Gil has paid tribute to northeastern music with the release of the CD *As Canções de Eu, Tu, Eles* (*Songs from I, You, Them*), featuring covers of many Luiz Gonzaga hits originally recorded in the 1940s and 1950s.

The last decades of the twentieth century witnessed a remarkable flourishing of new Afro-Brazilian styles and trends in Salvador da Bahia, always noted as a center of musical innovation. New phenomena appeared in the circuit of popular music for consumption via show, record, radio, and television, having emerged from local urban folk and Carnival-specific sources. In 1982, the first of a long series of recordings of new Afrocentric Carnival music of Salvador (afoxé and bloco afro) was distributed nationally. Of particular importance was the development of samba–reggae in the mid-1980s and its subsequent dominance in Salvador's Carnival. Growing out of the bloco afro tradition, this new sound featured a "back to Africa" drumming and singing texture. One particular group, the Olodum Carnival group, was most responsible for the emergence of this new approach, which soon established associations with the local, national, and international popular music industries. The essence of the style is located in the interlocking patterns of low surdo drums with high-pitched tarol, *repique,* and *timbales* on top. Commercial Bahian bands such as Reflexu's and Banda Mel were among the first to make commercial adaptations (in the late 1980s) of the samba–reggae by translating the drumming patterns to ensembles based on guitar, keyboard, percussion, and vocals. In the 1990s, Olodum (represented by a scaled-down professional touring band) gained international attention via its work with Paul Simon (on his *Rhythm of the Saints* album) and Michael Jackson and Spike Lee ("They Don't Really Care about Us"), which linked the new Bahian sound to the world music phenomenon.

Collectively, new Afro-Bahian sounds of the 1980s and 1990s came to be known as axé music, and it became a force in the national music industry. Ironically, its most commercially successful star was Daniela Mercury (a white Bahian woman), whose 1992 release "O Canto da Cidade" (written by black singer–composer Tote Gira) sold over 1 million units in less than a year. Later developments include the ascendance of Carlinhos Brown and his eclectic Carnival performance group Timbalada, which added the distinctive timbal (a conga-like, cone-shaped drum with a thin plastic head) to the domain of axé music. Timbalada is both an urban folk music expression (with weekly open rehearsals using fifty to seventy drummers) and a media-savvy commercial music entity putting out yearly recordings.

In Recife, the 1990s saw dynamic changes in the city's popular music scene, which led to the eclectic artistic movement called mangue beat that exploded onto Brazil's national popular music landscape. Spearheading the movement was a band named Chico Science & Nação Zumbi, which mixed the percussion-heavy local traditions of maracatu and the côco with funk, rock, metal, punk, rap, and hip-hop. The creative fusion of Chico Science and other bands in the mid-1990s put Recife's new musical scene at the forefront of Brazilian music. Other local bands in Recife include Mestre Ambrósio, Cascabulho, and Chão e Chinelo, whose members have engaged in ongoing musical dialogues with the musicians of venerable local traditions as they reinterpret and revitalize the musical heritage of their region.

PART II

Creating Music in Brazil

"Creating Music in Brazil" takes a closer look at the interplay of music with racial identification and the development of northeastern regional identity by investigating three important realms of northeastern musical culture framed within regional and national contexts. Building on concepts discussed in Part I, Chapter 3 highlights the importance of Candomblé religious practice as fundamental to an understanding of African identity and music in Brazil. Next, the chapter explores the historical trajectories and musical specifics of afoxé and maracatu—two important Afro-Brazilian urban Carnival traditions linked directly to Candomblé. In Chapter 4, the frevo, a hybrid carnival music from Pernambuco performed by brass and percussion bands, is traced from its multiracial origins among nineteenth-century marching bands and Afro-Brazilian capoeira groups to its present status as a vibrant marker of Pernambuco cultural identity. The chapter reframes the Brazilian nationalist narrative of the positive nature of racial and cultural mixture (discussed in Chapter 1) within in a regional context. Chapter 5 reframes regionalist narrative to the national level by discussing the creation of northeastern popular music within the context of the national music industry located in Rio de Janeiro (southern Brazil). We will first trace the early twentieth-century impact of northeastern musicians in Rio's music scene and then discuss the advent of Luiz Gonzaga and his baião in the 1940s and 1950s, which contested the dominance of samba as the singular national musical symbol of Brazilianess.

CHAPTER 3

Afro-Brazilian Musical Traditions: Candomblé, Afoxé, and Maracatu

Brazil without Africa is inconceivable. Portuguese participation in the transatlantic slave trade for more than 350 years produced a society in the eastern half of the South American continent in which roughly 50 percent of the people are of African descent. Indeed, modern Brazil is second only to the West African nation of Nigeria in the size of its black population. It is, therefore, not surprising that African traditions and cultural heritages greatly shaped the development of the Brazilian cultural landscape—its music, dance, religion, food, visual art, linguistic patterns, modes of social interaction, and ways of experiencing the world. Within Brazil, the impact of Africa was first felt in the northeastern coastal areas, where a thriving monoculture of sugarcane was established. The Northeast played a formative role in defining the early configuration of the New World colony and in cultivating cultural practices that were closely linked to African heritage. In addition to the African-inspired musical traditions and aesthetics that were sown deep into the Brazilian soil, European-derived musical traditions in Brazil were transformed through intimate relationships and intercultural exchanges between Afro- and Euro-Brazilian communities. Because of extensive interchange, an African-inspired musical orientation and specific modes of performing music were embedded in the fabric of daily life in the colony. Patterns of social and cultural interaction have made Afro-Brazilian music ubiquitous in the musical landscape of modern Brazil. Put another way, to speak of Brazilian music today is to speak of Afro-Brazilian music. Brazilian music without the African musical heritage is unthinkable.

Although almost all forms of Brazilian music have been impacted by the African musical heritage in one way or another, a few Afro-Brazilian musical practices serve as core symbols of African identity in Brazil. These traditions have their Brazilian roots in the northeastern coastal areas. In this chapter, I will investigate three of the quintessential

Afro-Brazilian musical traditions of the Northeast that have influenced national conceptions of African identity in Brazil. First, the highly participatory style of the music of Candomblé, Brazil's dominant African-related religion, will be discussed. This religious tradition and its music provide the primary template for Afro-Brazilian identity—a template modeled on a universalist type of African identity in which the concept of Africanness is expressed through cultural competency in music and dance. Practiced in private temple houses, Candomblé has become a powerful source of African identity within Brazil. I will then address two highly public manifestations of Afro-Brazilian identity that have emerged within the context of Carnival in Brazil. In the urban Northeast, Carnival traditions in the black population formed soon after the abolition of slavery in the late nineteenth century, as newly freed blacks took to the streets in celebration and spectacle. The two most enduring Carnival manifestations of black culture are the maracatu of Recife and the afoxé of Salvador. Both of these traditions drew inspiration directly from Candomblé. In the Carnivals of Recife and Salvador, they became local and national symbols of Afro-Brazilian identification. Before beginning my investigation of these three core Afro-Brazilian traditions, I will discuss the way in which Afro-Brazilian musical culture emerged as an important element in Brazil.

Afro-Brazilian Chronology

1525–1851	Transatlantic slave trade from Africa to Brazil
1590	Approximate date of the beginning of *Quilombo de Palmares* in Northeast Brazil, a settlement of runaway slaves that lasted for almost 100 years and housed some 20,000–30,000 individuals
1666	First written description of the Rei de Angola and Rei de Congo, the colonial practice of crowning black kings in Brazil
1695	Death of Zumbi, famous warrior/leader of the Quilombo de Palmares
1830s	Founding of the earliest known Candomblé centers in Bahia
1872	Ventre Livre (law of the "free womb") passed by the Brazilian parliament freeing children born of enslaved parents
1888	Lei Aúria ("Golden Law") signed by Princess Isabela establishes the total abolition of slavery in Brazil
1890s	Afoxés and maracatus begin parading in the Carnivals of Bahia and Pernambuco
1905	Public displays of "African" music, dance, and costuming banned in Salvador, Bahia
1920s–1930s	Frequent police raids of Candomblé centers
1949	Afoxé Filhos de Gandhi founded in Salvador, Bahia
1974	Ilê Aiyê, Salvador's first *bloco afro* founded in the neighborhood of Curuzu
1977	Gilberto Gil releases *Refavela*, inspired by African and Afro-diasporic traditions

Conceptualizing Afro-Brazilian Musical Culture

Recent scholarship has recognized—and sometimes overemphasized—the element of resistance embedded in forms of Afro-Brazilian expressive culture. For close to 500 years, Afro-Brazilian cultural practices have provided important spaces for embodying African heritage, for maintaining the social memory of enslavement and discrimination, and for voicing overt resistance to the structures of domination in Brazilian society. Black Brazilians have a long and proud history of effectively manipulating even the direst of situations in their country by using artistic/cultural expressions to construct their identities and to socially mobilize confrontations, diversions, and resistance within society. Black artists in Brazil have also been effective in establishing the aesthetic space for their own creative innovations. In the field of Brazilian popular music, the social linkages forged by black cultural mediators such as the popular musician Pixinguinha (Alfredo da Rocha Vianna, Jr.) have been crucial for the establishment of Brazilian national culture and the acceptance of blacks themselves in social arenas previously dominated by whites. The adoption and appropriation of black cultural forms in Brazilian national culture is so pervasive that, in some respects, Africa is taken for granted in Brazil. It is so embedded in daily life and society that African influence becomes invisible to many Brazilians; that is, they may experience many things as Brazilian and not African. Historically that has allowed a cover for not acknowledging the importance of African cultural heritage. But though this is generally true of Brazil's national culture, the core of Afro-Brazilian identity itself stands in a location removed from the main halls of national society. This core is located within the African-based religious traditions of the Northeast.

Afro-Brazilian religion is frequently conceptualized as a kind of parallel, alternative world within Brazilian society that articulates and maintains a pure vision of Africa and provides the essence of Africanness in Brazil. The concept involves the idea of a powerful set of African cultural practices that resist the encroachment of non-Afro-Brazilian elements. This essentialized view of Afro-Brazilian religion has become part of the discourse of the contemporary black movement in Brazil. In recent years, black political activists have attempted to redefine the Candomblé religion and its symbols as pure and authentic expressions of Africa. For many of them, the music and dance associated with the religion have become strategic cultural forces in their struggle to combat the historical discrimination of black people in Brazil and the appropriation of their culture. They reject the depiction of Afro-Brazilian religion as mere "folklore" and something that can be appropriated and instead see it as a tool of political resistance. They also point to the history of samba and the way in which the dominant sector of Brazilian society (largely white and from the south of the country) forged national sentiment by appropriating the hillside samba of black poor people and transforming it into the primary emblem of Brazilian national identity. Clearly, the Afro-Brazilian cultural landscape is a contested terrain where musical practices, styles, and aesthetic forms are closely linked to the formation of racial identities and to the values of competing forces within Brazil.

Given the historical, social, and aesthetic complexities, defining African heritage in the musical traditions of Brazil is a difficult task. One approach is to begin the discussion by identifying the three interrelated levels of African tradition in Brazil:

- African musical traditions that were transplanted to and then preserved faithfully in Brazil, with little or no European influence
- Neo-African music that, although firmly based on African models, developed into unique forms in Brazilian territories
- Acculturated hybrid forms of Afro-Brazilian music that were created in Brazil as the result of the blending of African and European—and to a lesser degree Amerindian—elements.

Peter Fryer,[1] following John Storm Roberts's ambitious work on the influence of African musical heritage throughout the Americas,[2] has adopted this basic model and distinguished five types of neo-African music in Brazil in which "European influence is either absent or negligible" from acculturated styles that were central to the development of the country's traditional and popular music. This kind of common-sense model is useful, but it creates the false perception that authentic African musical traditions and essential aesthetic qualities have been frozen in time and preserved in Brazil with little or no change since the earliest Africans arrived on the shores of South America. This misconception leads to assertions that, for instance, sacred drum rhythms have been passed down completely unchanged in Brazil for some 450 years.[3] It is more likely that some sacred African drum rhythms are treated *as if* they were passed down unchanged for hundreds of years. This is an important distinction involving the motivation to reproduce significant cultural practices in an orthodox manner. It is also probable that Brazilian drummers have passed down, updated, and elaborated elements of their African musical heritage over time. As new rhythms and performance practices emerged, elements of the old repertoires were probably lost, forgotten, or discarded. Although we often have sketchy historical data on such matters, it is fairly clear that a rather restricted repertoire of drum patterns based largely on Yoruba and Fon traditions from West Africa was codified in the late nineteenth century in Bahia. These patterns came to define the dominant canon of a musical orthodoxy for Candomblé religion.

Thus, many of the assumptions about the historical age and immutable nature of African practices in Brazil paint an inaccurate picture. This is not to deny the fact that members of the Afro-Brazilian community frequently treat drum patterns, song texts, and dance styles as authentic expressions of an African heritage that their ancestors maintained against all odds in Brazil. Indeed, they often do, and many people hold on to the idea that Candomblé represents an unbroken religious tradition straight from Africa. One famous priestess of Candomblé, Mãe Menininha do Gantois, interrupted an important religious ceremony when she determined that one of the percussion rhythms was not being performed in a precisely accurate manner.[4] This kind of imposed orthodoxy leads us to realize that Afro-Brazilian religious "traditions" have been maintained through active guidance and oversight of the artistic elements that define African religious identity in Brazil. Drum rhythms can be quite important in this struggle to define Africa in Brazil.

The African-based religions of Brazil provide what José Jorge de Carvalho has called the dominant "matrix" of Afro-Brazilian identity in Brazil.[5] However, this matrix is not based on biologically or geographically determined concepts of racial identity; rather, it is founded on the aesthetic competency demanded of social participation within Afro-Brazilian religions. This cultural competency finds its primary expression through the modes of dancing, singing, and drumming in Candomblé. African-based religious music and dance also provide major reference points for Afro-Brazilian musical identity in the larger context of the civil society. Although the direct transfer of specific drumming patterns or melodic material from Afro-Brazilian religious repertoires into mainstream Brazilian popular music has not been widespread, the general musical style of Brazilian religious ceremonies conditions many musicians from an early age. For many musicians, performing artists, and audiences throughout the country, Afro-Brazilian religious drumming, singing, and dancing are key components of their aesthetic education. Composers and musicians in Brazil constantly draw from Afro-Brazilian religious practices for their musical and spiritual inspiration. Understanding the basic nature of such practices lays the foundation for understanding Afro-Brazilian music in general.

Candomblé: Afro-Brazilian Religion and Music

Brazil is home to a number of religions founded on models from Central and West Africa. The best-known and most thoroughly researched is the Candomblé from Bahia. The term *Candomblé* typically refers to an assortment of historically related religious practices that developed in Brazil (especially in Bahia and Pernambuco) with West African belief systems involving a pantheon of deities (Orixás and Voduns). Separate lineages of Candomblé are organized into "nations" (*nações*), linked loosely according to African ethnic associations established in colonial times in Brazil. The main Candomblé nations that persist today include the Ketu, Ijexá, and Nagô (Yoruba groups originating in southwestern Nigeria and central Benin); the Gêge (Ewe-Fon groups from Benin); and the Congo-Angola (Bantu groups from Central Africa). In Brazil, the term *Nagô* is frequently used as the generic designation for all Yoruba groups. The dominant role of West African (Yoruba and Ewe-Fon) beliefs and practices in Candomblé relates to the fact that during the final phase of Brazilian slavery (from 1700 to 1850), most of the enslaved Africans transported to Brazilian soil came from Yoruba and Fon areas in West Africa. African-inspired religious traditions linked to Bantu areas of Central and South Africa are more dispersed; during colonial times in Brazil, these were blended into West African systems. As a result of the large numbers of West African slaves in the final period of the slavery era, Afro-Brazilian religious life was dominated by the Yoruba and Ewe-Fon systems in the nineteenth century. In addition to Candomblé, important regional Afro-Brazilian religions were also established in Maranhão (Tambor de Mina) and Pará (Batuque). Highly syncretic forms also emerged, blending the African Orixás with Brazilian spirits of both indigenous and Afro-Brazilian inspiration. These syncretized forms included the Candomblé de Caboclo in Bahia, Pajelança in Belem, Jurema in Recife, Macumba in Rio de Janeiro, and Umbanda, which is popular throughout the country. Elements from Catholicism and spiritist traditions were also mixed into these religions. The proliferation and cross-influences of African-inspired religious groups in Brazil produced a complex situation, which makes it difficult to draw definitive lines between these various Afro-Brazilian denominations.

Figure 3.1 Dancing at a Candomblé ceremony, Recife, Pernambuco, 2000 (photo by Sylvia Crook).

Candomblé and the Aesthetics of Participation

In the Northeast, both Recife and Salvador have thriving communities of African-inspired religious groups, who trace their origins to the nineteenth century. The most famous—and the most researched—are those in and around Salvador, which have been examined in numerous anthropological studies, documentaries, feature films, and literary works as well as media stories and tourist industry promotions. In Recife, Candomblé religious houses are less researched and publicized than their Bahian counterparts, but they also represent a major religious community. One characteristic linking all Afro-Brazilian religious expressions is the fundamental importance placed on a religious experience achieved through participatory music making involving drumming and singing and dancing. Indeed, music and dance are the vehicles through which religious fulfillment is achieved.[6]

In Candomblé, a restricted number of African Orixá deities are worshiped in private and public rituals and ceremonies held in their honor. Each of the Orixás has a particular personality; distinct likes and dislikes; and associations with natural forces, colors, food, musical preferences, and characteristic styles of dance. In the orthodox houses of Candomblé, the Orixás are exclusively African in racial identification and form a small community of religious deities.

Orixás in Brazil

Some of the most popular Orixás in Brazil and their common attributes are given in the following list. Variations in color and other aspects exist in different areas of Brazil.

- *Ogum* is a powerful deity of war and the protector of all who work with iron. He dances while armed with a sword and wears blue with green.
- *Xangô* is the god of thunder and lightning and of justice. He dances with a double-headed axe and wears red and white.
- *Omolu* (also known as *Obaluaê*) is the god of medicine and contagious diseases, especially smallpox. He dances with a small staff and wears straw and the colors red, white, and black.
- *Oxossi* is the young brother of Ogum. He is the god of the hunt and carries a bow and arrow and whip while he dances. His color is green.
- *Iemanjá* is the goddess of the sea and mother of Xangô and Exu. She is unpredictable, wears light blue, and dances with a fan.
- *Iansã* is the goddess of the wind and storms and a wife of Xangô. She dances with a small whip, and her color is a reddish-brown.
- *Oxum* is the Orixá of rivers and is associated with fertility and vanity. She dances with a hand mirror to see herself, loves gold, and is a favorite lover of Xangô. Her colors are yellow and light blue.
- *Exu* is the servant of the other Orixás and acts as a mediator between them and humans. He controls points of access and opens the way for ceremonies and rituals. His colors are black and red.

During the public celebrations at Candomblé houses, the African Orixás are called down to earth to possess religious initiates (*iaôs*). The celebration in which this activity takes place is referred to rather generically as a *festa* (festival or feast), and the structured ceremony involves a sequence of ritual acts, invocations, songs, and dances collectively called a *xiré* or a *toque*. The term *toque* also refers specifically to the patterns played on the sacred drums, underscoring their paramount importance within the religious ritual.

Personal relationships to African deities are manifest in highly charged moments of spirit possession brought about through dancing and singing accompanied by the ubiquitous sound of drumming. Spirit possession by one's own Orixá involves a response triggered by the drumming patterns and sacred songs of Candomblé; it is the result of many years of aesthetic training and educational preparation in the social values rooted in West and Central African cultures but developed in a unique way on Brazilian soil. In a very real sense, the Candomblé houses found in Salvador and Recife are an important social space for keeping alive "a powerful world of form, symbols, aesthetic values, experience of transcendence, and communal solidarity."[7] This has been Brazil's sacred space for maintaining African identity. But what kind of African identity has been maintained in Candomblé?

In the world of Candomblé, biologically determined racial identity and the separation of humans into racial categories such as black and white are minimized. In fact, an ideology of universalism seems to prevail in which anyone, regardless of race (or gender), may be chosen by an Orixá to become a member of the religious family of the Orixás. As Carvalho stated: "From the point of view of ethnic identity, the Candomblé does not establish social, racial, or color distinctions: everyone is a potential member, since all human beings have *orichas* [orixás]; so, blacks or non-blacks, 'preto' or 'negro,' Brazilian or non-Brazilian, are oppositions that do not make sense in the world of the *orichas*; they are just African, on the mythological level; and on the level of individual identification, they are simply universal."[8]

The ideology of universalism stressed in Candomblé extends to the Orixás themselves, who, though they are typically depicted as powerful African beings, also derive much of their imagery from Roman Catholicism. The imposition of Roman Catholicism and its symbolic images on Afro-Brazilians during slavery resulted in the accommodation of such mixed imagery as well as the parallel linking of specific Orixás with Catholic saints. Carvalho also noted that Candomblé's religious discourse is noticeably silent on the historical issue of slavery in Brazil, focusing instead on the all-powerful nature of the African Orixás and on the Afro-Brazilian leaders who established the religion in Brazil. Although the Orixás are conceived as universal Africans who mix the imagery of Africa and Europe, the music to which they respond is uncompromisingly African in inspiration. There is very little to suggest that much influence of European music is found in the Candomblé. Additionally, the Candomblé music has the potential to manifest an Afro-Brazilian identity in anyone who can master its aesthetic demands. In other words, not only is religious fulfillment achieved through music and dance, one also becomes symbolically African, in a religious sense, through the process of aesthetically responding to the music. This reinforces the notion that participation is essential in Candomblé.

Candomblé in Recife

The first organized houses of African-inspired religion in Recife were begun by slaves and free black Brazilians and emerged in the second half of the nineteenth century in neighborhoods near the center of the city. By the early twentieth century, new houses were being founded by former slaves and free blacks who occupied sprawling shanty-towns on the outskirts of the city near the Bebiribe River.[9] These were small, independent religious centers (known as *terreiros*) established by and for the poorest segment of the city's population. As in other areas of Brazil, local civil authorities considered African religious practices an affront to public morality, felt the loud drumming was barbaric, and treated the various activities of the groups as offensive and even criminal behavior. The Catholic Church also condemned the ritual practices of the terreiros as witchcraft. The Afro-Brazilian religious community of Recife was subjected to official and unofficial persecution, police harassment, confiscation of its sacred objects (including musical instruments), and the public humiliation of its members. It is testimony to the strength of the Candomblé community that it continued to flourish through these times. And flourish it did. René Ribeiro's important research—carried out in the 1940s and 1950s—registered more than 100 independent Candomblé centers in Recife.[10] In and around Recife, the Candomblé community was dominated by the Nagô (Yoruba) nation, and Xangô became the most important Orixá deity in the area. The word *Xangô* itself also came to refer to the African-inspired Candomblé of Recife; according to Roger Bastide, it was the name that local whites used to refer to the houses.[11] During my own research in Recife in the 1990s, the terms *Candomblé* and *Xangô* were used interchangeably to refer to the religious houses considered traditionally "African." In addition, the more syncretic religion known as Jurema was also quite popular in the area and mixed Amerindian spirits (known as Caboclo) and Afro-Brazilian spirits (known as Preto Velho), which were worshiped alongside the distinctly African Orixás. Among the general population of Recife, it is common to hear both Xangô and Jurema referred to as Xangô or, increasingly, as Candomblé.

Candomblé houses operate independently but are linked as a religious community of shared beliefs and practices. The unifying belief system involves three categories of spiritual beings who interface with humans: Orixás (African deities who link humans to the Yoruba supreme deity, Olorun), Ori (an individual's guardian angel), and Eguns (souls of the ancestors). The primary religious activities of each Candomblé center take place in a terreiro, or sacred compound. Public and private rituals and ceremonies occur in the terreiro house, where sacred objects including musical instruments are stored with care and where the spiritual essences of important ancestors are believed to reside. During public rituals in which the Orixás are summoned, initiates of the religion (the symbolic sons and daughters of the Orixás) dance and sing in their honor while specialist initiates perform the sacred drumming. In Bahia, the drummers are referred to as *alabê*; in Recife, they are called *ogan*.

The Candomblé religious house Abassa Igibale was founded in Recife in 1979 by Luiz Carlos, who is also known as Lula de Oiyá. According to Lula, the name of the house is Gêge (Ewe), meaning "House of Iansã." Iansã is Lula's primary Orixá, his main deity. Although the house is described by Lula as Gêge—that is, of the Gêge nation, with a lineage from the old West African kingdom of Dahomey—the intermixing of various lineages as well as non-African traditions is also evident there. Lula's own background provides insight into the syncretic nature of the house.

Lula de Oiyá did not begin his religious life in Candomblé; he was first drawn to the Espiritualismo or spiritism of Alain Kardec. Kardec (1809–1869) was a French spiritist whose writings influenced the development of Umbanda in Brazil. Growing in a different spiritual direction than the religion, in 1967 (at the age of seventeen) Lula left Umbanda and entered the world of Candomblé. He went through the initiation process in the

Figure 3.2
Luiz Carlos and
the Candomblé
Abassa Igibale
House, Recife,
Pernambuco,
2000 (photo
by Larry Crook).

religion and eventually became a *babalorixá* (priest). Lula went on to establish one of the important terreiros in Recife and is well respected within the city's Candomblé community.

The public ceremonies of the Candomblé houses are planned months in advance and represent the culmination of private ritual activities such as the initiation of new sons and daughters of the Orixás. Such a celebration is a public ritual and performance of the immediate religious group in the presence of invited guests. It is common for the leaders in the Candomblé community to attend important public ceremonies of their counterparts. This was the case for two festas I attended at Lula's Abassa Igibale terreiro. Drumming, singing, and dancing are the primary mechanisms for achieving spirit possession by the Orixás in these ceremonies, which involve a suite of musical offerings and dances structured around the Orixás. During public ceremonies, each Orixá is addressed with the singing of specific songs, dancing, and corresponding rhythmic patterns played on sacred drums. Further, each Orixá has a repertoire of favorite songs and rhythms as well as choreographic dance movements, all of which are expressions of the deity's temperament. Twelve different patterns of drumming played during the public festivals of Xangô in Recife have been identified.[12] When the songs and rhythms of an Orixá are performed, children of that deity may be moved to emotional states, followed by spirit possession.

I observed a strong communal ethos of music making and dancing among participants at the ceremonies I attended at Lula de Oiyá's Abassa Igibale house in Recife. On those occasions, up to forty participants were simultaneously dancing and singing vigorously while five to six musicians shared time on the sacred drums and the large gourd shakers used at this house. Although the ceremonial performance was clearly led and sustained by the initiated members of the Abassa Igibale house, the sons and daughters of the Orixás from other Candomblé also danced and sang enthusiastically. Over a period of six hours, about twenty individuals were possessed in each of the ceremonies. My field notes from October 28, 2000, illustrate how I reflected on my own experience of one of those ceremonies:

> Lula de Oiyá said there would be three appearances of the Orixá Iansã during the night that would form the basic structure of the ceremony. As it turned out, the three appearances took place over about a five and one half hour period. This festa was one in which there were about twenty individuals possessed by Orixás. Possession came in waves with some of the most energetic ones occurring soon after a young man was possessed by Xangô. After that possession, there were a number of people who fell into possession. When this happened, each individual let out a cry and then fell down to his or her knees with shoulders trembling rapidly. Eyes were closed and on the face was a kind of scowl in which the lower lip was pushed out and the teeth clenched while the lips were closed.
>
> The amount of possession surprised me. As I was observing it I was thinking about how, for many of these people, the experience of possession must be a main focus of their lives. In light of the upcoming municipal elections and the local police strike in Recife—some of the important current issues confronting these people in their daily lives—these kinds of ceremonies must provide a mechanism for letting go and at the same time allow them to take control of their situation if only for a night while dancing and singing. The whole ambiance of the house was conducive to completely letting go within a safety net provided by the Candomblé community. I could feel a strong sense of caring in this community. When a person was possessed, there always seemed to be someone close by to take care of the person, removing eyeglasses, rolling up pants legs, wiping sweat from the brow, keeping that person from hurting himself. Then there was a cloth tied around the person's chest that I think indicated through its color the Orixá that had taken possession of the body. When this caring activity was complete, the possessed person usually danced into the center of the room, the attendant close by. In the case of one possession by Xangô, the dancer stood motionless, facing the drummers for about a minute or two before vigorously entering the dance.[13]

Figure 3.3
Possession by
Xangô at a
Candomblé,
Recife,
Pernambuco,
2000 (photo
by Larry Crook).

   The possession experience is a strong expectation among the participants at Candomblé ceremonies. For these initiated sons and daughters of the Orixás, possession is an emotional state of reattachment to their deity. The role of music in provoking emotional states in preconditioned individuals and in controlling possession underscores its important position within Candomblé. Competence in dancing, drumming, and singing is more than the ability to produce aesthetically satisfying sounds and choreography; it is a core element of the religious experience. Moreover, the care that is exhibited toward the person undergoing possession within the ceremonies reminded me of the kind of care one might show to a younger sibling. The notion of caring for the ones who are undergoing possession extends to the way the drummers act when possession occurs. Reflecting on the moment during a ceremony when an Orixá possesses someone, one drummer told me:

It's like I said, no one remains silent. The Orixás only come during moments when there is a lot happening and when there is a strong sense of vibration. And that is why the ogan [drummer] is important. It is through the hand of the drummer that the vibration comes. And from the vibration comes happiness and energy. The Orixá radiates energy. A person inside the circle of the dance is dancing, is dancing around and begins to radiate energy. The spirit of that person begins to leave the body in order to leave space for the entrance of another spirit. Then the body of that person begins, as we call it, to surupembá [be possessed].

When the drummer sees that, then he really starts to put his hand into the drum [to play intensely] so that that person will manifest the Orixá quickly. So that he will not suffer because that state is terrible. Because you lose your senses, your sight leaves, and then returns. So the drummer plays with more force and feeling. They start to sing with more feeling and with more vigor. With more vibration.[14]

A feeling of discomfort in the moments just before possession takes place is a common experience for many Candomblé practitioners and can involve crying and other visible signs of emotional states. The central role of the music and the musicians in controlling the possession flows from the highly participatory and inviting nature of the music.

Music of Candomblé

The music that accompanies the ceremonies is patterned on a socioaesthetic matrix in which a small ensemble of three drums and one or two percussion instruments is combined with vigorous singing and dancing. The rhythmic relationships established among the performer–participants emphasize tight coordination and a communal ethos. Although the singing and dancing involve abundant participation from the extended group of people at Candomblé ceremonies, the drumming is performed exclusively by a small number of musical specialists (always male), who must undergo special initiations into the religious society. The drums on which they play are also baptized in ritual preparation for their essential roles in achieving the proper religious experience. The Orixás never possess the drummers while performing their musical duties.

The acoustic texture of drumming and singing without any additional melodic or harmonic instruments is strikingly different from Roman Catholic religious music, in which an organ or stringed and wind instruments typically accompany voices. The drumming and vocal texture of Candomblé follows the general aesthetic preferences of West and Central Africa. Thus, whereas secular forms of music making among Afro-Brazilians developed during colonial times by incorporating and adapting string, wind, brass, and other instruments of a European musical heritage, African-inspired religious music making tended to resist such influences as it carved out its own unique aesthetic space in the Brazilian context. The dominant influence of Yoruba and Fon-Ewe traditions in the nineteenth century served to solidify and codify these qualities as an aesthetic canon of Africanness in Brazil. The sound produced by this musical texture marked a distinctly African musical identity within Brazil and provided the uncompromisingly African feel to Candomblé.

Instruments of Candomblé

The basic Candomblé ensemble is a family of two or three similarly shaped drums, with the largest (and lowest-pitched) instrument functioning as the lead member. On this instrument, rhythmic variations, improvisations, and cues are performed by a lead drummer, who directs the other drummers, singers, and dancers. The smaller drums (the medium- and high-pitched instruments) and one or more instruments, such as an agogô or an *agbe*, combine to provide a repeating rhythmic structure performed in strict metric time that sets a basic time cycle or rhythmic groove in motion. In the traditional Candomblé of Bahia (Gêge-Nagô), a drum ensemble of three instruments (lê, rumpi, and rum)—known collectively as atabaque—is the most common. These tall, barrel-shaped drums are somewhat like conga drums but use thin goatskin heads and are played with thin sticks (*aguidavi*) and with the hands. In shape and design, these drums bear a close resemblance to contemporary Anlo-Ewe drums from southeast Ghana. In fact, the rum is almost identical in shape and size to the lead *atsimevu* drum of the Anlo-Ewe set. When Ewe master drummer Godwin Agbeli was in residence at the University of Florida (in 1994 and 1995), I observed the similarity not only of the drums but also of the

Figure 3.4 Ogan drummers at a Candomblé ceremony. In the picture are the three atabaque drums and an agbe beaded gourd, Recife, Pernambuco, 2000 (photo by Sylvia Crook).

drumming techniques he used and the drumming techniques employed in the Candomblé, which involved complex stick and hand patterns on the lead drum. Each drum has a single skin attached to the wooden shell by means of lacing, wooden pegs, or mechanical iron tensioning. Accompanying the drums is the agogô, the double bell made of metal.

In Recife, a set of drums known as ilu, an agogô, and an agbe are typically used for the Candomblé known as Xangô (Nagô houses) and for the more syncretic religion of Jurema. Like the atabaque, the ilu is a set of small-, medium-, and large-sized drums (melê, melê-ankó, and ilu inhã). Many of these names are used among the Yoruba of Nigeria to designate the individual drums of drum ensembles, such as the hourglass-shaped talking drums (dùndún) and the double-headed batá drums that are sacred to the Orixá Xangô. The ilu are double-headed cylinder drums of a large diameter with thin goatskin heads and are played exclusively with the hands. Today, drum makers construct the ilu drums out of a plywood shell with metal rims and long metal bolts used to tighten the skins. These instruments are readily available for purchase in religious shops devoted to Xangô and Jurema in Recife. According to several drummers in Recife, the modern plywood construction and metal tensioning replaced an older solid wood or barrel construction and roped tensioning for the skins in the 1950s. Photographs taken in 1938 in Recife by a government-sponsored cultural mission from the southern state of São Paulo appear to corroborate the oral testimony of these drummers. Headed by writer and musicologist Mário de Andrade, the mission collected and documented several drums from Recife's Xangô houses. Photographs of these instruments (published in 1946) show double-headed drums with rope tensioning over barrel-shaped wooden shells.[15]

Candomblé songs are linked to the specific activities of the private and public rituals of the religion and to specific Orixás as well. The words of the songs of the traditional Candomblés are in Yoruba or Fon (or in a combination of these languages) and are sung in a solo-responsorial manner, with a lead singer (frequently the head priest) alternating solo phrases with choral responses from members of the congregation. This musical organization structures a social ethos of communal participation among the singers, who are also simultaneously dancing in front of the drummers. Everyone sings the same melody, without harmonization. The drummers provide specific rhythmic patterns (toques), often featuring a twelve-beat cycle divided simultaneously into shifting patterns of four and six. It is often difficult to determine exactly where the main beat falls: such is the shifting nature of the music, which provides a dynamic quality in constant motion. The lead drum improvises and plays with the elusiveness of the rhythmic structure. This is set precisely to interact with the rhythm of the singing, which delineates a structure that occurs within four repetitions of the drumming's basic pattern and alternates lead and responding parts. Simultaneously, the lead drum performs variations that continually shift the metric feeling of the music and coordinate the choreography of the dance.

These examples of Candomblé help to illustrate the fundamental importance of music as an active ingredient in Afro-Brazilian religious aesthetics. The next section, on the Afro-Brazilian musical expressions that developed in the more public arenas of Carnival, will demonstrate that these religious expressions also played a vital role in the broader context of civil society.

Afoxé and Maracatu: Two Afro-Brazilian Carnival Expressions

Late in the nineteenth century, soon after the abolition of slavery, processions celebrating African heritage entered the annual Carnival celebrations of Brazil's major cities. In both Recife and Salvador, the parading of black Carnival groups highlighting "African" themes heralded an initial flourishing of African consciousness within the new Republic. Through public events, blacks sought an active and visible role in establishing cultural values that would define modern Brazilian society. However, by the early 1900s, the dominant sectors of society called for state intervention to prohibit the "barbarous" African-related practices, which they feared were "Africanizing" the country's Carnival. In Bahia, the newly formed black parading groups ranged from large, well-organized associations (*clubes uniformizados*) to small, spontaneous groups of revelers (batuques and sambas de roda) to groups directly linked to Candomblé (afoxés). In Recife, some blacks who were members of the city's Candomblés organized their own processional groups known as maracatus. In this section, I will explore the histories of the Afro-Brazilian Carnivals of these two cities and examine how black communities in both Recife and Salvador developed public expressions glorifying African history, religion, and culture through processions with costuming, music, and dance. Rather than the relatively private and sacred nature of the Candomblé ceremonies, which took place indoors and within individual terreiros, these Carnival traditions were performed openly in the streets of the cities, and they played important roles in defining black identities in the context of the larger society.

Afoxés in Salvador da Bahia

> *Afoxé É*
> *The afoxé is a seed*
> *Planted by those who once wanted*
> *Planted by those who may yet want*
> *You have to put your faith in the bloco*
> *You have to enjoy walking on foot*
>   (Gilberto Gil)

In Salvador, a variety of black parading organizations emerged in the 1890s. There were large and well-organized clubes uniformizados as well as small and spontaneous batuques and afoxés. The big clubs, such as Embaixada Africana (African Embassy) and Pândegos da África (African Merrymakers), selected and mixed elements of the elite Euro-Brazilian Carnival with imagery, themes, and music drawn from Afro-Brazilian and African cultural heritage. The small and spontaneous groups of blacks also participated in Carnival by performing vernacular Afro-Bahian music and dance, such as the samba de roda and the batuque. In addition, the members of Salvador's Candomblé religious community danced in the streets, singing songs in Yoruba and Fon and playing music on drums and percussion instruments derived from their religion: atabaque and ilu drums, agbe and afoxé beaded gourds, and agogô bells.

Writing at the turn of the twentieth century, Nina Rodrigues, Brazil's first anthropologist to systematically study and analyze Afro-Brazilian culture, said the following about the black Carnival groups that were flourishing in Bahia (my translation):

> Lately, Bahian Carnival celebrations have been all but limited to African clubs organized by some Africans, negro creoles, and mestizos. In the last few years the richest and most important [of these] clubs have been: *Embaixada Africana* and the *Pândegos da África*. Furthermore, in addition to the smaller clubs like *Chegada Africana, Filhos de África,* etc., there are scores of anonymous African groups and isolated masked groups of negros. The formats of [all] these clubs reveal two distinct sentiments. In some, like the *Embaixada Africana*, the main idea of the more intelligent or better-assimilated blacks is to celebrate an old practice or a tradition. They take their characters and their subjects from the educated peoples of Africa: Egyptians, Abyssinians, etc. In the other types of groups, [even] if, on the part of the organizers, there is an occasional desire to revive [older] traditions, their success among the common people is due to their nature as true vernacular African celebrations. The theme [for these groups] is the uneducated Africans who came in an enslaved state to Brazil.[16]

This description makes it clear that the black Carnival groups reflected two broad segments of the Afro-Brazilian population: (1) the educated and assimilated blacks, and (2) the uneducated masses. Consulting articles and letters published in the popular press of the day, Rodrigues detailed the prevailing opinions held by the dominant sector toward the black population of the city and their attitudes about the Africanization of the city's Carnival. It appears that those black cultural organizations that highlighted the notion of an educated Africa and conformed to the accepted codes of civilized behavior set by the dominant sector of Salvador's society were accepted as examples of authentic African culture. However, those black Carnival groups that drew on the vernacular expressions of black culture (so foreign to Euro-Brazilian aesthetics) were deemed incompatible with Brazil's development as a modern nation. A letter to the editor from a local teacher, published on February 12, 1901, in the *Jornal de Notícias*, provides further clues to the prevailing attitude of the white elites toward vernacular black culture (my translation):

> I refer to the great Carnival celebrations and the abuse that has been introduced into them through the presentation of badly prepared masks, indecent and dirty, and also the way this great civilized celebration has been Africanized among us. I am not referring to the uniformed clubs like the Embaixada Africana, the Pândegos da África, and the like, which are faithful to African customs. However, I think that the authorities should prohibit these [other] batuques and Candomblés that, in great numbers, spread though the streets on these days, producing an enormous amount of noise, without [musical] tone or sound, as

> if we were in the Quinta das Beatas or in the Engenho Velho, like this group of
> masqueraders dressed in skirts and head scarfs, singing the traditional samba, in
> as much as all of this is incompatible with civilization.[17]

The reference to poor neighborhoods of Salvador where the city's black population predominated (Quinta das Beatas and Engenho Velho) underscores the strategy of the upper class to establish and maintain social and cultural distance from the poor masses. It was in such neighborhoods that the city's most venerable houses of Candomblé were located.

The willingness of the Bahian elite to accept, on the one hand, the large, organized clubs of black revelers who presented African-related themes in Europeanized formats but to disparage, on the other hand, the smaller, spontaneous batuques and Candomblé afoxés reflected the prevailing Brazilian racial ideology of the time known as branqueamento (whitening). The primary thesis of this ideology was the assumption that whites were biologically (and culturally) superior to blacks; this "self-evident truth" would naturally lead to the eventual whitening of both the general population and the culture of Brazil. The whitening thesis was widely accepted among Brazilian elites during the first fifteen years of the twentieth century. Under this supposedly enlightened racial theory, blacks would be accepted into the national community as long as they conformed to the dominant sector's (white) values. At issue in Bahia's Carnival was the cultural component of racial identification: blacks were expected to present themselves during Carnival in an orderly and well-dressed manner conforming to Euro-Brazilian aesthetics. The disorderliness and non-Europeanness of the batuques and the afoxés were targeted for public condemnation and legal action. In essence, blacks were expected to behave like whites and to demonstrate their blackness in color only.[18]

Salvador's dominant sector was formed almost exclusively by whites of European descent: members of traditional families, wealthy merchants, high-level government employees, and politicians. At the bottom of society's economic scale were the masses of predominantly black and mulatto working-class poor. The small middle sector also included mulattoes and a few blacks. The handful of blacks and mulattoes who rose socially and economically did so by "whitening" themselves culturally, that is, by conforming to the accepted codes of public behavior established by the dominant sector. Within Carnival, the emergence of the large uniformed clubs of blacks and mulattoes reflected the strategy of their members to adopt values from the dominant sector while simultaneously creating symbolic elements (themes, costumes, music, dance) evocative of their African heritage.

White elites also employed cultural practices to define themselves as modern and to maintain social distances among Salvador's population. The abolition of slavery had heightened the desire of the dominant white sector to solidify the social boundaries that distinguished them from the lower-class black population. For instance, in the late nineteenth century, members of Brazil's upper middle class adopted European music and dance forms as expressions of their own cosmopolitan social standing. Salvador's annual Carnival celebration was the city's major public occasion in which established social hierarchies were directly confronted by the emergence of black uniformed clubs. These clubs represented a subtle—yet perhaps more fundamental—challenge to the established social order than did the relatively small batuque or Candomblé afoxé groups. Initially, however, the dominant sector aimed its anger only against the smaller groups of black revelers and their "uncontrollable" practices, partly because the music of black vernacular culture represented a clear and present affront to the accepted codes of moral behavior and was deemed incompatible with civilized Brazil.

The descriptions and accounts of contemporary Brazilian intellectuals make it clear that the well-assimilated (educated) blacks who organized large Carnival associations were capable of skillfully negotiating social ascension. Their strategy was to create representations that depicted African heritage as civilized and noble. Meanwhile, working-class and poor blacks were less concerned with using cultural resources for social ascension and presented their batuques and Candomblé afoxés in unadulterated fashion, which, to the elites, symbolically represented the barbaric, uneducated, and uncivilized side of Africa. The symbolic opposition of civilized and barbarous cultural practices within the Afro-Bahian Carnival highlights the complexity of the social and intellectual context in which the black community existed in the late nineteenth century. Vernacular Afro-Bahian practices (for example, batuque, Candomblé, and capoeira) were branded as violent and uncivilized behaviors of an inferior race, and they were subjected to legal prohibitions and police action. It is not surprising that, struggling to achieve fully empowered citizenship in post-slavery Brazilian society, some blacks accommodated themselves to dominant cultural values by creating "civilized" Carnival practices evoking their African heritage around the idea of an educated and noble past. Other, less assimilated blacks maintained the vernacular expressions of Afro-Brazilian communities—practices that had developed during the era of slavery in colonial Brazil and were directly related to the experiences of the country's enslaved population. In 1890, in an effort to erase the official memory of slavery in post-abolition Brazil, the Brazilian government ordered the destruction almost all official records on the slave trade. A more subtle mechanism for erasing the legacy of slavery was to disparage and prohibit the batuques, sambas, capoeiras, Candomblés, and afoxés of the black population. In other words, they sought to erase those core traditions that defined the black population.

The clash of cultural values resulted in increased calls for police intervention to control the unruly black masses, and on February 24, 1905, the *Jornal de Notícias* published the following official notice (my translation):

> By order of the Secretary of State, chief of public security, and, for the knowledge of all, let it be known that no club shall be allowed to present itself publicly in the streets of the capital without the approval of their critiques [satirical themes] by the police and that the following will absolutely not be permitted:
>
> 1. the exhibition of African practices with *batuques*;
> 2. the exhibition of personally and socially offensive critiques;
> 3. the use of masks after six o'clock in the afternoon, except at balls until midnight.
>
> The vagabond and inebriated masked groups shall be placed into custody, just as the municipal rules should be rigorously enforced relative to the entrudo.[19]

This official notice addressed "to the public" made it clear that, from that point forward, Afro-Bahian cultural practices would be treated as common unlawful acts perpetrated against the public good and in violation of community standards. Between 1905 and 1914, the Bahian police banned Carnival expressions with African music, dance, and costuming. This forced the batuque and afoxé groups out of the city's official Carnival. The legal prohibitions and police repression also led the large, organized African clubs to disband. The newspapers of the time were virtually silent on the continued presence of African-related groups in Salvador, but it is likely that at least some of the afoxés and the informal batuques continued in the poor neighborhoods of the city. Additionally, the breakup of the large Carnival clubs may have led to the transfer of aesthetic elements and members of these associations into the afoxés and batuques. The transfer of new ideas and membership from the well-organized, middle-class clubs into the afoxés and batuques of the working-class further suggests the adaptability of Salvador's black population in the face of increased racial discrimination. Police repression against the Candomblé religious community in the first half of the twentieth century was systematic and a part of the society's resistance to the cultural values of its Afro-Brazilian community. Police repression was certainly one of the most difficult obstacles for the religious black community to overcome, requiring a variety of strategies, ranging from pure and simple confrontation to negotiation and accommodation. In the arena of Salvador's official Carnival, the black community was also resilient, despite continued discrimination and police repression. Beginning in the 1920s, mentions of "African" Carnival practices once again appeared in Bahian newspapers. The *Diário de Notícias* of February 5, 1921, for example, reported (my translation): "From the lands of Guinea will come, also, to enjoy the three days of Carnaval, among us, the Nagô Revelers, making heard their African songs and teaching the ways of sorcery, evil eye, bad luck and other abuses now in vogue, that belong to the uneducated people."[20]

The mention of sorcery and other "abuses" clearly referenced the Afro-Brazilian Candomblé religion, which was the target of intense police aggression in Salvador in the 1920s. Here again, the black Carnival clubs were associated with the uneducated masses and undesirable African elements that were considered a curse on civilization.

Throughout the 1920s, there was an occasional mention of black Carnival groups such as the Africanos em Folia and Congo Africano in Salvador's newspapers. From these and other historical records, the extent to which European elements were incorporated into the groups' Carnival parades is not entirely clear. However, in the early 1930s, the groups Ideal Africano, Lordeza Africana, and the revived Pândegos da África appear to have reverted to a traditional African format with Candomblé alabê musicians singing, drumming, and leading the parades. The participation of the alabês as musical leaders of the Carnival groups suggests that the groups must have performed music and dance influenced by (if not directly related to) Candomblé. As respected musical specialists of the Candomblé religion, the alabês would have commanded quite a bit of musical and religious authority in the black communities that marched in Carnival. However, we know very little of the actual repertoire and musical performance styles of these groups. In addition, a variety of other black Carnival groups also proliferated in Salvador. The distinction between the afoxés and these other groups from the 1930s through the 1950s was rather fluid, as indicated by the proliferation of names used to describe them. New developments in the Carnival of Rio de Janeiro also impacted Salvador's Carnival during this period, especially the new institution of the samba schools.

The terms *batucada*, *cordão*, and *bloco* were used to refer to the many different types of Afro-Bahian groups that paraded in Salvador's Carnival. Batucadas were neighborhood-centered groups that formed among working-class blacks in Salvador and employed many of the Afro-Brazilian percussion instruments that were part of the samba schools of Rio de Janeiro: the tamborim, cuíca, agogô, pandeiro, and ganzá. That there were cross-influences between the poor black communities of Rio de Janeiro and Salvador was not surprising because of the extensive migration and travel between the two cities. News of the developments in the Carnival of Rio de Janeiro was probably carried first-hand by family members and friends in the two cities. In addition, radio and newspaper coverage spread news of Rio de Janeiro's Carnival and its samba schools to black Carnival revelers in Bahia. The batucada groups of Bahia reflected this interregional circulation of cultural practice. The first officially designated samba school in Bahia was the Escola de Ritmistas do Samba, founded in 1957.[21] There were other terms applied to black Carnival groups: *bloco* and *cordão* (literally meaning "cord") could also refer to informal Carnival groups of working-class blacks and mulattoes in Bahia. Some of these parading groups included small ensembles of wind and brass instruments in addition to drums and percussion. In a book on Brazilian race relations, the American sociologist Donald Pierson described official Carnival parades that he observed in Salvador in the mid-1930s; in them, the large, elite Carnival clubs of whites were preceded and followed by black groups:

> In 1936, as for some years previously, three clubs competed in presenting floats on the opening and closing evenings of Carnival. The rivalries, especially between Cruz Vermelha and the Fantoches, are intense, the Innocentes em Progresso appearing to be rather generally admired.
>
> Before, during and following the parade, Negro *batucadas* and *cordões* pass through the milling crowds. The *batucadas* are usually composed of fifteen to twenty young men, invariably blacks or dark mulattoes, who carry small drums, *cuícas*, and *xaques-xaques* [described by Pierson as metal instruments with small pebbles inside], and parade in single file. The music is one toned and monotonous, reminiscent of the Candomblé ritual. A *cordão* usually consists of fifty or sixty people of both sexes and all ages, invariably blacks and dark mulattoes, enclosed within a roped quadrangle, some marching, rather informally, some constantly whirling and dancing, all singing African songs and beating their palms. A banner, usually of silk and velvet, bears the group's name. It may be Outum Obá de Africa, Ideal Africano, Onça, or some similar designation. The group also includes ten to fifteen musicians with brass instruments, a few blacks in African costume, and a dancer bearing an animal's head (tiger, lion, onça, etc.).[22]

Pierson was a sociologist (not a musician), and his comments regarding the similarity of the batucada music he observed and the music of a Candomblé ritual need to be evaluated with caution. Perhaps the batucadas reminded him of the Candomblé because of the acoustic texture of the drumming and singing (without additional melodic or harmonic instruments). These characteristics would have surely distinguished the music from the Carnival music coming from Rio de Janeiro and spread throughout Brazil via radio broadcasts during the 1930s. The music was also different from the musical accompaniment to the cordão groups, which featured wind and brass instruments. It is likely, too, that there was a wide degree of variation in the musical repertoire and instrumentation of the various Afro-Bahian Carnival groups of the time. The cordão that Pierson described as composed of fifty or sixty individuals accompanied by a band of fifteen musicians playing brass instruments was probably performing sambas, Carnival marches, and other commercial popular music of the day. It is also worth noting that Pierson never actually used the term *afoxé* to describe any of the black Carnival groups. That designation may not yet have been widespread in Salvador's Carnival. In the mid-1930s, Edison Carneiro, a noted Brazilian ethnographer of Afro-Bahian culture, mentioned that the afoxé was among the secular dances performed in the Bahian Carnival.[23] In a later source, Carneiro maintained that usage of the term *afoxé* to designate the Carnival groups was rather recent and was unknown during the early part of the century.[24] Nonetheless, though use of the term may have been rather recent, the groups themselves maintained a tradition stretching back at least into the nineteenth century.

Relying on the oral testimony of his primary informant, Hilário Reimídio das Virgens, whom he described as an "old black Bahian man closely connected to all the popular manifestations of the city," Carneiro concluded that "after the splendor of the late nineteenth century, the *afoxés* began presenting themselves more modestly in Carnival."[25] Hilário informed Carneiro that the following afoxés had been active at the turn of the twentieth century:

- Folia Africana (African Merrymakers)
- Lembrança Africana (African Memory)
- Papai Folia (Daddy Merrymakers)
- Guerreiros de África (African Warriors)
- Lanceiros de África (African Spearmen)
- Mamãe Arrumaria (Mommy Arrumaria)
- Lordes Ideias (Ideal Lords)
- Africanos em Pândega (Africans in Revelry)
- Lutadores de África (African Fighters)
- Congos de África (Congos of Africa).

As is clear from these names, issues of African identity, heritage, and resistance were important among these groups. As mentioned earlier, the initial flourishing of African-related thematics in Salvador's Carnival was met with a backlash from the city's dominant sector, which forced the activities of the black community underground. However, though no longer part of the official Carnival of Salvador, these manifestations of African cultural awareness never went away, just as Brazil's population was never transformed into a homogeneous "race" through the process of whitening. Nor was the promise of a racial democracy in Brazil realized.

Another important ethnographer of Afro-Brazilian religion, Roger Bastide, conducted extensive field research among Salvador's Candomblés during the 1940s and 1950s. He described the afoxé as a recreational manifestation of Candomblé during Carnival (my translation):

> One still encounters the expression "recreational Candomblé" within the *afoxé*. Most *afoxés* are from the Bantu nations, but I know at least one that is Nagô. It consists, in essence, of religious groups manifesting themselves in the noisy streets of the city, now no more than an ensemble of priests and the faithful, but in the old days it was a royal court, with a king, a queen, princes, guards, ladies of honor. However, this courtly procession in the middle of the exuberance of Carnival is preceded by a *padê* de Exu [an obligatory prophylactic ritual that begins a ceremony, intended to ensure a safe and successful process and outcome] and by a series of songs, sung one by one, in honor of the entire pantheon of African Orixás. Even here, this is "recreational Candomblé." Nonetheless, its primarily function was serious. With the result, the most celebrated of these [older] *afoxés* was that of Otum, Obá de Africa, at the Gantois Candomblé house. The two terms *obá*, king, and *otum*, right-hand chief, indicate quite clearly that the primitive form of this procession was the visit that the sovereign made to his people during the time of their celebrations, in which case the Candomblé [ritual] that preceded it was nothing other than the symbol of the religious festival realized before the secular festival. Pure African survival.[26]

The close connection between African religious practices and Carnival afoxé was evident here. Was Bastide describing the efforts of turn-of-the-century blacks in Salvador to construct, through their uniformed clubs, a "civilized" image of a royal African heritage?

During the 1940s and early 1950s, blacks and mulattoes continued to parade in several kinds of Carnival groups in Salvador—blocos, cordões, ranchos, batucadas, and afoxés. Photographs of these groups taken in those decades show the variety of musical instruments that were in use: several sizes of barrel-shaped drums being played with sticks and with hands, cuícas, agogô bells, agbe beaded gourds, metal shakers, and wind and brass instruments. Among these Carnival groups, the afoxés were unique in that they utilized atabaque and ilu drums drawn from Candomblé.

FILHOS DE GANDHI: THE BIRTH OF A NEW AFOXÉ

At the end of the 1940s, a group of striking dock workers from the Port of Bahia founded the most enduring and popular afoxé of all time: Filhos de Gandhi. The official website of the Filhos de Gandhi includes a page titled "Como Nasceu" ("How It Began") and offers the following description (my translation):

> The Carnival Association Filhos de Gandhi, was founded on the 18th of February of 1949. Inspired by newspaper headlines about the death of the great Indian leader Mahatma Gandhi, a group of stevedores from the Port of Salvador

created the bloco Filhos de Gandhi. As Gandhi had struggled non-violently for the independence of his country, the group decided to march in white, symbolizing peace. The bloco prohibited the presence of women and alcoholic beverages in order to avoid fights and other problems during its presentations. Initially known as a bloco, the Filhos de Gandhi was later defined as an *afoxé*, due to the fact that it could not compete as a *bloco* because of the instruments it used. For its first parade in 1949, the group wore sheets, sandals, and onion straw wrapped around the head, which gave its members an Arabic look. The *afoxé* was inspired by the Indian leader Mahatma Gandhi.[27]

Early on, the group used the same musical instruments employed by other blocos of Salvador. Consistent with the preceding description, most of the founders recount that Filhos de Gandhi began as a bloco of revelers singing Carnival sambas and marches and only later became an afoxé, when members incorporated musical instruments and songs of Candomblé. However, there is controversy regarding the early years of the Filhos de Gandhi, as a few of the founders maintain that the group was actually an afoxé from its inception. Regardless of the precise sequence of events, by the early 1950s, Filhos de Gandhi had established direct links to Candomblé and was parading in the Bahian Carnival as an afoxé, performing songs in a mix of Portuguese and Yoruba and playing Candomblé-derived rhythms on agogôs, ilus, atabaques, and afoxés. (The term *afoxés* also refers to the small beaded gourds used by the groups.) Many local priests of Candomblé participated in the Filhos de Gandhi, and the group established a long-standing relationship with one of the city's most important Candomblé terreiros: Axe Apô Afonjá.[28] In addition, in 1951, the members voted to select as their "god-mother" one of the city's most prominent Candomblé priestesses, Mãe Menininha do Gantois.

Ijexá Rhythm

Example 3.1 Basic rhythmic scheme for the ijexá rhythm as played by the Carnival afoxé Filhos de Gandhi. In the ilu part, noteheads with an *X* refer to slap strokes played on the drums.

During the 1950s and 1960s, the term *afoxé* became the accepted designation for Carnival groups associated with Candomblés of the city, and more specifically, it came to indicate a musical rhythm derived from the Ijexá nation within Candomblé. The ijexá rhythm, as it came to be known, is a deceptively simple rhythm based on syncopated interplay between the three primary percussion instruments (Example 3.1).

Unlike many of the Gêge-Nagô rhythms of Candomblé, which use thin sticks (*aguidavi*) on the atabaque drums, the ijexá rhythm is performed exclusively with the hands. The basic rhythm—relatively easy to master—was accessible to the many non-specialists who paraded during the Carnival. The short melodies of the afoxé songs were also conducive to group participation. In a small pamphlet published in 1976 by Fundação Nacional de Arte (FUNARTE), Brazil's national arts foundation, Raul Giovanni Lody described the afoxé songs, which he called *orô*, as having melodies similar to songs sung in the Candomblés of the Ijexá African nation.[29] My own analysis of afoxé song repertoires also reveals stylistic similarities to the songs and the singing style of Candomblé: scales with five pitches, call-and-response vocal organization, and syncopated phrasing emphasizing offbeats. In addition, afoxé song lyrics are sung primarily in Yoruba and pay homage to many of the Orixás of Candomblé.

It is not clear how many afoxés were active during the 1960s and the first half of the 1970s. Lody mentioned seven groups he considered traditional African afoxés (Império da África, Filhos de Odé, Mercadores de Bagdá, Cavaleiros de Bagdá, Filhos de Obá, Congos da África, and Filhos de Gandhi) and three afoxés de caboclo (Índios do Brasil, Tribo Costeira da Índia, Índios da Floresta). The afoxés de caboclo were linked to the syncretic Candomblé houses, the Candomblé de Caboclo, that mixed indigenous and African elements. By the early 1970s, however, the afoxés represented a marginalized folkloric presentation of Afro-Bahian culture during Carnival. This situation was about to change, as a new generation of young Bahians would help revive the afoxé tradition in the process of searching for their own African cultural roots. This process of revitalization would include the involvement of non-Candomblé members who would introduce changes into the "traditional" afoxé. Changes were met with criticism. In 1974, soon after that year's Carnival, anthropologist Juana Elbein dos Santos published a newspaper article titled "O Afoxé e o Africanismo Baiano" ("The Afoxé and Bahian Africanisms") in which she lamented the changes then occurring in the afoxés of the city (my translation):

> Of the five afoxé groups, three were based on Indian themes with feathers, spears, and war dances, constituting blocos that had absolutely nothing to do with the afoxé. . . . The other two groups, in spite of using elements derived from Nagô culture—rhythms, songs, instruments, etc.—do not represent afoxé, because the most fundamental part was absent: the Babalawô [diviner of the future] and his activities that provide the traditional content to the revelry.[30]

Despite such criticisms, the revitalized afoxé tradition became an important site for young Bahians to rediscover themselves, and many changes were soon on the horizon. One significant event was the participation of Brazilian pop star Gilberto Gil in the revival of the Filhos de Gandhi afoxé. Recounting his own involvement with the group during the early 1970s, Gil stated (my translation):

In truth, the afoxé, in which I have now marched for six years, was my own way of reconciling with Carnival. . . . Only upon my return from London, within that process of reclamation, of rediscovery, of the sophistication of my taste, did I go and specifically search for the afoxés, because, even in the Carnivals of my youth, they [the afoxés] seemed to me to be a calming element, an oasis of peace amid that chaos of the street. I remember that when I returned [to Brazil], I was told that the afoxés were no longer parading. And, in fact, I went and encountered some twenty members of Filhos de Gandhi, with their drums on the ground, in a corner of the Praça da Sé. They did not have the resources or the energy to maintain their space in the Bahian Carnival. I went to find them in order to join the afoxé, it was like a devotional thing, a vow, a desire to use my position of prestige to advocate for that beautiful thing that is the afoxé. And I paraded for six years, doing the entire twelve-hour preparation, singing and playing [music], stopping at the devotional locations, obeying the discipline, which is quite rigorous. And, last year, there were already 1,000 Filhos de Gandhi, and there were other afoxés, some very new, like Badauê, that is a type of youth afoxé, a pop afoxé, progressive.[31]

In an article published in the January–February issue of *Viver Bahia*, Gil described the afoxé experience as (my translation) "something stronger, superior, it's the spiritual side of carnaval. It counters the violence of the *trio elétrico*, it's something much more profound, magic even. It's as if all of the saints, all of the orixás, were there, in the middle of the people, taking control of the Carnaval, with all of its power."[32] For young Bahians in the late 1970s, the afoxé, like the venerable Candomblé religion itself, provided an important link to Afro-Brazilian culture. Gil and other youthful Bahians of the day were ready to affirm pride in their own black heritage. In Chapter 7, I will investigate the advent of an entirely new type of Carnaval association among Salvador's blacks during this period, known as the blocos afro (Afro blocs). But the reinvigorated afoxé tradition was also a mechanism to express black identity during Carnaval. Gil helped foster the revival of the Filhos de Gandhi by parading with the group during Carnival and by recording the song "Patuscada de Gandhi" (with authorship attributed to the afoxé Filhos de Gandhi) on his seminal album *Refavela*, released in 1977. On Gil's recording, the piece was arranged and performed in a style closely approximating that of an afoxé group performing during Carnaval.

Gilberto Gil also collaborated with João Donato on the song "Emoriô," which was recorded by Sergio Mendes & Brasil '77 in 1976. With increased media attention because of Gil's participation, membership in traditional afoxés such as the Filhos de Gandhi grew rapidly, and other new, politically minded afoxés were formed. Art historian Daniel J. Crowley listed a total of twenty-three afoxés participating in Salvador's Carnaval of 1983. Nineteen of these had been founded between the years 1970 and 1982.[33] The largest of all the afoxés, Filhos de Gandhi, marched that year with 3,500 members. Newer groups such as Badauê (founded in 1978) marched with 1,000 members, and Monte Negro (founded in 1981) counted 3,000 individuals among its membership. These progressive afoxés quickly infused new aesthetic ideas into the tradition. While firmly committed to the idea of highlighting Afro-Bahian heritage, the new groups minimized the roles of the Candomblé leaders. According to Antônio Risério (my translation):

> The new afoxés ... are led by young people, who, in principle, practically eliminated the creative and leadership roles of the babalorixás and other individuals in the hierarchy of the terreiros, generally the eldest people. The musicians are no longer necessarily alabês, instrumentalists who have been consecrated and confirmed (in the religious sense of these terms). In the same way, the songs are no longer chosen from the liturgical repertoire—the afoxés [now] have their own teams of composers. For their part, the dances are stylized, freer, and less restricted than the dances of the Orixás (only the basic movement is maintained).[34]

Although they did minimize the direct involvement of the religious authority, the creative young leadership in the new afoxés did not sever their ties with the Candomblé houses (in fact, many of the progressive afoxés maintained symbolic as well as active relationships with Candomblé). What they did was to expand the afoxé tradition in new directions that took advantage of the contemporary popular culture of Bahia. The most innovative new afoxé of the late 1970s was Badauê, led by Moa de Catendê. The group broke the established "rules" of the traditional afoxés in several areas, including musical style and repertoire. Risério provided valuable information on the subject when he quoted Catendê: "In the first place, we do not sing music from the sect, from Candomblé. We create our own music, we select the best songs during a festival, and we sing them in the streets, the opposite of singing music of the terreiro."[35] In addition, the composition of new songs involved freely mixing Yoruba with Portuguese, making the lyrics more relevant to the Bahia's young Carnival public. Badauê was also the first among the afoxés to utilize sound amplification during its parades, as it mixed new rhythms and instrumental sounds into the afoxé tradition. Risério again quoted Catendê: "The rhythm is different too, it's something else, it has more of a swing. Instead of staying tied to that 'ta-kum-kum,' there's always a variation, a counter rhythm, and it has the participation of other instruments."[36] Recalling the assessment of Gilberto Gil regarding the "pop" qualities of the new afoxés, Badauê arranged and rehearsed the repertoire in a manner that moved the afoxé in the direction of the aesthetics of popular music. Badauê was also featured on a 1982 compilation recording (*Alegria, Alegria, Carnaval da Bahia '82*) that included a track by the Filhos de Gandhi. Unlike that track, Badauê's offering, titled "Festa de Magia," was well rehearsed, arranged, and tightly performed. "Festa de Magia" is built around the alternation of two distinct rhythmic/melodic sections. The first section is set to a 12/8 rhythm reminiscent of the Candomblé toque known as *batá*. Section two is set to the ijexá rhythm. In addition, a berimbau is added to enhance the sound. The inclusion of the berimbau references the general symbolism of black resistance of the capoeira martial arts and dance form. These and other creative components incorporate a wide range of African-related images and symbols into the afoxé. The solo and choral voices are clear in the sound mix, the result of skilled studio recording and mixing techniques. In addition to responsorial singing (characteristic of the afoxé), a countermelody balances the main melodic phrase of the song. Likewise, the drums are recorded with attention to capturing their tonal qualities and sound, somewhat similar to congas, in the overall mix. Attention to the aesthetic dimensions of the sound recording and to the compositional parameters distinguishes the sound of Badauê from the traditional, street-oriented afoxés.

The trajectory of the afoxé tradition, from the early flourishing of African groups in the 1890s through the founding of the Filhos de Gandhi to the revival and renaissance of new afoxés in the 1970s and early 1980s, reflected the changing nature of the country's thoughts on racial identification. By the 1970s, voices from within Salvador's black community were demanding equal participation in the racial democracy that had been promised but not delivered. The progressive afoxés were part of this growing racial consciousness. The main cultural component that foreshadowed and mobilized political activity in the country was centered in Salvador and involved the emergence of new Carnival groups in the city, with social and political agendas. I will return to this issue in the final chapter of the book. Now, however, I will address the maracatu of Recife, whose history has paralleled that of Salvador's afoxé tradition.

Maracatu in Recife

> *Nagô, Nagô*
> *Our queen has been crowned*
> *Our king came from Mina*
> *Our queen has been crowned*
>   (Nação Porto Rico do Oriente)

These are the lyrics to one of the most popular songs of the maracatu Nação Porto Rico do Oriente. During colonial times in Brazil, *Mina* referred to the Fanti-Ashanti territories of West Africa. In the songs of the maracatu, the term is used to conjure up the image of an original African homeland for the imaginary African nations. Other terms, such as *Luanda,* are also invoked in maracatu songs. The *maracatu de baque virado* (maracatu of the turned-around beat) is generally acknowledged as the oldest and most "Africanized" element of Recife's Carnival. The maracatu in Recife preserves an old practice from colonial days featuring a procession with a symbolic African royal court, complete with dignitaries, musicians, and guards. The lyrics to the song just cited attest to the continued importance of kings and queens in the maracatu procession. In this section, I will trace the history of processing with invented African courts in Brazil and the transfer of this tradition into the Carnival of Recife as the maracatu de baque virado. As this name implies, a main component of these groups is an identifiable beat, supplied by large and loudly played drums that acoustically invade the areas where they perform. Much of the association of the maracatu groups with the idea of Africa resides in the powerful nature of the drumming, which draws on Afro-Brazilian musical aesthetics. Over the course of the twentieth century, this powerful music provoked both public scorn and adoration.

Figure 3.5 Dona Elda, queen of the maracatu Nação Porto Rico do Oriente during Carnival, Recife, Pernambuco, 2001 (photo by Larry Crook).

HISTORY OF A ROYAL FORM

Paralleling events in Salvador, the blacks and mestizos of Recife inundated their city's Carnival with newly formed parading groups soon after Brazil's abolition of slavery in 1888. Many of Recife's blacks, mestizos, and whites formed large pedestrian walking clubs (*clubes pedestres*) in the 1880s, featuring capoeira practitioners dancing in front of military marching bands. From these multiracial organizations, the unique Carnival music from Recife known as frevo evolved, to be exalted as the city's signature music and dance genre in the twentieth century. In addition to the multiracial pedestrian clubs, black Carnival associations linked directly to the city's Candomblé houses also took to the streets. These groups, like the Candomblé from which they sprang, were conceptualized as African "nations" and were called maracatu. The maracatus drew directly on the colonial practice of crowning black kings and queens and became the primary mode of highlighting African heritage in Recife's Carnival.

The colonial practices that predated the Carnival maracatu were called the *Rei de Angola* (King of Angola) and the *Rei de Congo* (King of the Congo) in Brazil. These were originally linked to the black Catholic brotherhoods, especially Nossa Senhora do Rosário dos Pretos (Our Lady of the Rosary of the Blacks) in both Brazil and in Portugal. In Portugal, enslaved Africans held festivals accompanied by African music and dance during the fifteenth and sixteenth centuries, in which they elected their own kings and queens. Members of Portugal's black community entered the brotherhood of Nossa Senhora do Rosário in the late fifteenth century and participated in its many public festivals. Documents from this same Catholic brotherhood in Recife first recorded the election of a rei de Angola in 1674. On special days in the colony, blacks held festivities just outside church grounds to celebrate their coronations with public processions of singing, dancing, and instrumental music. The earliest evidence of a coronation of a rei de Angola in Brazil comes from a description by Urbain Souchu de Rennefort, a Frenchman who was in Recife in 1666. He wrote (my translation): "In spite of the hard state of servitude in which they lived, the negros do not refrain from celebrating on occasion. On Sunday, September 10, 1666, they had a feast in Pernambuco. After some four hundred men and one hundred women attended mass, they elected a king and a queen, they marched through the streets singing and reciting verses that they themselves improvised, preceded by atabaques, trumpets, and tambourines."[37]

To the ears of the seventeenth-century Frenchman, the singing of these improvised verses by a black man and several women no doubt appeared exotic and certainly non-European. Although we do not know specifically what was being sung on that occasion, Rennefort's description could apply to a host of African song forms in which set choral refrains are alternated with solo improvisations by one or more lead singers. This type of vocal call-and-response organization is a hallmark of African music. Outside the church grounds, religious leaders and slave owners in rural and urban areas permitted and even encouraged blacks to hold such festivities in which they elected their own kings and queens. They even allowed blacks to parade through the streets performing music and dance. The most compelling reason for this leniency was that in the slave society of Brazil, the institution of black kings and queens served a useful function for administrators: it helped keep civil order among the enslaved and free black population. On special occasions, such as the festivities surrounding Catholic patron saint days, the black kings and queens presided over both secular and sacred activities. The church tolerated many of the non-Christian elements that were included in the festivities in order to attract the black population to the "true" faith—Catholicism. That is, church leaders tolerated what, in their eyes, were surely pagan African practices of music and dance as long as these did not conflict directly with church dogma or directly confront Christian moral sensibilities. The church's colonial policy toward blacks in Brazil held that Africans were like children and had to be "attracted by music, which they loved; by dancing, which was their great diversion; and by their liking for titles and grandiose positions."[38] Henry Koster, an

Englishman, wrote the following account of the crowing of a rei de Congo, which he witnessed in Pernambuco in 1814:

> In March took place the yearly festival of our Lady of the Rosary, which was directed by Negroes; and at this period is chosen the King of the Congo nation. . . . The Congo Negroes are permitted to elect a king and queen from among the individuals of their own nation; the personages who are fixed upon may either actually be slaves, or they may be manumitted Negroes. These sovereigns exercise a species of mock jurisdiction over their subjects, which is much laughed at by the whites; but their chief power and superiority over their countrymen is shown on the day of the festival.[39]

Koster went on to note:

> About eleven o'clock, I proceeded to the church with the vicar. We were standing at the door when there appeared a number of male and female Negroes in cotton dresses of colors and of white, with flags flying and drums beating; and as they approached, we discovered among them the king and queen and the secretary of state. Each of the former wore upon their heads a crown, which was partly covered with gilt paper and painted of various colors. The king was dressed in an old-fashioned suit of diverse tints, green, red, and yellow; coat, waistcoat, and breeches; his scepter which was of wood, and finely gilt, was in his hand. The queen was in a blue silk gown, also of ancient make; and the wretched secretary had to boast of as many colors as his master, but his dress had evident appearances of each portion having been borrowed from a different quarter, for some parts were too tight and others too wide for him.

The emergence of the black religious brotherhoods in colonial Brazil provided blacks a mechanism to maintain and develop African practices under the cloak of Catholicism. The vague phrase "drums beating" in the preceding description does not tell us much about the type of drums or style of drumming that occurred in these processions. Was it African-style drumming on European-style drums? Drawings and paintings from the time suggest that European-style drums were common for these kinds of events. Annual celebrations for the patron saints of the brotherhoods provided the opportunity for an "African" royal court to lead processions of danced presentations with drumming, singing, and costuming. When African costuming was discouraged or banned, the processional groups incorporated European-style dress, which may have also camouflaged the underlying meanings of these practices for the black population.

As mentioned in Rennefort's comments, cited earlier, improvised singing and instrumental music were present at these events as well. Some of the black and mulatto musicians were also active performers of European musical repertoire and played in charamela ensembles, which also participated on these occasions. Such intercultural connections had a significant role in the development of hybrid forms of popular culture in the Recife area. Though we do not know how the instrumental music actually sounded for the processional events, numerous reports from colonial Brazil described the mixing of African-derived instruments, such as marimbas, drum types, idiophones, and shakers, with Portuguese wind, string, and percussion instruments. The mixing of African and European elements of music, costuming, and dramatic presentation was an important aesthetic and social strategy within the black population, and these public processions became a primary vehicle for the development of Afro-Brazilian performing arts. Within this context, it is likely that the drumming that accompanied the crowning of black royalty was derived, at least partially, from African musical heritage.

Beginning in the late eighteenth century, the Catholic Church looked with increasing disfavor on the Afro-Brazilian processional dances in Pernambuco that were associated with the rei de Angola and rei de Congo. There was also a growing trend among the upper-class urban and rural elites of the time to regard the gatherings of large groups of blacks in urban areas as potentially dangerous and threatening to the stability of the society that they administered. This growing fear coincided with the Haitian revolution, which sent shock waves throughout the hemisphere. Rather than seeing the processions and the institution of the rei de Angola and rei de Congo as convenient mechanisms of control, the Brazilian slaveholders now considered them dangerous activities through which the black community was able to mobilize itself in large numbers. One of the consequences of this change in attitude was that, by about 1850, the direct links of the rei de Angola and rei de Congo to the religious brotherhoods of the Catholic Church had become quite weak. During the course of the nineteenth century, Recife's Afro-Brazilian religious community gradually took over the processional and ceremonial elements of the rei de Angola and rei de Congo traditions, turning them into public manifestations of Afro-Brazilian religion. As noted earlier, in the final phase of the transatlantic slave trade (in the late eighteenth century and the first half of the nineteenth century), the majority of Africans who were enslaved and transported to Brazil came from Yoruba and Fon-Ewe territories of West Africa. This fact resulted in the establishment of a strong Nagô and Gêge presence among the Afro-Brazilian population. This period of West African influx also coincided with the emergence of the early houses of Candomblé in Recife, which were dominated by the Nagô (Yoruba) traditions. Nagô religious affiliations and influences came to dominate the Afro-Brazilian religious houses of Recife, but the diversity of the various African ethnic groups in Pernambuco continued to be reflected in the division of the black population into nações, or nations. The term nação was also applied to the parading groups associated with Candomblé houses in Recife. Further, the term maracatu became associated with these processional groups around the same time that they were taken over by the Candomblé houses.

Despite scholarly attempts to link it to earlier Amerindian and African sources, the term maracatu most likely developed sometime during the nineteenth century in Recife. In that century, the word appeared frequently in Recife newspaper articles. Most of these articles dealt with police actions arising during the social gatherings of large groups of blacks in the area. One article published in the Diário de Pernambuco on May 27, 1851 reported that Recife's chief of police had received a petition from the "black African Antônio Oliveira, with the title of Rei do Congo, complaining about another leader who had publicly assembled his own nação for entertainment without submitting to [Oliveira's] authority. The goal [of the petition] was to cause the police official to make arrangements so that such gatherings, popularly called maracatus, would stop occurring, because of the unfortunate things that happen at them" (my translation).[40]

It is worth noting that the public gathering of blacks was referred to as a maracatu (in which "unfortunate" things occurred) and also that it was a member of the old black "aristocracy"—a rei de Congo—who was lodging the complaint. The mid-nineteenth century was the time in which the colonially sanctioned institution of the rei de Congo disappeared and the new nações and their maracatus emerged. It was also the time in which Recife's paper published notices written by members of the local elite that condemned the maracatu practice as a form African barbarity. For instance, the *Diário de Pernambuco* edition of May 18, 1880, published the following notice (my translation):

> *Maracatu*, the stupid African merrymaking for which a certain segment of our society shows itself to be insatiable, not withstanding appearing in the municipal register and police records, has been growing in this city and in its outskirts, and it seems that, if not with their collusion, at least with the permission, of police authorities.
>
> Meanwhile, this alleged entertainment—where abjectly immoral scenes are observed, devoid of any good customs—is the motive for fights and it is not rare for the participants to leave with knife wounds. Moreover, as we have already said, and we will repeat, the [maracatus] are extremely inconvenient for the neighbors of the locations where they hold reunions, not only because the beating of the barbaric instruments and the out-of-tune voices of the singers are deafening and go on for hours, but also because when the participants leave the area, they occasionally shout obscenities and dirty sayings.[41]

As this newspaper article made clear, the term *maracatu* in nineteenth-century Recife was closely associated with crime, disorderly conduct, and loud noise coming from the Afro-Brazilian communities of the city. The dominant sector demonized the instruments themselves as barbaric and regarded the powerful drumming as threatening. The noise of the drumming, together with the "out-of-tune" singing, must have been quite an affront to the European aesthetic sensibilities of the members of Recife's dominant class, who valued all things European as they sought to make themselves and their city modern. This maracatu noise of the lower classes was certainly not music to their ears. About thirty years later (in 1908), the Recife folklorist Pereira da Costa would echo some of the same aesthetic value judgments when he described the musical accompaniment of the maracatu in the following manner (my translation):

> In the rear came the instruments: drums, megaphones and other African things, that accompanied the songs and marches and diverse dances with a horrendous noise. The song of the march, performed by the whole entourage with the noisy accompaniment of the instruments, consists of a song fit closely to the dance, with words constantly repeating, as you can see from the following verse, that we offer as a feature of these particular songs:
>
> > *Aruenda qui tenda, tenda,*
> > *Aruenda qui tenda, tenda,*
> > *Aruenda de totororó.*[42]

Such opinions regarding the sound qualities of the maracatu did not change much in the early twentieth century. By the 1930s, the term *maracatu* was also intimately associated with Afro-Brazilian religion in Recife, and both were considered matters requiring swift police action. In a work on the Xangôs of Recife, Albino Gonçalves Fernandes cited numerous police raids against the religion that were written up in the newspapers of Recife. The following article appeared in the Recife paper *Diário da Tarde* on September 1, 1933 (my translation):

> Cognizant that Afogados was infested with these centers of witchcraft, Mr. Edson Moury Fernandez . . . went into that area of town yesterday night determined to establish order. Under protests that these were houses of *maracatu*, the *macumbeiros* [Afro-Brazilian cult members] arrived agitated, in large numbers. The first group of *catimbó* [another designation for Afro-Brazilian religion] sighted by the police was the "*maracatu* Estrela Baiana," located on the S. Mangueira street, in Afogados. In that location, the *macumbeiros* were caught in the act by the police [who] confiscated various bottles of palm oil, [and] copper coins covered with rice. . . .
>
> After this raid, the police went to the African Center of Noberto Costa, known as Pai Noberto. . . . In the main room of his house . . . is an altar in front of which the *macumbeiros* profess their mysterious and sinister liturgy. They separate couples, harass their enemies, break up marriages, in other words, they practice an endless series of frightfully dreadful things. . . . To the sound of African songs, in honor of S. Budun, the *macumbeiros* sacrifice sheep, pigs, goats, chickens, and other domestic animals.[43]

The mocking, even contemptuous tone of this newspaper account depicted members of the Xangô Candomblé community as common criminals, child molesters, and purveyors of African witchcraft. Police brutality was a severe and constant fact of life for the Candomblé community during the first half of the twentieth century. One strategy that the members of that community developed to minimize the harsh punishment resulting from police raids was to camouflage their religious rituals under the guise of the Carnival maracatu. In the account just cited, practitioners of the two "suspect" houses that were raided in 1933 claimed they were only practicing maracatu. In truth, it is likely that the two houses were simultaneously houses of Candomblé and the headquarters of maracatu nations.

In the 1930s, one of Recife's leading *babalorixás* (male priests of Candomblé) gave oral testimony about the origins of the maracatu to Gonçalves Fernandes (my translation):

> Adão, speaking about the Maracatu, told me that many years ago, in the time of his grandfather, the negroes of all the nations in Recife, would get together . . . to dance in front of the doors of the churches. When it was time to end the dancing they would say "MARACATUCA," which meant: let us leave. Students enjoyed hanging around those dances and, hearing this word, created, together with the negroes, a similar dance, calling it MARACATU. . . . Today, because the maracatu is a Carnival association, before any parade through the city

streets, they pay homage to Our Lady of the Rosary, dancing at the door of the churches.[44]

When Pai Adão told Gonçalves Fernandes this story about the origins of the term *maracatu*, the Candomblé priest was already in his sixties and was describing events that, in all likelihood, had been told to him by his own grandfather (also a prominent Candomblé priest). If this line of reasoning is accurate, the events that Adão described would have occurred sometime in the second half of the nineteenth century, perhaps in the 1850s or 1860s. This time line corresponds accurately with the years in which the rei de Congo tradition was separating from the Catholic brotherhoods and being adopted into the Candomblé houses of Recife. The danced procession involving the royal court, musicians, and dancers was not abandoned but was adopted by members of Recife's Afro-Brazilian religious community, perhaps marking the "beginning" of the maracatu tradition as told by Pai Adão.

It is instructive to consider the symbolic importance of the intercultural collaborations between the students (white) and the maracatu performers (black) that Pai Adão embedded in his story. From the perspective of a Candomblé priest in the 1930s, Adão may have wanted to embellish the origin of the maracatu to match the contemporary idea of racial and cultural mixture that was becoming so important in Brazilian intellectual thought at the time. In his book, Gonçalves Fernandes mentioned that Pai Adão was also a good friend of Gilberto Freyre during the 1930s. In that decade, Freyre published his famous book *The Masters and the Slaves,* in which he articulated his theories on racial and cultural mixture as a positive component to Brazilian national identity. It would be wrong to assume that Pai Adão was incapable of conversing intellectually with Freyre about such matters. Apparently, Adão was a well-traveled individual, having visited Nigeria and Europe in 1906. Gonçalves Fernandes also noted that, because of religious convictions, Adão refused to participate in the First Afro-Brazilian Congress, organized by Gilberto Freyre in Recife in 1933. Following the logic of Adão's statement, one could read into the story the symbolic birth of the maracatu tradition through the union of white and black participants of Pernambuco society. In the second half of the nineteenth century and in the early twentieth century, the streets of Recife provided many opportunities for that kind of intercultural and multiracial mingling. The most celebrated Carnival music of Recife that came to symbolize this intercultural and racial mixing was the frevo, which will be investigated in detail in Chapter 4. In the context of the present discussion, it is important to note that by the 1930s, the frevo had already entered Brazil's national music industry as a form of regional counterpoint to the samba and the Carnival march from Rio de Janeiro. The development of the maracatu in Recife gained much of its meaning in relation to the frevo. Although the frevo was venerated as Recife's great symbol of cultural and racial mixture, the maracatu was representative of the African heritage of the area. However, it was also, as Pai Adão's story makes clear, a likely site for potential cultural and racial mixing. In the Carnival of Recife, there were many opportunities for creative mixture among members of the maracatu community and other traditions. However, somewhere between 1890 and 1930, the public image of the maracatu became nestled within a set of ideas that linked the tradition exclusively to a kind of purified and frozen African heritage. Dismissing the dynamic process of cultural hybridity that was actually occurring at the time, Brazilian folklorist Pereira da Costa described the maracatu in 1908 in the following manner (my translation):

> If the *maracatu*, ready to self-destruct by freezing itself out, in a time that Africans are no longer present [in the maracatu], and their descendents have a preference for second-hand imitation of white society in their intimate dance gatherings; if the *maracatu*, thus, already becoming rare, only appears in a modest manner during Carnival, there was a time not so long ago that it was performed in large numbers, more or less well organized, displaying a truly splendid pomp and luxury.[45]

Thus, already in 1908, the intellectual elite conceptualized the maracatu as a vestige of Recife's dying African culture. Furthermore, intellectual discourses of authenticity located the maracatu's identity in the idealized premodern past of the country, an era before urbanization radically altered the national way of life. It should be noted that Pereira da Costa was writing some twenty years after the abolition of slavery and perhaps only fifty or sixty years after the maracatu had emerged. By the time Pai Adão was informing Gonçalves Fernandes about the tradition's origin, the maracatu was already considered somewhat of a museum tradition that preserved African folk culture within Recife's Carnival. In this regard, it is significant that the 1930s also witnessed the first attempts by Recife composers to create a popular musical genre called maracatu. During the same years in which Recife's police force was raiding Xangô Candomblé terreiros and arresting the members of the Afro-Brazilian religious community and their maracatu nations, the Federação Carnavalesca Pernambucana (Pernambuco Carnival Federation), under the state's Ministry of Culture, was awarding prizes to composers to produce compositions in the newly created maracatu genre of written music. This genre translated the drum and vocal music of the traditional maracatu nations to a radio-orchestra format emphasizing brass and wind instruments, with minimal percussion accompaniment. Local frevo composers Capiba (Lourenço da Fonseca Barbosa) and Nelson Ferreira both wrote in this new genre. Capiba won prizes for the compositional maracatus "É de Tororó" (1935), "Onde o Sol Descamba" (1936), and "Êh! Uá Calunga" (1937). Ten of his maracatu compositions were later published in the book *Danças Pernambucanas*.[46] However, unlike the success experienced in creating a commercialized genre of samba in the national music industry of Rio de Janeiro, the attempt to make a similar adaptation of the maracatu did not generate commercial success. Maracatu remained a regional, state-supported phenomenon.

Codifying a Tradition: Maracatu de Baque Virado

By the first years of the twentieth century or perhaps even a few years earlier, the musical configuration of the traditional maracatu nations was codified. The strong association with African rhythmic sensibilities is suggested by the name applied to the musical components of the tradition: maracatu de baque virado. Minor innovations in music, dance, and costuming may have occurred, but from about 1900 to 1985, the maracatu remained relatively frozen in its basic format. This stability was noted by the folklorist Katarina Real in the 1960s when she wrote (my translation):

To sum up the situation . . . we still have in Pernambuco survivals of the ancient "African nations" whose Carnival manifestation is the "regal court" with kings and queens today called the "maracatu." The most extraordinary aspect about this regal court has been its great stability over time—that is, for more than one hundred years, the court of the maracatu-nation has remained entirely stable, virtually without modification. If we compare the dazzling presentations of the maracatu-nations of today, in the decade of the 1960s, with that famous description of the maracatus that Pereira da Costa wrote in the first years of the century, we will see that the parades of today are almost identical to those of 1900.[47]

Real then quoted part of Pereira da Costa's description of the maracatu, published in 1908, to emphasize her point (my translation):

The procession begins with a standard bearer flanked by guards, followed by two rows of beautifully adorned women with turbans of ribbons of various colors, small mirrors and other accessories, representing, in the middle of these rows, various characters, who carry religious fetishes—a wooden rooster, a stuffed alligator, and a doll in white clothing with a blue veil; and soon after this, formed into lines, come the dignitaries of the court, ending the procession are the king and the queen. These two characters, displaying the royal insignia, such as crowns, scepters, and full capes held up by servants, march under a large parasol and [are] protected by guards.[48]

The descriptions from Pereira da Costa that appear throughout the work of Katarina Real all mention the splendor of the traditional maracatu groups and their vaunted place within the Recife Carnival. The Brazilian composer and self-taught folklorist César Guerra-Peixe produced the most comprehensive study of the traditional maracatus. While in Recife from 1949 to 1952 as musical director of a local Recife radio station, he conducted extensive field research and then published a book titled *Maracatus do Recife*, originally issued in 1955.[49] His research was carried out primarily with the maracatu Nação Elefante (recognized as the oldest maracatu nation in Recife, tracing its founding to 1800), but he also worked with other venerable groups in the area: Leão Coroado, Porto Rico do Oriente, and Estrela Brilhante. He also researched the relatively new hybrid type of maracatu known as *maracatu de orquestra* (maracatu orchestra), that mixed African and indigenous elements. In addition to substantial descriptions of the social components of the groups and a thorough review of the written research on the maracatu, the most impressive aspect of Peixe's work is the detailed musical notations and the stylistic descriptions of the drumming and singing. Many of the same basic rhythmic patterns and melodies that he notated in the 1950s were still in evidence among the maracatus during the 1980s and 1990s when I was conducting field research in the area.

According to Peixe's informants, Nação Elefante's heyday occurred during the 1920s when João Vitorino was the crowned king of the maracatu nation.[50] At the time of Vitorino's death in 1928, the group was reported to have performed with about ninety members, including the following types of characters:

- Queen and king
- Four ladies of honor
- Princess and prince
- Ambassador and minister of state
- Duchess and duke
- Countess and count
- Eight vassals
- Three *damas de paço* (ladies of the palace), each carrying a *calunga* doll (a representation of an important ancestor of the maracatu)
- Master of ceremonies
- Flag bearer
- Slave, crown guard, bodyguard
- Secretary
- Thirteen lance carriers
- Twenty caboclos (Indians)
- Twenty baianas (female figures dressed as initiates of Candomblé)
- Fifteen *batuqueiros* (musicians).

Through the 1980s, the large maracatu nations were still appearing in Recife's annual Carnival in an elaborate form quite similar to this description. When I first observed the Nação Elefante and the Nação Porto Rico do Oriente in the Carnivals of 1987 and 1988, the structure of the two groups involved the royal court of a king and queen with all of their lesser dignitaries (princes and princesses, dukes and duchesses, ambassadors, counts and countesses, and so on). In each group, a "slave" held an elaborate parasol over the royal couple, and Roman guards circled around the court carrying spears. A number of baiana women were in costumes based on the full dresses and accessories of the Orixás during Candomblé ceremonies. One or two of the women (the damas de paço) also carried calungas, the special wooden dolls that represented the ancestors of the group. Finally, the batuqueiros carried large, double-headed drums (*alfaias*); snare drums; metal shakers (*mineiros*); and a metal bell (*gonguê*).

Track 1 of the CD features music I recorded during the 1988 Carnival in Recife. I was in the downtown area of the city the week before Carnival on an evening billed as the "Night of Maracatu." The entire Nação Porto Rico was performing, and the sound was extremely powerful. Everyone in the procession danced, but it was the baianas and the damas de paço who were the most expressive and intense in their dancing.

The role of the queen in the maracatu has become particularly important. The most respected maracatu queens are invariably female priestesses (*ialorixás*) in Candomblé who have their own terreiros. Among the powerful women who reigned over maracatus in Recife during the twentieth century were Dona Santa (Nação Elefante) and Dona Elda (Nação Porto Rico do Oriente). When I interviewed Dona Elda in 1998, she emphasized the link of the maracatu nations to African heritage and her own role within the history of the Nação Porto Rico:

> There was a certain time that it [Nação Porto Rico] was inactive, stopped. Then
> ialorixá Elda reorganized it. It was organized by Elda, that's who I am. You see,

the elders, the Africans, Francisco do Iatá and Pereira da Costa, they had their own members who were those old Africans, those people who worked in the sugarcane fields, they were fishermen . . . and went onto the rivers, navigating and playing the atabaque drums, making offerings to the Orixás. They made [religious] vows with rice, beans, corn, and that kind of thing for the Orixás. And everyone around there was enjoying themselves and dancing. . . .

Among them, the first was José da Farinha, and later came José da Ferida, and then those old Africans died. However, others continued [the Nação Porto Rico]. It was placed in the hand of Elias Arruda, and Elias Arruda—who was a babalorixá—died and passed it on to Elda, the ialorixá Elda. So, it's because of this history that I tell you that it was transferred to the city of Recife. There was a time when it was not active . . . and then it was revived by Elda, the current president, and queen. Its headquarters are located on Eurico Vitrúvio street, number 483, in the neighborhood of Pina.[51]

Under Dona Elda's leadership, Nação Porto Rico became one of the top maracatu de baque virado groups, winning championships in the Carnival competitions of Recife. In 1989, the group was chosen as a representative of Recife's culture and traveled to Europe to perform. By that time, Dona Elda's son Shacon Viana was sixteen years old and was already an accomplished drummer in the group. In the mid-1990s, he took over the musical leadership of the group. In 1998, I worked with Shacon and learned some of the maracatu de baque virado drumming style.

The powerful nature of the drumming is built around a highly syncopated scheme of rhythms that seem to turn the beat around in your mind as you listen to it. A list of the instruments of the maracatu de baque virado follows:

- *Alfaias* are large, double-headed bass drums that come in three sizes (large—*trovador*; medium—*rompinor*; small—*melê*). These instruments are the heart and soul of the maracatu and provide the unrelenting bass of the ensemble. There can be as many as thirty of these powerful drums.
- The *caixa* (a deep snare drum) and the *tarol* (a shallow snare drum) play repeating sixteenth notes and give the initial call (*chamada*) for the group.
- The *gonguê* is a large iron bell played with a thick stick. The gonguê provides a syncopated time line that helps hold the entire ensemble together.
- The *mineiro* is a metal shaker that plays repeating sixteenth notes.

Within a maracatu de baque virado, the drummers are called batuqueiros, and the rhythmic patterns they perform are referred to as toques or baques. According to Shacon, there are five basic baques: the *baque virado, baque Nagô, baque martelo, baque parado,* and *baque de Luanda.* These baques are all in 2/4 meter and are subtle variations of the same basic pattern. The baques are performed by themselves and also as accompaniments to songs, which are known as *loas* or *toadas.* Most maracatu pieces begin with a call (the chamada) performed on the caixa and accented by the alfaia bass drums. The chamadas are often in a triple meter before modulating to the duple meter patterns that set the rhythm of the maracatu. This opening pattern can be heard on *Track 1* just after the voice begins.

Figure 3.6
Maracatu Nação
Elefante
batuqueiro
drummers during
Carnival with alfaia
drums, Recife,
Pernambuco,
1988 (photo by
Larry Crook).

Example 3.2 Chamada of the baque virado played on snare drum and bass drums

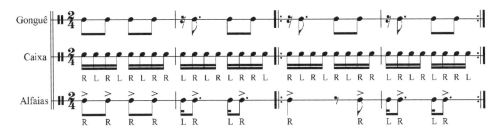

Example 3.3 Basic baque virado rhythmic scheme of Nação Porto Rico do Oriente. The common sequences of sticking on the caixa and the alfais are given (L = left hand, R = right hand).

This pattern functions as an introduction and is immediately connected to the baque virado pattern or one of the other baques of the group. The baque virado pattern of the Nação Porto Rico is given in Example 3.3.

This pattern continues until the end of the piece, with the drummers of the largest of the alfaias (the trovadores) playing elaborated variations emphasizing syncopated patterns.

Unlike the lyrics of the Bahian afoxé songs, the lyrics of traditional maracatu songs are almost exclusively in Portuguese. They are also typically quite short and comment on events such as the crowning of kings and queens, the beauty of the maracatu, and trips across the sea. One of the old songs of the Nação Porto Rico is "Segue Ambassador."

"Segue Embaixador" (an old loa sung by the Nação Porto Rico)

Continue Mr. Ambassador
Show me the signal
Our flag is of the nation

I'm going to Luanda
To look for the beads of Saramandá.

Another of the old songs in the repertoire of the group is "Beira Mar" ("Seashore").

"Beira Mar"

Ô lê lo ê
Ô lê lo á

Ô lê lo ê
I left from the seashore
The seashore
It is from my heart
This *maracatu* Porto Rico
It is of distinction.

Allusions to places in Africa in these songs (Luanda, Angola, Mina) strengthen the relationships of the maracatu community's members to their ancestral homeland. The idea of a journey across the sea also underscores the historical travails of their ancestors, who were uprooted from their homes, enslaved, and transported to Brazil. The repertoire of traditional loas of the maracatus make subtle references to the history of slavery and contemporary discrimination in Brazil, but a new repertoire of songs began emerging in the late 1980s that connected with the growing black consciousness in the country. New and revitalized maracutu groups at that time began making more overtly political statements through their music. This development coincided with the national black consciousness movement in Brazil. Effects within the traditional maracatu nations could also be seen. According to Shacon, the song "Zumbi dos Palmares" of the Nação Porto Rico is a recent addition to the group's repertoire. Written by Jaime, the musical leader of Nação Porto Rico until the mid-1990s, the song invokes the image of and pays tribute to the famous leader of black resistance in Brazil—Zumbi.

"Zumbi dos Palmares"

The nation is Nagô
It comes flying through the air

The nation of Porto Rico
Salutes Zumbi of Palmares

From Africa come our traditions
If Zumbi were here
He would applaud this nation
Our king, save the queen
Save the ambassador
Save the king
Save the queen
Save our emperor
Make our nation
A nation of value

Although the songs of Candomblé have remained silent on the issue of slavery and racial discrimination, maracatu texts now make subtle references to that history and to the contemporary position of blacks in the country. Never overt repudiations of the promise of a racial democracy, the allusions to figures such as Zumbi, a mythologized black hero of seventeenth-century slave resistance in the Northeast, indicate the growing awareness of members of these traditional maracatu groups. As the main emblem of African heritage in the Recife Carnival, the maracatu is a powerful resource for black cultural awareness that has never been fully tapped within Recife. However, a vibrant new popular music movement developed in the city in the early 1990s—the mangue beat—

and adopted the maracatu rhythm and drums as part of its hybrid sound. The mangue beat will be investigated in the final chapter of this book. In Chapter 4, we will focus on the frevo, Recife's signature Carnival music. Drawing on the Afro-Brazilian martial-arts dance of capoeira and the European marching band tradition, this highly animated music became an important regional expression of the nationalist discourse on mixture (cultural and racial) as a positive element of Brazilian identity.

CHAPTER 4

Making Multiracial
Carnival Music: The Frevo

Frevo is a form of music and dance unlike anything else in the world. CD *Track 4* is a modern recording of the frevo "Freio à Óleo" ("Brake Oil"), written in 1949 by band-leader and composer José Menezes. This kind of instrumental frevo for a wind, brass, and percussion band is called a *frevo de rua,* or street frevo. Based on two musical sections, the horn and wind sections of the band play interlocking syncopated melodies while percussion punctuates the melodies with loud rim shots and stops. In Recife during Carnival time, the streets and airwaves are full of frevo. First emerging at the turn of the twentieth century in Recife among the multiracial working-class Carnival clubs, the frevo soon became Pernambuco's premier Carnival music and a symbol of the cultural and racial mixture of the northeastern city. The frevo drew from two important cultural traditions in Recife: European band music and the Afro-Brazilian martial-arts dance known as capoeira. At its core, the frevo is a highly syncopated instrumental music performed by marching bands that animate hundreds of revelers in the streets of Recife during Carnival. In the 1920s and 1930s, the frevo entered Brazil's national consciousness through the country's newly formed recording and broadcast industry, centered in Rio de Janeiro. Composers from Recife sent their compositions south to Rio, where they were recorded by studio orchestras and released on 78-rpm phonodiscs. Like the samba, its better-known cousin from Rio de Janeiro, the frevo also became an emblem of the racial and cultural mixture that was emerging as a unifying element of Brazilian identity. However, the frevo represented not the national but rather a regional expression of this idea. Unlike the samba, the frevo was never a viable candidate to fulfill the role of the unifying emblem of Brazil's national consensus culture. Rather, it served as a variation on the theme of Brazilianess, as a regional musical counterpoint to the centralizing discourses involving Brazil's national cultural essence. Furthermore, the intellectual production of a narrative story regarding the frevo's origins did not include an attempt

Figure 4.1 José Menezes and his frevo orchestra perform during Carnival, Recife, Pernambuco, 2001 (photo by Larry Crook).

to locate the music's "authentic" prototype exclusively in Afro-Brazilian cultural roots—as was the case for the samba. Instead, the notion of collaboration among Recife's multiracial lower-class populations (blacks, whites, and mulattoes) during the city's street Carnival of the early twentieth century was privileged as the source and site of the so-called authentic frevo. In this chapter, I will investigate the multiracial roots of the frevo in the nineteenth century and then trace the history of this music over the course of the twentieth century.

The Frevo and Recife's Carnival, 2001

I first met José Menezes in Recife in 2000 when I attended a rehearsal of his orchestra as it prepared for the upcoming Carnival season. During the Carnival of 2001, I heard the group perform several times in the Recife area. One evening of Carnival, I was backstage listening to Menezes and his orchestra perform when a young frevo bandleader turned to me, pointed at Menezes and the players in his orchestra, and said simply, "The professors!" When I asked what he meant by that, he replied that Menezes and the musicians of his generation had taught practically everyone else how to play frevo. *Track 4* on the CD showcases the style of frevo created by José Menezes, Duda (José Ursicino da Silva), and the other composers/arrangers of their generation. This track is a remake of Menezes's classic frevo de rua "Freio à Óleo" (first recorded in 1950) and comes from the 1998 CD *Frevos de Rua: Os Melhores do Século, Vol. 1* (Street Frevos: The Best of the Century). Frevo lover, pianist, and composer Luiz Guimarães produced the recording. Guimarães is one of a handful of promoters of frevo in the Recife area. The recording features the Orquestra do Maestro Duda, with a modern arrangement provided by Menezes. For this project, Menezes wrote a new arrangement of the piece, which he explained as merely a "redistribution" of the voicings for the winds and brass. The extended jazz chord at the end, which the brass and winds hold for several seconds, is an example of the "modern" extended chords introduced by the progressive composers of Menezes's generation in the 1960s.

During Recife's Carnival 2001, hundreds of musicians were on the streets performing the frevo. Perhaps the large number of musicians was not surprising given the official theme of that year's Carnival, "*O Frevo Vai Brilhar*" ("The Frevo's Going to Shine"). According to Zé da Flauta, head of the music division in the mayor's office, 864 amateur musicians and 530 professional musicians performed frevo during that Carnival. A few of the select "orchestras" performed on stages, but the majority of the bands played in the street for parading dancers.

In Recife's Carnival the street bands that play frevo are called *fanfarras* (fanfares) and use standard arrangements of traditional frevos, performing them in a non-stop manner with connecting cadences played by the percussion section. Many of the written arrangements for the fanfares date from the 1960s and earlier, and the sheet music parts that the musicians use have been copied and recopied hundreds of times. However, most frevo musicians memorize these standard arrangements and have no need of the written music when they perform. In the street, the idea is to animate the crowd with pieces that everyone already knows. The fanfares are the heart and soul of frevo in Recife. The instrumentation of fanfares harks back to the early twentieth century: the *requinta* (small clarinet), clarinet, trumpet, saxophones, valve trombones, bass tubas, tarol, surdo, and pandeiro.

Meanwhile, another kind of Carnival group, the bloco carnavalesco, specializes in the frevo de bloco. These groups are accompanied by the pau e corda, or wood and string, ensembles of guitar, cavaquinho, mandolin, flute, clarinet, saxophone, surdo, tarol, and pandeiro. While these musical organizations animate the street parades with frevo, a select few professional *orquestras de frevo* (frevo orchestras), such as the José Menezes orchestra, are hired by the cultural office of the city to perform forty-minute shows on outdoor stages set up primarily in the downtown area. The frevo is alive and well in Recife.

Military and Civic Bands in Nineteenth-Century Brazil

At the turn of the nineteenth century, military music in Brazil lagged behind European military music and suffered from official neglect, inadequate musical training of instrumentalists, and a general lack of professionalism among the ranks of musicians. This situation would change rapidly, and by the end of the nineteenth century, military and civic bands were thriving in all of Brazil's major cities and in scores of small towns dotting the countryside. During this period, the band movement became not only a vital component of the country's musical culture but also an important social institution that connected diverse sectors of Brazilian society. Military bands served as models for the creation of municipal civic bands with widespread and diverse public participation. Social historian José Ramos Tinhorão commented (my translation):

> The fact is that the valorization of bands from the troops of the First Line and of the National Guard gave hundreds of musicians of common origin the opportunity to earn a living by means of their abilities and talent. Through the music played on outdoor bandstands and during civic festivals, they helped common people identify with a type of instrumental formation quite similar to the orchestras of the elite. Proof that the military band extended its activities beyond its precise [military] functions lies in the fact that civilians imitated its formation, creating similar bands for dance music or bandstand music in the town square and, [later,] from the beginning of the twentieth century, for recording the first phonodiscs, as was the case of the Banda de Casa Edson, founded at the end of the preceding century, still the time of the cylinder gramophone.[1]

The bands played a key role in linking diverse sectors of nineteenth-century society and perhaps were the first truly national form of musical entertainment. In the 1800s, bands helped foster national sentiment among the Brazilian population, being the only type of musical ensemble that performed annually for the three main national holidays: Independence Day, Holy Week, and Carnival. This "Brazilian ritual triangle," to use Roberto da Matta's phrase, combined "festivals devoted to celebration of the most institutionalized component of the nation-state (the armed forces), festivals controlled by the Church (another crucial component in the construction of Brazilian society), and, finally, Carnival, dedicated to what is believed to be the most disorganized component of Brazilian society, the people or the masses."[2] Military bands thus connected the multiple contexts in which the state, the church, and the celebratory spectacle of the masses were invoked. To understand the role of the band movement in Brazil and how it affected the development of frevo music in Pernambuco, we must trace the history of military music in the country.

Short Chronology of the Frevo

1800	Modern European-style band instruments introduced into Brazil
1824	Two complete sets of band instruments imported into Pernambuco from France
1831	Establishment of the National Guard Bands in Brazil
1880s	*Clubes pedestres*, carnival clubs of mixed race urban laborers form in Recife, Pernambuco and participate in carnival accompanied by marching bands and capoeira
1880s–1910	The *polka-marcha* transformed into the *marcha-frevo*; the *fanfarra* wind, brass, and percussion ensemble develops; passo steps arise from capoeira movements
1890	Brazil's new Federal Penal Code prohibits the practice of capoeira
1907	The term "frevo" appears in print for the first time
1920s	*Blocos carnavalescos* emerge among the middle-class of Recife singing *marchas de bloco* accompanied by wind, string, and percussion instruments
1929	Nelson Ferreira's frevo-inspired song "Não Puxa Maroca" recorded by the Orquestra Victor Brasileira in an arrangement by Pixinguinha for RCA Victor
1930s	Annual competitions for frevo begin in Pernambuco; frevos written by northeastern composers enter the Brazilian music industry; Rádio Clube de Pernambuco expands and hires Nelson Ferreira as musical director
1952	Discos Rozenblit, Pernambuco's first recording studio, opens and establishes the Mocambo label
1957	Nelson Ferreira's marcha "Evocação no. 1" becomes Rio de Janeiro's biggest carnival hit of the year
1960s	Era of the radio is replaced by television and the modern orquestra de frevo is developed

Prior to the nineteenth century, the most common musical instruments used for military purposes throughout colonial Latin America included trumpets (clarions, cornetts), shawms (charamelas), fifes, and several varieties of European drums. In many areas of Brazil, however, the only instruments available for militias and regiments were fifes and drums. The rudimentary state of military music in Brazil at the beginning of the nineteenth century was evident when Prince Dom João VI arrived with the Portuguese court in 1808. On disembarking in Rio de Janeiro (the capital of the colony), the royal entourage was received not by a well-appointed, modern military band but by "the cheerful striking of bells, the sounds of the drums and other musical instruments, mixed with the noisy racket of gunfire, exploding fireworks, and applause from the crowd."[3] The other musical instruments that greeted the entourage probably included charamelas and trumpets. This archaic musical reception must surely have seemed unbefitting a

European royal entourage of the nineteenth century. However, things changed quickly in Brazil. Ten years later (in 1818), when Dom João VI was confirmed as king of Brazil, four modern military bands performed for the occasion. Subsequently, the state of military band music witnessed a rapid development, as Brazil was transformed from a colony to an independent sovereign nation-state. The main advances in musical life in Brazil occurred first in the capital city of Rio de Janeiro and then filtered out into the vast and remote territories of the nation. In Pernambuco, the situation of military and regimental ensembles was more favorable than in most other areas of the country beyond the capital.

In Pernambuco, a regimental ensemble was established as early as 1645—a type of charamela ensemble, which included oboe-like charamelas, flutes, trumpets, and a variety of drums (see Chapter 1). In 1697, a music school was opened at the cathedral in Olinda. By the last decades of the eighteenth century, the modern instrumentation of the European military bands began replacing the early forms of regimental music in Pernambuco. During the administration of Governor Tomás José de Melo (1787–1798), large wind and percussion bands were created in the municipalities of Recife, Olinda, and Goiania to accompany the regimental militias that were stationed in Pernambuco.[4] The instrumentation of these military bands included two fifes, two clarinets, a bassoon, two trumpets, snare drum, and two bass drums (surdo and zabumba). These expanded forms of regimental bands would soon take over the role of the older charamela ensembles in many public functions sanctioned by the state and the church. Beginning in the second decade of the nineteenth century, the older-style straight trumpets, cornets, timpani, and charamelas began to disappear in Recife's public festivals. In their place were new regimental bands.

Church record books indicate that between the years 1810 and 1840, the new style of regimental bands in Pernambuco were being paid to perform for many church-sponsored festivals, which were community-wide public events. This development coincided with Brazil's independence as a nation-state (achieved in 1822), stimulating the subsequent creation of many bands for the newly formed military regiments of the new country. The beginnings of this new band movement in Brazil also coincided with the advancement of technology in brass and woodwind instrument making in Europe, which progressed quickly during the nineteenth century. The development of valved brass instruments (trumpets and other horns) around 1830 and mechanically keyed wind instruments (first the flute and clarinet and later the saxhorn and saxophone) by mid-century gave a greater amount of musical flexibility to the military regimental bands and increased the technical possibilities of their instruments. In Europe, military bands of the day expanded in size and quickly incorporated these new, fully chromatic instruments (that is, instruments able to play sharps and flats). With their larger size, the bands began grouping instruments into several sections, a practice derived from string orchestras. The expanded bands also required a musical director to coordinate the larger ensembles and an increased musical literacy among the musicians. In Brazil, military bands soon copied these European advancements, and Recife was at the forefront of band innovations in the country.

Two complete sets of band instruments (as well as sheet music from Europe) were imported directly from France to Pernambuco in 1824 for use in the area's military bands.[5] A complete set for a French infantry band of that time would have included two flutes, four oboes, fourteen clarinets, six bassoons, four horns, and two trumpets. Although the exact number of specific instruments is not known, it is likely that the instrumentation imported into Pernambuco was roughly equivalent to that of the French bands of the time. A large ensemble of that type would have required a musically educated and literate bandmaster (mestre) capable of coordinating the band and its various sections into an orchestra-like ensemble. The musical training necessary for this was connected to sacred music of the church and to the more elite string orchestras of the day. The earliest bandmaster in Recife for whom we have documented evidence was Francisco Januário Tenório. An accomplished musician, composer, musical theorist, and conductor, Tenório was born in Recife sometime in the latter half of the eighteenth century and was likely a student of Pernambuco's leading composer of the day, Luiz Álvarez Pinto.[6] Tenório was familiar with counterpoint and composed sacred church music and had an active career in the military as a bandmaster. He was a remarkably well-rounded musician, and his achievements were recognized at the highest levels of the governing administration in Pernambuco, as evidenced in an official correspondence dated November 15, 1822, from Pernambuco's military commander—Brigadier José Correa de Melo—to the local governing council requesting that all military bands in the province be put under Tenório's control. The transcript of this letter provides a number of revealing facts about Tenório's biography and musical accomplishments (my translation):

> [Tenório] enlisted in the military on the 27th of May 1793, in the Regiment of Olinda, where he organized and taught a class in music and formed a regimental band. Later he organized another regimental band for the artillery regiment. In 1810 he was contracted and enlisted as the leader of the Regimental Band of Recife, where he served until 1817. In that year he was nominated by General Luís do Rego to be bandmaster of the Division Band and traveled to Rio de Janeiro, with the monthly pay of 24,000 réis. By order of the same general, he organized the bands of the First and Second Militia Battalions of the second line, teaching and composing music for the same bands and, later, served in the Third Caçadores Battalion where he was assigned the same duties.
>
> In 1821 he received his discharge, but in the following year, because there was no other musician in the province who was capable of teaching, organizing, and composing for marches and other music necessary for the military bands, he accepted a new commission in the Second Caçadores Battalion with a salary of 11,000 réis on top of his soldier's pay of 290 réis.[7]

From this correspondence, it is clear that Tenório was a leading figure in Pernambuco's newly developing band tradition and possessed the multiple skills needed to organize large ensembles. His background in sacred music and in composition provided him with a solid foundation in European musical tradition. Furthermore, in traveling to Rio de Janeiro in 1817, Tenório would have been exposed to an urban musical environment unequaled in all of the Americas. Because of the invasion of Portugal by Napoleon I, the Portuguese court was in exile in Rio de Janeiro from 1808 to 1821. This period coincided with Tenório's visit. The relocation of the Portuguese Crown to Brazil brought with it an infusion of European musicians of the highest order in Rio de Janeiro. Marcos Portugal, the leading Portuguese composer of the day, moved to Rio de Janeiro in 1811, and Austrian composer Sigismund Neukomm, a former student of Franz Joseph Haydn, resided in the Brazilian capital from 1816 to 1821. Tenório's time in Rio de Janeiro also overlapped the presence of a German band brought to the Brazilian capital in 1817 as part of the entourage of Archduchess Carolina Josepha Leopoldina for her wedding with Prince Regent Dom Pedro, later crowned emperor of Brazil. Commenting on the city's musical scene and on the impact of the German band in Rio de Janeiro, Manuel de Oliveira Lima wrote (my translation):

> Musical inclination was powerful not just among the educated class in Brazil: it also revealed itself without artifice and learning in the character and spontaneity of popular music. What was lacking [in Brazil] was merely the schooling. Padre José Maurício and other talented Brazilians of the kind were very useful, the proof of which is affirmed by the influx of the German band that remained with the royal princess and helped to establish good taste and musical style among us, determining intelligent training and knowledge [about music] without which numerous professional vocations would have been lost.[8]

Padre José Maurício Nunes Garcia (1767–1830), the most distinguished Brazilian composer of his day, was closely associated with the Portuguese court of Dom João VI and with the reign of his son, Emperor Pedro I. Other talented Brazilian musicians— including the visiting Francisco Januário Tenório from Pernambuco—would have benefited greatly from the opportunity to observe and learn some of the latest instrumental techniques of the day from the German band. The influx of these musicians and the contemporary European trends in music they brought with them helped establish and solidify the new band tradition in Brazil. It also reinforced the modern European image of band music.

Brazilian bands followed European developments in instrumentation and began expanding their repertoires from hymns, marches, and other patriotic pieces to include light European classical and popular music genres as well. The Brazilian National Guard bands, established in the 1830s, were some of the first to expand their repertoires into these realms. In the following decades, these bands would provide the model for creating civic bands in municipalities throughout the country. Music bands were important components of a growing cultural cosmopolitanism, which linked new concepts of modernity (that is, European civilization, industrialized technology, and commercial activities) to local cultural practices in Brazil. The military and civilian bands that formed quickly became a staple of the musical landscape of the country and spread the new styles and genres of modern music throughout Brazil. As noted in Chapter 2, the new bands shared the stage with string orchestras at the elite masquerade balls that took place during Carnival time. They also played for community-wide religious processions and civic events. For a nineteenth-century Brazilian, whether living in a small town of the interior or in the urban environs of a large coastal city, the military and civic bands provided musical education, training, and entertainment that cut across the class and racial lines of the country. The bands increasingly carved out a kind of popular middle ground for entertainment, between the art music of the elite and the folk music of the common people. The military bands also created a network of musicians throughout Brazil's vast territories who played wind, brass, and percussion instruments. Accompanying the military units to which they were attached, the military bands were periodically relocated from one area of the country to another, spreading musical repertoires, performance techniques, and musical theory. In local communities, they functioned like music conservatories, transmitting knowledge of written music, large-ensemble coordination, and instrumental tradition. The bands represented the first musical institution in Brazil with a truly nationwide scope and popular appeal. Military musicians such as Tenório would have had the opportunity to travel and interact with musicians from throughout Brazil.

Most forms of music making in that period, whether elite (concert, opera, and salon) or vernacular (rural and urban folk and popular), articulated distinct social, economic, and racial sectors of Brazilian society, but the music bands cut across such divisions. In addition to bands for regimental and National Guard units, civic bands, which utilized semi-professional musicians (of all races and all social classes, from both military and civilian ranks), were created from the 1840s onwards in municipalities throughout Brazil. As in Europe, these mixed wind bands represented and stimulated a new literate tradition of instrumental ensemble music making among amateur and semi-professional musicians drawn largely from the ranks of the working class. Indeed, the increasing appeal of the bands in both Europe and Brazil among the so-called common people partly arose because the roster of band musicians reflected the diverse population of local communities.

Throughout the country in the second half of the nineteenth century, municipalities, urban trade guild workers, religious brotherhoods, and military and police detachments formed music bands to participate in community celebrations, including religious processions, political ceremonies, and civic parades. The bands also performed for a new set of leisure activities such as Sunday concerts on outdoor stages (*coretos*), at elite social gatherings and private balls in theaters and salons, and for the modern Carnival parades and celebrations emerging in Brazil's cities. In short, performances by music bands were an essential element of modern community life throughout Brazil in the nineteenth century. They became an expressive means for articulating and reinforcing pride in neighborhoods and local communities even as they served to establish connections with national and international trends in musical culture. The role played by the music bands in linking province to empire was evident in the visit of Dom Pedro II (the second monarch of the Brazilian empire) to Pernambuco in 1859. During the month-long visit, the military and civic bands of the area received the royal entourage repeatedly. It was a matter of municipal pride when a newly formed band received an invitation to perform in honor of Dom Pedro II and his wife, Tereza Cristina. In *Tradicionais Bandas de Música* (Traditional Music Bands), José Pedro Damião Irmão recounted one such invitation (my translation): "In September of 1859, the [band] '7 de Setembro,' with barely one year of existence, had received an invitation: 'The organizers of a reception for the Emperor, have the pleasure of inviting the Musical Band "7 de Setembro" from Timbaúba to enliven, together with its counterparts from Goiana, 'Curica' and 'Saboeira' the parties in honor of His Majesty D. Pedro II who will visit the Goiana area very soon.'"[9]

Like other parts of the country, the Northeast witnessed the founding of numerous municipal and other civic bands during the second half of the nineteenth century. At the time of the royal visit, there were a total of five National Guard battalions, two cavalry squadrons, and two army regiments, each with its own music band in Recife alone. Local communities took pride in their bands; sometimes, such pride was carried to an extreme. The two oldest music bands still in existence in the state of Pernambuco are the Curica (founded 1848) and Saboeira (1849)—both from the town of Goiana, close to Recife. An intense rivalry between the bands (including their many followers) existed from the early days, as evidenced by an article that appeared in the *Jornal do Recife* on August 24, 1871 (my translation): "On the occasion of the procession that left from the church of Soledade, when the music brought forth the honor guard for the quarter, street kids showed their enthusiasm with shouts of 'Viva Curica, die Saboeira' and vice versa. They engaged in heated confrontations and yielded clubs, some departed wounded. Two or three of the disorderly leaders were put in jail to be disciplined."[10]

In Pernambuco, revelers frequently accompanied the bands with chants, songs, and dances as they marched through the streets, especially during Carnival parades. This public performance context nurtured a new form of music and dance at the end of the century that was unique to the Carnival of Recife. Although the music band as an institution was linked primarily to the European musical heritage, the movement and dance that accompanied the Carnival parades were directly connected to Afro-Brazilian street culture and, more specifically, to the form of martial-arts defense known as capoeira.

Capoeira and Band Rivalries

Capoeira originated among Afro-Brazilians as a mechanism of both direct and indirect resistance to the oppressive controls and violence of Brazil's slave culture in the country's colonial era. Based on African models derived from the Congo–Angola area of Central Africa, its earliest center of activity in Brazil was in the state of Bahia. There, capoeira developed as a fighting game among the enslaved male populations on the sugarcane plantations; it involved acrobatic movements of advance and retreat by two contestants, accompanied by a repertoire of songs and rhythmic patterns among the participants. Forbidden to carry firearms, the black males who engaged in capoeira became experts "in the use of daggers and knives, but, above all, in head-butting, tripping, kicking of the feet out from under the adversary, which characterized the type of fighting known as capoeiragem."[11] Early in Brazil's colonial history, there were also clandestine communities of runaway slaves known as quilombos where practices related to capoeira may have also developed. The largest and most famous of these fugitive black communities was the Quilombo de Palmares in the Northeast near Pernambuco, which lasted for almost the entire span of the seventeenth century and was led by the famous black resistance fighter Zumbi. During the nineteenth century, the one-stringed musical bow called the berimbau (an instrument derived from African models) assumed a dominant role in capoeira's musical accompaniment. The Bahian style of capoeira, which also includes the use of other Afro-Brazilian percussion instruments, became the dominant form of capoeira in the twentieth century and has been exported around the world. I took the picture in Figure 4.2 in New York City, where the Brazilian capoeira master Jelon Vieira, from Salvador, Bahia, now resides.

Figure 4.2 Capoeira master Jelon Vieira (playing the berimbau) and his students during a roda de capoeira in New York City, 1999 (photo by Larry Crook).

By the late eighteenth century, capoeira was emerging in the main urban areas of Brazil, where it became part of the street culture of blacks and mulattoes. Government authorities and the urban elites of Brazil considered capoeira a plague on the country's civilized citizenry. In their view, capoeira was a barbaric African practice among vagrant gangs of black urban thugs who perpetrated violence and other criminal activities on the general population. Brazilian historian Caio Prado Júnior described the nineteenth-century urban context of capoeira in the following manner:

> In the cities, the vagrants were more dangerous and delinquent, since they did not encounter the hospitality of the rural areas; nor were there any rural bosses to take them on and provide them with an outlet for their aggressive feelings. In Rio de Janeiro it was dangerous to travel in secluded parts alone and unarmed, even in broad daylight. The city's first chief of police, appointed after the arrival of the Court, was Paulo Fernandes, who made an energetic attempt to grapple with the problem. Nevertheless, the social evil continued, and only in the Republic were the notorious capoeiras, offshoots of the colony's vagrants, eliminated from the capital.[12]

Various connections existed between the black urban practitioners of capoeira and the military and police forces during the nineteenth century. The Royal Guard Police, created in 1808 during the sojourn of the Portuguese court in Rio de Janeiro, was directed by

Major Miguel Nunes Vidigal, a military man reported to be adept at capoeira himself.[13] However, after his appointment to the administrative post, Vidigal became a staunch enemy of the capoeira gangs in Rio de Janeiro and waged a campaign against the practice. During that era, one of the most common charges against enslaved black males in Rio de Janeiro was for the "offense" of capoeira.

In Recife, capoeira was also considered part of the criminal and vagrant activities of enslaved blacks, free blacks, and the mulatto population. The city council of Recife passed ordinances in 1831 aimed at restricting various public "nuisances" associated with the city's black population, including a restriction on capoeira, an offense subject to a penalty of two to six days in jail for free blacks and twelve to thirty-six lashes for slaves.[14] In Recife, capoeira was also closely linked with the musical life of the city. Music making occasions in Recife's public areas, especially the parading of the music bands, appear to have been the favored public contexts for capoeira. In a passage describing the close relationship that existed between capoeira and popular forms of music entertainment, Valdemar de Oliveira wrote (my translation):

> Their [the capoeira groups'] preference for music was manifest, not through a passive inclination, but, because it functioned like sugar attracting a fly: there was the guitar playing on small stands, serenades on streets dimly lit by gas lights, the virtuosity of the harmonica, berimbau, and ganzá shaker on long nights. Primarily, they were [attracted] to the military bands that entered the streets to parade with their regiments, for roll call, for Church novenas, processions, for horse races in the neighborhoods of Derby, in Hipódromo, and in Lucas, and at the dock ramp for the arrival and departure of important people. No celebration occurred without a music band. And there was not a music band without capoeira. [15]

What distinguished the capoeira tradition of the nineteenth century in Recife from its manifestations in Bahia and Rio de Janeiro was precisely the close association that it maintained with the performances of the area's music bands. Increased police repression in Rio de Janeiro made capoeira all but extinct in the capital city by the beginning of the twentieth century. In Recife, police repression resulted in the camouflaging of capoeira under the guise of a new dance form—the frevo. Heated rivalries between marching bands provided the context for the initial transfer of capoeira movements into new dance forms. In the 1850s and 1860s, two important military bands in Pernambuco rivaled each other for prominence in the Recife area: the Fourth Artillery Battalion's band, known popularly as the Quarto (The Fourth), and the National Guard band, given the monicker Espanha (Spain) because of the Spanish heritage of its bandmaster, Pedro Francisco Garrido. Violent encounters between the capoeira groups that marched in front of the two rival bands became so heated that Garrido was reportedly murdered. Oliveira cited an editorial article that appeared in the December 15, 1864, edition of the *Diário de Pernambuco*, addressed as a plea to the commanding colonel of Recife's military in the area (my translation): "The worthless custom adopted by the slaves of this city, of accompanying the military bands and exchanging shouts of 'live' and 'die,' have fostered disgraceful conflicts that go back for years. Yesterday, a partisan of one of these bands, a black slave [named] Melquídes, stabbed another black slave named Elias, claiming to be the partisan offender of one of the bands."[16]

Bands developed loyal and partisan followers, who marched along whenever the groups paraded through the streets of the city. In front of each one of the music bands marched a group of capoeira revelers singing songs. They also carried sticks, clubs, and knifes and performed capoeira movements. In 1908, Francisco Augusto Pereira da Costa published a description of the capoeira groups that marched in front of the Espanha and Quarto bands during the 1860s, recalling some of the chants that they sang to accompany the marches (my translation):

> The capoeira groups showed their enthusiasm for certain musical pieces [of the bands], to the point of composing verses to sing that were appropriate for double stepping, like the following, [and] were contemporary to the era in which the two rival groups were formed, chiding their adversaries:
>
> > Espanha doesn't get this
> > Espanha doesn't get this
> > Espanha only gets this
> > There behind Saint Francisco
>
> And others, sung during the trio section of a dobrado march of the 4th Artillery Battalion, a piece they called *Banha cheirosa* [Fragrant pomade], a dobrado march that put the partisans into a delirium, especially when the part of the piece arrived that included a loud explosion simulated on the bass drum in the trio section of the piece.[17]

Other authors also have mentioned the strong effect that the dobrado marches of the military bands had on the Recife public. Discussing his experiences as a child in Recife in the 1890s, writer Mário Sette remembered (my translation): "In 1897, with the 27th, it [the Fourteenth Infantry Regiment of Pernambuco] left Recife for Canudos where, as it was said, Antonio Conselheiro wanted to restore the monarchy in Brazil. My young eyes saw them pass by, pulled along by a solemn dobrado march, with the capoeiras weilding their clubs and knives in front of the music, and with a small group of women crying behind the rear guard."[18]

Many musicians, journalists, and historians in Recife have pointed to the creative interplay between the black and mulatto capoeira revelers and the military bands during the last few decades of the nineteenth century as the critical context in which the city's new Carnival music, the frevo, emerged. The story of the frevo became reinforced as a kind of urban origin myth and was used to validate the belief that everyone in Recife, regardless of racial background, had a place in the construction of the new society. Emerging just a few years after the abolition of slavery, this was a powerful message of inclusion. Intercultural collaboration among African and European elements was selected as the core metaphor for the almost spontaneous way in which the frevo developed. As capoeiristas (practitioners of capoeira) blurred the lines between their martial arts and a newly devised dance, it is likely that the acrobatic movements of attack and defense used in capoeira were gradually adapted and transformed into the individualistic dance steps that would become the frevo dance. At the same time, bandmasters and other band musicians transformed the performance practices and stylistic characteristics of the marches and other musical genres in the band repertoires in order to inspire dancing and collaborative audience participation during Carnival parades.

Unfortunately, no musical manuscripts survive (or have been discovered) from this formative era to illuminate the specific musical means through which this creative process grew. Nevertheless, it is clear that marching bands and parades in Pernambuco became creative laboratories where composers, arrangers, and performing musicians developed hybrid musical forms mixing local and international elements. This was the case in both Rio de Janeiro and Recife. In Rio de Janeiro, this creative process of artistic hybridity among musicians led to Brazil's first national form of popular dance music, the maxixe, and later the samba. In Pernambuco, the process led to the most important regional Carnival music dance: the frevo. And just as the samba would eventually come to symbolize the racial and cultural mixture of Brazil's self-chosen identity on a national level, the creative and hybrid nature of the frevo's origin would be highlighted as a regional northeastern manifestation of that same racial and cultural mixture.

Frevo: A Mixed Carnival Music in Pernambuco

A New Music for a New Century

The opinions expressed by the Recife writer Leonardo Dantas Silva summed up much of the prevailing conventional wisdom regarding the sequence of the frevo's early musical development (my translation):

> Initially called a "march," later the "Pernambuco carnaval march," and by some composers even today the "frevo march," . . . the frevo as a form of music has its origins in the repertories of the military and civic bands in existence in Recife in the second half of the nineteenth century: the modinha, the maxixe, the tango brasileiro, the quadrille, and, most particularly, the dobrado and the polka, they were combined and melted together, yielding as a result, the FREVO, a popular rhythm that even today is still evolving rhythmically and choreographically.[19]

The emergence of the new frevo as a unique musical form coincided with dramatic economic, political, social, and cultural changes in Brazil. As the new century approached, slavery was abolished (in 1888), a new republic was proclaimed (in 1889), and the southern part of the country underwent rapid urbanization and industrialization. The beginnings of a national entertainment industry were seen in Rio de Janeiro, and that city's Carnival celebration became the country's national festival, with regional variants in the cities of Recife, Salvador da Bahia, and São Paulo.

Recife's Carnival at the turn of the twentieth century provided three main options for revelers. Black, lower-class urban dwellers who were part of the Candomblé community formed Carnival associations called *nações de maracatu* (maracatu nations), which paraded through the streets during Carnival days in the form of African royal entourages, complete with powerful drumming and dancing. As discussed in Chapter 3, these groups were directly descended from the colonial practice of crowning African kings and queens, and their inclusion in Recife's Carnival represented the flourishing of Afro-Brazilian consciousness that followed the abolition of slavery. For upper-class members of the urban society (predominantly white Euro-Brazilians) there were new Carnival associations called *sociedades de alegorias e críticas* (allegorical and satirical societies), which paraded publicly with horse-drawn floats and carriages during the day and held masked balls at theaters and private social clubs during the evenings of Carnival. These elite-leaning associations had their roots in the cosmopolitan masquerade balls and parades of mid-nineteenth century Brazil. The new societies in Recife formed in the 1880s and were very popular at the turn of the century. A third option for Recife's Carnival revelers was to participate in a new type of association that developed around the city soon after the abolition of slavery. These groups were the clubes pedestres, or walking clubs; they were formed among the new classes of urban laborers (including recently freed blacks) and were made up of coal shovelers, ironworkers, street cleaners, dockworkers, and the like. In membership and cultural practice, the pedestrian clubs opened up creative new options for Recife's urban masses. Membership in these clubs cut across racial categories: especially prominent were the multiracial mulatto populations of the city. Capoeiristas joined their ranks and marched in front of the groups, transferring much of the movement style they had developed in front of military band processions to the new Carnival clubs. Prominent citizens also served as patrons and benefactors of the clubs.

The cultural practices of both the sociedades de alegorias e críticas and the clubes pedestres—the music, dance, costuming, and songs—were eclectic and reflected the influence of both elite and vernacular traditions. For the public parading and various types of performances during Carnival, bands provided the musical accompaniment with military marches, dobrados, polka-marchas, Carnival marches, maxixes, and even popular selections from operas. Dancing among the crowds of revelers who attached themselves to the public parading of the clubs incorporated the movements of capoeira and the physical demands of negotiating passage through the crowded streets of Recife during Carnival. Leonardo Dantas Silva gave an apt description of the eclecticism of the Carnival clubs in Recife at the turn of the twentieth century (my translation):

> During Carnival, groups of urban workers with friends and neighbors from the same quarter of the city took to the streets with dozens of revelers in front, clearing the way through the masses. Two majorettes, who were responsible for maneuvers of the group, led the club's members who wore costumes made of Japanese silk and flannel pants. Standard-bearers wore costumes in the style of the court of Louis XV and four staggered lines opened to present the group's standards. The more distinguished members were in fine silk, with parasols covered in the same fine material and patent leather shoes. . . . In the center the "Father of the Club"—a fat character, costumed as a circus clown, with a bouquet of flowers in one hand and a staff in the other, graced the people—and, closing the procession, a "banda de música" in military formation. At prearranged locations, the procession stopped in order to intone opera arias.[20]

Parading through the streets during Carnival, the elite clubes de alegorias e criticas attracted the general public and helped stimulate a creative atmosphere in which new forms of artistic expression were created. Silva continued (my translation):

> The presentation of these Carnival groups, with their songs and movements exhaustively rehearsed, demonstrates the strong influence of the theater, with its reviews, operettas, zarzuelas and even opera, on the street Carnival in Recife. ... The [Cara Dura] club was formed by Military officers and members of the Fireman's Corp, led by lieutenant Chaves and commander Passos, who, together with a few civilians, entered the streets in cars pulled by pairs of horses causing a great stir among the population. On one of the cars was installed a stage, and on the second musicians were seated, as if in a moving outdoor bandstand, performing accelerated marches and polkas causing the throng of people that were following the route of the club to go delirious.[21]

Although the elite clubes de alegorias e criticas such as Cara Dura certainly had an influence on the development of the frevo, it was among working-class pedestrian clubs that the main contours of the frevo were worked out in the early twentieth century.

With the abolition of slavery in 1888 and the declaration of the new Brazilian Republic in 1889, thousands of freed blacks joined other urban workers and took to the streets in jubilation for Recife's Carnival. The 1880s and 1890s witnessed the founding of a number of pedestrian clubs, such as Clube dos Caiadores (Whitewashers Club) in 1887, the Bloco das Pás de Carvão (Bloc of Peace of the Charcoal Workers) in 1888, and the Clube Vassourinhas (Little Broom Sweepers Club) in 1889. In research carried out in the 1960s, folklorist Katarina Real spoke with several elder members of these early clubs, who gave oral testimony about numerous turn-of-the-century clubs among ironworkers, dusters, street cleaners, trash collectors, and individuals in dozens of other professions in the city.[22] There were likely close to 100 pedestrian clubs that celebrated the Carnival of 1900.

Among these walking clubs, the capoeira groups adapted and transformed their martial-art moves into soloist dance steps known as passos, which became the basis for the repertoire of steps that slowly evolved into the frevo. These steps were adopted and partially developed by the general dancing public that accompanied and participated in the parades. The revelers who marched with the clubs also developed vocal calls and chants that were aimed at the rival groups of Carnival clubs that they encountered on the street. It was also in this context that the celebratory energy of the new working-class pedestrian clubs stimulated bandmasters and their musicians to transform military marches, dobrados, and polkas into a faster, more syncopated music. In these years, the term frevo and its cognates began appearing in Recife's newspapers around Carnival season.

According to Recife Carnival historian Evandro Rabello, the word frevo first appeared in a Carnival announcement of February 9, 1907, printed in the Recife paper Jornal Pequeno. The announcement listed the musical repertoire of the club Empalhadores do Feitosa for that year's Carnival as consisting of marches, arias, and tangos; one of the marches was titled "O Frevo." The Empalhadores do Feitosa hired members of the Banda da Polícia Militar (Military Police Band) to perform the club's repertoire. This is perhaps the first documented usage of the term *frevo* in print, but Recife's public had already been using slang terms derived from the Portuguese verb *ferver* (to boil over) to describe the effervescence of the new style of music and dance. Words such as *frevança* (to boil over + dance), *frevolência* (to boil over + violence), and *frevióca* (a group of Carnival revelers) were commonly used in vernacular speech to describe the raw energy of the music and the social atmosphere in which Recife's Carnival clubs performed. It is clear that the frevo represented the high energy, delirium, and ethos of social participation that came to characterize the Recife Carnival and its clubs in the early years of the twentieth century.

The quick acceptance of the term *frevo* to capture the social exuberance, musical form, and dance movements of the pedestrian clubs coincided with increased police vigilance against the practice of capoeira, which was part of the revelry. Authorities blamed the capoeira groups for escalated rivalries and violence among pedestrian clubs during Carnival days. In 1906, the police in Recife cracked down more vigorously than before and put in place a prohibition that lasted until 1911. In that year, the I Congresso Carnavalesco Pernambucano (First Carnival Congress of Pernambuco) was established in order to improve relations among the various clubs. In an attempt to further camouflage and stylize the movements of attack and defense into a more dance-like choreography and thus avoid police recriminations, capoeiristas gave birth to the first steps of the frevo.

Starting in 1908, journalist and Carnival aficionado Osvaldo de Almeida, writing under the pseudonym "Pierrot," published a regular column devoted to Recife's Carnival in the local paper *Jornal Pequeno*. Through this column, he helped popularize and publicize the term *frevo* for the Recife reading public. The *Jornal Pequeno* announced the opening day of Carnival in 1909 with a front-page graphic including the headline "Olha o Frevo!" ("Look at the Frevo!"). The year before, the composer Ernesto Oliveira had written music for the upcoming Carnival titled "Olha o Frevo," which became part of the repertoire of the Club das Pás.

Forging a Street Music: From Polka-Marcha to Marcha-Frevo to Street Frevo

Bandmaster and composer José Lourenço da Silva (1889–1952) is often credited with making critical innovations that transformed the hybrid polka-marcha—used by the music bands in conjunction with the participation of the crowd singing along during Carnival—into the purely instrumental marcha-frevo. In the late nineteenth century, bands performed a number of hybrid march and dance genres, with lyrical sections sung by the participating crowds as they paraded during Carnival. According to Mário Melo, it was da Silva, popularly known as "Zuzinha," who first altered the older format of the polka-marcha, which featured a fast instrumental introduction followed by a lyrical second section that was slower in tempo, into a new type of march in which two instrumental sections were played in fast tempo. Here is how the hybrid polka-marcha form that became the basis for the frevo was described in an article originally published in 1938 in the *Anuário do Carnaval Pernambucano* (my translation):

> It was the time of polkas. There was not a single composer who did not write a polka, and there was not a single young girl who did not dance it in the ballroom. If only the people who dance the fox-trot today [1938] could have known the

polka! There were the [polkas] with jumping, and the ones where rhythm was not quite so violent. The latter kind acquired the name of a marcha-polka or a polka-marcha. It was like a march, only faster, or like a polka but less violent. And the pedestrian clubs began to adopt the marcha-polka and it was becoming an independent [dance].[23]

If Melo's account is correct, musicians around the turn of the twentieth century performed polkas in at least two styles and creatively mixed the genre with marches and possibly other musical forms. One result of this creative fusion was the polka-marcha, the direct forerunner of the frevo. Continuing his story, Melo added:

During this time . . . Zuzinha, today called Captain José Lourenço da Silva, was the director of the 40th Battalion Infantry band stationed at the Five Points Fort [and] an instructor in the Military Brigade of the State. He was the one who established the dividing line between what later was called the *frevo* and the marcha-polka, with a composition that was popular in its time, which I later played on my little harmonica during my academic days. At the time, I thought that this composition, even today distinctly etched in my memory, was by Benedito Silva, another noted composer. But, once, while conversing with Zuzinha, singing the melody of this, the most ancient *frevo*, he confessed to me that he had composed the piece.[24]

This account did not provide the title of Zuzinha's frevo, nor did it suggest a date on which the venerable bandmaster may have composed the piece. Most frevo aficionados in Recife with whom I have spoken believe that Zuzinha probably penned the piece during the first few years of the twentieth century.

Like most of the early composers of frevo, Zuzinha had a musical background that was intimately linked to the music band tradition. He was born in the interior of Pernambuco in the town of Catende and moved to Goiana with his parents as a child. By the age of seventeen, he was already an accomplished musician, had composed several pieces, and was able to play all of the band instruments, specializing in the flute. Zuzinha was director of the famous Saboeira band of Goiana. Was it during this time that he composed the piece "Divisor das Águas," which later musicians and historians recognized as the first true frevo? Zuzinha held his position until, in 1916, he moved to Recife and became the director of the music band of the Polícia Militar de Pernambuco. He later served as the director of the band of the 40th Battalion, stationed in Recife, and was an active figure in the city's musical scene until his death in 1952. Whether or not he was, in fact, the first to develop the new instrumental frevo form out of the polka-marcha, Zuzinha's name has become enshrined into Recife's pantheon of frevo composers.

Information is rather sketchy regarding the precise size and instrumental makeup of the military and civic bands that Carnival clubs contracted to accompany their street parades during the early years of the twentieth century. Apparently, bandleaders operated as freelance contractors during Carnival season, hiring individual musicians to form the Carnival bands. The ensembles they organized were referred to as fanfarras, or fanfares. Newspaper accounts, interviews with musicians, and historical writings on the frevo suggest the fanfares that marched in Carnival varied in size from about ten to thirty-five musicians. For instance, the famous Vassourinhas pedestrian club is reported to have been the first frevo group to employ a military band.[25] For the Carnival of 1907, this club contracted members of the Fourteenth Infantry Battalion's band, which included thirty-four musicians, and another club, Lenhadores, hired a private orchestra with eighteen members.[26] These early Carnival fanfares typically consisted of at least the following wind and brass instruments: a requinta (a small clarinet in B flat) a clarinet, a trumpet, two trombones, two horns, two tubas, and a bombardino (a tenor tuba in B flat).[27] The tarol (a shallow snare drum) and the surdo (a deep bass drum) made up the standard percussion section for the fanfares in the early years. This combination of wind, brass, and percussion instruments paralleled the military and civic bands of the era. In addition, the pandeiro (tambourine) was added to the fanfare ensembles and became an indispensable part of the frevo percussion section. This percussion instrument was extremely popular and used widely in musical styles associated with both European and African traditions in Brazil, including capoeira, samba, choro, and the côco. As such, pandeiro musicians who entered the fanfares probably served as cultural intermediaries, bringing new musical ideas into the band tradition. This interaction represented the heart and soul of the creative process of cultural mixture. Coming from the oral folk musical traditions of Brazil, the pandeiro players had never been part of the formalized musical instruction of the music bands. Neither were they part of Candomblé, and hence their instrument was not restricted by the orthodox ideology and sacred rhythms of the Afro-Brazilian religion. Techniques and rhythmic patterns on the instrument were fluid and passed from one tradition to another. The pandeiro's role as an important accompaniment instrument in capoeira suggests that the capoeiristas who marched in front of the music bands may have led to its incorporation into the fanfarras. Equally important was the pandeiro's use in European-style processions of folk Catholicism (such as the pastoril) that were being introduced into Carnival at the beginning of the century.

Another important element that the pandeiro players brought into the bands was an intimate familiarity with the dance traditions of the area. The pandeiro player's role as a social and cultural intermediary between the music bands and a variety of dance traditions remained relatively unchanged over the twentieth century. During my visit to Recife in 2001, I met dozens of pandeiro players from many different musical traditions. In June of that year, I interviewed one of the city's best frevo pandeiro players, Luciano Ricardo Maciel da Silva, known throughout the frevo world of Recife as "Mamão." During the interview, Mamão told me about his musical background as a pandeiro player and highlighted his early familiarity with several dance traditions of the area.

Larry Crook: What made you want to become a musician?

Mamão: I was like many other musicians, I danced frevo. I already was dancing, dancing frevo, maracatu, ciranda, forró. I had an uncle who was a *coquista* [performer of the côco], one of the best coquistas around. I lived in the middle of all of this. It was from that point that I began opening my head up to the music, I began playing in a local samba school, I also played with Preto Velho in Alto da Sé.

LC: Playing pandeiro?

M: No. I played tamborim, repique, surdo. Later, I entered the Bairro Novo group, which is another samba school, and I also was with the samba school Brown and White. And during that time, I was waking up to the beauty of the pandeiro when it was played.

LC: When was this, more or less? What year?

M: It was 1983, 1983 to 1987 that I played samba. After that, I began to play the pandeiro, in 1988. I went into a music store, but I didn't know how to play. I picked up an instrument, played around on it, and I was able to get an okay sound out of it. I really liked it; I admired people who played in frevo and in the samba schools. From that point on, I opened up, I bought a pandeiro, began to practice, and discovered my own style. My style is very personal.[28]

Figure 4.3 Pandeiro player Mamão performing frevo during Recife's Carnival, Recife, Pernambuco, 2001 (photo by Larry Crook).

The process of learning on one's own through observation and participating in dance and percussion sections is common among pandeiro players. Musically, then, the fanfares combined the European band traditions of written musical instruction, composition, and organization for the brass and wind instruments with principles of percussion derived from both European folk tradition and African rhythmic sensibility.

Many authors note that the Carnival clubs and the general public of Recife had a distinct preference for low brass—especially the trombones of the fanfares. One of the reasons often cited for this is that the expanded number of trombones in a fanfare gave the band a more powerful bass range to its sound and allowed a club to compete more favorably with rival groups. Additional trombones were added to the fanfares to achieve an overall aesthetic that is referred to as *peso* (weight). This weight is still admired as one of the qualities of fanfares that march in the streets during Carnival.

By the second decade of the twentieth century, the trombone-heavy fanfares were definitely the preferred type of ensemble to accompany the pedestrian clubs. Some bands marched with up to fifty trombones. With the addition of the pandeiro to the percussion section, the basic format of the fanfare ensemble was set, and it would remain relatively unchanged throughout the twentieth century. I encountered many ensembles with

Figure 4.4 Trombone section of a frevo fanfare performing in Carnival, Recife, Pernambuco, 2001 (photo by Larry Crook).

essentially the same instrumentation marching in the streets of Recife during Carnivals I attended in the 1980s and 1990s.

The instrumental street frevo performed by the fanfares developed into a short, two-part form that featured syncopated melodic writing idiomatic to the brass and wind instruments and retained the basic duple meter (two beats) common to both the military march and the polka. The two-part form consisted of a first section (A) of eight to sixteen measures in length and a second section (B) of a comparable duration. In performance, fanfares usually played each of the two sections twice, yielding a simple form that can be labeled AABB. A brief connecting passage of from two to eight measures in length usually separates the two parts. The entire AABB structure was repeated several times before the bandmaster cued the ending, which typically involved a sustained chord built on the tonic note. One of the characteristics that came to define the frevo was the use of syncopated and tightly interlocking parts between the brass instruments (trumpets, trombones, tubas) and the winds (requintas, clarinets, saxophones). This simple yet effective structure can be heard in José Menezes's frevo titled "Freio à Óleo" on *Track 4*. Although this is a modernized version of the frevo, with additional harmonic complexity not typical of the earlier frevos, the basic plan of the form and the interlocking brass and wind sections have been retained without much alteration as essential components of the music.

Another important characteristic of the early fanfares that played the frevo in the streets was the improvisatory role of the requinta clarinet player, who was expected to improvise melodic variations on the primary melody of a frevo during the many repetitions of the AABB structure. Saxophonist and composer Edson Rodrigues believes that the requinta's role in the fanfares was directly descended from the military band tradition in which clarinets were expected to improvise variations on the melodies of standard dobrados, marchas, and polkas. The role of the small requinta clarinets within the fanfares reflected the combination of written and non-written traditions within the ensembles. In addition, the sound of these high-pitched clarinets and their improvisatory role paralleled the earlier colonial charamelas of Brazil. In both cases, the intersection of written and oral modes of musical performance led to creative fusions of traditions. The percussion that was used in the fanfare bands also reflected this same kind of fusion of musical ideas.

Distinct from the written arrangements that the bandmasters and musicians worked out for the brass and winds instruments, the oral tradition of learning and working out parts was relied on exclusively by the musicians in the percussion section. This characteristic of the frevo percussion remains largely unchanged today. Most of the drummers I have met have only a rudimentary knowledge of musical notation. They learn their parts by relying on a well-developed sense of musical memory. The basic rhythmic patterns for the three percussion instruments is notated in Example 4.1.

As indicated by the notation in this example, the low-pitched surdo provides strong strokes on beat two of each measure, whereas the tarol snare drum (the middle line) syncopates the measure with accents that cut across the main pulse. The pandeiro (the top line) adds a third dimension to the rhythm and is free to vary and depart from the set pattern notated in Example 4.1. This basic pattern lies behind almost all of the frevo played by fanfare bands. Between individual pieces, the percussion section plays rhythmic

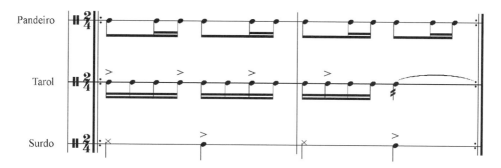

Example 4.1 Basic percussion patterns used in the instrumental street frevo

cadences. During these breaks, the drummers elaborate their basic rhythm to heat up the revelry of the Carnival crowds. On *Track 5* on the CD, a drum cadence that I recorded during the Carnival of 2001 can be heard. I was in the historic downtown area of Recife known as Recife Antigo, attending a Carnival club's parade. Featured here are the *ritmistas* (percussion players) of the Orquestra José Menezes marching down the street. They were positioned just behind the brass and wind players of the group and in front of hundreds of dancing participants. In this recorded example, one can hear the driving rhythm as it connects directly to the beginning of the popular frevo titled "Três da Tarde." This track offers a good example of the sound that has animated Carnival in Recife for about 100 years.

The street frevo that I have been describing so far, played instrumentally by the fanfare bands to accompany the pedestrian clubs, did not develop in a vacuum during the early years of the twentieth century. There were other frevo-like march pieces called *marchas carnavalescas* (Carnival marches) that mixed instrumental sections with lyrical sung sections during Carnival. These pieces represented a continuation of the practice of crowds singing along with the marching bands. The practice went back at least to the mid-nineteenth century and included a common repertoire of songs such as "Banha Cheirosa," cited earlier in this chapter. As mentioned previously, it was partly from these kinds of sung marches that the purely instrumental street frevo—via the polka-marcha—first developed. At the time of the turn of the twentieth century, these sung marches coexisted with the instrumental frevo, and they were also important components of the repertoires of the fanfares when they marched with the Carnival clubs. Like the instrumental frevo, the marcha carnavalesca acquired more syncopated rhythmic attributes than the military march in response to the demands of the Carnival dancers and other revelers. Rather than providing a coordinated rhythm for marching in lockstep, the new syncopated march styles favored individualized expressions of dance and rhythmic elaboration.

A number of sung Carnival marches emerged at the turn of the twentieth century. The most famous of these pieces is the Vassourinhas Carnival club's "March Number One." Today, this piece is referred to simply as "Vassourinhas." Matias de Rocha and Joana Batista are credited with its authorship, but this is a matter of some dispute. The fact that assigning authorship to the lyrics and melody was an issue indicates the impact the

Figure 4.5 Frevo drummers from the José Menezes Orchestra perform on the street during Carnival, Recife, Pernambuco, 2001 (photo by Larry Crook).

popular music industry had in Brazil and its blurred relationship with elements of popular culture that were in the public domain. The melody of the lyrical section of this piece may well have been in existence long before the Vassourinhas Carnival club was founded in 1889.[29] Nonetheless, 1889 was first perpetuated through oral history as the year in which the Carnival march "Vassourinhas" was written. Recent research has uncovered a receipt of payment (dated November 10, 1910) by the Vassourinhas club, paid to Matias de Rocha (for the music) and Joana Batista (for the words) for the rights to the "Vassourinhas" march.[30] Recife's Carnival historian, Rafael Rabello, also discovered a notarized document in the archives of the Office of Titles and Documents in which Batista declared that "Vassourinhas" was composed in January 1909. Whatever its origin, this piece remains the most popular of all frevos, and it is the de facto hymn of Recife's Carnival. In addition, the piece was possibly the first of the sung Carnival marches to be called a frevo. Recounting the oral testimony of João Batista do Nascimento, one of the first members of the Vassourinhas club, Mário Filho, wrote: "'Vassourinhas' . . . came forth as the first marcha-*frevo* that was adapted rhythmically to Carnival. Clearly, the other clubs performed marches, but they did not have the characteristics of the *frevo* 'Vassorinhas' and of other pieces that emerged later."[31] These characteristics undoubtedly included the rhythmic vitality of syncopation that was essential to the instrumental street frevos of the day. In form, the marchas carnavalescas most likely included an instrumental introduction played by the fanfare band, followed by a more lyrical second section in which the instruments of the band accompanied the choral singing of the revelers in unison.

At this point, it may be useful to summarize the state of the frevo at around the year 1920. Purely instrumental street frevos were played by fanfares and featured a two-part structure with syncopated melodic and rhythmic characteristics. There were also marchas carnavalescas, which were sung in a somewhat slower tempo and combined instrumental and sung sections. Both types of music were performed in the streets and accompanied by individualized dancing, featuring a repertoire of dance steps called passos derived from capoeira. The specific passos that accompanied the frevo were later codified into a standard repertoire of steps. Because of the frequently violent encounters of the pedestrian clubs during Carnival, members of the middle and upper classes of Recife looked unfavorably at the street frevo. The elite of Recife increasingly opted to segregate themselves from the urban masses during Carnival and attended exclusive Carnival balls held at theaters and private clubs. At these balls, the frevo (instrumental and sung) was presented on stage by the city's most professional bands and orchestras. Meanwhile, a growing middle class of Portuguese and Italian families began forming new Carnival associations in the city that sought to separate themselves from the raucous nature of the street frevo. It was among these middle-class associations that a new, re-Europeanized form of the frevo developed.

Blocos Carnavalescos and the Frevo de Bloco

Excluded from the Carnival balls and parades of the elite and increasingly alarmed at the violent nature of the crowds surrounding the street frevo, middle-class revelers in Recife began forming new Carnival associations called blocos carnavalescos, or Carnival blocs, in the 1920s. These Recife groups were similar to the *ranchos carnavalescos* (Carnival wanderers) that emerged in Rio de Janeiro's Carnival at the end of the nineteenth century. Similar groups were also forming in Salvador da Bahia. In addition to incorporating elements from the frevo of Recife's Carnival, the blocos carnavalescos also drew on the venerable tradition of the pastoril, which involved young girls as shepherdesses who sang songs in unison as they danced in honor of the birth of Christ. The pastoril derives from Iberian folk plays depicting the visits of shepherds (*pastores*) to see the baby Jesus in Bethlehem. In Pernambuco, the girls who participate in the pastoril dress as shepherdesses and dance, sing songs called loas, and accompany themselves on pandeiros. It is also common for several stringed instruments (such as the guitar, violin, and cavaquinho) as well as light winds (such as the flute and clarinet) to accompany these groups.

Unlike the pedestrian clubs (largely composed of urban laborers working in the same profession), the blocos carnavalescos of the 1920s were formed primarily along family lines and among close neighbors of the city's petite bourgeoisie (especially Portuguese and Italian families in the neighborhoods of São José, Santo Antônio, and Boa Vista). Considered by Recife's middle-class families to be more respectable than the unruly pedestrian clubs, the blocos—constituted as family affairs—provided a safe and protected environment in which the young girls and women of the families could participate in the public Carnival of Recife. Female relatives, especially teenage girls, formed singing groups (*corais femininos*) that were reminiscent of the pastoril. The men specialized in an ensemble called the *orquestra de pau e corda* (wood and string orchestra), which featured various combinations of the flute, clarinet, mandolin, cavaquinho, guitar, banjo, violin, pandeiro, and surdo. Many of the young men who participated in the orquestras de pau e corda also sang romantic and sentimental songs from the modinha repertoire for nightly diversions. The overall sound of the orquestra was well suited to accompany the women's voices of the coral feminino, such that neither the instrumental nor the vocal group overpowered the other. The sound of the bloco carnavalesco was soft and much less aggressive than the street frevo played by the fanfare bands.

The music played and sung by the blocos carnavalescos was eclectic at first and included national popular songs and genres such as the samba, tango, and Carnival marches. The eclectic nature of the repertoire is evident from this note published in the *Diário de Pernambuco* on February 20, 1924 (my translation):

> Raul Moraes, one of the most ardent Carnival revelers of Recife, has just completed some interesting marches and sambas for the upcoming Carnival, each having appropriate words and most of them dedicated to the charming bloco of Avenida Lima e Castro, the following musical pieces are available for purchase at the Casa Ribas: O Sabiá, samba; Regresso, marcha; Aí tamborete, samba; Marcha das Flores, marcha; Se tem bote, tanguinho; Agüenta firme, marcha; Andorinha, samba; Fica por aí dizendo, samba; Ela não qué, marcha; Apachinete, marcha.[32]

The "charming bloco" mentioned in the quote was the Bloco das Flores, one of the first of the new blocos carnavalescos in the city. The inclusion of marches, sambas, and one "little tango" among the pieces that Raul Moraes had dedicated to the bloco—of which he was a member—reveals the cosmopolitanism linking these groups to similar middle-class groups in Rio de Janeiro known as ranchos. For instance, the original members of the Batutas de Boa Vista (reportedly the first bloco carnavalesco in Recife), witnessed parades of ranchos in Rio de Janeiro's Carnival before founding their own group in Recife in 1920.[33] Increasingly, the moderately paced marcha de bloco became the signature musical genre of Recife's blocos carnavalescos. In later years, these sung marches would acquire the name *frevo de bloco* (frevo of the bloco) as a commercial label when the song form entered the recording industry. The codification of the marcha de bloco gave the blocos carnavalescos of Recife a regional musical identity distinct from the ranchos of Rio de Janeiro and a local musical identity distinct from the pedestrian clubs of Recife.

Some of the musical characteristics of the marcha de bloco included a slower tempo and softer volume than the frevo de rua, a slightly syncopated march rhythm in 2/4 meter, the predominant use of minor keys, and an instrumental section that separated each verse/refrain. Less syncopated that the street frevo, the marcha de bloco's short instrumental introduction of eight measures was played in unison by the melodic instruments of the orquestra de pau e corda ensemble. After the instrumental introduction (usually performed twice), the coral feminino sang one verse and one refrain of the song in a binary form (AAB or AABB). The B section of the song was typically in a contrasting key (frequently going from the minor key to the parallel major or to a closely related key). At the completion of each verse/refrain, the instrumental introduction would return in ritornello fashion, followed by another verse/refrain. Table 4.1 represents the formal structure of the marcha de bloco.

Table 4.1 Representative schematic for a *marcha de bloco*

Intro	A A B	Intro	A A B	Intro
(instrumental)	(song)	(instrumental)	(song)	(instrumental)

Track 2 on the CD demonstrates the simple, formal design of the marcha de bloco "Alegre Bando." The cavaquinho and violão (bottom line in Example 4.2) provide the harmonic and rhythmic structure of the march while the pandeiro and surdo play a steady rhythmic accompaniment.

Example 4.2 Basic rhythmic accompaniment for the frevo de bloco. In the surdo staff, an *X* notehead indicates a muffled stroke.

An early marcha de bloco titled "Marcha da Folia" (written in 1924 by Raul Moraes) exemplifies the sentimental and bittersweet nature of the poetry that came to characterize the genre. The song begins with an introduction and first verse in the key of C minor.

Partial lyrics to "Marcha da Folia," by Raul Moraes

Bloco das Flores, wherever you pass by
With such grace, you plant the sound of beautiful songs
The splendors of that happiness
That enchants our souls
And impassions our hearts.[34]

The music then shifts to the parallel major key (C major) as the refrain comes in.

Refrain to "Marcha da Folia"

Long live the revelers of Carnival
Intense happiness without equal
That makes you forget the cruel suffering
And teaches us to smile and love.

The key then shifts back to C minor for a repeat of the introduction played by the orquestra de pau e corda, followed by the second verse.

Second verse to "Marcha da Folia"

In life we have only distastefulness
Sadness, bitterness, and the final disillusion
But overcoming the evil, we rise up
And forget our suffering as we party during Carnival.

The brief excursions to the parallel major key during the refrains of the song make the lyric progression from joy to pain to temporary triumph over the evils of life all the more bittersweet. Both the musical and poetic techniques in the song reflect and comment on the experience of Carnival in the lives of many Brazilians. For many, Carnival is a privileged moment "lost in time"—as Roberto da Matta has characterized the annual ritual—that occurs over three or four days out of each year, a time linked to concepts of universalism and transcendence and permeated with "all-embracing categories such as sin, death, salvation, mortification of the flesh, and sexual excess and continence."[35] Expressing the joy of Carnival revelry, this marcha de bloco song celebrates family communion among the members of the Carnival group. For the middle-class revelers trying to carve out a space for themselves within the raucous Carnival, the song lyrics and musical components of the marcha de bloco came to represent their family values rooted in European tradition.

The semi-erudite wording of such lines as "que olvidar faz a dor ferina" ("that makes you forget the cruel suffering") from "Marcha da Folia" further reveals the social location of the composers and performers of the marcha de bloco. Attempting to separate themselves from the lower-working-class groups that comprised the pedestrian clubs, the blocos carnavalescos marked their cultural distinction with the sophisticated trappings of such songs. This effort was also evident in the work of a new generation of Recife composers who specialized in the form. Raul Moraes (1891–1937), composer of "Marcha da Folia," and his younger brother, Edgard Moraes (1904–1973), composer of "Alegre Bando," were two of the most celebrated composers associated with the bloco carnavalesco tradition in Recife. In 2001, I met many of the daughters and granddaughters of Edgard Moraes. They had recently revived a family singing group, which they named Coral Edgard Moraes, to commemorate and keep alive their family tradition. *Tracks 2* and *6* on the CD are recordings of this group from their self-titled CD. The two patriarchs of the Moraes family, Raul and Edgard, were from a different musical world than either the military band tradition or vernacular Afro-Brazilian musical heritage. They represented a more sophisticated musical milieu of European tradition in the area.

The elder brother, Raul, received formal training in piano and taught music for ten years at the Academia de Canto e Música in the city of Porto Alegre, in the far southern portion of Brazil, between 1910 and 1920. After traveling throughout South America and Europe, he moved back to Recife in 1922 and became active in composing popular musical genres of the day, including marchas de bloco such as "Marcha de Folia." He was also a noted pianist in the area. Among his hits in Pernambuco were "Batutas Brejeiros" (1923) and "Saudade Eternal" (1925). In the late 1920s and early 1930s, several of his songs were also recorded and released nationally for the Brazilian Odeon and Columbia labels. Edgard Moraes learned music from his older brother and also established a distinguished career as a composer, having his compositions recorded by all of the major record labels active in Brazil between the 1930s and the 1960s, including RCA Victor, Philips, Odeon, CBS, and Mocambo. But the Moraes brothers were not the only composers from Recife who were interested in commercializing their music and entering the national scene.

By the early 1930s, Pernambuco's Carnival music was firmly embedded in Brazil's national recording and broadcast industry, located in Rio de Janeiro. This relationship would radically expand and alter the artistic and commercial production of Recife's frevo music as increased specialization among musicians, composers, and arrangers evolved and as distinct commercial categories were created by producers and marketing specialists.

Nationalizing the Frevo: Pernambuco Carnival Music and Brazil's Popular Music Industry

Recife's marcha de bloco, sung frevo, and the instrumental frevo de rua (street frevo) emerged at a time when the recording and broadcast industries in Brazil were in nascent states. The first sound recordings in Brazil date to 1902, and radio broadcasting began in the early 1920s. As the political and cultural center of the country, Rio de Janeiro dominated both industries. The music of a few composers from Pernambuco and the Northeast had been recorded before the 1920s, but Recife pianist Nelson Ferreira was the first composer whose music disseminated Pernambuco's new Carnival sounds to the country via Brazil's national music industry.

Ferreira's first recorded song was "Borboleta Não é Ave" (with words by his brother-in-law Jota Borges Diniz), which he wrote for the bloco carnavalesco known as Bloco Concórdia for Recife's Carnival of 1922. In 1923, Casa Edison (Odeon) recorded the music at its studio facilities in Rio de Janeiro. (This and other historical recordings of Nelson Ferreira have been reissued recently by the Revivendo label in Brazil as part of the series *Carnaval: Sua História, Sua Glória*; volumes 23 to 28 of the series are devoted to Ferreira's music [Revivendo RVCD-174]). For the recording, Odeon used one of Brazil's early recording artists, the singer Bahiano (Manuel Pedro dos Santos), accompanied by Grupo Pimentel; it marketed the song under the marcha genre label. At the beginning of the recording, an announcer states, "Borboleta Não é Ave, marcha carnavalesca, Casa Edison, Rio de Janeiro." Written without an introduction, the piece was a simple march in two parts with a refrain and four verses set in the key of D major. The instrumental accompaniment on the recording included piano, cavaquinho, guitar, and saxophone. Recife's music historians frequently cite "Borboleta Não é Ave" as the first *frevo-canção* (frevo song) to be recorded. In reality, the piece more closely resembled a Rio de Janeiro-style sung march (*marchinha*) than a frevo. It was not until the end of the decade (in 1929) that Nelson Ferreira would score another hit recording, with a piece titled "Não Puxa Maroca."

Recorded by RCA Victor and marketed under a new genre designation, *marcha nortista* (northern march), this recording featured the newly formed Orquestra Victor Brasileira under the direction of Pixinguinha (Alfredo da Rocha Viana Filho). Pixinguinha was one of Brazil's most celebrated musicians of the day. He was an accomplished flutist, saxophonist, bandleader, arranger, and composer. His wide-ranging influence on the development of Brazilian popular music was comparable to the impact Louis Armstrong had on American music. Pixinguinha was a musician in and bandleader of several important musical groups during the first two decades of the century, including the Os Oito Batutas group that toured throughout Brazil, South America, and Europe. As Hermano Vianna (1999) pointed out, Pixinguinha, a black Brazilian, was a pivotal figure in the process of cultural mediation occurring during the years in which samba became Brazil's primary national musical form. The cultural mediation provided by musicians such as Pixinguinha established important links between socially and racially defined segments of Brazilian society in the early twentieth century. Equally proficient in written and improvised forms of music making, Pixinguinha performed in the social environments frequented by elite as well as popular classes of Brazil. Furthermore, as an arranger and musician in Rio de Janeiro's recording studios of the day, he was in a key position in the industry. He was familiar with a wide range of regional and international styles of music and freely mixed stylistic elements from these sources into Brazil's emergent national popular music. His role in arranging, orchestrating, and directing the music for Nelson Ferreira's "Não Puxa Maroca," recorded in July 1929 at the Casa Edison studio in Rio de Janeiro, exemplified Pixinguinha's intercultural mediation. The recording of "Não Puxa Maroca" was reportedly the first Carnival piece arranged by Pixinguinha for the new RCA Victor label.

A year before the studio recording was made, Ferreira had entered "Não Puxa Maroca" in a Carnival competition at one of Recife's elite private clubs, the Clube Internacional. The piece took first prize. Ferreira's role within Recife's musical and social environments was similar in many ways to that of Pixinguinha. In 1920, Ferreira became the pianist in the orchestra of the Teatro Moderno movie house in Recife. The theater's orchestra was led by Zuzinha, the famed bandmaster who is credited with transforming the polka-marcha into the marcha-frevo. With the well-seasoned Zuzinha, he would have learned the stylistic intricacies of the street frevo as well as many other aspects of the band tradition. This tutelage may have led Ferreira to incorporate the bass tuba into his own popular orchestra in the mid-1920s. Ferreira was, in fact, the first bandleader in the Recife area to add that instrument to a "jazz" orchestra. This addition may have been an attempt to mix the local fanfare band sound with the popular orchestra format. When Zuzinha stepped down as leader of the theater's orchestra, Ferreira took over as its musical director. During his tenure in that position, he likely first crossed paths with Pixinguinha, who was in Recife for a thirteen-day engagement in 1921 (from July 6 to 19) at the Teatro Moderno with his group Os Oito Batutas. By 1928, Nelson Ferreira was a pianist and orchestra leader of renown in Recife and also an important figure in the blocos carnavalescos of the city. His orchestras were apparently in high demand for dances at the city's most exclusive private clubs. Through his various musical activities in the 1920s, he was responsible for bringing contemporary trends in national and international popular music, especially American jazz, to the Recife public. Ferreira blended these diverse influences in his piece "Não Puxa Maroca."

The piece was actually a hybrid song form, in which Ferreira mixed the instrumental frevo de rua, or street frevo, with the marcha de bloco. Analysis of the piano/vocal score to the piece reveals an instrumental first section of sixteen measures, which features highly syncopated melodic material reminiscent of the opening sections of the street frevos as performed by fanfares in Recife's Carnival parades. Played two times, the first section is followed by a second section that begins with four-part chordal writing (soprano, alto, tenor, bass) for the first eight measures, suggesting a semi-erudite rendition of the marcha de bloco song form. The second section concludes with eight measures of a highly syncopated, single-line melody (no longer the semi-erudite, chordal-style writing). Although it is not clear exactly how Ferreira might have arranged the piece for his own popular orchestra in Recife, he likely incorporated some of the idiomatic elements drawn from the fanfare bands and the orquestras de pau e corda of Recife's Carnival of the day. His later orchestrations featured experiments in which he further combined elements drawn from the frevo de rua and the marcha de bloco. Ferreira was a well-trained professional mulatto musician from Recife who explored the commercial potential of his musical background. Not afraid of experimenting, he was crucial in the development of the frevo into several categories that were adopted by the music industry. For the national music industry, these were fresh sounds from the urban Northeast. But the recording of the northeastern urban sounds required close collaborations with southern musicians such as Pixinguinha.

For the recording of "Não Puxa Maroca," Pixinguinha arranged the piece instrumentally for flute, violins, trumpets, clarinet, tuba, and drumset but did not include the vocal components of the song. His instrumental resources for the Orquestra Victor Brasileira in 1929 included piano, violin, trombone, saxophone, clarinet, trumpet, guitar, banjo, cavaquinho, drumset, and pandeiro. Other instruments were brought in when needed, including the bass tuba. Why did Pixinguinha set the piece instrumentally and not for voices and orchestra? According to Henrique Cazes, Pixinguinha experimented with various instrumental combinations between 1928 and 1932 in the hope of establishing a typical ensemble sound capable of representing Brazil on a national level.[36] Was he experimenting at the time he recorded "Não Puxa Maroca"? The newly opened RCA Victor record company in Rio de Janeiro had just hired him as its studio arranger/orchestrator in 1929—the year the company recorded "Não Puxa Maroca"— and Pixinguinha quickly assembled the Orquestra Victor Brasileira as its studio orchestra.

Did the RCA Victor executives give Pixinguinha the option to use a singer and a chorus for the recording? Perhaps he was just interested in exploring the possibilities of translating the new frevo and its energetic fanfare performance style with his own studio musicians. This style of music was certainly more syncopated and rhythmically interesting than Rio de Janeiro's march music. Perhaps Pixinguinha envisioned a new musical form that could rival the samba. Apparently, he had a personal affinity for Recife's music; a number of unedited instrumental frevos of his authorship are in existence.[37] In any case, Pixinguinha succeeded in producing an innovative arrangement of "Não Puxa Maroca" and the recording became a hit for the Carnival of 1929, which helped establish the instrumental frevo on a national level. Within a few years, this new frevo variant had a foothold as a commercial genre in Brazil's national popular music. Two more of Nelson Ferreira's instrumental frevos—"Carrapato com Tosse" and "Vamos Chorar, Nega?"—were released in 1931 on the Victor label. Both of these recordings featured the Orquestra Victor in arrangements that emphasized a sectional interplay between brass and winds reminiscent of the street frevo of the fanfare bands. The addition of strings, piano, and other instruments rounded out the instrumental recorded sound and gave the music a closer affinity to the production values and aesthetics of the national and international music industry. During the early 1930s, this variety of instrumental frevo on national recordings was referred to under various marketing labels: *marchinha carnavalesca pernambucana*, *marcha pernambucana*, *marcha nortista*, and *frevo pernambucano*. This plethora of names with either the state (Pernambuco) or the regional (North) association suggests that the industry was searching for a marketing identity that would complement the mainstream national music of the day. Between 1933 and 1938, the popular recording group Os Diabos do Céu, directed by Pixinguinha, released a total of eight instrumental frevos for national consumption. By 1936, the industry had firmly established the connection of the instrumental frevo with the Northeast region of the country, and thereafter, the commercial designation became simply *frevo*. However, as with the development of samba as a commercial popular music, a parallel solo song form was developed to serve as a vehicle for Brazil's popular crooners of the day.

During the 1930s, the frevo-canção evolved as a commercial song genre of the frevo. Brazil's most popular vocalists of the day recorded frevo songs written by Pernambuco composers. Chief among the popular song composers of Recife who excelled at the new form was Lourenço da Fonseca Barbosa, known under the name "Capiba." Capiba scored national hits with singers Mário Reis, Aracy de Almeida, and Francisco Alves. The Pernambuco song-writing team of the Irmãos Valença (Valença Brothers) also had many frevo song hits during the 1930s. Although these hits were produced and recorded in the studios of Rio de Janeiro, the compositional activity took place in Recife, where the composers continued to reside. Meanwhile, Recife slowly built up its own industrial infrastructure to support the recorded and broadcast entertainment media.

In Recife, the 1930s ushered in the era of the radio, as the Rádio Clube de Pernambuco installed a new 2-kilowatt transmitter and built an auditorium/soundstage for live broadcast. Under the call letters PRA-8, the Rádio Clube de Pernambuco became the major disseminator of Pernambuco's Carnival music. The powerful radio station in Recife provided access to the primary market for the recordings of frevo emanating from the studios of the major record companies in Rio de Janeiro, and PRA-8 also supported its own house orchestra under the direction of Nelson Ferreira. From 1931 through the mid-1960s, Ferreira was in charge of practically all the artistic elements of the radio station. He composed, arranged, performed, and directed thousands of hours of music in all genres and for hundreds of national and international guest artists. The top musicians in Recife all passed through Nelson Ferreira's orchestra.

By the early 1940s, the frevo was represented by two separate but interconnected contexts of social/artistic production. One context was the street Carnival of Recife, which included two subgenres of frevo music: (1) the street frevo, or frevo de rua, performed by fanfare bands that continued to animate the pedestrian clubs and large crowds of revelers/dancers, and (2) the marcha de bloco performed by female choruses and orquestras de pau e corda of the blocos carnavalescos. The second context encompassed the commercial frevo, linked closely to the recording and broadcast industry but also performed on stage at elite Carnival balls and other private events. As noted earlier, the commercial recording of frevos written by composers from Recife flowed through the studios and other production facilities of recording companies located in Rio de Janeiro. For the artistic production of these records, the Victor, Odeon, Parlaphon, and Columbia studios employed arrangers and performers largely from southern Brazil. Rio de Janeiro was like a magnet attracting musicians from throughout Brazil, and many of the musicians who worked in Rio's studios came from Bahia, Pernambuco, and other states of Northeast Brazil. Thus, although the industry was located in Rio de Janeiro, the environment was one of national scope. The role that such interregional musical collaboration played in developing Brazil's nationalized popular music, including the so-called regional styles such as the frevo during the first four decades of the twentieth century, has not been studied extensively but was undoubtedly decisive. Within the Northeast, however, resistance to the centralized control of the nation-state and the perceived cultural domination of the South led to a regionalist rejection of Rio de Janeiro's "frevo."

After being arranged, recorded, and manufactured in the South, the recordings of frevo were disseminated via broadcast and record sales primarily in the Northeast. In Recife, the commercial recordings of frevos were consumed by local audiences as records, and the pieces were also performed live by the city's own radio orchestras and society orchestras comprising Recife's top instrumentalists and vocalists. In this way, local audiences had the opportunity to compare the national recordings, made in Rio de Janeiro, with the local products, performed by northeastern musicians. The radio orchestras that played the frevo were influenced by but distinct from the fanfare bands of the street.

The *frevo de orquestra* (frevo of the orchestra)—as the socially elevated style of the radio frevo was sometimes called—involved primarily two subgenres: (1) the frevo (an orchestrated frevo performed instrumentally), and (2) the frevo-canção (an orchestrated frevo with an introduction followed by a solo song). These two branches—street and studio—intersected and cross-pollinated in a variety of ways, including the overlapping of musicians and repertoire. However, several social and artistic commentators in Recife saw the two worlds as quite separate.

In an article published in 1946, Valdemar de Oliveira articulated the viewpoint of many frevo purists in Recife, who felt that the "authentic" frevo was suffering from the negative impact of American jazz during the 1930s and 1940s. The American influence was cited for smoothing out and and stripping the frevo of its primitive virility. Specifically, the saxophones had romanticized the texture, the trombones had been minimized, and the whole ensemble had been "feminized." Oliveira cautioned the Pernambuco public in the following manner (my translation):

> If you want to hear a typical *frevo* from Pernambuco, do not go to the radio or to an artificial society ball, where all you find is a jazz band and never a fanfare, but locate a pedestrian club parading, with its musicians in [the frevo's] true ambiance. That is where you can hear the *frevo* and see the *passo*, at the real source. Accompanying the "peso" of a requinta, three clarinets, three saxophones, three trumpets, ten trombones, two horns, three bass tubas, two tarol drums, one surdo. Anything else is false.[38]

Writing in the mid-1940s, Oliveira was articulating a historical perspective that created an aura of authenticity around the street frevo as performed by the fanfares of the pedestrian clubs. This was contrasted to the frevos played by the jazz bands and orchestras that had become common by the late 1920s in Brazil. These latter instrumental groupings, which added vocalists, string instruments, piano, string bass, and other musical instruments, were precisely the ensemble arrangements favored for elite social balls held at private clubs, for the radio orchestras of the day, and for the studio orchestras of the recording industry in Rio de Janeiro. Like the music bands in the nineteenth century, the society orchestras in Recife played a wide variety of popular and semi-classical musical genres. Regarding this context of international musical activity as anathema to the true frevo, Oliveira identified—in naturalistic terms—the social and cultural characteristics of the street during Carnival as the authentic context of the frevo. Comparing the frevo to a wild animal in its natural habitat, he went on to describe the acoustic urban environment in which the frevo's characteristic sound was developed (my translation):

> A savage animal is only comfortable—and can only be truly observed—in the jungle, free. The large *clubes pedestres* of Recife can come into the center of the city, to present themselves. But, their [natural] habitat is elsewhere. . . . In [the neighborhood] of São José, the *frevo* finds a good "atmosphere." It is curious; the *frevo* does not work well in open spaces, on broad streets, on avenues. Because they lack resonance, the resonance that echoes off tall houses on narrow streets, where it was created. . . . Moreover, on the avenues, there is too much space. And the compressed mass of humanity is the *frevo* itself.[39]

Many pundits of Recife's frevo felt that the commercial recordings made in Rio de Janeiro had emasculated the frevo. In musical terms, the characteristic roles of the low brass, together with the strongly syncopated rhythmic drive of the fanfare bands, were missing from the frevos played by the studio orchestras in Rio. Responding to the overt commercialization of the music, Brazilian composer César Guerra-Peixe made the following insightful comments in 1951 in the *Diário da Noite* (my translation):

I am familiar with the environment of urban popular music in Rio de Janeiro. I know that the success of any new and original music causes a deluge of vulgar imitations. The success of any little foreign musical ditty is further proof of this. In addition to not being foreign, the *frevo* is also one of the richest types of our popular music of which the *carioca* is not familar. I am referring, of course, to the authentic *frevo*, and not to the false interpretations, that are heard on numerous recordings of irresponsible orchestras, full of "variations" under the guise of jazz, that have nothing to do with the dance.

One particularity has resulted in the *frevo* retaining its rhythmic vigor, its self-confident orchestration, and its characteristic form: the fact that the composer [of frevo] is not musically illiterate, but is always a musician who conceives of the orchestration in his imagination and immediately notates his inspiration. The result is that in the composition of a *frevo*, the orchestration is also the composition. Except in rare occasions, the composer of a *frevo* is also its orchestrator.[40]

Guerra-Peixe's perception of the uniqueness of the frevo's compositional process within Brazil's popular music landscape was well informed. One of the country's leading art music composers of the day, he had been an active arranger, composer, and performer of popular music within the broadcast and recording industry in Rio de Janeiro during the 1930s and 1940s. In 1949, he went to Recife to serve as musical director of the newly opened Rádio Jornal do Commércio. In that capacity, which he held from 1949 to 1952, Guerra-Peixe interacted directly with many of the city's top frevo composers and performers. He established a particularly close relationship with Capiba, Recife's foremost composer of the frevo-canção. During this time, Capiba took private lessons in orchestration and harmony from the respected composer. In addition, Guerra-Peixe actively researched Recife's folk and popular traditions, resulting in the publication of a number of scholarly articles and monographs. Active in all of these arenas (folk, popular, and art music), he was a uniquely qualified observer of and commentator on Recife's musical community. His perspective on the compositional process of the frevo accurately reflected the close link that frevo composers maintained to the music band tradition.

Since the early years of the century when the polka-marcha was transformed into the marcha-frevo, frevo composers and musicians had come primarily from the ranks of the military and civic bands of the area. Partly because of the common musical background of composers and musicians, both the performance style and the formal structure of frevo had co-evolved within the context of Recife's Carnival. A primary element of a frevo's identity became its characteristic orchestration—the interlocking of brass and wind sections. As Guerra-Peixe noted, a frevo's orchestration is part of the composition itself. However, even though the style and formal structure of the frevo were forged largely within the context of street parades played by the fanfares, the street was not the only musical context in which frevo musicians participated. From the start, some of the most talented composers and musicians of the Carnival fanfares also performed in the elite orchestras of the area. As noted earlier in this chapter, Zuzinha, the widely acknowledged father of the marcha-frevo who had a long career as a military musician, was also the musical director of the house orchestra at the Teatro Moderno in Recife in

1920, when Nelson Ferreira was hired as the group's pianist. Zuzinha arranged and performed all kinds of popular music in that context. It is highly unlikely that he operated in a musically schizophrenic manner, separating the two musical worlds. As I have already observed in relation to Pixinguinha, intercultural artistic mediation was also common in Recife and was embodied in the work of musicians such as Zuzinha and Nelson Ferreira. Another component to this was the diverse backgrounds of the pandeiro players within the frevo groups. Drawing on musicians familiar with a variety of traditions, they brought wide-reaching knowledge of European- and African-related musical heritages. The two major traditions that led to the frevo—the European band music and the Afro-Brazilian capoeira—further underscore the mixed and hybrid form. Guerra-Peixe's knowledge of the folk, popular, and art musical heritages of the country may have provided him with the perspective needed to penetrate the nature of the frevo rather cogently.

However, like most of Recife's intellectuals of the 1940s and 1950s, Guerra-Peixe's views were part of a romanticized narrative of the frevo's origin that minimized the productive interminglings of elites and commoners and simultaneously disparaged the foreign influences that were involved in the very beginnings of the frevo. In the origin narrative, intellectuals selectively reinforced the notion of hybrid intercultural collaboration among simple music band musicians and capoeira practitioners. Rather than having an authenticity located in an agrarian past among an idealized peasantry, the frevo was rooted in the cultural mixture of the lower-class multiracial urban population. It became Recife's own musical example of the hybrid nature of the Brazilian nation itself, so forcefully articulated by the city's leading social thinker, Gilberto Freyre. This position was simultaneously advanced against the national context in a regionalist critique of the centralized and dominant influence of the culture of Rio de Janeiro embodied in the samba. The true heartbeat of Brazil lay in the Northeast, the area of the country where a pure and uncorrupted citizenry could be found. This historical gaze into the creation of the frevo linked the idea of authenticity exclusively to the idealized values and aesthetics of the lower classes, the common people of Recife. Again, this view was most forcefully expressed by Valedmar de Oliveira (my translation):

> Frevo composers belong to, and always did, a special class, far removed from those who dedicate themselves, for example, to the *samba*. [Frevo composers are] people who have never attended the theater or a grand ballroom, they never mixed with others and were only interested in their yearly roles: as bandmasters . . . assistant bandmasters . . . band musicians . . . good trumpet players . . . good clarinetists . . . trombonists . . . and a few shady characters. Without that special knack, no one attempts to write a *frevo* in Recife. . . . Composers of the famous "Pernambuco waltzes," of "pas-de-quatre" and of the many beautiful cançonetas of Recife during the illustrious early years of the twentieth century (not to mention the pianists and other artists who were afraid of the genre), never messed with the *frevo*, never. Those that tried, failed. Some of them were drawn to other modes of the frevo. But to the street *frevo*, never. Among these I include myself.
>
> One after another, the unique style of the *frevo*, which not everyone gets, escaped them. Even in a *frevo* competition, organized by the Carnival Federation

of Pernambuco, around 1937, there was a well-constructed composition, very well written, that wanted to be a *frevo*, but was a long way from actually being one. . . . The composition was proof that the erudite musician is incapable of writing a *frevo* that the common people of Recife will accept with open arms. This has only been achieved by a limited number of popular composers who know the musical architecture of the genre, who can play around effortlessly with the timbres and who know how to produce its prime character.[41]

Oliveira's view of the "real" frevo as being confined to a few local culture bearers uncontaminated by erudite refinements and mass commercialization is an interesting counterpoint to the discourses on authenticity that were created by Brazilian intellectuals to explain the emergence of samba. As Hermano Vianna pointed out, Brazilian chroniclers and anthropologists frequently agreed that samba "was restricted to the *favelas* [slums] until abruptly triumphing in the musical taste of a social elite previously quite distant from Afro-Brazilian popular culture."[42] Origin myths constructed by Pernambuco's elites to explain the frevo, by contrast, never located the genesis of the form exclusively in the Afro-Brazilian culture of the favelas of Recife. Rather, the frevo's origin was narrated as a story of social and artistic alchemy, which took place in the laboratory of the streets of Recife. It was there, mixing equal parts of Afro-Brazilian capoeira and Euro-Brazilian marching band music, that Pernambuco's cultural essence sprang forth in the form of the frevo. It was also in the streets of Recife that the commercial attempts to capture and domesticate the frevo's true character were doomed to failure.

In this construction, the frevo emerged as Pernambuco's primary urban cultural symbol of resistance against the nationalizing efforts of Brazil's state-supported cultural machine from Rio de Janeiro. Local responses of resistance took several forms. From the 1930s through the 1950s, Recife's newspapers chronicled the invasion of the carioca (that is, from Rio de Janeiro) samba on Pernambuco's beloved Carnival, provoking heated debates among musicians and cultural pundits. Starting in the 1930s, local government and business interests joined forces in Recife to sponsor annual competitions for the creation of new frevo compositions. The city's two major newspapers (the *Diário de Pernambuco* and *Jornal do Commércio*) underwrote these competitions in the early 1930s. After 1935, the competitions were officially sanctioned by the Federação Carnavalesca Pernambucana and included the private patronage of the local media and other businesses. The statutes establishing Pernambuco's new Carnival Federation included the following goals: "to mold the Carnival in the sense of historical and educational traditionalism, in order to revive our customs, our history, facts that educate us" and "to collaborate with public powers for the regulation of traffic, in order that it not hinder the *frevo*, which deserves support so that it can be preserved in its typical form."[43] The traditional form, only some thirty to forty year old at the time these statutes were written, was found in the streets of Recife during Carnival.

In 1951, the Vassourinhas frevo club—complete with dancers and a sixty-five-piece band of musicians chosen from the Banda da Polícia Militar de Pernambuco—was dispatched to Rio de Janeiro. Although this trip was lauded by many, the frevo's marginal position within the Brazilian music industry had changed little since the early 1920s. In an interview with the popular frevo composer Carnera for a newspaper column titled *Na*

Retaguarda do Frevo (The Rearguard of the Frevo) in 1951, journalist Antônio Guilherme Rodriguez asked for his opinion regarding Pernambuco's Carnival music in relation to the music "imported" from Rio de Janeiro (my translation):

> As an artistic expression, Pernambuco's music constitutes a point of pride for us, because, in addition to its musical value, it has an extremely original choreographic interpretation whose defense is permanently guaranteed, because it is entrusted to its legitimate interpreters: the common people. And these people will never stop dancing the passo. . . . As to [commercial] production, our music competes with little more than 10 percent of the market while the remaining 90 percent is devoted to the music of Rio. The fight is, as they say, very unequal. While a composer from here puts out two pieces of music at the most, there are composers from Rio who put out close to twenty pieces of music in order to have one success, or at times no success at all.[44]

The 1950s saw a dramatic change in this situation. In 1952, José Rozenblit opened Recife's first recording facility, Discos Rozenblit, and established the local label Mocambo. Fittingly, the name of the label was the term for a slave hideaway in the colonial era. The first record released on the Mocambo label was ready for the Carnival of 1953. Side one of the 78-rpm disc was a frevo de rua by Nelson Ferreira titled "Come e Dorme" ("Eat and Sleep"). On side two was "Boneca," a frevo-canção by Aldemar Paiva and José Menezes. Both sides featured the Rádio Clube de Pernambuco's PRA-8 orchestra, under the direction of Nelson Ferreira. With the opening of Discos Rozenblit, Recife's composers no longer needed to send their compositions to Rio de Janeiro. During the 1950s, Mocambo became a safe house for northeastern musical forms that were marginalized in the national industry, especially for the frevo. Recife's popular music journalist José Teles recently summed up the impact of the Discos Rozenblit (my translation): "In short, the Rozenblit [record company] was the savior of the *frevo*, recording practically the entire opus of Capiba and Nelson Ferreira. It released records with the music of Levino Ferreira, Zumba, Felinho, Irmãos Valença, Raul and Edgar Moraes, it paved the way for new creators such as maestro Duda, Edson Rodrigues, José Menezes and Clóvis Pereira, still active today in Recife."[45]

The opening of Rozenblit Records marked a critical juncture in the history of the frevo. From that point on, the frevo exhibited two main tendencies: (1) an extreme traditionalist tendency that was overtly conservative and valued the frevo of the past, and (2) a more progressive tendency that was forward-looking and valued a modicum of musical innovations within the frevo. On the traditionalist side, the Mocambo label provided a forum for recording and re-recording some of the classic frevos of Pernambuco's Carnival. One expression of this traditionalist tendency was the recording of street frevo by various military bands in the Recife area. Cultural purists in Recife's frevo community considered only the freva de rua played by military bands as an authentic frevo. For example, Nelson Ferreira's 1957 recording "Vem Fervendo" (Mocambo 15.185-A) featured the Banda da Polícia Militar de Pernambuco. The revival of traditional frevos—sometimes recorded for the first time—reinforced nostalgic and sentimental values within the frevo community and also led to the creation of a new commercial genre, the frevo de bloco, based on the marcha de bloco of the blocos carnavalescos. Ferreira's 1957 song titled "Evocação No. 1" (the first frevo de bloco) became Mocambo's best-selling record of all time. The impact of the song reached all the way to Rio de Janeiro, where it became the biggest hit of Rio de Janeiro's Carnival of 1957, surpassing even the recordings made in Rio that year. Ferreira's classic pumped new energy into the blocos carnavalescos in Recife and ushered in a renaissance of this nostalgic and sentimental music. The Coral Edgard Moraes, which sings on *Track 2,* grew partly out of this tendency. *Track 6* was recorded by the same group. The latter song ("Poeta da Aurora"), an homage to the memory of the great composer of the marchas de blocos that are now labeled frevos de blocos, was written by Luíz Guimarães and Alvacir Raposo. Since the mid-1990s, Guimarães has become Recife's main supporter and producer of frevo music. A pianist and composer, he supports both the traditionalist and the more progressive elements within the frevo community.

The progressive tendency of the frevo was initiated by a new generation of composer/arranger/orchestra leaders who increased the instrumental and harmonic possibilities of both the frevo de rua and the frevo-canção. This group of innovators included José Ursicino da Silva (Duda), Edson Rodrigues, José Menezes, Clóvis Pereira, and Guedes Peixoto. In their hands, the harmonic vocabulary of the frevo was expanded to include extended chords and jazz voicings in the winds and horns. Menezes told me that the jazz-arranging method of the Berklee College of Music was particularly influential in the 1970s among the select group of Recife arrangers that included Duda, Pereira, Peixoto, and himself. Both Duda and Pereira also learned advanced harmony in the early 1950s from César Guerra-Peixe. During the 1960s and early 1970s, these and other bandleaders in Recife also developed the modern orquestra de frevo for recording and live stage presentations. These orchestras differed from the military bands by: (1) replacing the bass tuba with electric bass; (2) streamling the brass section to three or four trumpets and three or four trombones; (3) deleting the flute, requinta, and clarinet in favor of a larger saxophone section (two altos, two tenors, a baritone); and (4) establishing a percussion section of a pandeiro, two surdos, and a drumset. The basic instrumentation of the orquestra de frevo (with minor variations) remained the same from the late 1960s through the end of the twentieth century. José Menezes helped bridge the gap from Nelson Ferreira's generation of composers to the younger, progressive frevo composers of the 1960s and 1970s. A brief look at Menezes's musical biography will illuminate this transition.

A Seasoned Master of the Frevo: José Menezes
José Chavier Menezes (b. 1923) grew up in the town of Nazaré da Mata, located about 60 miles northwest of Recife. Of his early musical experience, he recalled: "I began in the band. My father was a band musician too, so it began at home. I was taught at home, and later I went on to the band. I studied with the maestro of the band. And I began to study the instruments. I began on the horn and later switched to saxophone." (The quotations and the information in this section come from an interview I conducted with Menezes in Recife on February 6, 2001.)

In 1943, at the age of twenty, he was invited to Recife by members of the Jazz-Band Acadêmica and asked to become part of their group. Capiba and other student musicians in Recife had formed the group in 1930, and by the 1940s, the band was considered among the city's top orchestras of the day and performed throughout the Northeast. The jazz band included a mixture of instruments, such as the piano, guitar, cavaquinho, banjo, violin, accordion, flute, clarinet, saxophones, trombones, bass tuba, and drumset. Menezes joined the band as a saxophone player.

> I came to Recife to play saxophone, alto saxophone. Well, this was an organization, an orchestra that rehearsed where all of us lived. The guys in this group all lived there together. All of them were young men, single, students. You had to be a student, had to study. That's why it was called the Jazz-Band Acadêmica. So I went to school and played in the group. . . . It was one of the best orchestras around here, in the city in those days. We played in the clubs, the Internacional, Clube Português, and the money we earned was enough for our living expenses, going to school, hiring a maid.

During those years, the U.S. military presence in the area was strong. Because of its strategic geographic position, Recife was the location of a U.S. Air Force base, and many American airmen were stationed there. The Jazz-Band Acadêmica played for numerous dances held on the base and at other locations around the city where Americans were frequently in the audience. Musicians from Recife also had the opportunity to hear American military bands and American jazz bands. José Menezes interacted with the musicians in these military bands on many occasions: "When the American orchestras came, from the ships, they came to play. We made good friends with them, and we played music together, the reed players. One American musician even gave me a book of hymns from all over the world. The book was in English and in Japanese. I love American music."

The influence of American music, especially the big-band sounds of Glenn Miller and other orchestras of the 1940s, is mentioned by many frevo musicians of José Menezes' generation. Menezes himself listened to recordings and was impressed by the full arrangements of the bands and the orchestrations. By the end of the decade, he was ready for new musical opportunities: "I stayed in that group until 1949 . . . and then I moved on to Rádio Clube with Nelson Ferreira. Maestro Nelson Ferreira invited me there as a saxophonist and as an arranger. . . . He invited me to work in the orchestra of the Rádio Clube because he was the director. So I went there as a saxophonist and arranger to help him."

The Rádio Clube de Pernambuco was one of Recife's top radio stations and the location of much of the city's modern musical activity. As Ferreira's assistant, the young saxophonist/arranger was exposed to many contemporary trends in commercial popular music: "Every day was the same . . . working at the radio station. In the afternoon, we went in to the radio station to rehearse [with] singers who arrived from Rio, São Paulo, for the program, to be on the live radio program. All of the programming was live, we never recorded. So we rehearsed in the afternoon, starting around one thirty or two o'clock and rehearsed until four or five. And at night we played the program, from seven or eight until ten at night. That was the schedule every day."

Menezes also wrote musical arrangements for the singers who came to perform on the nightly programs. Like other professional radio orchestras of the day, the PRA-8 was a large orchestra that included flute, oboe, clarinet, bassoon, four saxophones, horn, three trumpets, two trombones, drumset, percussion, eight violins, two violas, two cellos, double bass, and piano. During Carnival season, a smaller orquestra de frevo was extracted from the larger orchestra and utilized only the brass, winds, and percussion.

While gaining valuable experience by orchestrating and arranging popular music for singers, he was also composing original frevos. In 1949, he won a local competition with his frevo de rua "Freio à Óleo." In 1950, RCA Victor in Rio recorded this with Zacarias e Sua Orquestra. Three years later, he teamed up with poet Aldemar Paiva to produce the frevo-canção "Boneco," which was recorded at Discos Rozenblit in Recife and released on the Mocambo label. It did not hurt that Nelson Ferreira was the artistic director of Discos Rozenblit. During those days, frevo arrangements were typically restricted to chord voicings that did not extend much past the basic triad and the occasional dominant seventh chord: "These older composers, Nelson Ferreira, Levino, Zumba, they wouldn't let you even put a sixth in the final chord. Not even a sixth. . . . When I began, at the age of 20, 25 years old, he [Ferreira] was already forty or forty-five years old. He was like twenty years older than me. I considered him old, I considered him square. Whenever I wanted to modernize something, he would censure me saying: 'No, it can't be done that way young man.' Later on, things changed."

Those changes occurred in the 1960s. Not only had radio been replaced largely by television but innovations in instruments, the influence of rock, and newer forms of American jazz also impacted musicians such as José Menezes. In 1960, he became musical director at the TV Rádio Clube in Recife, and in 1961, he founded his own frevo orchestra. During the 1960s and 1970s, he recorded many frevo records with his orchestra and played regularly for Recife's elite Carnival balls at the Clube Internacional and Clube Português in Recife.

Postscript: A Bygone Era?

Beginning in the 1970s, the frevo suffered from several rather unsophisticated attempts to market the music via recordings and radio play as Discos Rozenblit steadily declined and finally closed its doors in 1980. The 1980s saw a new series of recordings called *Frevança*, featuring the winners of frevo competitions held annually in Recife. Each year, the competition generated a large number of entries in the four official categories: frevo de rua, frevo-canção, frevo de bloco, and maracatu. After selecting the best entries, a panel of experts chose the top three compositions for each category in a festival competition in which an orquestra de frevo and local singers performed the pieces before a live audience. The first Frevança competition, held in the fall of 1979, resulted in a recording that was released in 1980. Both the live competition and the recording featured an orquestra de frevo led by Edson Rodrigues. After the selection process was concluded each year, a studio recording was made featuring the winning compositions. However, the Frevança competitions were poorly recorded and insufficiently marketed and generated little interest among Pernambuco's most popular composers. Concurrently, projects were undertaken to bring the frevo in line with the production values of the modern recording industry, among them the *Asas da America* series of LPs in which some of Brazil's most popular singers were contracted to cover frevos-canções. These singers included national MPB stars Gilberto Gil, Chico Buarque, Caetano Veloso, Elba

Ramalho, and Alceu Valença. The *Asas da America* series was launched by CBS and then taken over by Sony Music and resulted in a total of five recordings. The series gained a small following among the university crowd but was rejected by the conservative frevo purists in Recife for its excessive rock influences. By the end of the 1980s, the frevo seemed to be an enjoyable part of Recife's Carnival but not a dynamic element of the future. It was a nostalgic music, a music to be celebrated once a year during Carnival.

In the early twenty-first century, the frevo is once again being discovered by a new generation of musicians and audiences. Chief among the new wave of musicians taking the frevo to new heights is Inaldo "Spok" Cavalcanti Albuquerque. Spok and his twenty-piece band (SpokFrevo Orquestra) have infused new life into the frevo by taking the traditional repertoire and form of frevo as a point of departure for instrumental improvisation, technical virtuosity, and new harmonic complexity. The influence of jazz and desire to develop the frevo in new directions is particularly strong among members of the group. As bandleader, composer, and saxophonist Spok puts it (my translation): "[We've had] a few opportunities to tour throughout Brazil and the world, . . . we were able to play . . . at some jazz festivals, and observed that while the frevo was well received and appreciated for being a unique music, that even with the special magic that the frevo has, with its melody, harmony, and performance style unique to Pernambuco, I always felt and observed a certain lack of freedom, that the musicians needed to solo and improvise. I started dreaming of doing this with the frevo."[46] Listen to the SpokFrevo Orquestra's CD *Passo do Anjo* if you want to hear the direction that the frevo may take in the twenty-first century.[47]

CHAPTER 5

Inventing Northeastern Popular Music for the Nation

Oh no! There's no moonlight, like the moonlight of the sertão!
("Luar do Sertão," by Catulo da Paixão Cearense)

The Northeast's style of popular music attained national commercial success in the late 1940s, a time in which Brazil's popular culture was being widely and critically examined for excessive foreign influence. Questioning and condemning non-Brazilian influence on the country's primary index of national cultural identity, the samba, critics and mass audiences turned to northeastern traditions to renew Brazil's "authentic" musical heartbeat. The new popular music was aimed primarily at the mass population of caboclo migrants, who flowed back and forth from the interior of the Northeast to the promised lands of the industrial South. This music was identified and marketed under the name of its signature genre, the baião; it was also known under the more generic designation of *música nordestina* (northeastern music) and later transformed into the broad category of urban working-class dance music known as forró. The key figure in the emergence and success of this national phenomenon was Luiz Gonzaga, an accomplished accordion-playing singer from the far western corner of Pernambuco, deep in the sertão region of the Northeast. Together with several songwriting partners, Gonzaga combined nostalgic lyrics of his homeland with musical styles from the rural Northeast to address the dreams, desires, concerns, and fears of northeastern migrants living in the large cities of southern and central Brazil. The success of Gonzaga's musical regionalism in the popular culture arena provided a way in which Brazil's rural poor could participate in the national dialogue to redefine the country's racial and cultural identity. The creation of the new popular music from the Northeast region added to the racial, cultural, and regional contradictions embedded in the state's attempt to forge a homogeneous consensus culture for the nation. Highlighting musical traditions with characteristics deeply rooted

149

in notions of rural authenticity that were assumed to be more resistant to foreign influences, Gonzaga and other northeastern musicians provided an alternative to the singular dominance of the samba. The commercial success of Gonzaga's music also stimulated the creation of a network of northeastern-style forró dance clubs and other performance venues in Rio de Janeiro, São Paulo, and throughout the nation. Comparable to urban honky-tonks and juke joints in the United States, these forró clubs catered primarily to working-class audiences in Brazil and later were adopted by wider segments of the population. Before turning specifically to the era of Luiz Gonzaga and the incredible mid-century success of his signature genre, the baião, we will first examine the influence that Catulo da Paixão Cearense, João Pernambuco and other northeastern musicians had on burgeoning styles of Brazil's national music industry located in Rio de Janeiro.

A Brief Chronology of Northeastern Popular Music 1910–1950s

1910s	Catulo da Paixão Cearense and João Pernambuco adapt the themes and styles of northeastern music for Rio de Janeiro audiences; "Luar do Sertão" (1915) helps usher in a vogue of Brazilian country songs
1921	Os Oito Batutas (including João Pernambuco and Pixinguinha) sent to the Northeast to perform and collect folk music
1930s–1940s	Embolada and other northeastern country genres popularized nationally through recordings and broadcasts
1946	Luiz Gonzaga and Humberto Texeira's "Baião" becomes a hit song and begins the baião era in Brazilian popular music
1950s	Luiz Gonzaga establishes the trio format of triangle, zabumba drum, and accordion for música nordestina; forró dancing clubs established in Rio de Janeiro and São Paulo catering to working-class migrants from the Northeast

Creating Images of the Nation: All Roads Lead to the City

During the nineteenth century, musicians and poets (elite and popular) in Brazil were developing urban musical forms that incorporated romantic images of the country's rural-based traditions. It was on the rural areas of the Northeast (and, to a lesser extent, those of the South) that elite Brazilian composers focused most of their attention. Mixing urban lyrical song forms and popular dance music with genres, styles, and themes of the rural hinterlands of the country, a vogue of things "folkloric" emerged at the turn of the twentieth century. Including music written for theatrical stage presentation, for the salons of the wealthy, for street serenading, and for dissemination through the new recording industry, this diverse musical repertoire was aimed primarily to satisfy the tastes of urban middle-class audiences in southern Brazil. Occurring precisely as the first phonograph recordings appeared in Brazil (in 1902), a folkloric musical style entered on the ground floor of the new Brazilian music industry, with headquarters located in Rio de Janeiro. One important branch of this folkloric popular music was a romanticized folk song style, which had itself grown out of the Brazilian sentimental song tradition.

Sentimental art and popular songs known as modinhas, or little songs, had been present in Brazil and Portugal since the late eighteenth century. Accompanied by instruments such as the viola, harpsichord, and piano, the modinha spanned vernacular and elite contexts and their associated performance styles from its beginnings. Domingos Caldas Barbosa (1738–1800), a viola player and poet of mixed race from Rio de Janeiro, popularized the Brazilian-style modinha (adapted from Portuguese song traditions) and the closely related *lundu* (derived from African dance music traditions) in Lisbon and in Rio de Janeiro in the late eighteenth century. The son of a European father and an African mother, Barbosa had a playing style on the viola that featured distinctive Afro-Brazilian musical characteristics, which he had learned directly from black and mestizo street musicians in Rio de Janeiro. The lundu was originally an Afro-Brazilian dance form before it was cultivated in the elite salons of Rio de Janeiro and Lisbon. In nineteen-century Brazil, the modinha was transformed into a sentimental romantic song genre in the salons of upper-class society, where it incorporated cosmopolitan aesthetics of the Italian opera aria. Simultaneously, Brazilian modinhas circulated in oral tradition among rural and urban popular musicians throughout the country, who accompanied themselves on stringed instruments such as the guitar, or violão. Among this diverse cast of musicians from throughout the country, regional performance practices mixing both Afro- and Euro-Brazilian elements emerged. The development of the modinha thus traversed class divisions and cultural styles associated with the complexities of racial heritage in Brazil.

In Rio de Janeiro, social and artistic collaborations between urban middle-class writers and lower-class popular musicians in the mid-nineteenth century took place during informal performances of modinhas. From about the 1870s, the lyrical modinha also appeared in the popular serenades among strolling urban musicians (*chorões*) and in other urban contexts for audiences of mixed social ranks. The sentimental, lyrical style of the salon modinha, heavily influenced by cosmopolitan European aesthetic qualities, embodied the Brazilian romantic style of the nineteenth century, which became a model for the nationalized popular song repertoire. By the late nineteenth century, song lyrics depicting the rural life of the countryside were becoming common in the modinha repertoire, including stylized naturalist themes from the rural musical landscape of the northeastern interior. The poet–musician generally credited with reforming the modinha and creating a popular vogue in this style of regionalist "folk song" during the first decades of the twentieth century was Catulo da Paixão Cearense (1863–1946).

Born in São Luiz do Maranhão, Catulo moved from the Northeast to Rio de Janeiro with his family in 1880 when he was only seventeen years old. In the capital city, the young northeasterner was attracted to both the cosmopolitan culture of the city's elite and to the urban popular music of the street, where cultural interactions among diverse segments of the population took place. The son of a well-educated goldsmith and an avid reader of the classics, Catulo fitted comfortably into the intellectual literary circles of the city and was at home among the educated elite of Rio de Janeiro. He wrote poetry, which included modinha song lyrics (he even translated poems from French to Portuguese), and edited several songbook collections of lyrics of the popular songs of the day. Catulo also played flute and guitar in informal music sessions known as *rodas de choro* (choro circles) where musicians from a cross-section of Rio's population interacted. Hermano Vianna described the well-connected Catulo da Paixão Cearense in the following manner:

> A friend of politicians, writers, and millionaires, he also maintained contact with musicians less famous than himself, including many of the future inventors of the samba, and he frequented the house of the famous Bahian woman Aunt Ciata, one of the fabled cradles of Rio's samba culture. As a legitimate northeasterner, Catulo eventually took advantage of this new interest in the folk culture of the northeastern backlands. But his initial repertory was composed primarily of modinhas, of which he became the acknowledged master—most especially because of a celebrated 1906 performance at a soiree given by Mello de Moraes Filho. . . . In 1908, he took his guitar to the National Institute of Music, that bastion of high culture, and sang modinhas there. And in 1914, Catulo sang at the presidential palace.[1]

In the quest to define the cultural outlines of their new nation, many members of the cosmopolitan elite society of Rio de Janeiro's belle epoque had first looked to European culture and music. Simultaneously, these urban cosmopolitans distanced themselves from what they felt to be Brazil's "backward" rural traditions and from the emerging popular culture traditions of the country's urban areas. However, during the early twentieth century, encounters between elite and vernacular culture increased as performing and literary artists such as Catulo da Paixão Cearense presented the (stylized) vernacular traditions of Brazil in elite contexts and as the country's art music composers sought to nationalize the inherited European musical forms. Additionally, popular culture was exploding in public events such as Carnival and in new forms and contexts of the popular entertainment industry. Catulo was a central figure in this two-way cultural interaction and sang sentimental modinhas with guitar accompaniment at soirees held in the homes of Rio's most influential artistic patrons. In such lofty milieus, he interacted with artists and literary intellectuals, including writers, critics, and folklorists such as Afonso Arinos, Sílvio Romero, and Mello de Moraes Filho. Adapting the sentimental modinha to the folkloric vogue of the day, Catulo da Paixão Cearense also introduced the guitar itself into the homes of the elite and into the premiere concert halls of the city. As noted by Vianna in the previous quote, Catulo's many activities included a performance at Brazil's National Institute of Music, which was under the direction of composer Alberto Nepomuceno at the time. Catulo would later write that "it was practically impossible to book the main room of the Institute because the guitar was not [yet] an official instrument."[2] The guitar—a favorite instrument of lower-class rural and urban musicians of the time—was looked on with disfavor in elite circles. However, in the streets and in other venues of the country's musical life, the guitar was quickly becoming one of Brazil's most characteristic and popular instruments. Like the modinha, the guitar was now developing into an instrument that traversed class divisions in Brazil. By the 1920s, the instrument would be accepted at all levels of society; by the 1960s, the guitar was viewed as quintessentially Brazilian.

At the same time that he was performing in elite and popular venues of the city, Catulo also scored a string of hit songs in the new recording industry by setting some of his poems to the music of well-known Brazilian composers of the era, including Anacleto de Medeiros and Ernesto Nazareth. Reflective of the diverse musical realms in the early recording industry, Medeiros came from Rio de Janeiro's band music tradition, whereas Nazareth was a pianist and composer who straddled the popular and art music fields. Catulo's early song hits incorporated the mix of cosmopolitan international popular genres and local musical forms that were then in vogue, including the polka, schottische, waltz, modinha, tango, *tango-brasileira*, and lundu. Only after about 1910 did his lyrics begin to focus on northeastern themes and his music tap into northeastern styles. This shift coincided with the advent of his partnership with João Teixeira Guimarães (João Pernambuco), a rather unassuming guitar player from the state of Pernambuco. After meeting the phenomenal guitarist, Catulo began incorporating lyrics and music more specifically identified as northeastern into his own modinhas and other folkloric compositions. João Pernambuco was a pivotal figure in the history of the flow of musical material from the Northeast to Rio de Janeiro in the first two decades of the twentieth century.

João Pernambuco

As a young man, João Pernambuco had moved to Rio de Janeiro in 1904 after spending his formative years in Recife, Pernambuco. Whereas Catulo was a well-educated man and a literate poet and singer who easily adapted to the elite society of Rio de Janeiro, Pernambuco was a simple man with no formal education. However, he could play the guitar like few others. This talent was highly appreciated in Rio de Janeiro's diverse urban environment, where a swelling population of migrants from all over the country now resided. Pernambuco came from humble origins and had learned the traditional viola (ten-string guitar) and the guitar directly from musicians in Recife. Such musical interactions had provided him with first-hand experience in the rich musical traditions of the Northeast. It was João Pernambuco who brought this intimate knowledge of northeastern folk traditions to Rio de Janeiro's musical scene and exposed Catulo to many beautiful northeastern melodies and songs. Over the course of his own career, João would also influence the development of Brazilian instrumental music (especially the Brazilian choro) and become one of the country's most significant guitar players of the twentieth century. A brief look at his life will help to illuminate his key role in bringing the vernacular musical traditions of the Northeast to national audiences.

João was born in the sertão of Pernambuco in 1883, the third son in a family of eleven children.[3] Severe droughts in the sertão and the death of João's father in 1891 resulted in the family moving to the city of Recife in search of a better life. At that time, Recife was a growing regional metropolis with a diverse culture. By the age of twelve, João was playing viola in the city's open-air street markets. It was here that caboclo singers, *violeiros* (viola players), *emboladores* (embolada singers), and other popular musicians from the sertão and the rural areas surrounding Recife went to perform for local audiences. Recife was an important regional crossroads for musicians throughout the Northeast. There, João heard and learned a rich repertoire of northeastern folk and popular styles, such as cantoria, côco, and *embolada* (a tongue-twisting song form). He would also likely have been exposed to the emerging frevo and the maracatu Carnival traditions of the city. Eventually, he decided to focus on the six-string guitar and began learning from noted local guitarists Manuel Cabeceira, Cirino da Guajurema, Bem-Te-Vi, Madapolão, Serrador, Cego Sinfrônio, and Falcão das Queimadas. In 1904, João left Recife and moved south to Rio de Janeiro in search of employment as an ironworker. In Rio, he worked as a laborer during the week and played music at nights and on the weekends. During informal musical get-togethers of choro musicians in which modinhas, polkas, waltzes, maxixes, tangos, and other genres were performed, João met musicians who would become important figures in Brazilian music, including the composer Villa-Lobos and the popular musicians Pixinguinha, Donga (Ernesto Joaquim Maria dos Santos), and Catulo da Paixão Cearense. He also participated as a musician in grand society balls sponsored by Rio de Janeiro's elite Carnival clubs, such as the Democráticos, Fenianos, and Tenentes do Diabo. Through his many musical activities, João formed important social connections and established a reputation for his mastery of the guitar and for his wide knowledge of folk and popular music from his natal land of Pernambuco. This time in João's life coincided with the increased appreciation for the regional folk traditions of Brazil among the Brazilian public. It was also during this period that João Teixeira Guimarães acquired the nickname "João Pernambuco," a moniker reflecting his artistic and cultural identity, which was rooted in the image of the Northeast as the country's most traditional region. Though this image was created around the notion of an idealized agrarian caboclo culture, it was crafted and manufactured in the urban environment of Rio de Janeiro.

When he met Catulo da Paixão Cearense in Rio de Janeiro, João had already composed numerous *toadas sertanejas* (country songs) and instrumental choros and had performed in a wide variety of musical contexts in the city. After meeting, the two northeasterners began performing in the homes of Rio de Janeiro's elite patrons of the arts. João could play for hours, singing songs from Pernambuco and improvising over the northeastern musical styles he knew. He relied on an excellent musical memory, advanced improvisatory skills, and a phenomenal guitar ability to quickly establish a reputation as one of the city's best guitarists. He was instrumental in his collaborations with Catulo da Paixão Cearense in bringing northeastern music into vogue, and he also made important contributions to the development of Brazil's instrumental choro music and to Brazilian guitar music in general. He was a member of several key musical groups in Rio de Janeiro, including Caboclos de Caxangá, Turunas Pernambucanos, and the Oito Batutas group led by Pixinguinha. Brazilian composer Heitor Villa-Lobos was also one of his most avid admirers. However, with no formal musical training—he did not read or write music—João was unable to notate on paper the music he performed. This would be a point of contention between the two northeasterners. Catulo da Paixão Cearense never acknowledged the major role that João played in several of the poet's songs, yet there is reason to believe that the guitarist's contribution was substantial in the issue of authorship. According to José de Souza de Leal (my translation):

> In 1913, music was composed that would create the first controversy between João Pernambuco and Catulo da Paixão Cearense. This was "Cabocla de

Caxangá," the huge hit of the Carnival of 1914, which was performed by the Grupo Caxangá in their public appearances. This work was [legally] registered under the name of Catulo da Paixão Cearense, but, according to the friends of João Pernambuco, the music was written by him, and Catulo had only written the lyrics.[4]

Recorded in 1913 by Eduardo das Neves, "Cabocla de Caxangá" was reminiscent of the emboladas sung by popular cantoria singers from the Northeast to the accompaniment of the pandeiro. Though closely resembling an embolada, the 1913 recording of "Cabocla de Caxangá" was listed on the recording as a *batuque sertaneja* (country batuque). This genre designation is evidence of the hybrid nature of popular music of the era. The term *batuque* was applied rather broadly at the time to almost any Afro-Brazilian dance music with strong percussive components. The term *sertaneja* (literally meaning "from the sertão") indicated an association with the rural country music of the interior. Putting the two terms together conflated the two primary domains of northeastern cultural heritage: Afro-Brazilian and caboclo. Lyrics to the song make mention of a number of place names important to João Pernambuco's life, including Jatobá, his birthplace deep in the sertão of Pernambuco. Two years later (in 1915), Catulo scored the biggest hit of his career with a song titled "Luar do Sertão" ("Moonlight of the Sertão"). According to Jairo Severiano and Zuza Homem de Mello (my translation): "'Luar do Sertão' is one of the greatest successes of all time in our [Brazilian] popular music. Easy to sing, it is embedded in the memory of every Brazilian, even in those who are not interested in music. As with the majority of songs that praise rural life, it enchants listeners primarily through the ingenuity of its verses and through the simplicity of its melody."[5]

The simplicity of the folk-like melody was the direct result of João Pernambuco's influence. In fact, even though Catulo da Paixão Cearense took credit as the sole author of "Luar do Sertão" (and for "Cabocla de Caxangá" as well), the music was most likely written by João Pernambuco based on northeastern melodies that the guitarist had performed for Catulo. In the case of "Luar do Sertão," the melody itself was reminiscent of a traditional northeastern embolada titled "Engenho é de Humaitá," which was in João's repertoire. In subsequent years, a considerable controversy arose concerning the authorship of the music to "Luar do Sertão." Catulo registered both the lyrics and the music under his name in 1914. However, it is likely that João Pernambuco actually composed the music, based on a traditional folk melody from Pernambuco. Heitor Villa-Lobos was one of the many supporters of João's later claims of coauthorship for the song. The lyrics of "Luar do Sertão" paint a nostalgic view of the natural landscape of the northeastern sertão and evoke a sense of inherent values linked to the rural life of the area. The timeless quality of the natural landscape of the rural Northeast illuminated by a bright moon contrasts with an anonymous cityscape where the moon is dark.

Partial lyrics to the refrain and first verse of "Luar do Sertão," by Catulo da Paixão Cearense

English translation by Larry Crook.

> There is no, I'm telling you, oh! no,
> Moonlight like that of the sertão!

> Oh! How I long for the moonlight of my homeland, in the mountains,
> Turning the dry leaves on the ground white!
> This moonlight here in the city, so dark,
> Doesn't have that same yearning passion of the moonlight of the sertão.

Probably based on one or more folk songs from the Northeast, Catulo da Paixão Cearense claimed sole authorship to this song in 1915 and there followed a history of disputes as to authorship. Numerous recordings of this song have been made.

As the last verse of the song makes clear, the soul and essence of Brazil do not lie in the darkness of the city but rather in the moon of the sertão.

Partial lyrics to the last verse of "Luar do Sertão"

> But only in the *sertão* on nights when the moon is full,
> When the moon is like an amaryllis, is a spring flower,
> Is when the poet, singing the entire night,
> Sees in the Brazilian Moon, the entire soul of Brazil.

Drawing on João Pernambuco's intimate knowledge of northeastern traditions, Catulo da Paixão Cearense introduced such music into Rio de Janeiro and the national music scene. The releases of the recordings of "Caboclo de Caxangá" and "Luar do Sertão" in 1914 and 1915, respectively, ushered in a vogue of *canções sertanejas* (country songs) that would flourish into Brazil's urban country music over the next few decades. This country folk song style drew on repertoire from both southern and northeastern Brazil. Catulo went on to become one of Brazil's most popular poets, and João Pernambuco established himself as an important figure in Rio de Janeiro's popular music scene.

Before the success of "Cabocla de Caxangá" and "Luar do Sertão," João Pernambuco was actively involved in bringing a northeastern sound to Rio's Carnival celebration. In 1912, he had organized a group of six musicians to perform during Carnival dressed as northeasterners. Calling themselves the Grupo do Caxangá (named after a suburb of Recife), the group members paraded in Rio's Carnival while performing a wide variety of popular music, specializing in northeastern material composed and arranged by João himself. They dressed in straw hats, bandanas, thong sandals, and rolled-up pants, and they played guitars, violas, and mandolins. The northeastern-style hats that the Grupo do Caxangá used were patterned after ones worn by northeastern bandits, especially a gang from Pernambuco headed by the notorious Antonio Silvino. Silvino's lawless exploits were widely reported in the Brazilian press of the day, and the northeastern bandit had become a folk hero of Robin Hood-like stature throughout Brazil. In 1914, at the height of his exploits and in the same year as the release of the song "Cabocla de Caxangá," Silvino was captured and imprisoned in Pernambuco. The choice of the wide-brimmed hats for Carnival reinforced this popular northeastern imagery for João Pernambuco's group.

By 1914, the group had expanded and taken to the streets of Rio de Janeiro performing the hit "Cabocla de Caxangá" by Pernambuco and Cearense. One of the banners that accompanied the group members as they paraded down Avenida Rio Branco in the center of Rio de Janeiro read: *A Embolada do Norte* (The Embolada of the North). Among the members of the group at that time were some of the top popular musicians in Recife: Pixinguinha, Donga, Nelson Alves, Jacob and Raul Palmeiri, Jaime Ovale, and Quincas Laranjeira. Most of these musicians were active in choro circles and other venues, where a popular form of the urban samba was developing. Drawing from European- and African-influenced musical styles, the Rio de Janeiro musicians acted as cultural mediators linking diverse social contexts and racial segments of the city. One particularly important center of musical and cultural activity was around a part of town called Praça Onze (Plaza Eleven), where a large concentration of black immigrants from Bahia resided. According to Sérgio Cabral (my translation):

> For the carnival of 1917, the Grupo Caxangá was once again in the newspapers. Quite different from its earlier manifestation, it now rehearsed at the headquarters of the club Kananga do Japão, at Praça Onze, and had in its repertoire the outstanding piece "Pelo Telefone," considered the first recorded samba and whose authors (in the middle of a grand polemic about the true authorship of the song) were Donga and the journalist Mauro de Almeida. The club Kananga do Japão was frequented by all of the members of the group and was located near the house of Tia Ciata (Hilária Batista de Almeida), the location of daily and obligatory reunions of the black musical community in Rio. In that house, Pixinguinha would remain in the front room playing choro while his samba friends would go to the back of the house to play, dance, and sing.[6]

Pixinguinha, Donga, and other members of the Caxangá group—probably including João Pernambuco—were frequent participants at Tia Ciata's house. The house served as a central meeting point for musical gatherings and other forms of intercultural collaboration among diverse segments of the city's population. It was in such places that modinhas, polkas, tangos, lundus, maxixes, choros, marches, canções sertanejas, emboladas, and other genres mixed with Afro-Brazilian drumming and singing styles from Bahia. Out of the artistic creativity found at such locations came the beginnings of the urban samba.

Grupo do Caxangá was active in Rio de Janerio until 1919, when two important members of the group, Pixinguinha and Donga, were asked to select several musicians from the group to perform at the prestigious Cine Palais movie house in Rio. The new group they formed was named Os Oito Batutas (the Eight Masters) at the suggestion of the manager of the theater, Isaac Frankel. The performance of Os Oito Batutas (a racially mixed group) at the Cine Palais generated a scandal of sorts at the time. Some members of Rio's social elite objected to dark-skinned men performing maxixes, lundus, canções sertanejas, and batuques in a context that had been the preserve of European musical heritage, epitomized by refined classical music. Other members of Rio's upper class, including prominent politicians such as Rui Barbosa, became supporters of Os Oito Batutas.[7] João Pernambuco was closely involved in this mixed and controversial group from the start and was a member from 1919 to 1921. The Oito Batutas repertoire— including many musical selections billed as emboladas, desafios (cantoria song duels), and canções sertanejas —was influenced greatly by the northeastern repertoire that João Pernambuco had developed for the Grupo do Caxangá. That repertoire had been based not only on his musical memories from childhood but also on later trips he had taken to the Northeast to collect music of the region. These trips were financed by elite patrons of Rio de Janeiro.

As early as 1913, Arnaldo Guinle, a millionaire patron from Rio, had financed a trip by João Pernambuco, Pixinguinha, and Donga to Recife in order to collect typical music of the northeastern region. In 1921, Guinle would once again send the musicians, now members of Os Oito Batutas, on a performing and collecting trip to the Northeast, where they would visit Salvador da Bahia and Recife. During both trips, João Pernambuco was the key individual, with knowledge of the local traditions and personal connections with musicians. After the trips, he returned to Rio de Janeiro with fresh musical material from the Northeast. Guinle's patronage, with the goal of collecting the folk heritage of the Northeast, was consistent with the growing attention given to the regional folk traditions of Brazil by the elite of the country. This also points up the fact that Rio de Janeiro's upper class was not completely dismissive of "backward" local Brazilian traditions, as has often been claimed. Although many cultural elitists in Rio de Janeiro did look primarily to Europe for their cultural models, a countercurrent of national regionalism, represented most clearly by a fixation on the Northeast region of the country, was also present. This form of national sentiment gave great value to searching for authentic, home-grown Brazilian culture. In fact, the early years of the twentieth century witnessed the publication of several books on Brazilian folklore by numerous authors, including Mello de Moraes Filho, Sílvio Romero, and Pereira da Costa. These men became the leading scholars looking into the ancient soul of the Brazilian nation through the window of its folk traditions. Furthermore, the country's first conferences and festivals on Brazil's regional folklore (defined primarily as rural and non-European urban phenomena) took place during these same years. Together with the activities of poets and musicians such as Catulo da Paixão Cearense and João Pernambuco, this scholarly attention made regional "rural" Brazil a growing fad among the middle and upper classes of the southern cities. Because of the emergent success of northeastern music, a fad that he had helped usher in, João Pernambuco received invitations to perform for many events organized by the elite. One was the culminating concert of a conference exploring Brazilian folk traditions, organized by Afonso Arinos. The conference took place in 1915 at the Teatro Municipal in São Paulo (one of the country's citadels of high art). For the musical engagement, João organized a small group of musicians to perform urbanized country music for the elite audience. Advertising Pernambuco's group Troupe Sertaneja a year later, press coverage described the earlier event in the following way (my translation):

> Today . . . a well organized sertanejo group makes its first appearance in the popular theater, led by the celebrated artist João Pernambuco, whose success reached Sao Paulo when he took part in the conference—Brazilian Folk Tales and Traditions—organized by our beloved man of literature Afonso Arinos in the Theatro Municipal. The Troupe Sertaneja is composed of able players of violão, viola, bandolins, and cavaquinhos, and possesses a vast repertoire of modinhas sertanejas, so appreciated in our country. The Troupe included the participation of João Pernambuco, Juvenal Fontes, Luiz Pinto da Silva, José Alves da Lima, Joao Martins, and Octávio Lessa, for whom the press in São Paulo was unanimous in giving its highest praise. For this reason it is hoped that the Troupe Sertaneja, the only one of its kind touring in our state, may receive the most sympathetic reception in Campinas.[8]

Troupe Sertaneja's instrumentation of guitar, viola, mandolin, and cavaquinho reflected both northeastern string traditions and the urban choro groups from Rio de Janeiro. In Rio, João Pernambuco was intimately involved in instrumental choro music and was a regular at places such as the famous music store Cavaquinho de Ouro, one of the main locations where choro musicians congregated to perform. Together with fellow Pernambucan Quincas Laranjeira, João helped elevate the solo and ensemble possibilities of the guitar. This helped establish the artistic credentials for the instrument and greatly influenced Brazil's leading classical composer, Villa-Lobos (also a guitarist), who frequented choro gatherings as well. Commenting on João Pernambuco's influence on the composer, Henrique Cazes wrote (my translation):

> From associations with these choro musicians who played guitar, and primarily from João Pernambuco, Villa-Lobos extracted the basis for his guitar works, considered the most important for the instrument in this [twentieth] century. Prior to writing his studies and preludes, Villa-Lobos paid homage to the choro musicians with his Suite Popular Brasileira, composed in 1908 and in 1912 and constituted in five movements: "Mazurca-Choro," "Schottisch-Choro," "Valsa-Choro," "Gavota-Choro," and "Chorinho." This suite, and the "Choros Number 1," dedicated to Nazareth, are the works in which Villa-Lobos comes closest to the style of the choros.[9]

João Pernambuco mixed northeastern music with the choro form to develop the repertoire for the various groups in which he was involved; this extended into the repertoire of Troupe Sertaneja, Grupo do Caxangá, and Os Oito Batutas. João Pernambuco's own mastery of the guitar is evident in the handful of recordings he made for the Columbia label in the late 1920s and first years of the 1930s. (Several of these extraordinary pieces have been reissued on the CDs *Musique do Nordeste, vols.1 and 2.*)

When Os Oito Batutas came on the scene, the group capitalized on the success of northeastern music and scheduled tours throughout the Brazilian territories, featuring a repertoire of songs advertised as *emboladas do norte* (emboladas of the North). Their advertisements also highlighted the inclusion of the poetry of Catulo da Paixão Cearense, which would be sung and played by João Pernambuco and other members of the group. Clearly, the urbanized folkloric sounds of the Northeast were now becoming national in scope. Newspaper reports of their performances frequently mentioned the authentic "sertanejo" character of the music. For instance, when they performed at the Salão Conservatório Dramático Musical in São Paulo, their show was announced in the paper as "Uma Noite no Sertão" ("A Night in the Sertão"). As mentioned, in 1921, the patron Arnaldo Guinle once again sent João Pernambuco, Donga, Pixinguinha, and the other members of Os Oito Batutas to Salvador and to Recife in order to perform and to collect additional music typical of the northeastern region. While in Recife, the group performed at the cinema house Cassini Moderno to enthusiastic audiences, as reported in a local Recife paper, *Diário de Pernambuco,* in its July 3, 1921, edition (my translation):

> Sensational opening of the authentically national troupe that is celebrated and renowned: OS OITO BATUTAS with their original repertoire of SAMBAS, DESAFIOS, CANÇÕES, and SAPATEADOS SERTANEJOS. Sharing the stage are Alfredo Viana (Pixinquinha), the outstanding flutist, and Ernesto dos Santos (Donga), author of the tangos "Pelo Telefone," "Vamos Acabar com Isso," "Se a Bomba Arrebenta," and others. Today's program: 1) "Eu Vi Vovó" (samba); 2) "Cadê Ele!" (embolada); 3) "Segura o Gato" (choro); 4) "O Poeta do Sertão" (de Catulo Cearense); 5) "Bacatuba e Pedro Sabiá" (desafio); 6) "Urubu" (Grande Samba).[10]

Os Oito Batutas was Brazil's most influential popular musical ensemble of the 1920s, and it became the country's first popular music group to perform abroad when Arnaldo Guinle financed a performance tour to Europe; the group presented its repertoire of the rural and urban sounds of Brazil to enthusiastic Parisian audiences in 1922. Following this trip, Pixinguinha and Os Oito Batutas internationalized their sound by adopting instrumental elements of American jazz (saxophone, trumpet, trombone, piano, banjo, and drumset) and mixing this with Brazilian string instruments of choro and percussion instruments derived from Afro-Brazilian traditions. This mixed format laid the groundwork for the development of the instrumental ensembles that would feature prominently in the popular music recordings and radio broadcasts of the 1930s and 1940s. As mentioned in Chapter 4, Pixinguinha was one of Brazil's top arrangers and bandleaders for national recordings made from the 1920s to the 1950s. At the end of the 1920s, he formed the Orquestra Típica Pixinguinha-Donga and then, in the 1930s, Orquestra Típica Victor and Diabos do Ceu. These groups combined Brazilian-associated instruments (cavaquinho, guitar, mandolin, flute, pandeiro, and a wide variety of other percussion instruments) with piano, double bass, winds, and brass.

The flourishing of northeastern music in Rio de Janeiro and the South during the first three decades of the twentieth century and its impact on the development of Brazil's national music are frequently under-appreciated in historical accounts of Brazilian music. However, sounds from the Northeast were extremely influential in crafting the beginnings of Brazil's popular music. As influential as this early activity was, however, nothing could have predicted the impact of northeastern traditions in the next two decades. The 1940s would see the rise of Luiz Gonzaga, a popular musician from the far western corner of Pernambuco, deep in the sertão, who would change the face of Brazilian music and become one of the nation's most popular figures of the twentieth century. Increased migrations from rural to urban Brazil brought new waves of northeasterners to Rio de Janeiro and São Paulo in search of work and a better life. With the advent of national broadcasts in the 1930s, radio became the most effective means of mass communication in the country and the primary avenue through which national culture was codified and spread throughout the country.

Two main streams of regional music (flowing together frequently) developed out of the early vogue of folkloric sertanejo sounds popularized in the first decades of the century through the works of Catulo da Paixão Cearense, João Pernambuco, and others. One stream emanated from the rural country sounds of southeastern Brazil (especially from the states of São Paulo and Minas Gerais) and was first called *música caipira* and later *música sertaneja*. The other stream of regional music continued to flow down to Rio from the Northeast, especially from Recife. In the 1920s and 1930s, this northeastern "country" music continued to draw substantially on the instrumental and vocal traditions from Pernambuco and was represented nationally by popular singers who adapted the embolada and côco song forms to Brazil's national recording and broadcast industry in Rio de Janeiro.

Côco and Embolada in the 1920s and 1930s

While in Recife in 1921, Pixinguinha and João Pernambuco met several exceptional young northeastern musicians from that city who would soon make their own mark on Brazil's national music scene. Among these were José Luíz Rodrigues Calazans (Jararaca), Severino Rangel de Carvalho (Ratinho), and Luperce Miranda. In 1922, Jararaca and Ratinho formed a band named Turunas Pernambucanos and traveled to Rio de Janeiro to perform for Brazil's centennial celebrations. Comprising three guitars, saxophone, pandeiro, and *reco-reco* (a scraped percussion instrument) with each musician doubling on vocals, Turunas Pernambucanos was advertised to Rio de Janeiro's public as an authentic Brazilian caboclo ensemble with a repertoire of "songs of the sertão, emboladas, and desafios." The group was an urban ensemble of musicians, but its members nonetheless fit the southern image of northeastern caboclo musicians. An enthusiastic reception resulted in a six-month engagement for the group at Rio de Janeiro's Cine Palais and an invitation to record for the Odeon label. For the recording session, Turunas Pernambucanos was used to back up one of Brazil's most established popular singers, Manuel Pedro dos Santos (Baiano) and scored a hit with a northeastern-style embolada song titled "A Espingarda." The singer Bahiano (his name referred to his roots in Bahia) was a pioneer among Brazil's first generation of recording artists, having participated in the country's earliest recordings for Casa Edison in 1902. Born in Bahia, he recorded in all popular genres of the day and was the singer on the country's very first samba recording, titled "Pelo Telefone," in 1917. Carrying on the tradition established by Grupo do Caxangá and further developed by Os Oito Batutas, Turunas Pernambucanos set out on a tour of southern Brazil and Argentina, presenting the regional sounds of the Brazilian Northeast during the mid-1920s. One of the lead members of the group, Jararaca, also made solo recordings reflecting the fusion of northeastern music with samba (a hybrid genre he termed *samba sertanejo*). In the late 1920s, Jararaca and fellow bandmate Ratinho formed a musical duo presenting stylized emboladas and other regional repertoire within comedy routines that caricatured the rural folkways of the country. During the 1930s and 1940s, Jararaca and Ratinho became two of the country's most successful radio personalities and scored hit songs in a variety of genres. Once on the national level, the duo presented a rather generic and stylized image of the country's folk culture.

Another important Recife musician who had been influenced by the visit of Os Oito Batutas to Recife was the mandolin virtuoso Luperce Miranda. Only sixteen at the time of their meeting in 1921, Luperce impressed Pixinguinha with his virtuosity and command of the mandolin. Remaining in Recife until the late 1920s, Miranda participated in several local popular groups patterned on the Oito Batutas model, including the influential Voz do Sertão (the Voice of the Sertão), which recorded for the Parlaphon label. Miranda moved to Rio de Janeiro in 1929, formed the group Regional Luperce Miranda (Luperce Miranda's Regional Ensemble), and established himself as Brazil's first and foremost mandolin virtuoso. From the late 1920s through the 1950s, Luperce was one of the country's top recording and performing instrumentalists. His influential mandolin playing brought a distinctively northeastern feel to the commercial samba recordings of such top Brazilian singers as Carmen Miranda, Francisco Alves, and Mario Reis.

Vocalist Manezinho Araújo was another musician from Recife to gain national exposure through a recording and broadcast career in Rio de Janeiro. Known as the "King of the Embolada," Manezinho moved to Rio in 1933, where he made numerous recordings as a singer of emboladas and appeared on film and radio. The instrumental music accompaniment to most of his emboladas during the 1930s and 1940s featured the small ensemble format known as the *regional* (regional combo). The idea for the regional combo format originated in the northeastern-inspired ensemble sound of groups such as Grupo do Caxangá, Turunas Pernambucanos, and Os Oito Batutas. These small improvisatory groups emphasized plucked strings (guitar, cavaquinho, mandolin), the flute (and occasionally other melodic wind instruments), and the pandeiro (in addition to a few other Brazilian percussion instruments). The regional combos were distinct from the larger radio and recording studio "orchestras" of the day, which featured an international line up of string, wind, brass, and percussion. The regional combos provided a more distinctly Brazilian sound that was, at the same time, generically regional in orientation. The regional association was supplied primarily through connections to the musical culture of the Northeast. The regional musicians were accomplished improvisers who did not require fully written arrangements for their performances. In his book on the development of Brazilian choro, Henrique Cazes observed (my translation): "For a radio station of the era [1930s] the work of small 'regional' combos was indispensable, because, being a format that did not require written arrangements, these groups had the agility and the power of improvisation and were able to fill up the dead space and resolve whatever stops that might be called for in the accompaniment of singers."[11]

Arguably the most influential of the regional combos in Rio de Janeiro was the Conjunto Regional de Benedito Lacerda, which backed up Manezinho Araújo on many of his emboladas recorded at the Odeon studios. A classic example of the Araújo–Lacerda collaboration is the embolada "Arrisca um Olho" ("Take a Look"). Originally released in 1938 (Odeon 11339-b), this song has been recently re-released on the CD *Manezinho Araújo: Cuma É o Nome Dele?* Backed by Lacerda's regional combo featuring two guitars, flute, and pandeiro, the vocal melody of the piece is a rapid-fire succession of notes over tonic and dominant harmonies provided by the guitars. The singing and flute playing emphasize a perpetual rapid-fire rhythm of repeated sixteenth notes and rhythmic changes on the offbeats clearly patterned on the folk embolada, a form typically sung with the accompaniment of pandeiro and other Brazilian percussion instruments. The piece also conforms to the basic outline of the folk côco, with the alternation of verses and refrain.

Like many of the traditional emboladas from which the song derived, the lyrics to "Arrisca um Olho" relate a comical tale involving risqué subject matter and the use of many northeastern slang terms. In the song, a humorous incident occurs in a local church as a young female member of the congregation slips and falls from the balcony and loses her dress on the way down. After the admonition of the priest that anyone caught looking will be punished by blindness, one of the youngest boys in the congregation amusingly admits that he "just likes to watch." The story and the distinctively northeastern pronunciation of Manezinho's singing emphasized the stereotyped characteristics of northeastern culture. This and other emboladas sung by Manezinho established a national reputation for him as the "king of the Embolada."

From João Pernambuco through Jararaca and Ratinho, Luperce Miranda, and then Manezinho Araújo, the northeastern regional sound entered the national consciousness through the regional combo format within the recording and broadcast studios of Rio de Janeiro. However, these regional sounds represented only a small segment of the national music industry. That was about to change in the mid-1940s, when the nation's imagination was captured by an unlikely accordion-playing singer from Pernambuco.

Luiz Gonzaga and the Baião

Born in the far western portion of the state of Pernambuco in 1912, near the small town of Exú, Luiz Gonzaga was the son of poor rural caboclos of the sertão. His father, Januário, played the diatonic eight-bass instrument known as oito baixos, which was popular throughout the countryside. Luiz learned to perform on that instrument in his youth, played weekend forró country dances, and participated in the many rural festivities of the area. Through these and other experiences, the young Gonzaga became familiar with the full range of musical activities of the sertão: cantadores playing the viola and singing desafios and other song forms; dance music used to accompany the pageantry of folk dances, including the bumba-meu-boi and *quadrilha* square dancing; and bandinhas de pífanos playing for novenas and religious processions of folk Catholicism. Celebrations in the month of June were particularly animated in the northeastern interior. Popularly known as *festas juninas* (June-fests), the celebrations revolved around the cycle of Catholic feast days commemorating three important saints

(St. Anthony—June 13, St. John—June 24, and St. Peter—June 29). After the praying, hymn singing, and other religious activities were completed, the accordion and banda de pífanos musicians played social dance music until early in morning. This dance music included a repertoire of indigenous and "Brazilianized" foreign genres, such as the schottische, mazurka, *baiano* (from Bahia), and waltz. Gonzaga was already a well-known musician in his area when, at the age of eighteen, he sold his accordion, left the sertão of Pernambuco, and enlisted in the army.

The Brazilian army provided the young northeasterner the opportunity to travel and see the rest of the country. In addition to traveling throughout the Northeast, Gonzaga went south to Rio de Janeiro and then to the nearby state of Minas Gerais. While in Minas Gerais, he took up the guitar and passed much of his leisure time strumming and listening to the radio broadcasts originating from Rio de Janeiro. In 1936, Gonzaga befriended an accordion player named Domingos Ambrósio, who introduced the Pernambuco musician to the keyboard accordion. Until that time, Gonzaga was familiar only with the diatonic oito baixos type of button accordion that his own father played. Now, he began studying the more modernized keyboard accordion. The fully chromatic keyboard accordion (with a full complement of sharps and flats) allowed Gonzaga to learn Brazil's contemporary popular music directly from radio broadcasts. Soon, he was playing professionally, and by 1939, he had decided to leave the army in order to pursue a career in music. In March of that year, Gonzaga moved to Rio de Janeiro and began performing at bars, in dancing clubs, and for private parties with Xavier Pinheiro, a Portuguese-born guitarist. With Pinheiro, Gonzaga played *fados* (a Portuguese song form), tangos, waltzes, fox-trots, blues, and other international styles of music that were popular at the time. Eventually, Gonzaga started appearing on the radio talent shows in Rio de Janeiro known as *programas de calouros* (programs of amateurs). The programs served as a way for the Rio entertainment industry to discover new talent among the hundreds of musicians and actors who flooded to the city. These variety shows featured competitions of amateur musicians, some talented and some not. Imitating the repertoire and style of the mainstream popular music of the day, Luiz Gonzaga attempted to conceal his northeastern roots by adopting a *carioca* (meaning "like someone from Rio") persona. He performed practically everything *but* northeastern music during those days. In his own words (my translation):

> Nobody knew that I was a northeasterner. I was already a street-smart hustler; I hung around with blacks [*crioulos*], dressed like them. I even sang *sambas* in the *gafeiras* [popular working-class dance clubs in Rio]. I was interested in picking up the carioca accent. I had already lost the northeastern accent. Also, I had left the Northeast more than nine years ago. When I quit the army and moved away from Minas Gerais, I was already acting like someone from the state of Minas Gerais.[12]

These statements clearly highlight Gonzaga's desire at that time to become a fully modern Brazilian citizen through his attempts at gaining competence in Brazilian national forms of culture. His adoption of the speech patterns of the south-central area of Minas Gerais and then of the carioca accent of Rio de Janeiro indicates that the official, standard Brazilian speech pattern was defined as that of Rio de Janeiro. This was largely because of the advent of national radio broadcasts and music recordings emanating from the capital: all of the announcers and singers employed the accents of the South. As a musician, Gonzaga realized that the road to national commercial success also went through Rio de Janeiro and its popular culture establishment. However, he was not particularly well suited for singing in the internationalized national style that dominated the musical scene there. Additionally, he soon came to realize that there might be commercial potential, a certain niche for a regional music that was distinctly northeastern in orientation and that contrasted with the mainstream sounds associated with the samba. During the 1930s and 1940s, the commercial samba was increasingly criticized for being subject to excessive foreign influence, primarily from the United States. Regional sounds that were authentically rooted in Brazilian culture might be commercially viable, especially among the many migrant workers from the Northeast who were flooding into Rio de Janeiro and São Paulo. Remembering the songs and musical styles of his father, Gonzaga began incorporating polkas, mazurkas, *chorinhos* (little choros), and square-dance tunes from the sertão into his repertoire. He maintained that he first included this northeastern material into his repertoire after he met several students from the northeastern state of Ceará who were temporarily living in Rio de Janeiro. At bars where Gonzaga was performing, these students began requesting northeastern songs to remind them of their homeland. With newly found inspiration and a growing sense of northeastern pride, Luiz Gonzaga appeared on Ary Barroso's amateur-hour radio program *Calouros em Desfile* (Amateurs on Parade) at the Rádio Tupi in 1940. For the show, he performed a northeastern-inspired accordion piece titled "Vira e Mexe." He won first prize for his performance and subsequently became a regular on another popular radio show, *A Hora do Sertaneja* (The Sertaneja Hour). This program featured caipira country music from São Paulo and Minas Gerais as well as northeastern music, and it provided ample opportunity for Gonzaga to work alongside other important regional artists of Brazil. His career as a recording artist would soon develop, and in 1941, he recorded four pieces for the Victor label: "Vespera de São João" (a mazurka), "Numa Serenata" (a waltz), "Vira e Mexe" (a *xamego*—also spelled "chamego"—the term is slang for "lover"), and "Saudades de São João Del Rei" (a waltz).

The recording of the instrumental "Vira e Mexe" exhibited Gonzaga's exceptional accordion work, which was backed up by a regional combo of mandolin, cavaquinho, and pandeiro with the addition of triangle and a zabumba drum. These last two instruments gave the piece an instrumental quality that Luiz Gonzaga would later use to define a northeastern trio sound based on the tight interaction of accordion, triangle, and zabumba. Listed as a xamego, the piece was written in a fast duple meter with quickly running notes over simple chords (tonic and dominant). The overall effect is reminiscent of the fast, march-like dance music that accompanies square dancing in the Northeast. The term *xamego* was a slang expression for a passionate lover, and Luiz Gonzaga employed this word as a genre designation for several of his songs. Between 1941 and 1945, he recorded numerous instrumental pieces for the Victor label. He also appeared frequently on live radio programs such as the highly popular *Alma do Sertão* (Soul of the Sertão), where he became known as "the best accordionist from the Northeast."[13] Meanwhile, Gonzaga continued performing in Rio de Janeiro's bars and dancing clubs, where he perfected his northeastern-related material. In addition, in 1944, he began collaborating with his first songwriting partner, Miguel Lima. Although Luiz Gonzaga was a first-rate accordionist and an able composer, the artistic directors of Rio de Janeiro's radio shows and recording studios considered his voice too nasalized and northeastern in sound for the tastes of the general buying public. Gonzaga's attempts to sing during the programs and on recordings were rejected numerous times. To record his own compositions, he was forced to collaborate with other vocalists who interpreted his music. These singers included Carmen Costa, a singer from Rio, and Manezinho Araújo, "King of the Embolada." Araújo recorded "O Xamego da Guiomar" in 1945, with Gonzaga on accordion and a backup regional band of flute, guitar, trombone, cavaquinho, and pandeiro. (In addition, a bass drum and perhaps other instruments, including the violão, seem to be present in the recording. "O Xamego da Guiomar" has been rereleased on *Manezinho Araújo: Cuma É o Nome Dele?* [Revivendo RVCD-109].) Also listed as a xamego, the piece is in a slow duple meter reminiscent of the schottische of the Northeast.

Gonzaga's first recordings as a singer were made in 1945; he recorded "Dança Marequinha" (a mazurka), "Penero Xerem" (a xamego), and "Cortando o Pano" (also a mazurka), all co-written with his partner, Miguel Lima. The moderate success of these recordings established Gonzaga as a bona fide singer, but he was still searching for a distinctive repertoire and a lyricist who could convey the sentiments of the migrant workers' nostalgia for the sertão. In August 1945, Gonzaga met Humberto Teixeira, a lyricist from Ceará who shared the musician's orientation. The Gonzaga–Teixeira collaboration yielded immediate results with the song "No Meu Pé de Serra" ("At the Foothills of My Homeland"). Reportedly written in just ten minutes, Gonzaga's song is semi-autobiographical.

Reminiscent of the nostalgic songs of Catulo da Paixão Cearense some thirty years earlier, the lyrics to this piece treat the longing of a displaced northeastern caboclo for his homeland: Oh what sadness I have / I will return to my sertão. Such nostalgia would figure prominently in songs Gonzaga would co-write with Teixeira in the future. The choice of the xote (a Brazilianized northeastern form of the schottische) as the rhythm for the piece also linked it closely to the musical repertoire and characteristics of the sertão.

Though not exclusive to the rural northeast, the xote became one of the area's most widespread and popular social dances in the late nineteenth century. Additionally, a variety of cosmopolitan European social dance forms (polka, quadrille, waltz) and Hispanic social dance forms (tango, habanera) spread via Brazil's urban areas into the rural regions of the country in the 1800s. At roughly the same time, Italian immigrants introduced the accordion into southern Brazil, and from there, the veterans of the Brazil–Paraguay war carried the instrument back to the Northeast when they returned home in the 1860s. In the northeastern sertão, the diatonic eight-bass accordion known as the oito baixos became a favored instrument for country dances and social celebrations that featured the Brazilianized versions of the international dances. The accordion music replaced the fife-and-drum groups for these occasions. Luiz Gonzaga's own father, Januário, was a typical performer of this country-dance tradition and represented perhaps a third generation of accordion players in the sertão. Inspired by remembrances of the xotes played by his father during his youth, Gonzaga composed the melody and provided a basic idea for the lyrics, which, together with Teixeira, he transformed into the song "No Meu Pé de Serra." Gonzaga's recording of this song in 1946 featured the slow duple meter and the shuffle feel of dotted rhythms with a backbeat accent on two that characterized the northeastern-style xote. The recording highlighted Gonzaga's nasalized, "northeastern" voice and his expert accordion playing, backed up by a hybrid regional combo of cavaquinho, violão, and the zabumba drum. The inclusion of the zabumba, drawn from the banda de pífanos ensemble, reinforced the northeastern flavor of the music among migrant audiences already familiar with these sounds.

Luiz Gonzaga's commercial breakthrough came with the second piece he wrote with Humberto Teixeira, titled "Baião." First recorded in 1946 by the group Quatro Ases e um Curinga (Four Aces and a Joker), the piece became a national hit. Gonzaga later recorded his own version of the song in 1949. The growing popularity of Luiz Gonzaga and his music contested the theretofore unquestioned supremacy of the samba.

In the 1940s, especially after World War II, the mainstream samba suffered from the increasing influence of American and other foreign musical sources and was criticized by Brazilian nationalists for becoming too Americanized. The international popularity Carmen Miranda gained through Hollywood films during that era is a prime example. By the time that Luiz Gonzaga and Humberto Teixeira began composing northeastern-style songs such as "No Meu Pé de Serra," Brazilian national audiences and cultural critics were primed and ready to identify with a musical style that could claim a Brazilian pedigree untainted by foreign influence. Where better to find such a style than in the music of the northeastern sertão, an area identified since the last years of the nineteenth century as the wellspring of their country's "authentic" national character and the home of its "purest" traditional culture.

By the late 1940s, the Northeast clearly represented the so-called traditional side of the modern Brazilian nation. The South had solidified its position as the urban, industrial, economic, and political core of the nation; the image of the Northeast remained tied to an agrarian past, where droughts and economic crises forced its humble caboclo peasants to leave their traditional homeland and culture in search of jobs. From the 1940s onwards, the South acquired the reputation of an economic Garden of Eden among the poor souls of the Northeast who flooded to São Paulo and Rio de Janeiro to find work. Swelling the urban industrial areas of the South, northeastern migrants represented both a socioeconomic problem and a rich source of Brazilian cultural authenticity. Luiz Gonzaga, drawing directly from the musical traditions familiar to these migrants, created a series of new commercial musical genres to express the experiences, the hopes, and the dreams of the northeasterners. He also became the country's leading and most commercially successful popular musician in the years between the late 1940s and the mid-1950s, attracting a wide national audience and selling more records than any other national star.

Although Gonzaga's music was aimed squarely at rural migrants from the Northeast, his national appeal arose largely because of his ability to translate the experiences of the sertão to a broader audience. In so doing, he was able to reinforce the notion that the Northeast was truly the authentic source of Brazil's national culture. Gonzaga reached his audience through recordings, live performances, and nationally syndicated radio programs such as *No Mundo do Baião* (In the World of the Baião, on Rádio Nacional do Rio). During live broadcasts, he presented various musical genres (xote, baião, toada, xamego), which were clustered under the category of "música nordestina," or "northeastern music." Gonzaga's signature genre, the baião, came to represent northeastern music as a whole, and it achieved unprecedented commercial success on a national level through the radio broadcasts, live performances, and record sales. To build a national audience for northeastern music, the radio programs were carefully planned to address the listeners directly as "friends of the sertão." The live radio shows included didactic elements in which northeastern slang terms and common expressions from the sertão, precisely those found in Gonzaga's songs, were explained to the listeners. This strategy indicates that the audiences for the shows extended into the national realm, where such slang terms were not understood. Before a song was performed, the narrator frequently elaborated the theme and character of the piece and informed the audience of its significance. The intent to solidify Gonzaga's música nordestina as an authentic national style of popular music was evident in the introduction given before a performance of "No Meu Pé de Serra" during one radio broadcast (my translation):

> "There at the foothills of my homeland, I left my heart." That's how Humberto Teixeira and Luiz Gonzaga began the lyrics to the first song they ever wrote together. The success of this sentimental and heartfelt *xote* was responsible for the birth of the *baião* phenomenon, which is today an authentic national sensation within the field of popular music, as we all know. With its enthusiastic acceptance, folkloric northeastern music was planted in the large cities.[14]

Such introductions on the radio also linked the idea of rural authenticity directly to the baião and established the cultural continuity of the traditional values of the sertão to the new northeastern popular music of the cities. This music contrasted starkly with the foreign-influenced sound of the mainstream Brazilian popular music of the day. Narrations on the radio also helped to create a unified image for the various regional genres associated with the Northeast by elevating one of the genres, the baião, to the status of signature genre for the whole of música nordestina. In the mythical world created for música nordestina, the baião and its rhythm emerged from the premodern soul of sertanejo culture. Its mission and destiny was to become the heartbeat of all Brazilians. The introduction to the show *No Mundo do Baião* put it this way (my translation): "[The program] is going to focus on the customs, melodies and rhythms of the sertão. All of the original rhythms of the northern regions: côco, toada, xote, frevo, maracatu! And finally the baião, the rhythmic cadence that sprouted forth from the soul of the sertanejo to enchant the heart of all Brazil."[15]

By 1950, Gonzaga and his songwriting partners Humberto Teixeira and Ze Dantas were redefining the shape of Brazilian popular music. Two of their biggest hits were adaptations of traditional melodies and lyrics from the sertão: "Asa Branca" (1947) and "Juazeiro" (1949). The triumphant impact of the new northeastern style was the subject of Gonzaga's hit "A Dança da Moda" (The Dance of the Day), released in 1950. In the song (co-written by Ze Dantas), the new baião conquers Rio de Janeiro during the nights of the festivities for São João to become the "dance of the day."

However, it was the song titled simply "Baião," by Gonzaga and Teixeira that launched a craze that became a national obsession. For the creation of the new commercial genre that also came to be known as baião, Gonzaga drew on melodic and rhythmic elements of northeastern music that were distinct from the musical characteristics of European social dances such as the polkas, mazurkas, and schottisches. In various interviews, he stressed that the basic rhythmic idea he used for the baião existed in the sertão years before he utilized it in creating the new genre of popular music. For example, he stated (my translation):

> Before me, the *baião* already existed, but in a very indistinct and loose form. It was known as *baiano* in many parts of the Northeast. I mean, in its primitive form the *baião* was not a musical genre. It existed as a characteristic, as an introduction [played] by singers on their *violas*. It was a rhythm, a dance. Before tuning their viola, the singer plays an introduction.... When the singer ... feels that the viola is tuned properly, he beats [out a rhythm] on the soundboard, like this: t-chum, t-chum. I took the baião from this beat. [16]

Luiz Gonzaga and Humberto Teixeira based the rhythmic essence of the baião on this characteristic rhythmic pattern played by traditional viola players. As will be discussed in Chapter 6, in the improvised singing of cantoria, each performance segment of a desafio song duel is referred to as a baião. Before beginning each separate segment of the duel between the singers, a characteristic rhythmic pattern is played on the viola, which relates to the "baião" rhythm that Gonzaga referred to in the quote. This basic pattern is provided in Example 5.1.

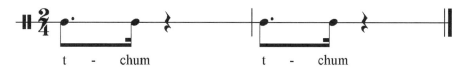

Example 5.1 Baião rhythm that Gonzaga extracted from viola players of the Northeast.

This simple syncopated rhythm features an accented stroke just before beat two (the "chum" Gonzaga mentioned) and became a distinctive marker and organizing principle for the baião. *Track 12* on the CD features this rhythm, played by the zabumba drum in the banda de pífano ensemble. The rhythm is closely related to similar rhythmic patterns present in numerous Afro-Brazilian music forms in the Northeast. One related cognate form is performed in a fast duple meter dance known as the *baiano* (literally meaning "someone from the state of Bahia"). The baiano genre is part of the musical repertoire that accompanies several danced dramas in the Northeast (caboclinhos, bumba-meu-boi, and cavalo-marinho). For example, in the cavalho-marinho popular in the coastal areas of Pernambuco, baiano dance tunes are played by an ensemble of rabeca (folk violin), pandeiro, cane scraper, and metal shaker. In addition, the dancers beat out the basic syncopated rhythm on their legs, using inflated bull bladders (*bexigas*), as shown in Example 5.2.[17]

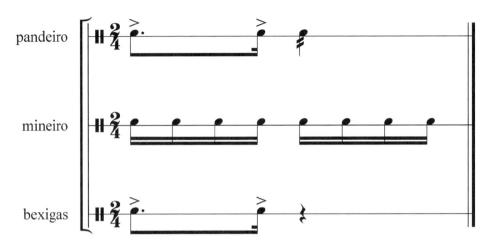

Example 5.2 Rhythmic accompaniment for a baiano as performed in cavalo-marinho.

Notice that the basic rhythm provided by the pandeiro and the bexiga (first and third lines) in the first half of the measure is identical to the pattern of the viola players that was incorporated by Gonzaga for the baião. Both the fast-paced baiano referenced earlier and the closely related *abaianada* (meaning "in the style of Bahia") rhythms are also present in the repertoires of the banda de pífanos ensembles found throughout the sertão. In an interview for a national weekly, Gonzaga himself once claimed, "When I was a kid, I used to play in those little *pífano* bands, and my instrument was the *zabumba* drum. When I decided to create the *baião*, I remembered the *zabumba*."[18]

In Pernambuco, the abaianada rhythm played by the banda de pífanos groups is also similar to a rural samba and employs systematic syncopation in the melodies and its rhythmic accompaniment. Informal dance parties in the rural areas of the Northeast where baianos and abaianadas are performed are frequently called sambas. John P. Murphy reported that in cavalo-marinho performances, the baiano may also be called *samba de matuto* (country hick or rural samba).[19]

During field research I conducted in Pernambuco between 1984 and 1988, several banda de pífano musicians informed me that the abaianada rhythm is much older than the baião. This information is consistent with the research of Brazilian folklorists. The same basic rhythmic pattern played on the zabumba drum that Gonzaga used to define the baião is also present in the côco, an Afro-Brazilian music and dance characteristic of the coastal areas of the Northeast. For the côco, the rhythm is performed on the pandeiro and the zabumba. On the pandeiro, the côco is performed in the manner indicated in Example 5.3.

Example 5.3 Côco rhythm on the pandeiro

The first two accented notes in Example 5.3 (the notes written below the line) are played with an open tone on the drum and articulate this same syncopated figure. By drawing on this rhythmic figure, so common among a variety of northeastern forms, Gonzaga was able to condense a wide range of musical experiences within the commercial baião that referenced both northeastern Afro-Brazilian and sertão culture.

The song titled "Baião" also featured a melodic quality that emphasized a lowered tone on the seventh note of the scale. Modal scales were introduced to the Brazilian Northeast during the early colonial period through the Catholic Church and missionary work. Modal scales were subsequently incorporated into many of the song and dance genres of the Northeast.

With the distinctive melodic and rhythmic qualities of the baião, Gonzaga could now lay claim to a uniquely Brazilian form that paralleled and exemplified the notion of Brazilian racial and cultural mixture. Clearly aware of its potential, he and his songwriting partners reinforced the idea of the baião's mixed nature through both musical and lyrical means. For instance, the lyrics to "Braia Dengosa" (written by Ze Dantas and Gonzaga) construct a mixed pedigree for the baião. In the song, the rhythm of the maracatu (described as a black dance) and the melody of the *fado* (representing Portuguese heritage) unite to produce the baião.[20]

Extolled as a national virtue since the 1930s, the notion of cultural miscegenation had also symbiotically accompanied the valorization and commercial success of the samba. Popularized through the mass media of radio broadcasts and recordings, samba had risen to dominate Brazil's mainstream commercial music. However, by the 1940s, mainstream samba was also increasingly influenced by contemporary trends in international popular music emanating from the United States and the Caribbean. Now, in the late 1940s, Brazil was ripe for a new musical style that could reconnect its citizenry to the country's regional roots. In this period, Gonzaga recorded the song "Baião" (1949), with a "regional" backup group featuring pandeiro, guitar, cavaquinho, gourd shaker, and zabumba drum. The sound of this music was far removed from anything emanating from Brazil's North American neighbors.

On recordings made between 1946 and 1949, Gonzaga experimented with several instrumental arrangements in order to refine the rhythmic accompaniment for the baião. For instance, on another release of 1949, titled "Vem Morena" ("Come Here Dark-Haired Woman"), co-written with his new partner, Ze Dantas, the percussion accompaniment included: (1) the addition of a triangle, which doubled the pandeiro part, and (2) an agogô bell, replacing the *xequere*. Additionally, the zabumba part was simplified, creating a more syncopated feel. These elements were present as early as 1947 with Gonzaga's recording of "Asa Branca." Though listed on the recording as a toada, the rhythmic accompaniment was, in essence, what would later be identified as the baião rhythm.

In Example 5.4, the zabumba drum provides that same distinctive "t-chum" syncopation that Gonzaga referred to in a quote earlier in this chapter.

By the early 1950s, Gonzaga had settled on a trio format of accordion, triangle, and zabumba drum that would distinguish the baião and other forms of música nordestina from the more generic "regional" combos of the music studios in Rio de Janeiro. In both visual and sonic dimensions, this instrumental format was distinct from the samba's

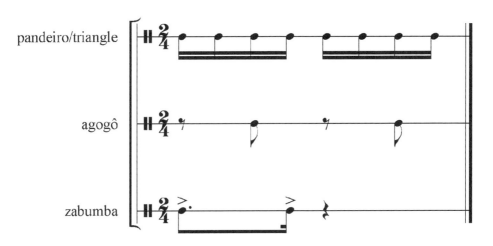

pandeiro/triangle

agogô

zabumba

Example 5.4 Rhythmic accompaniment to "Vem Morena" (1949)

instrumentation and served to solidify Gonzaga's northeastern music as a commercially viable alternative to Brazil's mainstream popular music.

For a period of ten years, from 1946 to 1956, Gonzaga's success was at its peak. During that period, Luiz Gonzaga was Brazil's most frequently recorded musical star. His success established so-called regional music as a commercially viable product in the Brazilian music industry, and it also made him the de facto national spokesman for the millions of northeastern migrant workers in the industrialized cities of central and southern Brazil.

Figure 5.1
Northeastern accordion trio (triangle, accordion, zabumba drum), Salvador, Bahia, 1982 (photo by Larry Crook).

Although Gonzaga remained the undisputed king of the baião and of northeastern music, other popular musicians from the Northeast rose to national prominence in the 1950s and 1960s. Chief among these new stars was Jackson do Pandeiro, who mixed the traditional regional sounds of the northeastern côco with the samba.

Jackson do Pandeiro, the Forró, and the Legacy of Luiz Gonzaga

Unlike Luiz Gonzaga, whose cultural roots were planted firmly in the soil of the northeastern sertão, Jackson do Pandeiro had grown up closer to the coast in the state of Paraíba, where the preferred social entertainment was the Afro-Brazilian côco, a lively music and dance genre closely related to the folk samba. The coastal area included more Afro-Brazilian influences. As a youth, Jackson played the zabumba drum at local côco gatherings, and by his early twenties, he was a professional singer and pandeiro player in nightclubs. In 1945, he joined the jazz orchestra of Rádio Tabajara in the state capital, and later, he moved to Recife, where he was a pandeiro player in the radio orchestra of the Rádio Jornal do Commércio. These professional experiences exposed him to a wide range of international dance music genres of the era (congas, boleros, tangos, blues, rumbas) and to the full range of Brazilian popular music.[21] Jackson began experimenting with commercial adaptations of northeastern genres, and he performed with local singer Benigno de Carvalho, who specialized in the embolada repertoire of Manezinho Araújo. In 1953, Jackson made his first record, with a côco titled "Sebastiana" and the *rojão* (an alternate name sometimes used for baiao) "Forró em Limoeira." Influenced by the advent of Luiz Gonzaga and the baião fad, these songs featured the distinctly northeastern regional ensemble sound of accordion, zabumba, and triangle, together with a prominent role for the pandeiro (Jackson's signature instrument), maracas, cavaquinho, bass, and agogô. Luiz Gonzaga's image evoked the country lifestyle and values of the rural Northeast, but Jackson do Pandeiro cut a more urbane and street-smart figure. After he relocated to Rio de Janeiro, he became one of Brazilian music's most colorful characters and scored a number of hits mixing his northeastern sound with samba. One of his most enduring and influential hits was "Chiclete com Bananas" ("Chewing Gum with Bananas"). The song is a satirical critique of excessive American influence and the typical failure of Americans to understand Latin American cultural diversity: "I'll only put bebop in my *samba*, / when Uncle Sam plays the *tamborim*, / when he grabs a *pandeiro*, / and a *zabumba*, / when he learns that the samba isn't the rumba."

Beyond his seminal contributions to the nationalization of northeastern sounds within mainstream urban Brazilian music, Jackson, along with Gonzaga, was also influential in stimulating new interest among migrant musicians. These musicians followed the lead of Jackson and Gonzaga and copied their music, and they employed variations of the trio format of accordion, zabumba drum, and triangle established by Gonzaga and expanded by Jackson as the core instrumentation for a neotraditional style of music called forró. Forró sprang up in the late 1950s in the informal urban dance halls of Brazil's major cities in the South that catered to audiences of northeastern migrants. The term *forró*, an abbreviation of *forrobodo* (an older term that had been used in the Northeast to designate dances of the common people), came to describe the social dancing events of the northeastern migrants. The name encapsulated not only the earthy yet urban musical style of forró itself but also the entire milieu of the working-class dance halls, the party atmosphere, and the expression of northeastern cultural identity through music and dance identified with that musical style.

During that period, forró was not just a single dance-music genre. Rather, it encompassed several genres, such as the xote, baião, waltz, arrasta-pé, and côco. This was largely the same set of country dances long favored by the rural population of the Northeast and those initially referenced by Luiz Gonzaga, Jackson do Pandeiro, and other popular musicians. Within urban areas, forró clubs became important sites of leisure activity for the working-class migrants: construction workers, domestic helpers, and others in low-paying occupations. Forró clubs first emerged in Rio de Janeiro soon after Gonzaga's initial success in the 1950s, and by the early 1960s, they appeared in São Paulo as well. The construction of the new capital of the country, Brasília, also drew thousands of northeastern migrant construction workers to central Brazil in the late 1950s, and forró clubs opened literally overnight.

Capitalizing on the new wave of northeastern music, many forró trios and other small combos emerged. Like garage band musicians, the members of these groups dreamed of landing recording contracts and scoring hit singles. For the most part, however, they performed covers of the songs made popular by the stars of northeastern music. By the early 1960s, a syncopated and slightly faster variant of the baião rhythm emerged, which itself came to be known as forró. This new genre, defined musically by the zabumba drum part, featured a loud muffled stroke before the second beat of the measure and a syncopated counter rhythm played with a thin stick on the underside of the drum.

The term *forró* had appeared in songs recorded by both Gonzaga ("Forró de Mané Vito" (1949)) and Jackson do Pandeiro ("Forró em Limoeiro" (1953)) in the late 1940s and 1950s. However, in these earlier manifestations, the term had been used in the traditional sense of a northeastern dance party. Now, in the early 1960s, the word referred to a genre as well and replaced the older term *baião* as the accepted designation of northeastern dance music in general.

Through their own innovations and their influences on other developments such as the baião and the forró, both Luiz Gonzaga and Jackson do Pandeiro helped establish northeastern popular music as an integral part of Brazil's national music. Gonzaga must be credited with taking the initial steps in this process and acknowledged as the key popular musician giving voice to Brazil's rural poor from the Northeast. With Gonzaga's national popularity, the marginalized segment of the population found a way in which to participate in the national dialogue, which redefined the nation's racial and cultural identity. After the advent of the baião, it was no longer possible to view the country as merely a homogeneous mestizo culture.

PART III

Focusing In: Intimate Portraits and the Reinvention of Brazilian Music

"Focusing In: Intimate Portraits and the Reinvention of Brazilian Music" presents in-depth portraits of contemporary musicians and musical culture in Northeast Brazil and highlights the ways in which they move among local, national, and international realms. Chapter 6 focuses on two rural-associated folk traditions: the *bandas de pífanos* (fife-and-drum bands) and the improvised sung poetry of *cantoria de viola*. Musicians João do Pife, and poet–singers Edmilson Fereira, and Antônio Lisboa are profiled. Chapter 7 explores contemporary urban popular music and musicians from Salvador, Bahia and Recife, Pernambuco. In Salvador, long regarded as the center of Afro-Brazilian culture, musicians in the *bloco afro* carnival groups highlight African heritage and diasporic identity through music and simultaneously contest the idea of Brazil as a racially egalitarian nation. The famous blocos afro Ilê Aiyé and Olodum are profiled. In Recife, the eclectic style of popular music known as mangue beat is examined through profiles of three important groups: Chico Science & Nação Zumbi, Mestre Ambrósio, and Cascabulho.

CHAPTER 6

Two Case Studies from the Northeast:
Banda de Pífanos and Cantoria de Viola

Those who visit the famous folk-arts market in Caruaru, Pernambuco, will possibly encounter a flutist named João do Pife. His main instrument is the pífano (or *pife* for short), an open-holed cane flute. *Track 7* on the CD is a recording of João performing with his friend Tavares da Gaita (playing on a percussion instrument he calls a bamboo reco-som). Tavares—a creative inventor of percussion instruments and a master harmonica player in his own right—often visits João at the market; he considers his close friend the best pífano player in Caruaru and maybe in all of Brazil. Many other people do as well. João and Tavares enjoy playing together, improvising around the tunes they have played for many years and composing other pieces on the spot. Listen to *Track 7* and notice how Tavares manipulates the sound qualities of his bamboo scraper to match João's improvisations on the pífano. João is a musical institution in Caruaru and has been making, selling, and playing pífanos at the folk-arts market in Caruaru since 1984; since the early 1990s, he has traveled to Europe and North America six or seven times to perform pífano music with his own group, the Banda de Pífanos Dois Irmãos (Two Brothers Band of Pífanos). He has also traveled by himself to the United States as a guest artist, performing and teaching about his musical love, the pífano. I first met João in the early 1980s, when I was traveling around the Northeast.

Until the advent of modern broadcast communications and better roads, the isolated northeastern interior of Brazil was an area comparable to the Wild West of the United States. After the prosperous sugarcane colonies along the coastal strip of the Northeast were established in the 1600s, the interior regions began to be settled as the cattle industry pushed westward and Portuguese settlers intermixed with the indigenous populations of the area. Villages and towns emerged along cattle trails and regional markets for the cattle trade established important locations for cultural and economic exchange among the rural-based caboclo populations. The decentralized nature of Brazil's colonial coastal

Figure 6.1 Picture of Juazeiro do Norte, Ceará, 1987 (photo by Larry Crook).

Figure 6.2 João do Pife selling pífanos at the artisan's market, Caruaru, Pernambuco, 1987 (photo by Sylvia Crook).

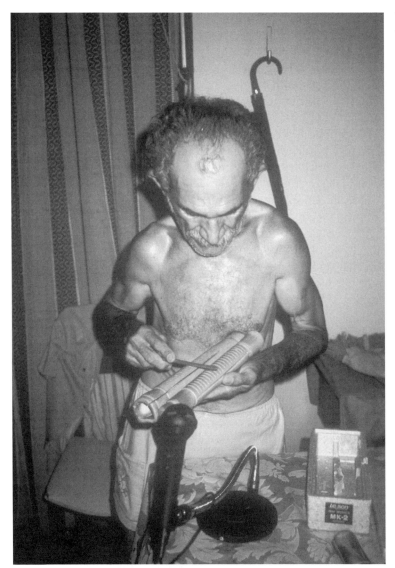

Figure 6.3
Tavares da Gaita
playing two
bamboo reco-som
scrapers, Caruaru,
Pernambuco,
2001 (photo by
Larry Crook).

society was paralleled by a largely unregulated life in the wild interior regions of the Northeast. In this environment, a domestic-centered, folk Catholicism with roots in medieval Portugal flourished. This religion was not the official Catholicism of the Roman Catholic Church but rather a popular form similar to the folk practices of Europe since the Middle Ages. The church's direct involvement in the life of interior communities was attenuated because of geographic isolation and poor travel conditions. There simply were not enough priests to minister to the rural populations, and those priests who were sent into the interior were left largely on their own. The result was the creation of a vibrant folk Catholicism led by lay specialists who focused their devotion on various "saints" (both recognized and unrecognized by the Roman Catholic Church).

The cult of saints that developed in the Northeast left indelible marks on the musical traditions of the area, and several distinct musical activities developed in conjunction with the folk Catholicism there. For example, hymns and praise songs were sung to the saints, and local instrumental practices were developed to accompany the rituals conducted in honor of those saints. In the nineteenth century, the cultural practices of the mixed-race caboclo population intertwined with military band music and accordions and brought European dance genres into the area. Local musicians playing on guitars, fifes, violins, drums, and the newly introduced accordions transformed these foreign sources into northeastern country dance music, which came to epitomize the rural folkways of the interior region. In addition, a rich tradition of improvised poetry also took hold among the singer–guitar players in the Northeast. These developments represent some of the core traditions that have musically defined the northeastern sertão region as a bastion of rural folkways and as the country's main cultural preserve of its agrarian past.

In this chapter, I will focus on two important musical traditions of the interior that represent the cultural folkways of the caboclo population. First, I will investigate one of the most revered instrumental traditions of the Northeast—the fife-and-drum ensembles known as the bandas de pífanos. This is the type of ensemble that João do Pife has played in since he was a young boy. These ensembles are the preferred musical accompaniment for a range of social and religious festivities of the caboclo population. Although identified closely with rural life, banda de pífanos musicians maintain close links to urban centers, where they perform as "folkloric" groups and present stylized enactments of rural folk culture. Next, I will discuss the poet–singer tradition of cantoria de viola, which draws substantially on medieval Portuguese heritage and features complex poetic forms and accompaniment by the guitar-like viola. Through an analysis of the poetic and musical components of this tradition and the biographies of Edmilson Ferriera and Antônio Lisboa, two contemporary musicians, one can gain an appreciation of today's cantoria and the way in which contemporary musicians operate in the rural and urban environments of Brazil.

João do Pife and the Banda de Pífanos

> I make the fife, I play the fife, I sell the fife, I eat money from the fife, and after I'm old I'll be totally fifed-out. Ha ha ha ha ha!
>
> (João do Pife, quoted to author)

João Alfredo dos Santos was born in 1942 in Sítio Chambá, a small hamlet about 40 miles northeast of Caruaru. His father worked the land as a farmer but had a passion for music. João's father played pífano and led an instrumental musical group named Zabumba Três Marcos. The small fife-and-drum instrumental group in the Northeast has traditionally been called the zabumba and more recently has acquired the name banda de pífanos (literally meaning "band of fifes"). Other names for this type of instrumental ensemble are *banda cabaçal, terno de zabumba,* and *esquenta mulher.* The musical group always has two pífanos, a zabumba bass drum, and a tarol snare drum. Frequently, other percussion instruments, such as a pair of hand cymbals, a small tenor drum, or a triangle, are also added.

Figure 6.4 Banda de Pífanos Dois Irmãos, Caruaru, Pernambuco, 2001 (photo by Larry Crook).

Small instrumental ensembles of fifes and drums have been common in the interior of the Northeast since at least the early nineteenth century and probably much longer. Among the rural caboclo population of the sertão, these ensembles are the preferred musical accompaniment for a range of social festivities and religious rituals, especially the *novena de casa* (house novena) prayer sessions given by individuals in honor of saints and other popular religious figures. The novena de casa is the most important traditional occasion for banda de pífanos music, and in the rural areas, many groups get together only when a novena is organized and they have been asked to perform. The musicians are invited to perform to help honor the saint during a religious procession and as part of a prayer session. They also are called on to animate the secular festivities of the party, which lasts until the wee hours of the morning. For some bandas de pífanos, these are the only public performances they give. The Zabumba Três Marcos of João's father was that kind of a musical group.

Pífano: A Blessed Instrument
By the time he was twelve, João was performing in his father's group at novenas de casa, together with his older brother. In 1987, I was living in Pernambuco and researching the

folk music of the area, and I asked João to tell me why bandas de pífanos are so frequently invited to perform for novenas de casa. He responded:

> This is the story of a novena procession. It's a tradition that comes sanctioned by God, our Father in heaven. What we believe, then, is that this is why we have the novena. Everybody praying and beseeching God. In other words, this is a tradition that has persisted. So, when it began . . . the mother of God with the young child God in her arms at the front, [she] said, "Let's have a procession." Then [she said], "Let's go ahead." An accordion player arrived, playing. And there she was with everybody praying, [João imitated the praying] "Our Heavenly Father, who art in heaven. . . ." And everyone else [praying] to her, "Ave Maria, Ave Maria, Ave Maria." So . . . there was this accordion player in the middle of the path. [He said,] "Well, I'm going to play along. You can't have a procession by itself. Not all by itself. [If it's] like that not everyone will pray. No, that won't do! [João imitated the sound of an accordion] Fa fa fa fa fa!" She [Mary] said, "No, not an accordion!" In a little bit, there came a viola, [João imitated the sound of a viola] "Ta ta ta ta ta!" A viola. Nossa Senhora said, "No! I don't want it." But is it possible? Is there going to be a procession and no one will play for it? I know that there was an accordion, a viola, there arrived more instruments, rabeca, all of the instruments that there are. "No, they won't do!" In a little bit, there arrived . . .

João then turned and looked directly at me as if to emphasize this next point and continued:

> This is a tradition. In a little bit, there arrived a person. With a pife, like this one [he held up a pífano]. There arrived a pife and a zabumba drum and a snare drum. Three, three arrived! Then, at that very moment, when the procession of Nossa Senhora arrived, a little old black man came along playing the pífano [João played the pífano]. Now, this is a procession! It didn't leave. It remained in the same place and then a zabumba, a snare drum, and a pair of cymbals arrived. Then it started. Nossa Senhora went on and said, "Good! Now the procession will continue." So our Eternal Father, Nosso Senhor—the young child God in her arms—said, "Let the procession continue forward. Let's go ahead. Because now there is a pífano playing." So I live from this instrument. It is a blessed instrument.[1]

Pifeiros (pífano players) such as João live with a strong sense of tradition. When he stopped his story about the first procession that used the pífano and emphasized that "this is a tradition," he was making sure I understood the importance of what he was relating. A tradition to João is something that has cultural authenticity and values passed down over the generations. His story in the form of a legend was a way for him to share with me some of the cultural logic that links his instrument, the pífano, to the fundamental religious values of caboclo culture. Pífano musicians do not earn much money playing at long and arduous novenas de casa. But they consider their devotion to pífano music as a religious devotion to the folk Catholicism of the area. For musicians such as João, the pífano is truly a blessed instrument.

Origins

The precise origins of the ensemble known as the banda de pífanos have never been uncovered. The most convincing hypothesis is that these caboclo ensembles were modeled on fife-and-drum groups first brought to Northeast Brazil by the Portuguese during the colonial period, perhaps as early as the sixteenth or seventeenth century. From the early settlements on the coast, they must have been taken into the interior by Portuguese settlers. In Portugal and Spain, musical groups called *bombos*, comprising bass drums, snare drums, triangles, and fifes, have performed for religious occasions for many years. In addition, military music from Portugal and Spain in the early colonial period featured fife-and-drum groups similar to the bandas de pífanos. Such Iberian-style musical ensembles likely served as the initial inspiration and prototypes for the development of the bandas de pífanos in Northeast Brazil. Pernambucan musicologist Jaime Diniz has cited expense records from the Santo Antônio Church in Recife to pay for hiring zabumbas for religious processions there as early as 1821.[2] Around that time, groups that featured charamelas (double-reed wind instruments brought from Portugal, see Chapter 1) and military drums also probably used the name zabumba. The ambiguity of the word *zabumba* continues to this day. The term can refer both to the large bass drum used in the ensemble and to the entire ensemble itself. In the past, the term may have also been applied to several different types of ensembles incorporating wind and percussion instruments. A possible African origin for the banda de pífanos ensemble has been suggested by Brazilian folklorist Abelardo Duarte.[3] Duarte has argued that when the Portuguese abandoned the sugarcane industry on the island of São Tomé off the west coast of Africa, many white and black colonists went to Northeast Brazil, taking with them not only the sugarcane industry but also the zabumba ensemble.

Many others cite the numerous flute traditions that were already present among the Amerindian Brazilian populations when the Portuguese first arrived in Brazil, asserting an indigenous origin for the banda de pífanos. Pifeiros themselves most often offer accounts of an indigenous origin for the instrument as well as for the banda de pífanos ensemble. João do Pife tells symbolically sophisticated stories connecting an indigenous origin to the development of the banda de pífanos tradition in the context of race relations and class formation in Brazil. Here is a story João told me in 1988:

> The banda de pífanos came from the Indian. And the zabumba drum, they took wood, those round tree trunks from the forest, killed animals, skinned [them] and then fastened the skin with vine. They made and played whistles from cane and fire. It [the pífano tradition] began from the breath of the Indian. Then later . . . the Indians were domesticated, working as house servants, and were teaching others [about the pífanos]. Because there were both savage Indians, those from the forest . . . and the ones that were already domesticated, that already married with Brazilian girls.
>
> So then [the Indian] was entering Brazil, teaching those old caboclos. Teaching, giving lessons, teaching about the zabumba. So from the start emerged the banda de pífanos. It was the creation of the Indians.[4]

In this story, João situated the origins of the instruments of the banda de pífanos within the national narrative of the emergence of the mixed-race caboclo population. The original flute came directly from the breath of the savage Indians of the forest. It was then domesticated, like the original caboclo population. The link to indigenous culture gives the pífano a profound sense of authenticity that ties it directly to the land of the Northeast. Simultaneously, João also linked the banda de pífanos to the class structure of haves and have-nots that emerged in Brazilian colonial society. On another occasion, João related:

> Bandas de pífanos, this was never anything among other types of people, it was born among the savage Indian, the Indian of the forest. . . . It was only the mulatto, the black, and the caboclo who took this up and played this here, . . . it's not something for whites.[5]

The class structure and system of racial identification that developed in Brazil over some 500 years articulated a socioeconomic system in which an upper-class, predominantly white European elite was economically and culturally separated from the non-elite population. It is not surprising that this situation was embedded in musical traditions such as the banda de pífanos. When João stated that the banda de pífanos was "not something for the whites," he was commenting on the historical factors involved in the construction of racial identities in Brazil. As noted in Chapter 1, racial and ethnic mixing was profound from the beginning of colonization and produced not only a miscegenated population but also dozens of terms for multiraced progeny. In Brazil, racial classifications conflate physical characteristics with the social, cultural, and economic status of individuals. Bandas de pífanos have always historically drawn their membership exclusively from the poor, rural inhabitants of the interior, and this link persists in contemporary Brazil. Although many pifeiros have moved to the cities and some, such as João do Pife, have even built successful artistic careers, these caboclo musicians continue to maintain lifestyles closely tied to their rural roots. And the pífano continues to be a blessed instrument for them.

Instruments of the Banda de Pífanos

Four core instruments make up a banda de pífanos: a pair of pífanos, a zabumba, and a tarol. These instruments are found in all bandas de pífanos and are considered the original components of the ensemble. In addition, the surdo, or small tenor drum, and a pair of hand cymbals (*pratos*) are commonly added.

The art of making pífanos has been handed down from generation to generation. The instruments are made from the taquara cane plant, which until recently grew abundantly in many forest areas of the Northeast. (In early December 2000, I traveled with João into rural southern Pernambuco in search of taquara. We encountered numerous hunters and farmers who informed us that the cane is becoming harder and harder to find.) Traditionally, pífanos were not tuned to a specific or absolute pitch. Rather, each pair of pífanos were made and tuned so that they could play together harmoniously in a single banda de pífanos. As João and other pifeiros showed me many times, pífanos come in three basic lengths: *meia-regra* (15 3/4 to 17 3/4 inches/400 to 450mm), *três-quartos*

Figure 6.5 João do Pife making a pífano in his home, Caruaru, Pernambuco, 1988 (photo by Larry Crook).

(18 3/4 to 19 1/2 inches/476 to 495mm), and *regra-inteira* (19 1/2 to 23 1/2 inches/495 to 597mm). Pífanos in all three sizes have seven holes, which are burned out with a hot iron poker. Six of the holes are for the fingers, and one is for the mouth.

To determine the length of the instrument and the position of the holes, pífano makers use different dimensions of their hands: the distance from the thumb to the forefinger, the width of three fingers, the width of the index finger, and so on. In various combinations, these measurements can be used to make the three sizes of pífanos. Because the hands of different pifeiros can vary greatly in size, the exact dimensions of pífanos can also vary from one maker to the next. Once made, a pífano is duplicated so that a second instrument is identical to the first. In a banda de pífanos, the identical tuning of two pífanos is needed to fulfill the musical requirements for playing together.

A brief explanation of the general tuning of the instruments and the way they play together is in order here. Even though the exact size and pitch varies, all pífanos have similar tuning characteristics related to the basic construction of the instrument. The basic scale produced on a pífano features seven notes. The scale produced by simply uncovering each successive hole is close to a major scale but with slightly lower second, third, sixth, and seventh scale degrees. This intonation produces scales that can be ambiguously between major and minor. Especially at the third and seventh scale degrees, pifeiros tend to produce notes almost evenly spaced between the major and minor third and seventh (in relation to the lowest note on the instrument). These qualities are further emphasized by the pifeiros, who bend the pitches by rolling the pífano and by half covering certain finger holes. These techniques and the intonation of the instruments give a distinct tonal quality to banda de pífanos music.

When two pífeiros perform, the second pífano plays a supporting role to the first. In many of the pieces that are performed, the first pífano plays the main melody and the second plays a parallel melody either higher or lower in pitch, usually at the interval of a diatonic third. In other words, each pífano plays essentially the same melodic contour but at different pitch levels. Because the two pífanos are tuned to each other, both instruments have the ability to conform to the same scale.

The traditional drums that accompany the pífanos are hand-made wooden drums with goatskin membranes. Recently, many musicians have adopted industrialized metal drums with plastic membranes. The zabumba drum is a double-headed instrument roughly 19 1/2 inches (495mm) in diameter and about 15 3/4 inches (400mm) deep. Traditionally, the shell of the drum was carved from a single tree trunk, but today, it is more common to fashion the shell by bending a piece of plywood into a cylinder and then nailing and gluing it in place. Two counter hoops of solid wood are also bent into a circle and serve to pull the skin membranes tightly over the main shell of the drum with rope lacing. The surdo and tarol can be made in essentially the same way but are of different sizes. However, an industrialized snare drum with plastic membranes and mechanical lug tensioning is preferred over the traditional wood-and-skin tarol because its tuning lasts much longer and produces a crisper sound. Finally, a pair of industrially produced hand cymbals complete the ensemble.

Music of the Bandas de Pífanos

> Until the hour of the novena [is over] we only play authentic music: a novena march, a dobrado, a procession waltz, prayer, praise song, these kinds of things, you know. Then, after the novena, our group has a drink, yeah. Then [the people] want something hotter, something that swings in a different way, forró.
>
> (Biu do Pife)

The music performed by bandas de pífanos can be grouped into two distinct repertoires: (1) religious music dedicated to the popular saints of Northeast Brazil, and (2) secular music for dancing and party merriment. Biu do Pife (another pifeiro from Caruaru) indicated this bi-stylistic distinction in repertoire in the preceding quote. The religious repertoire—called *música do santo* (music of the saint) or simply *música de novena* (novena music)—is performed during the religious portions of the novena de casa and derives primarily from Catholic Church hymns and from praise songs known as *benditos*. The religious repertoire also includes instrumental pieces that are modeled on the marches, *dobrados* (half-time marches), waltzes, and other genres popularized by military bands in Brazil. The main source of the secular repertoire is the social dance music of the Northeast, which features many genres of European-derived dances as well as uniquely Brazilian dance forms. This repertoire is partly shared with accordion-based ensembles and draws heavily on northeastern popular music. The modern strains of this repertoire are called forró.

Figure 6.6
A statue of Padre Cícero at a novena de casa, Caruaru, Pernambuco, 1988 (photo by Larry Crook).

MÚSICA DO SANTO—THE SAINT'S MUSIC

The *hinos* (hymns) and benditos that bandas de pífanos play are based on many well-known melodies sung in church, at religious festivals, for religious processions, and during the long pilgrimages to religious shrines in towns such as Juazeiro do Norte, Ceará. Women tend to dominate the singing and the praying that accompany the various manifestations of the folk Catholicism of the Northeast. This gender-specific role is related to cultural notions linking women to the domestic-centered folk Catholicism in that area. Women and men do not participate equally in the public performance of music. Almost all forms of music making (instrumental and vocal, private and public) are available to men, but this is not true for women. Traditionally, women's public music performance has been restricted primarily to the realm of singing. In rural-rooted musical traditions, women's participation in music making is generally further limited to the singing of religious music. Bandas de pífanos musicians (who are always male) frequently mention that the música do santo repertoire is based not only on the religious songs that women sing (a repertoire of specific melodies) but also on the characteristic way in which women prefer to sing these songs (a style of singing). These qualities of the religious repertoire of the bandas de pífanos nest this music within a symbolic domain that connects religiosity and women.

Figure 6.7
Women singing novena praise songs, Caruaru, Pernambuco, 1988 (photo by Larry Crook).

Contemporary pifeiros such as João do Pife also make a clear distinction between an older style of playing and a modernized one. According to this distinction, the older style is linked directly to the música de santo repertoire, whereas the modernized playing is linked to the social dance music repertoire. Stylistically, the música do santo is performed in a restrained manner, without melodic or rhythmic demonstrations of virtuosity. The pifeiros render their melodies in a simple, unadorned manner and connect the notes to each other in a smooth, legato fashion. This is precisely the way in which women sing songs and recite prayers at novenas de casa. In fact, hinting at the religious and pious nature of this style of singing, both praying and singing at novenas are frequently referred to with the verb *rezar*, literally meaning "to pray." On *Track 8* of the CD, which I recorded at a novena de casa ceremony, one can hear both the singing/praying of men and women and the instrumental playing of a banda de pífanos. This took place during the praying of one-third of the rosary in a novena de casa in a small town in the interior of Pernambuco. The praying moved directly into the singing of the devotional praise song "Bendita e Louvada Seja" ("Blessed and Praised May You Be"). As soon as the singing was complete, the banda de pífanos played an instrumental version of the same song.

Most of the hymns and praise songs that are sung at novenas de casa are formally structured into two simple melodic sections that correspond to the verse and refrain of the song texts. These two sections may be ordered in several ways. The most basic ordering is a simple alternation of the two sections (which can be represented by the letters *A* and *B*): *AB*. Other common combinations of the two sections of melody are *ABB*, *AABB*, and *AAB*. The songs are performed in a loose feeling of two or three beats (duple or triple meter). The exact length of the melodic phrases may vary from one song to the next and even among multiple performances of the same song. Banda de pífanos musicians refer to the tendency for such variability in musical phrasing, rhythm, and meter as "women's rhythm." When women (as well as men) sing these songs, the notes at the end of phrases often are held briefly, which temporarily suspends the duple or triple meter. Bandas de pífanos sometimes imitate this practice by adding extra beats at the end of melodic phrases when they perform a hymn or a bendito instrumentally.

Melodically, the música do santo songs emphasize stepwise motion from one note of the scale to the next with occasional skips of small intervals in the melody. These lyrical qualities derive from the hymn-singing tradition. Melodic sequencing (repeating the same short melodic contour in an ascending or descending sequence) is also common. The percussion accompaniment for the religious repertoire features simple rhythmic schemes coordinating the instruments to produce a strong emphasis on the main beats of the meter.

In performance, the drummers are expected to play their parts without overpowering the pífanos and without giving loud accents or embellishing the basic patterns. All of this is aimed at producing an overall sound that is aesthetically coherent with the devotional function of the music. Just as someone should not shout in church, a drummer should not give an excessively loud stroke on his drum during a novena de casa, at least not in front of the statue of the saint.

The banda de pífanos performs the música do santo repertoire with reverence and a sense of devotional obligation. In truth, many of the musicians themselves are devotees of Catholic saints, especially the religious figure Padre Cícero. They fulfill their own

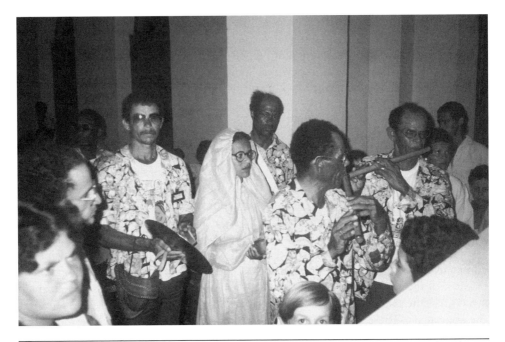

Figure 6.8 Participants at a novena de casa in Bezerros, Pernambuco, 1988 (photo by Larry Crook).

religious obligations through performing their music. A special act of supplication by the musicians is the *vênia do santo* (kneeling before the saint), a short musical offering made by a banda de pífanos in front of the saint. During a vênia do santo, the musicians kneel and symbolically kiss the base of the saint's statue and perform several pieces of music from the música do santo repertoire. In addition to performing instrumental covers of religious songs, bandas de pífanos also play religious music that is instrumental in both conception and performance. At novenas de casa, these pieces are performed mainly during the procession and during other religious events occurring outside the house. The percussion schemes for these pieces are structurally the same as the patterns used for the hinos and benditos. However, they are often performed at a quicker tempo and include more ornamentation and individual shows of technique on both the pífanos and the percussion instruments. Additionally, pifeiros play these pieces in a more staccato, detached manner. These pieces are grouped into different genres called *marchas* (marches), dobrados, *agalopadas* (galloped pieces), and *valsas* (waltzes). All of these genres except the waltzes are in duple meter.

In contrast to the lyric nature of the religious songs, the melodies of the instrumental pieces emphasize melodic skips, the outlining of chords, and rhythmic activity through the repetition of pitches. The "Marcha de Novena" by the Banda de Pífanos Dois Irmãos on *Track 9* of the CD illustrates these qualities. This melody is constructed over an alternation of the outlining of tonic to dominant harmonies. In the *B* section of the piece, the tonic triad and dominant seven chords are outlined. Another common feature of marchas and dobrados exhibited in this example is the symmetrical nature of the two sections and phrase lengths of even numbers. In "Marcha de Novena," both *A* and *B* sections are eight measures in length. Each section is further divided into two phrases or subsections of four measures each.

Although symmetrical sections and subsections are the norm for instrumental pieces, odd numbers of measures within sections and phrases are not unusual. For example, the marcha "Arrancada da Bandeira" ("Hoisting up the Flag") by the Banda de Pífanos São João has an *A* section of twelve measures and an irregular *B* section that is seven measures long. The *B* section is made even more irregular with the insertion of an added beat in its last measure, thereby transforming it into a measure with three beats. *Track 10* features the "Arrancada da Bandeira" piece.

Two instrumental genres closely related to the marcha are the agalopada and the *baiano* (Bahian piece). These are old genres that have disappeared from the repertoire of many bandas de pífanos. The melodic characteristics of these genres include the outlining of chords other than tonic and dominant and an occasional extension of harmonies to seventh and ninth scale degrees. In addition, sections and phrasing are not as clearly articulated in these genres as in the marcha. Finally, instrumental waltzes may also be performed for the various religious portions of the novena de casa. Set in triple meter, these pieces tend to be more lyrical in nature than the marchas, but in form and structure, they are quite similar.

FORRÓ: SOMETHING HOTTER

The music used to animate the secular party of the novena de casa—as well as the radio programs, tourist presentations, and occasional dance parties at which bandas de pífanos perform—is drawn from several sources. One is a repertoire of pieces unique to the banda de pífanos tradition called *brincadeiras* (games), which includes imitations of farm animals (goats, donkeys, roosters, chickens, bulls), insects (bees, wasps, fleas, mosquitoes), and especially songbirds of the Northeast. The banda de pífano tradition from Juazeiro do Norte, Ceará, is particularly rich in this repertoire. Trains, cars, and other objects may also be imitated. The most famous of such pieces is "Briga do Cachorro com a Onça" ("Fight of the Dog with the Jaguar"). This piece was popularized throughout Brazil when the group Zabumba Caruaru recorded it in the early 1970s. Since that time, it has become one of the signature pieces of the banda de pífanos tradition. Unlike the música do santo, most of the brincadeira pieces feature short, repeated rhythmic/melodic patterns (*ostinato*) played on the second pífano, leaving the lead pifeiro free to improvise variations. In the piece titled "A Dança do Araruna" ("Dance of the Araruna Bird") on *Track 11* of the CD, the song of the Araruna bird is imitated by the pífanos. This piece was recorded at a rehearsal of the group Banda de Pífanos Cultural de Caruaru.

The brincadeira repertoire is quite popular, but the primary source for the music that animates secular occasions—especially the secular party at a novena de casa—is the forró, the popular dance music of the Northeast. *Forró* is a broad term that describes a country dance party, a specific dance rhythm, and a series of dance genres, including the baião, xaxado, xote, arrasta-pé, côco, and, of course, the forró itself. Bandas de pífanos also perform a wide variety of non-forró popular and folk music genres from Brazil. These include the frevo (a fast Carnival march from Recife) and the choro (an instrumental genre from Rio de Janeiro performed in a samba rhythm). A forró dance party in its purely secular context—that is, apart from a novena de casa—is typically performed by accordion-led ensembles with a core instrumentation of three instruments: an accordion or oito baixos (literally meaning "eight basses"), an industrialized zabumba drum, and a triangle.[6] An oito baixos is a diatonic button accordion with eight bass-note buttons. Forró dances are notorious as occasions for excessive alcoholic consumption, displays of male bravado, sexual encounters, and fights. When bandas de pífanos perform forró music at a novena de casa, they are actively drawing on these elements to heat up the party. In contrast to the música do santo, which is devotional and submissive in style, forró is characterized by an emphasis on individual assertion, improvisation, virtuosic playing, and rhythmic intensity.

The forró music of the banda de pífanos centers on several related genres—which I will refer to as the forró complex—that are defined musically by an underlying rhythmic syncopation articulated most clearly in the zabumba drum and the surdo drum. The tarol snare drum also articulates this rhythm, in a more elaborated manner. This syncopation can be heard clearly on *Track 12* of the CD. The forró complex comprises several genres: abaianada, baião, and forró. Banda de pífanos musicians classify the abaianada as an old style of the baião and the forró as a modern syncopated version of it. As discussed earlier in Chapter 5, the baião itself was first popularized throughout Brazil in the 1940s by Luiz Gonzaga, widely acknowledged as the grandfather of forró music. Gonzaga, an accordion player, composer, and singer, grew up listening to bandas de pífanos in the far western portion of Pernambuco. Gonzaga claims that in creating the commercial genre that became the baião, he was inspired by the zabumba patterns from the banda de pífanos and by the rhythmic patterns played on the *viola* during *cantoria* between verses.

Banda de pífanos musicians consider the abaianada rhythm to be "less hot" than either the baião or the forró. In the abaianada, both the zabumba and the surdo perform essentially identical patterns and the tarol plays its part without dynamic accents. This produces a smooth, rolling feel to the rhythm. In contrast, the baião and the forró feature interlocking open and muffled strokes between the zabumba and surdo drums. Additionally, the tarol snare drum is performed with heavy accents in these two genres. The result is a strong, interlocking cross-rhythm. The CD's *Track 12* offers an example of the Bandinha de Pífanos Dois Irmãos playing this rhythm. The CD's *Track 14* is a contemporary urban example of the forró rhythm.

In the forró, considered the most modern and hottest of the rhythms, the zabumba and surdo reverse their muffled and open strokes and give additional interlocking syncopated strokes to fill out the rhythm. The rhythmic intensity of the music is a primary focus of the musician's verbal explanations of the forró style. Such explanations are coded in metaphors, which systematically link the semantic domains of heat, body motion, and sexual prowess. As I have explained elsewhere, "A core metaphor used to describe the rhythmic intensity of well-played *forró* is *quente* [hot]. This term, and its related verb form *esquentar* [to heat up] are also used to describe the physical and sexual effect that music has on women—'*esquenta mulher*' [it heats women up]. The phrase *ele é fogo* [he is fire] is used to describe a musician who is able to heat up a party through his intense performance abilities."[7]

Other terms extend the linking of heat to musical competence; for example, *ele toca como pimenta* (he plays like a hot pepper) or *ele toca fumando* (he plays [so well] he's smoking). Audience participants encourage musicians to play with more rhythmic intensity by shouting, "*Espalhe a brasa*" (Spread out the hot coals) or "*Rapa fogo*" (Catch fire). As Biu do Pife mentioned in the earlier quote, the people are asking for "something hotter, something that swings in a different way, *forró*."

On the pífano, hot playing involves embouchure techniques and special fingering patterns to "clean up the notes" and emphasize rhythmic intensity. Extra ornamentations, grace notes, and extensive improvisational ability are marks of a hot player. Some of these techniques include *bulindo a nota* ("shaking the note" to produce a trill) and *batendo o beiço* ("beating the lip" to produce a staccato note). The rapid-fire notes in the first pífano part exemplify what pifeiros call *rapando o pife* (cutting the pife into small pieces). Short improvised sections such as this are called *passagenzinhas* (little passages) and serve to demonstrate the instrumental prowess of pifeiros. The piece "Forró do Zabumba" on CD *Track 12* is illustrative and features João do Pífe's Banda de Pífanos Dois Irmãos performing for tourists in Caruaru.

Banda de pífanos musicians cherish both the *música do santo* and forró. Although playing the former fulfills religious obligations and connects them with the folk Catholicism so prevalent in their daily lives, performing the latter allows them to explore their artistic creativity. In addition, the repertoire of forró connects banda de pífanos musicians with the popular music that developed among accordion-based groups and linked northeastern folk traditions to Brazil's national music industry. Forró was the Northeast's first style of popular music to attain widespread, national commercial success, which came in the late 1940s with Pernambuco's musical star Luiz Gonzaga. Among rural and urban banda de pífanos musicians, Gonzaga and the advent of northeastern popular music served to validate and reinforce their traditions. It also modeled the possibility of expanding the horizons of the Northeast's traditions beyond regional boundaries.

Cantoria de Viola

History and Overview

Track 13 on the CD presents a song titled "A Família" ("The Family") by the poet–singers Antônio Lisboa and Edmilson Ferreira. This song, set in the poetic form of six-line verses known as *sextilhas*, is about the confrontation of traditional family values with modern Brazilian society. (See the Appendix for a complete transcription and translation of the lyrics to this song.)

Here are two of the verses from this song:

Two verses from "A Família"

The first *verse is* by Edmilson Ferreira and the second by Antônio Lisboa – *followed by my translations.*

    Não tem mais casal maduro
    orientando os guris (crianças)
    a televisão confunde

a escola contradiz
e nessa torre de babel
não há quem seja feliz

Nas famílias do país
as ordens não são cumpridas
os regimes muita abertos
as regras mal definidas
nem Freud nem Piaget
vão ajeitar essas vidas

There are no more mature couples
guiding their children
the television confuses
the school contradicts
and in this tower of Babel
no one is happy

In the families of the country
orders are not fulfilled
laws are very permissive
rules are badly defined
neither Freud nor Piaget
are going to fix these lives[8]

Lisboa and Ferreira are contemporary poets and musicians who specialize in cantoria de viola, a northeastern song tradition with historical links to the poet–musicians of medieval Europe. The main roots of cantoria—its foundation in improvised Iberian poetry and the use of the guitar-like viola—were carried to Brazil by the Portuguese, but the precise date and location of the first cantoria in Brazilian territory is not known. Otacílio Batista and Francisco Linhares consider the first cantoria singer to have been Gregório de Matos Guerra, a musician born in Bahia in the seventeenth century who sang improvised songs to the sound of the viola. The most complete study of the lyric content of cantoria is Câmara Cascudo's classic *Vaqueiros e Cantadores,* originally published 1939.[9] According to poet and journalist Orlando Tejo, cantoria de viola began in the early nineteenth century near Texeira, a town located in the interior of the state of Paraíba. But, the evidence to fully support the origin of cantoria in any one area of the Northeast is lacking. What most historians and the singers of cantoria agree on is that this form of singing developed in the Northeast interior.

A broad category of sung poetry, cantoria can be distinguished from most other northeastern song forms by the fact that it does not typically accompany any dancing, theatrical activities, or religious occasions. In the old days, *cantadores* (singers of cantoria) traveled from town to town singing their songs, telling their stories, and commenting on topical subjects in poetic form. They accompanied themselves on several instruments, including the rabeca folk violin, the pandeiro, metal shakers, and eventually the ten-string viola guitar. Cantoria de viola possibly developed in conjunction with several other related forms of cantoria singing. Reflecting the cattle-raising era in the Northeast, a beautiful a cappella singing of cantoria known as the *aboio* was first developed by northeastern cowboys as they sang to their cattle while out on the range. Typically, two cowboys sang back and forth to each other over long distances. Singing in a rhythmically flexible manner with long held notes and legato glides, the aboios singers possessed powerful and beautiful voices. This heritage is continued now by professional cowboy singers called *aboiadores*, who sing aboios and the closely related *toada de vaquejada* (rodeo songs) at competitions and demonstrations. These singers are regulars at northeastern rodeo events known as *vaquejadas*. The toadas de vaquejada are strophic songs sung in parallel thirds by the two singers, a musical detail reflecting Portuguese folk-singing characteristics. A number of exceptional aboiadores have made their own independent CD recordings. Another variety of cantoria is the embolada (tongue twister), a rhythmically energized form of improvised poetry sung by pairs of singers who accompany themselves on either the pandeiro or a metal shaker, the ganzá. The strict rhythmic accompaniment of the pandeiro emphasizes a syncopated pattern of either (3 + 3 + 2) or (3 + 2 + 3) quick beats. Over this rhythmic framework, the embolada song is sung as a kind of comical tongue-twister duel featuring many verbal put-downs and double entendres. The embolada is frequently performed in the open-air public spaces of street markets or on busy street corners in northeastern cities.

The final type of cantoria is the cantoria de viola, considered by many to be the latest and most advanced form of cantoria singing. Cantoria de viola—the act of singing improvised verses in a poetic dispute by two singers to the accompaniment of the viola—first became widely popular in the northeastern interior during the nineteenth century. Several regional centers of activity slowly emerged, including Juazeiro do Norte in the state of Ceará, Campina Grande in Paraíba, and both Caruaru and São José do Egíto in Pernambuco.

At first, cantoria de viola song duels (*desafios*) between two singers took place exclusively in intimate settings for attentive listeners. These locations included private homes in small towns or on ranches in the country. They also took place in small bars located next to a town's open street market. The singers gained a reputation for wanting to be seated with their backs to a wall in front of the listeners. Today, the term "*cantoria pé de parede*" (cantoria foot of the wall) describes cantoria de viola performed acoustically in an informal setting. Listeners interacted with the singers by requesting specific topics to be improvised and by encouraging the singers with shouts, laughter, and comments after a well-constructed verse. In addition, a listener could take an even more active role by making up a *mote* (a thought or subject expressed in the form of one or two lines of poetry) and then requesting that the poet–singers use it as the basis of an improvised duel. The close attention paid to verbal poetry is an essential component in this art form.

Repentistas (as these singer–poets are also called) functioned as social critics, historians, philosophers, and organic intellectuals commenting on the daily problems and social issues confronted by the rural and migrant populations of the Northeast. This traditional role has not changed in contemporary society. Cantadores still speak with authority on "the country people's" issues because most singers come from rather humble, rural origins and share the life experiences of their poor and often migrant audiences. This connection to common people and to issues of social equality is extremely important. Antônio Lisboa, a singer–poet who now lives on the outskirts of the city of Recife, related:

> I'm from Rio Grande do Norte. But not from Natal [the capital city of that state].
> I was born in Marcelino Vieira, a small city in the interior of the state. . . . Almost all cantadores have practically the same history: we're always from the interior, from the countryside, or from a small town. That is a life tied to the land. . . . Now, in the larger cities, they have cantadores, but most have moved there from the interior, from the hamlets close to the small cities. [These singers] are born and raised there, they begin singing in the country. Then they leave for a city, for a larger city, for one of the centers of cantoria, medium-sized cities in the interior where they can earn a living. Because when a cantador reaches a certain level, he needs to be in a location with communications media, ways of advertising his activities, a place that offers these conditions. A place that has one or two radio stations, television, newspaper, and that has good transportation infrastructure.[10]

In the twentieth century, the process of urbanization and the coming of radio created new contexts of performance for the singer–poets, but the basic structure of the cantoria de viola stayed relatively unchanged. Live radio programs featuring cantoria became quite common, and singers would travel for miles to appear on them. Aspiring young singers and aficionados of the tradition tuned in to the regular programming. Like other cantadores of his generation, Lisboa also grew up listening to regional radio programs featuring cantoria de viola:

> At the age of ten I was listening to cantorias on the radio and listening to the poems that were sung on the radio, the songs. I would listen one day, and the next day I'd listen again in order to learn it by heart. I learned things by heart in two hearings. I also learned all of the types [genres of cantoria] from the radio. I learned everything listening to the radio. . . . This was at the end of the 1960s, the 1970s, and into the 1980s that cantoria on the radio was strongest. And I remember that my mother listened to all of these programs, going from one program to another. Because they lasted the whole morning. And I remember that Cajazeiras had some eight programs on the radio.

Growing up listening to radio programs inspired the young Lisboa and helped him develop the memory and sense of poetic structure that would be necessary for cantoria singing. The radio has been important in the lives of many contemporary singer–poets. When I asked Edmilson Ferreira, a young poet–singer originally from the state of Piauí, how he began as a cantador, he responded:

> I had two influences that were fundamental. The first influence was my father, who was not a cantador but who always purchased *foletos de cordel* [pamphlets

on strings]. He memorized [them] and sang them for us. But the influence that I consider equally as important was the influence of the radio. We listened to many radio programs. Whenever there was a radio program of cantoria, we were always tuned in. Generally, these programs occurred early in the morning, from four o'clock in the morning until seven. My father woke up very early, and we stayed in bed listening. And also, at the end of the day there were more radio programs. Those radio programs were our daily entertainment. And that was enough to wake up an interest in me.[11]

Foletos de cordel are inexpensive, independently published booklets of poetry sold in markets in the Northeast. They derive their name from the practice of displaying these little booklets on string racks in street fairs. They often contain stories that originally developed in the oral tradition of the cantadores. The radio programs that both Lisboa and Ferreira mentioned were seminal in their early lives and part of their daily family experience. These programs developed loyal listeners and incorporated interactive elements for the audiences. Many programs were independently produced by the cantadores themselves, who purchased time on local radio stations. They could earn money by charging for the personal messages they read on the air, sent in by their listeners. Listeners also sent in their requests for cantoria improvisations in the form of motes. Commenting on the format of these radio programs, Antônio Lisboa also told me:

The cantadores bought an hour of radio time, they bought this hour from the station . . . and they then charged for each request that their listeners made. And the requests were for motes, songs, announcements, and other things. The programs of the *violeiros* [players of the viola] were the most popular that the radio stations had. Because it had this thing, it was a moneymaker for the cantador and functioned for him to publicize his work. And it also provided the public with a means to send messages to other people in the community.

Without a reliable telephone service or other means of instantaneous communication, the radio was one of the most useful mechanisms for the local population to send messages to each other, and it was still a popular means of communication in the early 1990s. In addition to its development through radio programs, cantoria also moved from more informal settings in private homes and small bars to the stage. With increased attention paid to the folk traditions of the rural areas of Brazil by elite cultural advocates, cantadores from all over the Northeast were soon invited to sing against each other in formal competitions. This phenomenon began in the late 1940s and coincided with the popularization of northeastern music on a national scale. A new context for the cantoria de viola emerged: the festival. In 1948, Ariano Suassuna organized what many cantadores believe was the first festival of cantoria de viola, which took place in Recife at the famous Teatro Santa Isabel. Official judges were chosen, and a formal process was instituted in which mote topics were written down and placed in sealed envelopes, replacing the older practice of calling out the motes. By the end of the 1970s, the festivals had become the dominant context for cantoria. Today, festivals are the primary means through which the poet–singers build their reputations, launch their careers, and earn their wages.

Figure 6.9 Antônio Lisboa with his viola dinâmica in front of his festival competition trophies, Recife, Pernambuco, 2001.

Festivals are formal competitions with invited cantadores who vie for prizes, trophies, and the prestige associated with winning a song duel. The festivals are frequently organized by municipal officials and/or by private patrons and feature a commission of judges. The competition may be several days in length or take place in a single night. In most, pairs of cantadores advance through the tournament structure as they eliminate their opponents. Each encounter between two cantadores takes the form of a song duel and features a sequence of cantoria song genres. The singers are presented with a new topic for each song type, which is delivered to them on stage in a sealed envelope. They must then begin their song duel, improvising their poetry on the given subject. A set amount of time (usually about five minutes) is devoted to each genre of singing. The art of cantoria centers on the fact that a singer's improvisations must conform to the detailed rules of meter, verse, and rhyme construction for each of the genres while at the same time exploring the given subject and simultaneously developing a cogent argument against an opponent. Some of the basic rules of cantoria are discussed in the next section.

Rules of the Cantoria

In a desafio song duel contest, the cantadores must improvise lyrics according to the rules of versification for various poetic genres. Each performance segment of a desafio is referred to as a baião and features one poetic genre. Researchers have discovered some seventy-four distinct poetic genres for cantoria, but about eight to ten are most commonly performed. Each one of the genres is defined by a set of rules that must be learned; these rules dictate the number of syllables per sung line, the number of sung lines per verse, and the exact rhyme scheme that each verse is to follow. Additionally, as already mentioned, audience members, radio listeners, or judges suggest the specific topics to be verbally disputed by the singers. Descriptions and examples of the most commonly used poetic genres of the desafio follow.

SEXTILHAS

Sextilhas are six-line verses that follow a rhyme scheme of *abcbdb*. Each line of the sextilha must be seven syllables in length. When two cantadores sing sextilhas in a desafio, they must alternate their verses. An obligatory rhyme, the *deixa,* must be maintained from one singer to the next in which the cantador must rhyme the first line of a new verse with the last line of the previous verse. Because sextilhas always rhyme the second, fourth, and sixth lines, the responding cantador can begin constructing the next verse as soon as the second line is sung by his challenger.

Desafios always start with the singing of sextilhas. To begin a desafio, the cantadores typically present autobiographical information about themselves in the first verses they sing. Two sextilha verses sung by Edmilson Ferreira and Antônio Lisboa show the obligatory deixa rhyme that must connect two verses:

Sextilha verses by Edmilson Ferreira and Antônio Lisboa

Verse	Rhyme	Line
A confusão das finanças	*a*	1
gera transtorno no leito	*b*	2
a mãe se sente culpada	*c*	3
o pai fica insatisfeito	*b*	4
quem não aprendeu correto	*d*	5
é raro ensinar direito	*b*	6
	deixa	
Todo casamento é feito	*a*	1
com duração vitalícia	*b*	2
termina com violência	*c*	3

juiz, divórcio, e polícia	*b*	4
todo mês atrasa a data	*d*	5
da pensão alimentícia	*b*	6

My translation:

The confusion of finances
causes problems in bed
the mother feels guilty
the father unsatisfied
he who does not learn correctly
rarely teaches others rightly

Every marriage that is made
for the duration of a lifetime
ends in violence,
judgment, divorce, and police
every month the date gets later
to receive funds for nourishment[12]

The sextilha is the most common verse form, and cantadores can virtually improvise in these poetic verse structures in their sleep. As a desafio progresses, the verse forms become longer and more complicated. Verses with six, eight, ten, and twelve lines are demanded of the singers. One staple of desafio singing is the use of poetic lines that are suggested by audience members.

MOTES OF SEVEN AND TEN SYLLABLES

Motes are topics in the form of two lines of poetry; traditionally, desafio audience members formulated motes in their minds and shouted them out to singers during performances. Technically, the motes are the final two lines of a *décima* (a poetic verse structure of ten lines). Motes come in two forms: one with seven syllables per line and the other with ten syllables per line. The mote must be sung as the ninth and tenth lines of each ten-line verse, whereas lines one through eight are always improvised. The rhyme scheme of the décima verse used for both types of mote is *abbaaccddc*. In festival competitions, a new mote is given to the singers in a sealed envelope immediately before they must sing it. The contadores get about a minute to formulate their ideas before they begin singing. One verse improvised by Antônio Lisboa incorporated the mote "O Tancredo morreu mas está vivendo no espírito do povo brasileiro" ("Tancredo died but is still alive in the spirit of the Brazilian people").

Lyrics to the mote decassílabo "O Tancredo morreu mas está vivendo no espírito do povo brasileiro," by Antônio Lisboa

Verse	Rhyme	Line	
O maior estadista da nação	a	1	
Não fez ponte, nem pista, nem asfalto	b	2	
Na subida da rampa do Planalto	b	3	
Quando ele chegou foi num caixão	a	4	
Vinha atrás uma grande multidão	a	5	
E ele em cima de um carro de bombeiro	c	6	
O palácio ficou sem seu herdeiro	c	7	
E sua faixa findou não recebendo	d	8	
O Tancredo morreu mas está vivendo	d	9	} mote
No espírito do povo brasileiro	c	10	

My translation:

The nation's greatest statesman
Constructed neither bridge, nor highway, nor asphalt road
Up the ramp to the Planalto
When he arrived there it was in a box
There came a great multitude behind
And he was on top of a fireman's car
The palace was without its heir
And he passed on without receiving his medal
Tancredo died but is still alive
In the spirit of the Brazilian people[13]

In this example, Lisboa was constructing a verse that had to fit into the poetic form and topic dictated by the mote.

Additional poetic genres of cantoria de viola

Numerous other genres can be sung in a desafio of cantoria de viola. Here are some of the most common ones. Clearly, the art of cantoria de viola is not for someone who has trouble finding the right words to express his or her thoughts.

The *galope à beira-mar* (seaside gallop) is considered the most demanding genre in cantoria de viola. Its difficulty lies in the fact that it is a ten-line verse with each line having eleven syllables. Trying to compose a line in English with eleven syllables illustrates the difficulty. The rhyme scheme of the ten lines of each verse is *abbaaccddc,* and the tenth line always ends with a variant of the phrase *galope na beira do mar.* To further complicate the matter, the ninth line is also a deixa, with which the responding singer must rhyme the first line of the next verse.

The *mourão* is actually a set of poetic genres in which each verse is sung in dialogic form. That is, the lines of each verse are divided between the two cantadores in a set way. There are several subtypes of this category. In a desafio, the most commonly used mourão is the *mourão de sete pés*, a verse of seven lines with seven syllables per line and with a rhyme scheme of *abcbddb*. The dialogic sequence is lines one and two (singer one); line three and four (singer two); and lines five, six, and seven (singer one). For each subsequent verse, the cantadores must reverse roles. Other types include the *mourão zebrado* (striped morão), the *mourão caído* (fallen morão also called *mourão de você cai*), the *mourão perguntado* (queried morão), and the *mourão respondido* (answered morão).

Treze por doze (thirteen times twelve) is another popular genre. This is a twelve-line verse with a changing number of syllables per line: lines one through six have seven syllables, lines seven and eight have eleven syllables, line nine has thirteen syllables, and lines ten through eleven have seven syllables. The rhyme scheme is *abba accd deed,* and the rhyme of the tenth line is a deixa for the first line of the next verse. This verse is not quite as complex as it might appear. Lines seven, eight, and nine are always the same: "*É treze por doze, é onze por dez / É nove por oito, é sete por seis / É cinco por quatro, mais um, mais dois e mais três*" ("It's thirteen times twelve, it's eleven times ten / It's nine times eight, it's seven times six / It's five times four, add one, add two, add three").

Oito pés a quadrão is an eight-line verse with seven syllables per line and a rhyme scheme of *aaabbccb*. The last line is always "*Nos oito pés de quadrão*" ("In the eight feet of the quadrão"), and the seventh line is a deixa.

Martelo alagoano (meaning "hammer from Alagoas") is a décima with ten syllables per line and a rhyme scheme of *abbaaccddc*. The sixth and seventh lines must rhyme with *ano* (pronounced "AH-new") because the tenth line is always "*E lá vão dez de martelo-alagoano*"("And there go ten [lines] of the martelo-alagoano"). The ninth line is also a deixa.

In a desafio contest, two cantadores match their wits by improvising over the sequence of poetic genres. The desafio might be compared to a legal debate in which two opposing lawyers present their oral arguments in a sung poetic form. Arguments, cross-examinations, and objections must all conform to the strict rules of construction known as the *regras da cantoria* (rules of cantoria). However, the art of cantoria de viola also involves the viola guitar and the melodic and rhythmic aspects of singing, to which I now turn.

The Viola and the Musical Structure of Cantoria de Viola

Old viola of pine-wood, companion of my soul

(Dimas Batista Patriota)

Figure 6.10 Edmilson Ferreira and his viola dinâmica, Recife, Pernambuco, 2001 (photo by Larry Crook).

One of the first stringed instruments that the Portuguese introduced into Brazil was a variant of the guitar known as the viola. In Portugal and Spain, four-, five-, and six-course guitars were popular from about 1500. The viola that developed in Brazil most likely derived from one or more of these instruments. The earliest mention of a viola in Brazil comes from the sixteenth-century Jesuit José de Anchieta, who described Indian children dancing in a Portuguese manner to the sound of drums and violas.[14] Today, the instrument is found throughout Brazil in many closely related forms. In the rural interior of south-central Brazil, the *viola caipira* (country-bumpkin viola) is a ten-string instrument slightly smaller than an acoustic guitar that is used to accompany many forms of music, including the *moda de viola* (moda accompanied by a viola). The moda de viola is south-central Brazil's counterpart to the Northeast's cantoria de viola. It is based on a pair of singers who accompany themselves on violas as they sing poetry based on four-, six-, eight-, and ten-line verses. The viola caipira is also the primary instrument of *música caipira* (country-bumpkin music), one of Brazil's most successful commercial musics. In the *Recôncavo* area surrounding Salvador da Bahia, capital of the state of Bahia, the *viola de samba* comes in several different shapes and with a varying number of strings and accompanies a type of samba known as samba de viola. In the Recôncavo, the playing of the viola accompanies both the singing of songs and dancing. But in the Northeast's interior regions, the viola is used almost exclusively to accompany the poet–singers of cantoria.

The violas used by cantadores come in two basic types: (1) the *viola simples* (simple viola), a wooden model slightly smaller than a classical guitar, and (2) the *viola dinâmica* (dynamic viola), an instrument with a wooden body and an internal, metal resonating disc and several circular sound holes. This variety is similar to the Dobro resonator guitar developed in the United States in the late 1920s. In Brazil, the instrument was manufactured in São Paulo by the Del Vecchio Company. Northeastern instrument makers began making their own violas dinâmicas after Del Vecchio ceased production. Both types of violas have provisions for ten metal strings organized into five double courses. The second variety is louder and quite metallic in sound.

The viola dinâmica's metallic sound is the result of its construction. Inside the main body of the viola, directly under the end of the strings, is a large aluminum disc. When the strings are played, this disc vibrates sympathetically, producing a metallic twang. The metal strings used on the viola further emphasize this sound. Small sound holes on the top of the instrument's soundboard help direct the sound out of the main body of the instrument. Although violas are constructed to have a total of ten strings (five courses of two strings each), in practice, most cantadores today only put seven strings on their instruments. Example 6.1 gives the tuning of the seven strings for the viola de cantoria.

From left to right, the note names of the open tuning are E, B, G, D, A, A, and A. Only one or two basic chords accompany most cantoria songs and serve as drones behind the singers with strong emphasis on the tonic by virtue of unison doublings and octaves. Simple strum patterns are used by the singers, and between verses they perform brief melodies and vary the rhythmic strums on their violas. The relatively simple accompaniment provided by the viola player is paralleled by the melodically and rhythmically simple nature of the song's melody. Cantoria songs feature a small number of tune melodies in which many repetitions of a few notes are given over a steady flow of rhythmic values. Melodies typically conform to seven-note scales with flatted sevenths or may involve the major diatonic scale.

However, singing features expressive alterations of the third, fourth, and seventh notes of a scale. That is, the singer is free to sing notes that are sharp or flat at those points of the scale. Singers consider these qualities to be expressive elements of their performances. Melodic and rhythmic phrasing must conform to the number of syllables per line as determined by the rules of cantoria. Musically, two or more lines of poetry frequently form a phrase, with the final syllable being held before the singer pauses for a breath. The

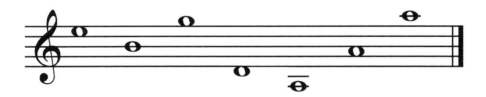

Example 6.1 Open tuning on the viola de cantoria

text is rendered syllabically (one note per syllable of the poetry) in even note values, with the final syllable held for a longer time value. This syllabic rendering is presented on *Track 13* of the CD; the lyrics can be found in the Appendix.

Most cantoria songs are sung within the total vocal range of an octave and feature tense and nasalized vocal production. This is a declamatory style of singing, in which the main focus is on the expression of the text and not the refined qualities of the voice. The expressive qualities of the voice are employed to emphasize key words and to stress the text's meaning. Likewise, the viola playing is only rarely developed beyond basic accompaniment. Between verses, as a singer formulates a poetic response, the viola is called on to play short melodies and to give brief rhythmic strums. Cantadores love their violas and would not think of performing without them. But the viola serves only to support and help interpret the poetry, not to overshadow it.

CHAPTER 7

Reinventing Africa and Remixing Hybridity: Blocos Afro and Mangue Beat

The last three decades of the twentieth century witnessed vibrant new musical and cultural currents flowing from two of Brazil's principal cities—Salvador da Bahia and Recife, Pernambuco. During the 1970s and 1980s, a renaissance of black musical activity centered in Salvador da Bahia emerged from the more general context of a growing black consciousness movement in Brazil. The confluence of social, political, economic, and cultural factors came to a critical juncture in 1988 during Brazil's official celebrations marking the centenary of the abolition of slavery in the country. Calling attention to what they believed to be an unbroken history of deep-seated racial discrimination in the country, Afro-Brazilian political and cultural groups throughout the country held demonstrations to counter Brazil's official celebrations of 1988. In Salvador da Bahia, widely acknowledged as the country's most "African" city, coordinated pressures from several sectors of the black community caused the government to cancel its official celebrations. Key among those protesting were the city's black Carnival groups (blocos afro) whose musical style—widely dubbed samba-reggae—had become a strategic resource for asserting black collective identity. Drawing on Afro-Brazilian musical heritage as well as African and black diasporic musical forms including Jamaican reggae, bloco afro groups such as Olodum and Ilê Aiyê ushered in a new musical era with transnational implications. Within the popular music industry of Brazil, Salvador's bloco afro groups—and other manifestations of the city's black cultural renaissance—garnered media attention and spawned a nationally and internationally recognized style of world music called axé music.

On the heels of Salvador's musical activities—and somewhat in that city's shadow in the media—Recife also witnessed the unfolding of a vibrant new cultural and artistic movement in the early 1990s. Musically, this movement coalesced around the mangue beat sounds of the innovative new band Chico Science & Nação Zumbi and its fusion of local northeastern traditions (especially maracatu, embolada, and côco) with global influences (especially North American funk, rap, hip-hop, and hard-core metal sounds). Subsequent musicians involved in Recife's new popular music scene (*nova scena*) have highlighted Pernambuco's regional difference as a strategy to reinterpret Recife's venerable local traditions while simultaneously engaging with national and global contexts of musical production. In this chapter, I will examine the historical trajectories of these two contemporary musical currents from the Northeast and explore how they became part of the international circulation of music at the end of the twentieth century.

Chronology of the Blocos Afros and Mangue Beat

1974	Ilê Aiyê, Salvador's first *bloco afro* founded in the neighborhood of Curuzu
1977	Gilberto Gil releases a cover of "Que Bloco É Esse" under the title "Ilê Aiyê" on the LP *Refavela*
1979	Olodum founded with headquarters in the Pelourinho area of Salvador
1984	With the help of Gilberto Gil, Ilê Aiyê records *Ilê Aiyê—Canto Negro*, the first LP by a bloco afro
1987	Neguinho do Samba's samba-reggae rhythms and the carnival theme "Egypt of the Pharaohs" help catapult Olodum to national prominence; Olodum records its first LP: *Egito/Madagascar*
1988	Brazil's centenary celebration of the abolition of slavery is contested by blocos afro and other groups of the black consciousness movement
1990	Paul Simon releases *Rhythm of the Saints* with the participation of Neguinho do Samba and drummers from Olodum
1991	Daniela Mercury popularizes axé music with the song "Swing da Cor"
1992	Carlinhos Brown forms Timbalada, which issues its first CD recording the following year
1994	Advent of mangue beat is marked with the release of Chico Science & Nação Zumbi's CD *Da Lama aos Caos*
1997	Chico Science is killed during Carnival in an automobile accident

Blocos Afro, Samba-Reggae, and Axé Music: Navigating the Black Atlantic

White man, if you only knew
The value that a black man has
You would take a bath of tar
So black you would be too
    ("Que Bloco É Esse?" by Paulinho Camafeu)

The rise of the blocos afro Carnival groups in Salvador da Bahia in the 1970s and 1980s reflected a conscious attempt by a large segment of the city's youth to carve out a uniquely black cultural space within the city's annual Carnival celebration. This social movement involved an aesthetic transformation in the city that gave increasing prominence to the creation of new music and dance styles influenced by local Afro-Brazilian heritage, translocal African cultural awareness, and international styles of black popular music. Participation in the local afoxé groups (see Chapter 3) was certainly an option for the young black population of the city, but by the late 1960s, that older tradition had come to symbolize a rather quaint folkloric representation of earlier Afro-Bahian values and aesthetics during Carnival time. The older style of afoxé did not seem particularly well suited for the contemporary expression of identity among black youth, and a number of new and politically motivated afoxés were formed. In addition, youth-oriented Carnival groups known as *blocos de trio* (trio blocs), featuring the electrified sound of *trios elétrico* (electric guitar bands playing atop sound trucks), connected more directly to the contemporary aesthetics of Salvador's emerging rock generation. However, the trios elétrico groups catered primarily to middle-class, often white, participants who formed large Carnival blocos to parade and dance around the amplified music during Carnival. First emerging in the 1950s, the electrified trios had initially transformed Pernambuco's frevo music into a local Bahian style of frevo performed on a trio of small-, medium-, and large-sized electric guitars backed up by drums and percussion instruments. By the 1960s, trios were playing a hyperactive electrified style known as *frevo baiano* (Bahian frevo) and generating interest among young rockers in the city. During the 1970s and 1980s, the trios elétrico bands became an important influence on Bahia's popular music and entered the national consciousness through Caetano Veloso and other popular musicians from Salvador.

During the 1960s, a large segment of the lower-class black and mestizo youth of Salvador also participated in local samba schools patterned on models from Rio de Janeiro. Samba had been supported as Brazil's national form of Carnival music since the 1940s, and samba school groups were present in all major Brazilian cities, including Salvador. They featured large batteries of percussionists, singers, dancers, and instrumentalists performing the national style of Carnival samba in the streets. In the latter part of the 1960s, an influential Carnival group from Rio de Janeiro named Cacique de Ramos (Chief of Ramos) provided the model for blacks in Salvador to form groups based on North American Indian thematics. In 1968, participants from several of Salvador's samba schools founded new Carnival groups of this kind, which were quickly labeled *blocos de índio* (Indian blocs). These "Indian" groups incorporated exotic imagery drawn from international popular culture (Hollywood westerns and comic books) depicting North American Indian nations such as the Comanche and the Apache. To Salvador's young blacks who were forming new Carnival groups, the savage Indian characters shown in the Hollywood films were non-white heroes who bravely resisted white cowboys and federal troops. The first bloco de índio formed in Salvador was the Caciques do Garcia (Chiefs of Garcia), created by members of the samba school Juventude do Garcia (Youth of Garcia). The second was the Apaches do Tororó, founded by members of the samba school Filhos de Tororó (Sons of Tororó). The transformation of these samba schools to blocos de índio heralded the search for new forms of identity among Salvador's poor black youth. In the streets during Carnival, the blocos de índio groups celebrated in their public show of power, which aroused both fear and respect from the city's general population. They marched by the thousands, dressed in Indian costuming, and engaged in aggressive dances. To some, this was youthful exuberance; to others, it was an outbreak of civil disorder. The samba music they performed was played on the ensemble of batucada percussion instruments derived from the samba schools. Violent encounters between groups such as the Apaches do Tororó and the police led to perceptions among middle-class and elite sectors of the city that the blocos de índio groups were little more than gangs of law-breaking thugs. In 1972, 5,000 members of the Apaches do Tororó paraded through the streets of Salvador during Carnival with wooden tomahawks and war paint. Labeled "inciters of violence" by the local press, members of an all-women's Carnival group registered a complaint with the police, accusing several members of the Apaches do Tororó of rape. According to João Jorge Santos Rodrigues, the president of Olodum (one of Salvador's largest bloco afro Carnival groups), "the complaint was sufficient reason for 3,000 people to be arrested in a single night. Anyone wearing Apache costuming—white and red pants, a white and red headdress, or stripes of white face paint—was subject to arrest."[1] During subsequent Carnivals in the 1970s, the Apache group was involved in several other violent confrontations with the city's police force.

By 1973, many blacks in Salvador were exploring new ways to express their identity as contemporary blacks living in a complex and interconnected world. Increased media saturation during the 1960s had exposed them to a wide range of world events, including several anti-imperialist revolutions in Africa and the civil rights movement in the United States. Media coverage and the expansion of mass communications had made available a host of black musical forms (for example, soul, funk, and reggae) from African diaspora communities. The international dissemination of cultural and political values associated with these black popular musics helped create an interconnected transatlantic community that Paul Gilroy referred to as the "Black Atlantic."[2] In Brazil, the country with the largest black population in the Americas, this Black Atlantic community was manifest in a variety of ways.

In Rio de Janeiro and in Salvador da Bahia, popular dances took place in poor black neighborhoods, featuring taped soul and funk music imported directly from the United States. These black soul–funk dances helped inculcate new forms of transnational racial identity in Brazil's poor black youth, who identified closely with the cultural styling of their counterparts in North America and in the Caribbean. This new generation of Brazilian blacks tended to opt out of traditional Afro-Brazilian practices such as the samba in favor of modern cultural forms linked closely to the civil rights and "black is beautiful" movements emanating from the United States. In Salvador, next to this modern black cultural activity, the older afoxés of the city represented an African heritage that seemed too folkloric and out of step with the tastes of the funk generation. Meanwhile, the imagery of the blocos de índio did not resonate with a sense of local or transatlantic African heritage. The time was ripe for a new type of Carnival association that would reflect the growing self-awareness of young black Brazilians. Logically enough, this new type of Carnival group—the bloco afro, or Afro bloc—would emerge in the historical center of Afro-Brazilian culture, Salvador da Bahia

Ilê Aiyê

In November 1974 in Salvador's large black suburb named Liberdade (Liberty), in the neighborhood of Curuzu, the first bloco afro was founded, with the explicit purpose of establishing an exclusively black-oriented Carnival group to express the values of the black race. The name the members chose for their group was Ilê Aiyê, derived from the Yoruba language of West Africa and meaning "House of Life." Many of the founding members of Ilê Aiyê had participated in a bloco de índio named A Zorra; others came from the Apaches do Tororó. According to Vovô (Antônio Carlos dos Santos), president of the Ilê Aiyê group, the black movement and black popular music from the United States were important influences on the group from its inception:

> When we created the group, the influence of the black movement from America was very strong. But we did not go around just talking about America, the United States. Instead, we chose [Carnival] themes about Africa. But . . . everything was always linked with the North American black movement. Everyone here was down with James Brown. There was a lot of music that was a point of reference. It was not a replacement for mother Africa [the African homeland]. Our day-to-day orientation, the orientation of the group was still Africa. But other things, like the Black Panthers, were also important. One theme that we used was Marcus Garvey; . . . we also spoke about Angela Davis, we spoke about Malcom X.[3]

That important figures associated with the black nationalist movement such as Marcus Garvey (an early twentieth-century leader of Pan-Africanism in the Caribbean and North America) and Malcolm X were mentioned indicates the intellectual awareness and militant stance under which Ilê Aiyê emerged. The group's founding in Salvador da Bahia is frequently cited as a milestone in the nascent black consciousness movement in Brazil. Indeed, the formation of this group actually predated the more overtly political associations in the black community in Brazil, such as the Movimento Negro Unificado (United Negro Movement), which was founded in 1978. Working in the cultural arena, Ilê Aiyê became a mechanism for Salvador's blacks to reinterpret and reclaim their historical and contemporary connections to Africa and to other African diaspora communities. In this process of re-examination, they drew freely from venerable Afro-Brazilian cultural practices and blended these with the sounds, ideas, and thematic images of Africa and the world of the Black Atlantic. In short, they conceptualized their own black community as part of a larger construct: the African world.

Each year during Carnival, Ilê Aiyê printed and distributed pamphlets containing the words to their songs and statements documenting the origins of their group. The following statement comes from Ilê Aiyê's pamphlet from the Carnival of 1984 (my translation):

> Ilê Aiyê [was] founded in November of 1974, by a group of young men and women from Curuzu that paraded in the street during Carnival in their African "kangas." From the beginning, some people were apprehensive about joining the bloco because of the oppression they were suffering, and in which only blacks

could participate. This restriction was not racism, but rather, a way to demonstrate, during Carnival, the value and the beauty of the blacks, a way of remembering the values of a race.

Today, Ilê Aiyê is more than a Carnival group, it is an institution known nationally, and internationally, which has year-round activities aimed at raising the consciousness of all people, but especially blacks. Ilê Aiyê has already marched [during Carnival] with themes about the Mali-Dogon, Zimbabwe, Cameroons, Ruanda, Watutsi, the Upper Volta, Ghana, always a Black African country and its people, bringing the history of black civilizations, our fights and glories.

According to Vovô, the founders of Ilê Aiyê initially considered calling themselves Poder Negro (Negro Power), among several other names. The reference to the militancy of the North American black power movement was overt. However, the group felt that such a name would probably inflame the local police, given the violence in 1973 surrounding the Apaches do Tororó group and the tense racial climate of the times. In light of these considerations, they settled on the name Ilê Aiyê. The strong Yoruba influence in Bahia—including the privileged position reserved for the orthodox Gêge-Nagô Candomblé houses of the area and their use of Yoruba as ritual language—made this an appropriate symbolic choice.

The lyrics of their songs spoke of an empowered black race operating openly in an African world. The first year that Ilê Aiyê members marched in Salvador's Carnival (1975), they sang the song "Que Bloco É Esse?" ("What Group Is That?"), written by Paulinho Camafeu. The refrain and first verse of the song made clear the group's relationship to a broader African world of negritude and black power.

Partial lyrics to "Que Bloco É Esse?"

What Carnival group is that?
I'd like to find out.
It's the black world
That we come to sing to you about
We're crazy blacks
We're really alright
We have kinky hair
We are black power.

Ilê Aiyê quickly became an important vehicle for exploring and expressing black pride within Salvador's Carnival. Initially seeking to open a new social space allowing blacks to participate fully in Carnival, the group decided to restrict its membership to the black population. In a society that believed deeply in the idea of the Brazilian racial democracy, this policy was controversial. Responding to a question about the discriminatory policy toward white Brazilians, Vovô stated (my translation):

People ask us about this a lot. With the passage of time, we have tried to educate ourselves more about how this came about. We created Ilê to combat the racism that already existed during that time, a time when a black person could only parade in one of the [city's] blocos as a musician or as someone pushing the parade floats. The exceptions to this were Gandhi [Filhos de Gandhi] and the blocos organized by the dockworkers. So, we thought to ourselves, "Seeing that we do not have access, let's create our own bloco too." But, we wanted to create a pleasing kind of space, a respectful space, without hoodlums and bad elements. We put the idea into the black man's head that he was important, that he should have self-esteem. With that, the bloco gained its own space and began transforming the lives of its members who then started to contest [things with] the police, the press, [and] the lawyers. In addition, people started to perceive us as a point of reference; the problems and the complaints of the community could be channeled through Ilê.[4]

This policy of membership based on racial identification sparked a quick backlash and provoked public indictments of reverse discrimination against Ilê Aiyê, despite the fact that other Carnival groups in Salvador had long excluded blacks from participation. Both the racially exclusive membership policy and the adoption of perceived foreign (for example, North American) cultural values resulted in criticisms and diatribes against Ilê Aiyê in the newspapers of Salvador in the 1970s. For instance, Ilê Aiyê was treated as a group of un-Brazilian racial agitators in an article that appeared in Salvador's newspaper *A Tarde* (my translation):

Carrying signs with inscriptions such as "Black World," "Black Power," and "Black for Yourself," the Carnival group Ilê Aiyê, nicknamed the Bloco of Racism, presented an ugly spectacle to this year's Carnival. Besides their inappropriate theme and imitation of North America, revealing enormous lack of imagination . . . the members of Ilê Aiyê—all people of color—went so far as to make fun of the whites and others that watched them from the official reviewing stand. . . .

Thankfully, we do not have a racial problem [in Brazil]. This is one of the great joys of the Brazilian people. It's clear that the harmony that reigns among the descendents of various ethnic groups [in Brazil] constitutes one of the reasons for the non-conformity of the agitators who would like to add the spectacle of a racial war to the class struggle. But, they will never accomplish this in Brazil.[5]

Such public comments pointed to the deeply ingrained nature of a myth that many Brazilians liked to tell themselves: that Brazil was a harmonious racial democracy. This notion minimized the importance of race as a factor of social and economic inequality and held that Brazil had no racial discrimination, only discrimination based on poverty arising from class-related issues involving the lack of full access to the economic, political, and educational resources of the country. However, by defining themselves as blacks first (not as Brazilians) and by implicitly comparing their situation to that of North American blacks, Ilê Aiyê members publicly contested the myth that

Brazil was a racially harmonious nation. This questioning went to the very core of the national identity itself.

Ilê Aiyê's formation was the opening salvo in an aesthetic revolution in Salvador described by Antônio Risério as the "re-Africanization" of the city and its Carnival.[6] Perhaps more aptly described as the "reinvention" of Africa in Salvador, this move began a process involving the construction of a socially engaged Afro-Brazilian identity that highlighted the art and beauty of Brazilian blacks as African descendants. Although the members of Ilê Aiyê had drawn their initial stimulus from the black movement emanating from North America, they drew much of their artistic inspiration from African and Afro-Brazilian coordinates. Involvement in Candomblé served as an important unifying element among group members. Many members of Ilê Aiyê participated in Candomblé houses, and Vovô's mother, Mãe Hilda, was herself an ialorixá priestess of a Candomblé house in the city. Mãe Hilda acted as a matriarch for Ilê Aiyê. Before each year's Carnival activities, the special Candomblé rituals she led prepared safe passage for the group's members to parade in the streets. Ilê Aiyê also focused their yearly Carnival themes on homages to black African nations and peoples: Mali, Rwanda, Angola, the Watutsi, and so on. Through the combination of a lived and imagined African heritage, they hoped to glorify the art and beauty of the black race.

Ilê Aiyê made its most dramatic impact on Salvador's culture in the area of music. From the beginning, a hybrid mixture of local and international Afro-related elements of music, poetry, and general symbolism played a vital part in Ilê Aiyê's music. Wanting to create something new, something that would distinguish them as a specifically black Carnival group, musicians in the group mixed samba instruments and rhythmic patterns with the ijexá rhythm derived from Candomblé that was popular among the afoxés of the city. Ilê Aiyê's first head of percussion—Bafo da Onça—was an alabê, or drummer, in Candomblé and hence quite familiar with the general principles and specific toques of the religion. However, as Vovô told me in an interview, the group did not sing any of the sacred songs or perform the sacred rhythms of the Candomblé religion on the street during Carnival. Rather, the members incorporated certain rhythmic and thematic elements of the religious repertoire to create what became, for them, an "Afro" sound. The Afro sound involved slowing down the fast samba patterns to a tempo that was more relaxed and syncopated, more Afro sounding. They also decided to maintain the acoustic texture of drumming, percussion, and vocals without adding any strings or wind instruments to the mix. This acoustic texture was aesthetically consistent with the basic performance ensembles of many African-related musical traditions that had been maintained within Brazil's black communities since colonial times. Drawing on this heritage was fundamental to the group's success.

The basic Ilê Aiyê style evolved among drummers, singers, and composers during the group's public rehearsals in the Curuzu neighborhood on Sunday afternoons. These community affairs, beginning some six months prior to Carnival, involved working out interlocking rhythmic patterns on the low surdo and high-pitched repique drums while singer–songwriters presented their songs to other singers who joined in on choral responses. This was a highly participatory format for learning and developing both songs and drumming patterns. Drummers developed Ilê Aiyê's basic *andamento* (accompaniment rhythm) and worked out *convenções* (conventions), that is, unique rhythmic cadences that served to punctuate the beginnings, the endings, and the important parts of songs.

The repique, a double-headed drum, was played with a stick-and-hand technique and provided a syncopated accent pattern reminiscent of samba de roda. The low surdo drums interlocked their parts and fused the samba de roda with a hint of the ijexá. This slow and lilting beat became Ilê Aiyê's signature *afro-primitivo* (Afro-primitive) style and distinguished the group's sound from the fast-paced samba played by the escolas de samba and blocos de índio on many of the same instruments. The afro-primitivo sound also involved the acoustic texture of drums, percussion, and vocals. Other drums and percussion instruments filled out the sound (snare drum, beaded gourds, timbal conga, cuíca), but no harmonic or melodic instruments (acoustic or electric) were permitted. This acoustically oriented texture with an emphasis on the low-pitched drums became a marker of the bloco afro sound of Ilê Aiyê and separated it from the trios elétrico.

Following Ilê Aiyê's lead, other bloco afro groups were soon forming in Salvador (Olodum and Malê Debalê in 1979; Ara Ketu in 1980; Muzenza in 1981). Daniel Crowley reported that there were sixteen blocos afro officially parading in Salvador's Carnival by 1983 and perhaps another twenty or so participating informally.[7] There were also twenty-three afoxés. As mentioned in Chapter 3, the long-standing afoxé tradition was also participating in the process of revitalization in the 1970s and 1980s, and many new, progressive afoxés were being formed. Salvador's Carnival was in the midst of an aesthetic paradigm shift emphasizing all things black—what Antônio Risério has also called *blackitude*. Another important element added to the mix was Jamaican reggae.

By the late 1970s, commercial recordings of Jamaican reggae were becoming widely available in Salvador. In the middle of the city's historical district, Pelourinho, and a short distance from the headquarters of the Filhos de Gandhi afoxé group, a reggae bar (Bar do Reggae) opened in 1978 and quickly became an important meeting place for a local Rastafarian and reggae counterculture. Earlier in the decade, popular music stars Caetano Veloso and Gilberto Gil had referenced reggae in their own music after they were exposed to Jamaican music while living in exile in London.[8] Veloso's LP *Transa* (1972) featured the first Brazilian reggae song, "Nine out of Ten."[9] Gilberto Gil incorporated a reggae-influenced song titled "No Norte da Saudade" ("To the North of Sadness") among other African and Afro-Brazilian sounds on his seminal *Refavela* LP (1977). This LP also included a pop version of Ilê Aiyê's song "Que Bloco É Esse?" (titled "Ilê Aiyê" on the record). The biggest hit of Gil's career came in 1979, when he covered Bob Marley's reggae hit "No Woman, No Cry" in a Portuguese version titled "Não Chore Mais."[10] All of this activity helped spread reggae's Pan-African messages, Rastafarian religious philosophy, and the sounds of Jamaican stars such as Jimmy Cliff and Bob Marley. Salvador's reggae phenomenon also included the founding of a new bloco afro, Muzenza, whose members established mythical links between themselves and Afro-Jamaican culture. Fittingly, the group's headquarters was located on a street in Liberdade that became popularly known as Kingston Avenue.

The trio elétrico tradition was also transformed within the general context of "blackening" Salvador's Carnival and its music. Bahian popular singer–composer–guitarist Moraes Moreira is credited with making the initial fusion of the electrified trio sound with the ijexá rhythm in the late 1970s. Unlike the blocos afro of the time, which played acoustically with hundreds of drummers marching in the streets, the trios elétricos were small ensembles that played atop elaborate mobile sound trucks that blasted their music into the throngs of Carnival revelers. Moreira had performed with several local pop groups, including the influential Novos Baianos. He also participated in trios elétricos. In 1979, Moreira released the song "Assim Pintou Moçambique" (co-written with Antônio Risério) on his LP *La Vem o Brasil Descendo a Ladeira,* which mixed the rock-influenced aesthetics of the trio elétrico with the ijexá rhythm. His next LP, *Bazaar Brasileiro* (1980), included the *ijexá*-influenced "Grito de Guerra" ("War Cry")(co-written with Risério and Toni Costa). Other popular music artists, such as Luiz Caldas and the group Chiclete com Banana followed Moreira's lead in the early to mid-1980s and further mixed international pop aesthetics, Caribbean dance music, northeastern caboclo traditions, and the Afro-based sounds of Salvador's Carnival into an electric band format. This pop music activity laid important groundwork for Bahia's popular music style that would explode onto the national and international scenes in the late 1980s. In addition, the ever-present Gilberto Gil further utilized his national influence as a popular music star in helping Ilê Aiyê organize the first LP recording by a bloco afro: *Ilê Aiyê— Canto Negro* ("Ilê Aiyê—Black Song") (1984). Gil participated as both producer and performer on the album and sang lead on the song "Que Bloco É Esse?"

By the mid-1980s, Salvador's Carnival comprised primarily a combination of electrified pop groups, with lead singers performing Afro-influenced music atop multimillion-dollar sound trucks; large street groups such as the blocos afro; and afoxés (also beginning to utilize sound reinforcement for singers). The city was exploding with various manifestations of its African cultural renaissance. At that time, a new synthesis of Afro-Caribbean and Afro-Brazilian music was first developed by members of a rising bloco afro named Olodum.

Olodum and the Development of the Samba-Reggae Rhythm

> *The drums were beaten*
> *The blacks cried out*
> *Olodum am I!*
> ("Olodum a Banda do Pelô," by Jaguaracy Esseere)

Olodum was founded in 1979 by several members of Ilê Aiyê who wanted to chart a new, modern direction for the bloco afro tradition. Olodum was a shortened form of the name of Olodumaré, the all-powerful Yoruba deity. A sociopolitical agenda of black consciousness, antiracism, and economic enfranchisement informed the creation of the group and its music. Music was only one part of an elaborate structure devoted to promoting social justice and fighting race-based discrimination in Brazil and the world at large. The Olodum structure would develop in the 1980s to include educational, political, and cultural components. Its ideological path was set by two primary influences: (1) the North American black movement (Black Panthers, Martin Luther King, Malcolm X), and (2) the African heritage. By the mid-1980s, after an initial reorganization of the group early in the decade, Olodum was publishing a bi-weekly journal and sponsoring seminars, lectures, and other public events in Salvador in addition to operating as a Carnival organization.

Figure 7.1
Colonial architecture
in the historical
Pelourinho district
of Salvador, Bahia,
1995 (photo by
Larry Crook).

Olodum's musical group was headed by drummer Antonio Luís Alves de Souza, nicknamed "Neguinho do Samba." (The biographical information on Neguinho do Samba in this section is derived primarily from my interview with him in Salvador on May 28, 1995.) Neguinho began playing music at the age of seven, taking after his father (who played bongos) and his older brothers (who also played percussion). By the age of thirteen, he was frequenting Candomblé ceremonies and participating as a musician in several blocos in Salvador that were primarily playing the rhythms and instruments derived from the samba schools. While participating in the percussion section for the large bloco named Lordes, Neguinho began experimenting with using two thin sticks made of the *vime* reed plant to play the high-pitched repique instrument. The repique drum was normally played with one snare drumstick and one hand. As Neguinho do Samba told me:

> Everyone in Lordes played with the other kind of stick, everyone in Salvador played with the same kind of stick that you use on a snare drum. That was the same stick that played the repique and other instruments. So I came to Lordes, with four of these [thin] vime sticks, and Jumar, who was the director of the band, he said, "No one plays with two sticks the way you do." I told him that I had a different background; my idea was to play something [different]. He put me in the last line of the drummers. One hundred men in the band and he put me into the last line. I was there at the end with those thin sticks, making a better sound than anyone who had those snare drum sticks.

Within two weeks, Neguinho do Samba was up at the front of the drum section. He also played in the bands of several other Carnival groups, including Ilê Aiyê during the 1970s and early 1980s. But none of the groups fully accepted his innovative style of playing, and they would not follow the other new ideas he envisioned for the rhythm. In early 1983, Neguinho left Ilê Aiyê to join the newly reformed Olodum group. By 1985, he and another drummer, Mestre Jackson, began experimenting with mixing the blocos afro samba patterns with Afro-Caribbean rhythms: salsa, merengue, and reggae. The results were the development of two new toques that involved interlocking patterns shared by four distinct parts played on the low surdo drums. From smallest to largest, the four low surdos are:

- The marcação de uma—a high-pitched surdo approximately 18 inches (450mm)in diameter that is played with one soft mallet
- The marcação de duas—a medium-pitched surdo approximately 20 inches (500mm) in diameter that is played with two soft mallets
- The fundos—two low-pitched surdos approximately 24 inches (600mm) in diameter, each played with one soft mallet.

The repique was played with two thin sticks of vime to effectively achieve a high, penetrating sound. The sound approximated the timbre of the atabaque drums of Candomblé, which were also played with two thin sticks.

The first of the new patterns that Neguinho do Samba developed was called reggae and was based on the loose duple feel of Jamaican-rooted reggae played in a slow tempo. In this pattern, a subtle shuffle feel gave the rhythm a characteristic swing.

The second rhythm developed from the adaptation of other Afro-Caribbean rhythms and featured an additive pattern of 3 + 3 + 4 + 3 + 3 played on the repique (the top line in Example 7.2) while the surdo drums interlocked their parts. The characteristic phrase of four sixteenth notes leading into the first beat of the beginning of the pattern on the surdo marcação de duas linked this rhythm to the merengue of the Dominican Republic. This rhythm became known in Salvador as the merengue.

Figure 7.2
An Olodum drummer
during a rehearsal at
the African Bar in
Salvador, Bahia,
1995 (photo by
Larry Crook).

Neguinho do Samba also added a set of three *timbale* drums (adapted from Cuban dance music) to serve as a lead instrument, with the role of providing cues to the other drummers. These musical innovations in the percussion section of Olodum, fusing Afro-Caribbean drumming traditions with Salvador's bloco afro samba, created new excitement among Salvador's Carnival participants. The new drumming style came to be known as samba-reggae. The innovations also reinforced some of the new thematic orientations of the city's blocos afro at the time.

During the 1980s, the annual Carnival themes chosen by individual blocos afro had expanded to include the struggles of disenfranchised black populations throughout the world and socialist movements in Africa and the Americas. For instance, Olodum's theme for the Carnival of 1986 was "Cuba." The new samba-reggae style invigorated Salvador's

Example 7.1 Bloco afro reggae rhythm as developed among Olodum's drummers

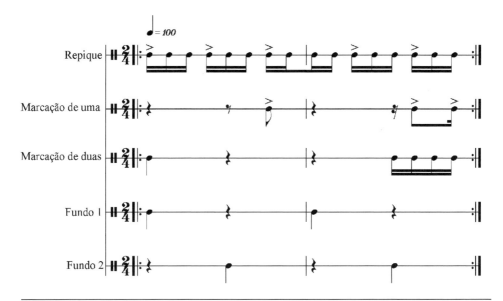

Example 7.2 Merengue rhythm as developed among Olodum's drummers

bloco afro community and catapulted Olodum to prominence in the city. The next year was unquestionably the year of Olodum and the samba-reggae. Olodum's theme for that year's Carnival was "Egypt of the Pharaohs," inspired by the controversial historical interpretations of Senegalese philosopher Cheikh Anta Diop. In Olodum's songs, ancient Egyptian culture was depicted as a universal black culture, with black pharaohs ruling over the lands. Using this theme was an attempt to raise consciousness by representing blacks not as victims but as rulers in dominant positions of state power. The hit song of Olodum's 1987 Carnival was "Faraó, Divindade do Egito" ("Pharaoh, Divinity of Egypt"), set to the group's bloco afro reggae beat. With poetry and melody written by Luciano Gomes dos Santos, the song asked Salvador's black community to awaken to the possibilities of an Egyptian-like renaissance in Pelourinho, the inner-city neighborhood where Olodum's headquarters was located.

Partial lyrics to "Faraó, Divindade do Egito," by Luciano Gomes dos Santos

Tutankamon, Akahenaton
Pelourinho, a small community
United by Olodum in the bonds of fraternity
Awaken yourself to Egyptian culture in Brazil
Instead of braided hair
We will see the turbans of Tutankamon
And liberty will fill our heads
The black community asks for equality
Leaving separatism behind.

The song and the thematic orientation of Olodum represented a symbolic shift in the bloco afro community from adherence to Afro-American models of black consciousness (Afros and braided hairstyles) and the separatist ideology of Ilê Aiyê to an ideology of inclusiveness. The new drumming style of Neguinho do Samba, which formed the rhythmic accompaniment to the songs of Olodum, ushered in the era of samba-reggae. Olodum's samba-reggae style became a major force in Salvador's Carnival and propelled the city's celebration to new national attention, including a dramatic increase in live television coverage of Carnival from Salvador. Although Rio de Janeiro still dominated national media coverage in Brazil, Salvador's Carnival gained on it substantially in the late 1980s. The incredible success of Olodum's music caused members of the local popular music scene to take note. The group obtained a recording contract with Continental records and recorded its first album, the LP *Egito/Madagáscar* (1987), which received airplay throughout Brazil. Included on the recording was the song "Faraó." Other prominent blocos afro in Recife also received recording contracts, Ara Ketu recorded the LP *Ara Ketu* (1987), and Muzenza recorded *Som Luxuoso* and *Muzenza do Reggae* (both released in 1988). Additionally, a number of pop groups in Salvador quickly copied the new Olodum style of samba-reggae drumming and adapted it to electric instruments (guitar, bass, keyboard) and drumset. Banda Mel and Reflexu's were two local popular commercial groups that released covers of bloco afro songs in an electrified samba–reggae style. Banda Mel's LP *Força Interior* (Inner Power) (1987) sold over 300,000 units, and Reflexu's *Da Mãe Africa* (From Mother Africa, 1987) sold over 1

Figure 7.3
Olodum drums stacked and ready to go for Carnival, Salvador, Bahia, 1995 (photo by Larry Crook).

million units. These commercial successes further influenced the city's trios elétricos bands to highlight bloco afro rhythms in their own repertoires. By 1988, Olodum and other blocos afro in Salvador were recognized not only for their social project of combating racism and raising black consciousness but also as a potential gold mine by the music industry of Brazil.

Axé Music: Bahia Ventures into the World Music Scene

> *I am the color of this city*
> *The song of this city is mine*

The ghetto, the street, the faith
I go walking around this beautiful city
The rhythm of the afoxé
And the force, where does it all come from?
No one can explain it
It is beautiful
("The Song of the City," by Tote Gira and Daniela Mercury)[11]

With the rising national prominence of Salvador's thoroughly "Africanized" Carnival and its exciting new samba–reggae rhythm, Bahia's musical currents began flowing steadily into Brazil's mainstream popular music industry in the 1990s. Since the 1970s, the city's popular music had unfolded in close relationship to Salvador's annual Carnival. The overarching trend of emphasizing Salvador's African cultural heritage, especially through its Carnival, was now also deeply ingrained in the city's popular music scene. By the late 1980s, Salvador's pop groups had developed a distinctive musical accent that derived from various mixes of bloco afro, ijexá, trio elétrico, and Afro-Caribbean-influenced dance music popular in the city (especially merengue, reggae, *soca* [a Trinidadian fusion of soul and calypso], and salsa). Much of Bahia's popular music was heavily dance-oriented, and much of the lyric content tended to center around love, partying, and the general notion of having a good time. However, lyrics also featured African-derived words (mainly from Yoruba) as well as references to Afro-Brazilian and Afro-Caribbean (especially Jamaican) cultural matters. The influence of the blocos afro and their cultural politics also brought issues of social justice, racial discrimination, and racial consciousness into pop song lyrics. In the press, the term *axé music* was initially applied in a rather derogatory manner to all of the Afro-related popular music flowing out of Bahia. Almost immediately, the nation adopted *axé music* as the umbrella marketing term for Bahia's new popular music. The name incorporated two important elements relevant to Salvador's popular culture in the late 1980s: (1) a widely dispersed black cultural identity built around Pan-African awareness, and (2) an increasing connection to international trends in popular music. For years, *axé* had been a vernacular term used in Salvador's black community. It is a Yoruba word that denotes spiritual force, power, and grace. Within Candomblé, the term describes the essence of the mystical life force. In Salvador, *axé* became a common term of greeting and leave-taking among members of the city's black community, a kind of hip street-speak marking an individual's awareness of and adherence to a wide range of black cultural values. The second part of the term, *music* (used in the English form, not in the Portuguese), reflected the international growth of a new category of global pop music that was then taking form around the concept of world music. Salvador's popular musical scene fitted nicely into the world music pattern of a local urban music style (typically from somewhere other than European or North American countries) that was rooted in the "authentic" sounds of a local, non-Anglo heritage and performed by urban popular musicians mixing rock instruments (electric guitars, drums, keyboard) with local instruments. The popular music of Salvador in the late 1980s fitted the bill and was about to be thrust onto the international stages of world music.

Key to axé music's perceived authenticity was its close relationship to African heritage via the music of the blocos afro groups in the city. The visual impact of the large blocos parading with thousands of costumed participants and the aural force of drumming corps featuring up to 200 members gave a potent, primal nature to the music. The blocos afro also provided a training ground for many of the percussionists of axé music who became performers with pop bands in the area. Tapping into Salvador's street-level rhythmic energy, electrified groups with lead singers translated the sounds of the blocos afro into a format for regional, national, and international audiences. At the end of the 1980s, numerous musicians and pop groups from Salvador were following this formula: Banda Mel, Banda Reflexu's, Chiclete com Banana, Luiz Caldas, Sarajane, and Gerônimo. This musical activity would likely have run its course relatively quickly—like so many other pop music fads tend to do—had it not been for the fortuitous collaboration between select drummers of Olodum and the American singer–songwriter–guitarist Paul Simon.

After the success of his Grammy-winning *Graceland* CD (1986), which featured artistic collaborations with black South African musicians, Paul Simon turned his attention to Brazil for his next international project. In 1987, he participated in Brazilian singer Milton Nascimento's *Yauaretê* recording in Los Angeles. At Nascimento's invitation, Simon traveled to Brazil four times over the next two years, accompanied by his recording engineer, Roy Hallie. Nascimento's own Brazilian record producer, Marco Mazzola, introduced Simon to local samba school drummers and other musicians in Rio de Janeiro. However, Simon was looking for something different, something exciting and captivating, and Mazzola informed him that some of the newest sounds in Brazil were coming out of Salvador da Bahia in the northeastern region of the country, the traditional center of African culture in Brazil. Simon went to Bahia in February 1988, where he was introduced to the Grupo Cultural Olodum. In the center of the city, in Pelourinho, he recorded a group of fourteen drummers from Olodum, led by Neguinho do Samba. The rhythms that Neguinho and Olodum played (based on the new samba–reggae style) were powerful and impressed Simon who used them for the basic rhythm track for "The Obvious Child," the lead song on Simon's next CD, *The Rhythm of the Saints* (1990).

Simon subsequently invited Neguinho do Samba and a group of Olodum drummers to tour and appear on American television with him to perform the song "The Obvious Child" (on *Saturday Night Live*, November 17, 1990). The media exposure of these activities bestowed international credibility on the Olodum group. As a result of the Simon collaboration, Olodum developed a professional show band (Banda Reggae Olodum) as one component of the larger cultural organization. This show band has toured extensively (in Europe, North America, and Japan) and has released CDs on an annual basis since 1987; by 2007 Olodum had released over twenty CDs. The Olodum group also collaborated with Michael Jackson and Spike Lee for the video "They Don't Care about Us" (1996). That event generated media interest and exposed Olodum to some 140 countries throughout the world. Working alongside international stars of Jackson's magnitude catapulted Olodum and Salvador's music into the world music arena while simultaneously giving them increased credibility in Brazil.

The international rise of Olodum also helped generate national interest in other ascending Bahian stars in the 1990s and placed Salvador on the world music map. The axé music diva Daniela Mercury's arrival on the scene solidified Bahia's new music within Brazil's mainstream music industry. Mercury began her career in the late 1980s as a singer for several trios elétricos and as a backup singer with Gilberto Gil and other prominent pop musicians from Bahia. Her debut solo album, *Daniela Mercury* (1991), became a national hit with the samba–reggae song titled "Swing da Cor" ("Swing of Color"), written by Luciano Gomes. The following year, she had another huge hit with the song "O Canto da Cidade" ("Song of the City"), co-written by Mercury and Tote Gira. Her album of the same name became the first Brazilian album to sell more than 1 million units, and the broadcast media saturated Brazilian airwaves with her music. "O Canto da Cidade" is set as a samba–reggae (merengue rhythm), with Olodum-style drumming prominently featured in the sound mix. In the first two lines of the song, Mercury, unambiguously white, proclaims, "I am the color of this city, the song of this city is mine." In their book *The Brazilian Sound*, Chris McGowan and Ricardo Pessanha wrote, "Some Brazilian critics suggested that much of Daniela's popularity was due to her being light-skinned and beautiful. Yet many black performers, including Gilberto Gil and Margareth Menezes, have defended Mercury's success and talent. Daniela is a kinetic performer with a sensual flair and effervescent charisma on stage."[12]

Daniela is certainly several shades whiter than the "color of the city" of Salvador, which is frequently described as the most African city in the Americas. However, her kinetic performance style derives fundamentally from the black aesthetics of Salvador's Carnival and its cultural life in general. It is intriguing to speculate on the relationships among her performance style, racial phenotype, and commercial manipulation of her image in the music industry. As samba–reggae and axé music gained more national and international recognition through the media and music industry, the possibility (and probability) of watering down the messages of African identity increased. One form this took was the promotion of non-threatening images of Bahia/Brazil (nationally/internationally) as a tropical paradise in which the races live together in harmony—the old myth of Brazil as a racial democracy raising itself through the pop music phenomenon of axé music. The video that was released for "O Canto da Cidade" featured Daniela as the lead singer–dancer, accompanied by several shirtless black male drummer–dancers referencing the bloco afro tradition as they danced their way through various parts of Salvador. A later album cover, *Feijão com Arroz* (Beans and Rice), featured a close-up of Mercury with an unidentified shirtless black man (or woman?) in a tight embrace. Had the black performance aesthetic merely been appropriated by Mercury and then transformed into Brazil's music industry category of axé music? Or had a black performance aesthetic become so thoroughly absorbed into Salvador's musical community that Mercury's performance style was the natural result of her participation in the city's cultural life? If in Candomblé, the bastion of Afro-Brazilian identity, anyone could become symbolically African through aesthetic and religious competence in dance and music (see Chapter 3), perhaps the same was possible in the field of popular culture.

Within the blocos afro community, a polarization of beliefs along separatist and integrationist lines persists. Ilê Aiyê's has tenaciously held on to an Afrocentric position of racial separateness, which it believes allows the group to maintain itself as a bulwark of black cultural resistance against the effects of continued white appropriation and domination. In Vovô's words (my translation):

I always say that here in Bahia there are two groups: one group that produces culture, that's us [the blacks], even with minimal resources and people to organize things. We make the music, the dance; we have the great composers, [and] all of this is appropriated and transformed through the media, like the *fricote* and *deboche* dances and rhythms were transformed, all the way up to *axé* music. It is telling that the kings and queens of *deboche* and *fricote* music never were blacks, or at least never presented themselves as real blacks. They adopted [cultural] paradigms in which the black man was not even a consideration.[13]

And Ilê Aiyê has continued to resist the adoption of string, wind, and electronic instruments into its ensembles. Other groups, such as Ara Ketu and Olodum, have "modernized" through the incorporation of additional electronic instrumental resources. The members of Olodum have also followed a distinctly different intellectual path in an attempt to assert themselves into the structural framework of the larger society in order to advance their cause of combating racism in all of its forms. As recounted by Olodum's long-time president, João Jorge:

Under the leadership of a new directorship in 1983 Olodum began to take steps to avoid the past errors of Ilê Aiyê, Badauê, Apache, the Filhos do Gandhi, Candomblé terreiros, political party members, Protestant church members, and members of the Catholic Church's Black Pastoral. And in so doing Olodum fulfilled an extremely important political role and wrote an important page in the history of Bahian music, culture, negritude.

The first thing we did was to admit whites and mestizos as members. Olodum would be made up of blacks, whites, and mestizos. The second thing we did was to insert ourselves into the political struggle. We knew that participating in Candomblé was good, that being a black artist or cultural producer was good. But something was missing. Previous revolutions and rebellions had taught us that it is not enough to acknowledge the value of our blackness and to say that we were beautiful. Above all we had to be strong. We had to have institutional strength and Olodum would fulfill this organizational role.[14]

Other Bahian artists more closely resembled the black phenotype typical of Salvador. For instance, Carlinhos Brown and his group Timbalada became a huge success within Salvador's Carnival, in the Brazilian national arena, and internationally as part of world music. After participating in almost all aspects of Salvador's musical life (as a percussionist, singer, and composer) and becoming known in Brazilian national music circles, Brown entered the international arena through the North American recording and release of *Bahia Black: Ritual Beating System* (1992). On this CD, he contributed five compositions, played guitar and percussion, and sang. The CD also included the Olodum group led by Neguinho do Samba as well as American jazz musicians Herbie Hancock and Wayne Shorter. Following this American project, Brown was tapped by the long-time exporter of Brazilian music Sergio Mendes, who featured the rising Bahian star on his Grammy-winning CD *Brasileiro* (1992). Subsequently, Brown developed the new Carnival organization Timbalada in the Candeal neighborhood of Salvador. The Timbalada group, like its leader, is extremely eclectic and incorporates multiple cultural and musical references from Bahia and the world in its repertoire. Its large drumming

Figure 7.4 Timbalada drummers rehearsing in the Candeal neighborhood of Salvador, Bahia, 1995 (photo by Larry Crook).

group is based on dozens of players of a conga-like drum called the timbal (hence the name Timbalada). Rows of percussionists also play cowbells and the combination of surdos, repiques, and snare drums typical of most blocos afro. They also incorporate an electrified band playing atop an elaborately wired sound truck. Singers move in and out of the drummers marching on the street with wireless microphones. Since issuing its first CD, *Timbalada* (1993), the group has released well-produced recordings every year.

The developments of Salvador's popular music of the last three decades of the twentieth century within the context of the black consciousness movement in Brazil had direct effects on the musical life of the Northeast's other main center for popular music, Recife.

Maracatu, Mangue Beat, and the New Scene of Recife

An Introduction and Manifesto

A new generation of musicians and artists from Recife burst onto the Brazilian popular music scene in the mid-1990s with a musical movement they called mangue beat.[15] Leading the movement was the band Chico Science & Nação Zumbi. The name of the band, like the name of the musical movement, referenced an eclecticism of style and an ideology assigning value to the hybrid and miscegenated nature of Recife and the Northeast. This alchemy combined scientific discovery with the tribal roots of an imaginary nation of Recife. The liner notes to the band's first CD, *Da Lama aos Caos* (From the Mud to Chaos, 1994), included a manifesto for the mangue beat movement. Originally written by Fred 04 (Fred Rodrigues Montenegro) and Renato Lins in 1991, the manifesto is titled "Caranguejos com Cérebro" ("Crabs with Brains") and is divided into three sections:

- "Mangue: The Concept"
- "Manguetown: The City"
- "Mangue: The Scene."

Together, these sections link the ecology and biological diversity of the local mangrove swamps (*mangues*) to the social, cultural, and economic realities of the greater Recife area. The importance of the biologically diverse estuary mangroves of the world is the focus of the first section. It is here that saltwater and freshwater flow in and out with the tides, replenishing some of the world's most fertile and productive ecological areas. Estimates indicate 2,000 species of microorganisms and vertebrate and invertebrate animals are associated with the diversity of the vegetation in the mangroves. In "Mangue: The City," Recife's urban landscape is conceptualized as being in a state of imbalance with the ecology of the local mangroves. Historically, Recife grew in an indiscriminate manner without concern for the consequences of invading, covering over, and destroying the mangroves. The so-called progress involved in becoming the regional metropolis of northeastern Brazil revealed Recife's ecological and economic fragility. As the manifesto puts it, "During the last thirty years, the syndrome of stagnation, linked to a continuing myth of the 'metropolis,' has only brought about the accelerated aggravation of misery and urban chaos." In the mid-1990s, Recife had the highest unemployment rate in the country, with over half of its inhabitants living in slums and flooded swamp areas. The manifesto cites the conclusion of an unnamed, Washington-based institute of population studies: Recife is considered the fourth-worst city in the world to live in. Finally, "Mangue: The Scene" provides a dramatic call to action (my translation):

> Emergency! A quick shock, or Recife will die from clogging! You need not be a medical doctor to realize that the easiest way to stop the heart is to clog its veins. Likewise, the quickest way to glut and drain the soul of a city like Recife, is to kill its rivers and cover up its estuaries. What can be done so that we do not worsen the chronic depression that paralyzes the city's people? How can we de-lobotomize to bring back the city's spirit and recharge its batteries? Simple! Just inject a little of the energy of the mud and stimulate what is left of the fertility in the veins of Recife.

> In mid-1991, a nucleus of research and production of "pop" ideas began to be generated and articulated in various parts of the city. The objective is to engender an "energy circuit" capable of linking the good vibes of the mangrove mud swamps with the global networks that circulate pop concepts. Symbol image: a parabolic satellite dish stuck in the mud.

> Mangue-boys and mangue-girls are individuals interested in comics, interactive television, anti-psychiatry, Bezerra da Silva, Hip Hop, mediotia [a made-up word suggesting the combination of *media* and *idiocy,* an interpretation suggested in Galinsky 2002], artism, music of the street, John Coltrane, chance, non-virtual sex, ethnic conflicts and all of the advances of chemistry applied to the alteration and expansion of consciousness.

It does not get much more eclectic that this! With the "Crabs with Brains" manifesto, the artists and intellectuals—the crabs with brains—envisioned the mangue movement as a jolt of energy for Recife, a wake-up call. They would combine the fertile local culture and artistic scene of Recife (symbolized by the city's mangrove swamps, where crabs and thousands of other creatures live) with global pop influences (symbolized by a satellite dish stuck in the mud collecting information from around the globe, perhaps even soaking up information from the universe). Mangue beat (originally proposed as mangue "bit," referencing a segment of digital information) evidenced the self-awareness of young Recife musicians living simultaneously in a technologically advanced age and in a Third World area with a rich and fertile local culture. Utilizing and exploiting the media through newspaper articles and liner notes, they created the initial appearance of a collective movement of artists with a "nucleus of pop ideas" dedicated to the regeneration of Recife's culture. In addition to Chico Science & Nação Zumbi, another band, Mundo Livre S.A., with an overlapping roster of musicians, was part of the initial mangue beat.

The advent of the mangue movement in the early 1990s coincided with the emergence of Recife from an extended period of economic and cultural stagnation. The artistic community of the area was awakening to possibilities of reviving and reinventing many of the Northeast's venerable folk traditions: maracatu de baque virado, *maracatu de baque solto* (maracatu of the free beat), banda de pífanos, cavalo-marinho, côco, embolada, *ciranda* (circle dance), caboclinho, and quadrilha. Northeastern folk instruments such as the rabeca (fiddle), oito baixos (diatonic button accordion), and pífano (cane fife) were receiving increased scholarly attention from folklorists and ethnomusicologists at the same time that young musicians and government-sponsored tourist agencies were "discovering" the traditional players of these instruments.

Other currents in Recife's musical scene had also emerged during the 1980s. The area's black population became increasingly conscious of the historical legacies of slavery and post-abolition racial inequalities in the country. In the 1980s, the blocos afro and afoxé Carnival groups and the samba–reggae musical style from Salvador became potent symbols of black identity and spread to other cities in Brazil as a grassroots phenomenon. This new model, based on using culture as a sociopolitical strategy of resistance, became a resource for black communities around the country. In the Recife area, percussion-based groups patterned on Salvador's blocos afro and afoxé began emerging. The first of these new Pernambucan groups was Afoxé Povo de Odé, founded in 1982. By 1991, there were at least twelve of these Afro groups participating in the Pernambucan Carnival. Following the lead of Olodum's slick new journal, an Afro-Pernambucan news journal named *Djumbay* was also founded in Recife in the early 1990s. The May 1992 edition of *Djumbay* reported four afoxés, six blocos afro, and fifteen bandas afro (afro bands) in the Recife area. All of these groups drew substantially on the new Afro-Bahian sounds. The afro bands mixed electronic instruments into their format, as similar bands in Salvador that were part of the emerging axé music did. Afoxés and blocos afro were constituted as black community service organizations, with music and dance as their primary activities to mobilize the youth. Within Pernambuco, this effort met with quite a lot of resistance and criticism from local cultural conservatives, who saw it as nothing more that a foreign invasion from Bahia. However, for Recife's young black and mestizo populations of the lower- and middle-class sectors, these new trends were both inspirational and fundamental cultural components of their own black identity.

Until the advent of the blocos afro such as Ilê Aiyê and Olodum from Bahia, which linked modern cultural production to issues of black consciousness and social awareness, most middle-class blacks in Recife were hesitant to participate openly in the city's local manifestations of black culture, especially in the venerable maracatu nations and in the Candomblés of the area. This activity was restricted largely to the culture of the lower-class blacks of the area. Following the lead of their Bahian counterparts, the afoxés, blocos afro, and bandas afro were formed at the community level in Recife to help stimulate interest in local African heritage among middle-class blacks and mestizos. They also began to spread to the white population, especially to university students in the area. The first local Afro-Pernambucan tradition impacted through middle-class participation was the maracatu de baque virado, one of the most potent symbols of African heritage in Recife (see Chapter 3). In December 1989, a new type of maracatu—the Maracatu Nação Pernambuco—was founded. Unlike the traditional maracatu nations of the area, the Maracatu Nação Pernambuco comprised well-educated, middle-class dancers and musicians, many of whom were white. The influx of middle-class youth (white, black, and mestizo) into the maracatu tradition brought new concepts of choreography and music. The Nação Pernambuco group was created on the pattern of a folkloric troupe that was not tied to the concepts of a traditional maracatu. Nação Pernambuco based its repertoire in the maracatu de baque virado but also included other folk traditions from the area. A small pamphlet published by the group in 1993 explains that the origin of the Pernambuco "nation" is found in the mixture of the African and the Amerindian and that its cultural, political, and social dimensions are derived from all people and races.

The founders of Nação Pernambuco were guided by the desire to revive the glory of the local maracatu and to create new possibilities that would help popularize Recife's rich artistic traditions. Led by artistic director Bernardo José, the group began performing stage shows and presentations throughout the year. It also released a self-titled first CD (in 1993) and began traveling in Brazil and Europe. Additionally, they traveled to the United States to perform at the New Orleans Jazz and Heritage Festival. Members of Recife's traditional maracatu nations reacted both positively and negatively to the commercial and folkloric developments represented by the Nação Pernambuco. Some criticized the group as a *maracatu de branco* (white man's maracatu) because several of its drummers were white. Others criticized the performances as too staged and the drumming and dancing as too stylized. A major issue was the fact that including the word *Nação* in the group's name implied that it was a traditional maracatu de baque virado connected to a Candomblé house. It was not. Despite these criticisms, the Nação Pernambuco opened up many new possibilities for some of the area's traditional mara-catus. The Maracatu Nação Estrela Brilhante (founded in 1906) began incorporating middle-class students (including several female percussionists) into its ranks in mid-1990s after it relocated its headquarters to the Alto José do Pinho neighborhood. Estrela Brilhante has become one of most popular of the traditional maracatus among middle-class audiences and musicians in Recife's nova scena. A number of prominent musicians from the city's bands have participated in the group, including Jorge Martins (Cascabulho) and Éder Rocha (Mestre Ambrósio). Another traditional maracatu,

Nação Porto Rico do Oriente (founded in 1916), has also incorporated women into its drumming corp and new performance aesthetics stimulated, in part, by the Nação Pernambuco model. According to many, the Nação Pernambuco was the initial seed from which Recife's mangue beat and its nova scena of the 1990s sprouted.

At the same time that the maracatu tradition was being reconfigured in response to the new models of cultural production from Bahia, underground scenes of hard-core metal, thrash, punk, funk, and other styles of music were popping up throughout the city. It was within this general eclectic milieu that the first impulses of the mangue movement emerged.

According to various sources, in 1990 or 1991, Chico Science first met percussionist Gilmar Bola Oito of the local Recife bloco afro group Lamento Negro (Black Lament). The group played mainly samba–reggae, and like Salvador's blocos afro organizations, it was involved in community-based activities. The members also were familiar with the local drumming style of maracatu. Lamento Negro's rehearsals took place at a local community center known as Daruê Malungo. In his book *Maracatu Atômico*, Philip Galinsky cited an interview with local instrument maker and former member of Lamento Negro Maureliano Ribeiro: "When Chico began music, he had a formal band of his own—drumset, bass, guitar. But he needed to do something new, different, for the sound he wanted to make. And he wanted to mix the culture. . . . So he went after Gilmar, who was a good friend of mine and such, we lived together in the same neighborhood, and he always asked Gilmar, 'Let's do it like this: an exchange with the drums.'"[16]

Chico attended Lamento Negro rehearsals for about a year before attempting to fuse the group's drumming style with electric guitar and bass. He enlisted the help of guitarist Lucio Maia and bassist Alexandre Dengue plus the drummers from Lamento Negro. This arrangement formed the core of a line-up that would later become the Nação Zumbi group. Chico Science's idea was to mix the Lamento Negro's drumming with music from his own background in classic North American black music styles (James Brown, Grand Master Flash, Funkadelic, and the Sugar Hill Gang were among his favorite performers). According to Recife music critic José Teles, both Maia and Dengue thought that the electric guitars would not work well with the sounds of Lamento Negro.[17] A few rehearsals proved that they were wrong.

Chico Science wanted to focus the group's attention on Pernambuco's rich musical heritage—primarily its rhythmic diversity—and mix this with a globally informed perspective. Galinsky noted, "Due to Chico's interest in reclaiming an unsung Pernambucan heritage, the influence of the Bahian samba-reggae was left behind in the band's efforts to couple regional sounds such as maracatu, côco, embolada, and ciranda, with heavy metal, rap, *ragamuffin*, soul, funk, psychedelic rock, electronic dance music, and samplers."[18] Chico would dub this rhythmic mixture mangue. The new style was to be based on principles of diversity, fusion, and global technology and the idea of reclaiming Pernambuco's regional cultural heritage. Experimenting with a wide range of northeastern rhythmic traditions, Chico and the group eventually settled into a close relationship with the instruments and the basic sound of the maracatu de baque virado. As Recife's oldest and most venerable Carnival music—something that was quite unique to Pernambuco, that had an unusually powerful sonic presence, and that symbolically represented the history of black cultural resistance—the maracatu provided an ideal vehicle for Chico Science and his group.

Changing its name from Chico Science & Lamento Negro to Chico Science & Nação Zumbi, the group pared down from about fifteen to eight musicians on electric bass and guitar, three maracatu alfaia drums, miscellaneous percussion, snare drum, and vocals. The name *Nação Zumbi* indicated associations both to the maracatu de baque virado tradition (with *Nação* designating the link of maracatu to Candomblé religion) and to the history of black Brazilian resistance symbolized by Zumbi, the legendary Afro-Brazilian leader of the Quilombo de Palmares runaway slave society. The influence of the maracatu tradition became most visible in the live performances of Chico Science & Nação Zumbi, with the distinctive alfaia drums played on center stage by three of the drummers of the group. One of the former members of the original Lamento Negro group, Maureliano, developed a modern version of the large double-headed drums that became a trademark of Nação Zumbi. Although made with the advanced woodworking techniques of cabinetmaking, Maureliano's drums used the rope tensioning and natural animal skins of the traditional maracatu drums.

The group's link to maracatu was also highlighted through creative CD packaging. The graphic layout on the back cover of Chico Science's influential second CD, *Afrociberdelia* (1996), prominently features an image of the band members framed inside the rim of one of Maureliano's maracatu drums. The focus on these drums was nearly ubiquitous in the sonic realm of the band as well. The maracatu de baque virado beat and other local rhythms were adapted largely to coordinated patterns played on the three large maracatu

Figure 7.5 Maracatu drums used by Chico Science, Recife, Pernambuco, 1998 (photo by Larry Crook).

drums and the snare drum of the ensemble, which worked well to create all manner of fusions between international popular music and regional folk traditions. The distinctive drumbeats played on the maracatu drums also gave mangue beat a distinctive musical style, and thus, it was able to serve as Recife's new entré into the world music scene. The international marketing of world music is founded largely on Western notions of premodern authenticity applied to selected Third World musical styles.[19] In the case of Chico Science & Nação Zumbi, the sense of premodern authenticity was conveyed through the use of the maracatu drums and the "primal" nature of the group's presentational style, rooted in a live performance aesthetic.

The group members, especially Chico Science, seemed to know where they wanted to take their sound, but translating it into a recorded format was not without its challenges. Brazilian rock music producer Liminha (Arnolpho Lima Filho) was chosen by Sony Music to produce the group's debut CD. Recounting the experience in an interview with Carlos Calado in 1993, Liminha stated (my translation): "One thing that impresses me a lot about the band is the heavy sound that they get. Those drummers play as if they are possessed. We're still going to experiment with adding samples to some things, but we're preoccupied with achieving a sound that can be reproduced live."[20]

From the perspective of a Brazilian record producer primarily familiar with rock, the problems associated with translating a complex studio sound into live performance had been an issue since the late 1960s; at that time, the Beatles had stopped touring because, in part, they could not reproduce live what they were creating in the studio. However, for Chico Science & Nação Zumbi, the more pertinent question was how to translate a complex live sound into the studio-based format.

In an interview with Walter da Silva, Chico Science emphasized the importance of the group's live shows and how its members had struggled to translate the energy of live performance to a recorded format.[21] Responding to a question about the difference between the group's first and second CDs, Chico spoke of giving a sense of "weight" to the recording, "a consistent kind of weight with everything in its place." He went on to stress that it was the specific sound quality of the drums—the maracatu drums—that needed additional attention in the recorded format. He added, "Listening to the first CD, playing shows, we saw how we could improve the sound by giving a new timbre to the drums." The acoustic power of the large maracatu drums was explored in the studio to create a distinctly Afro-Pernambucan accent to Nação Zumbi's music, which also made it appealing to world music audiences. The sound of maracatu drums runs throughout the two CDs that Chico Science & Nação Zumbi released. However, equally important for the construction of the mangue beat sound were the performance aesthetics, production values, and musical influences that linked the music to global popular youth culture. The booming bass of the maracatu drums matched the prominence of the low-end sounds in other international black popular music styles, such as hip-hop and reggae. The aesthetics of miscegenation also extended into transnational arenas with references to soul, funk, heavy metal, rap, ragamuffin, psychedelic rock, and electronic dance music and the use of sampling. Songs were often compositional pastiches moving from one style to the next. They also layered multiple influences, local and transnational, on top of one another. The distortion timbres of Nação Zumbi's lead guitarist, Lúcio Maia, were heavy-metal-tinged and reminiscent of Jimi Hendrix's guitar sound. The recitative-like rap vocal delivery and hip-hop physical stage presence of Chico Science, the unabashed celebration of electronic technomusic and computer technology, and the sampling all linked mangue beat to a postmodern aesthetic of the local/global context of artistic production. The creative fusion of these tendencies with the aesthetics of local traditions made Chico Science's importance extend well beyond the state of Pernambuco and the shores of Brazil.

After their first CD, Chico Science & Nação Zumbi experienced a meteoric rise in the world music scene. In 1995, the group appeared at the Montreaux Jazz Festival and in New York City's Central Park Summer Stage series, where they shared the stage with Gilberto Gil and other Brazilian artists. The career of Chico Science was tragically cut short when he died in an automobile accident on February 2, 1997, during Carnival in Pernambuco. But his impact on Recife's music scene proved indelible, as not only Nação Zumbi but also many other local artists continued creating a new wave of music based on creative fusions of local and international music. This scene includes highly electric, hard-core mangue bands such as Devotos do Ódio and Eddie as well as more roots-oriented groups such as Comadre Florzinha and Chão e Chinelo. The diversity of the post-Chico Science generation of popular music in Recife in the 1990s came under the broad designation of the city's nova scena.

Recife Unplugged: Mestre Ambrósio and Cascabulho

Among the most innovative of the nova scena groups to emerge on the Recife scene in the wake of Chico Science and the mangue beat were the bands Mestre Ambrósio and Cascabulho. These groups reinterpreted local folk traditions in a more unplugged manner than did Nação Zumbi. Though heavily influenced by the mangue beat of Chico Science and others, they also went through what John Murphy identified as a process of "self-discovery" involving a cleansing of extraneous elements from their music.[22]

Mestre Ambrósio, led by the rabeca player Sérgio Veloso (Siba), gives special attention to the northeastern folk fiddle known as the rabeca, which is particularly popular in the *zona da mata* (forest zone) cane-growing region surrounding Recife. The name of the group is taken from a central character in the local folk drama cavalo-marinho (literally meaning "sea horse"), in which the rabeca functions as the lead melodic instrument. The dance music that accompanies the cavalo-marinho features the lively baiano, a dance genre closely related to the baião. As mentioned in Chapter 5, Luiz Gonzaga drew on the baiano and other regional northeastern genres when he developed and popularized the baião in the 1940s and 1950s with his accordion-based ensemble. Subsequent innovations by Gonzaga and his followers led to the highly syncopated forró in the 1960s and 1970s. Parallel to the development of the accordion-based forró, other types of local ensembles in the Northeast also developed forró styles within their own repertoires. The forró played on the rabeca was little known outside the cane-growing area until Mestre Ambrósio and a handful of other bands in Recife began to play this music.

In the early 1990s, Siba was a student in music at the Federal University of Pernambuco when he met John Murphy, who was carrying out field research on the cavalo-marinho folk drama of the area. Together, they attended traditional performances throughout the sugarcane-growing region around Recife. It was there that Siba got his first extended exposure to the richness of the musical traditions involving the rabeca. Stimulated by the experiences, he went on to conduct his own research into the instrument, which involved learning to perform on it well enough to play for the all-night cavalo-marinho folk performances. Siba was also a guitarist and, like many other urban musicians, was interested in a wide range of rock, jazz, and classical forms. In the early 1990s, the nascent mangue beat movement was gaining momentum in Recife, and Siba teamed up with two other musicians (Hélder Vasconcelos and Éder Rocha) for projects mixing the maracatu with thrash-metal music. Out of these projects came Mestre Ambrósio, which was formed in 1992.

Early on, Mestre Ambrósio included both electric and acoustic manifestations, but the two separated entities were later fused. However, the members of the group eventually came to realize that they and their audiences identified more with the local regional styles in their music—especially with the sound of the rabeca—than with foreign (non-Pernambucan) sources. Reflecting on the situation, Siba explained: "To be truthful, for the music that we play today to be possible, we've been through a long process of self-cleansing. Cleaning ourselves of rock, of jazz, of art music. Cleaning, not in the sense that these things are good or bad, but in the sense that as we grow up with these other styles, living with them on a daily basis, we completely loose our meaning, our specific references, as musicians, as persons, and even as Northeasterners and Brazilians." He went on:

> And suddenly you see yourself, as I saw myself in my early twenties, studying at the university, where there was only room for art music, where I only played rock guitar and was starting to learn jazz. Everyone goes through this here. The process the band went through illustrates this. We started out with a very diverse sound, full of references, and started cleaning, cleaning, cleaning, until we arrived at a music that reflects the place where we live very well, and despite this has references to jazz, to rock—it's all there, in small proportions, for better or worse. But we had to clean ourselves. Not to put down or bracket off other styles, but to be able to see the real importance of each element.[23]

Crafting a predominantly acoustic sound that foregrounded the rabeca (played in a rhythmically active style related directly to the local forró tradition) with a pan-northeastern percussion line-up (zabumba, triangle, pandeiro, reco-reco, agogô), the group launched a type of forró that had never been popularized commercially: *forró de rabeca* (rabeca forró). The urban orientation of the music, embedded with rural aesthetics, is something the group came to refer to as *forró pé-de-calçada* (literally meaning "foot of the sidewalk forró"). This designation alluded to the phrase *forró pé-de-serra* (meaning "forró of the foothills"), referring to forró from the rural areas. It also recalled Luiz Gonzaga's famous recording "No Meu Pé de Serra" of 1946. In Mestre Ambrósio's forró pé-de-calçada, international influences have been gradually filtered out and various local traditions are highlighted to create the new kind of forró. The group's first CD, titled *Mestre Ambrósio*, includes the song "Pé-de-Calçada," which comments on this process.

Lyrics to "Pé-de-Calçada," by Sérgio Veloso (Siba)

Today I play forró in the city [*pé-de-calçada*]
In the midst of confusion going the wrong way
I went to the woods and returned to the city
From a *caboclo* I know my situation
Rabeca come and don't abandon me
Zabumba shake the earth, eat up the ground
When time is gone,
Transform the city [*pé-de-calçada*] into the country [*pé-de-serra*][24]

The "confusion" of the second line is perhaps an overstimulation resulting from too many influences and options in the city, a situation that can result in the loss of a well-centered identity. Making a pilgrimage to the woods and learning from a caboclo tradition bearer was the road to self-awareness: "I know my situation." Instrumental markers of traditional music (the rabeca and zabumba) are invoked to help embed the country in the city. This aspect of Mestre Ambrósio recalls the efforts of Luiz Gonzaga half a century earlier. CD *Track 14* presents Mestre Ambrósio performing "Pé-de-Calçada."

Cascabulho is another band in Recife's nova scena that honors local musical traditions by recasting them within its own urban musical fusion. Like their colleagues in Mestre Ambrósio, the members of Cascabulho have chosen a particular set of local coordinates to draw on. Like Chico Science, they are involved in experimentation with technology. The back cover of their first CD, *Fome Dá Dor de Cabeça* (Hunger Gives You a Headache), has the following inscription (my translation):

> We are not a rock band. Neither are we a "forró" band, much less a folklore group. Our roots: they're in the mud of Pernambuco, of which we are made. Our influences: we're suburban guys from the periphery of Recife, fertilized by the industrial winds blowing all over the planet. From Jackson do Pandeiro: we try to capture and follow his magisterial aesthetic conception, his bold stylistic originality, his extraordinary technical spontaneity, his profound musical sensibility, his virtuosic rhythm, the high artistic quality of his work that is always up-to-date and fresh. In truth, we're crazy about music! We're Cascabulho!

As the inscription makes clear, Cascabulho is inspired by the music of Jackson do Pandeiro, a legendary singer from the Northeast who rivaled Luiz Gonzaga for national prominence in the 1950s. In addition, members of the Cascabulho group have established ongoing relationships with the maracatu, banda de pífanos, and cantoria communities in Recife.

Cascabulho originally formed in 1995. The group was fronted by singer Silvério Pessoa, a former teacher from the zona da mata region, near Recife. Pessoa was an energetic singer who could stylistically pull off the rapid côco de embolada style that Pandeiro had popularized. Two talented young percussionists, Jorge Martins and Wilson Farias, anchored the rhythm for the band. The electric bass player (Lito Viana), electric guitar player (Marcos Lopes), and electric keyboard player (Kleber Magrão) all doubled on vocals and northeastern percussion instruments. In 1997, the group participated in Recife's premiere rock festival (Abril Pro Rock), and it was quickly proclaimed one of the most promising bands in the city's nova scena. The members then traveled to New York to perform at the Central Park Summer Stage series, sharing the stage with Mestre Ambrósio, Banda de Pífanos Dois Irmãos, and Lenine. Cascabulho was on an impressive trajectory for a band that was yet to record a CD. The first CD was released in 1998 for the local label appropriately named Mangroove. An eclectic variety of northeastern styles are pulled together on the CD, unified by what might be described loosely as mangue forró. The opening track, "Vovó Alaide," written by Silvério Pessoa, pays immediate tribute to the master with a sample of Jackson do Pandeiro, followed by an up-tempo *forró-côco*. Other styles referenced on the CD include the maracatu de baque virado, maracatu de baque solto, côco, cantoria de viola, and ciranda. The group won prestigious Prêmio Sharp awards (a Brazilian equivalent to the Grammy awards) in 1999 in two categories—Best Regional Group and Best Regional Song—with the song "Quando Sonei que Era Santo" ("When I Dreamed That I Was a Saint"). The band was also chosen to represent Brazil in the Panamerican Games in Canada, and it later performed at the Montreal Jazz Festival and the Vancouver Folk Festival. In the same year, it performed at the WOMEX (World Music Exposition) in Germany. The next year, 2000, saw the group traveling to the United States, with performances in California, Texas, and at the New Orleans Jazz and Heritage Festival in Louisiana. The group reformed itself after returning from the U.S. tour.

In its new formation, Cascabulho delved deeper into its instrumental repertoire, with several new musicans. One of the new members was Guga Santos, an eighteen-year-old percussionist from Olinda who had grown up participating in the maracatu de baque solto, a form of maracatu with ties to the syncretic religion called Jurema, which mixed Candomblé, Amerindian, and spiritist practices. Guga Santos was directly involved as an ogan drummer in the syncretic religion. Another young musician, flutist José Manuel, also joined Cascabulho. In 2000, Manuel was studying flute at the Federal University of Pernambuco. At the time, he told me that he favored baroque music, especially the music of Georg Philip Telemann and Bach. He was also interested in playing the pífano and hence brought ideas on incorporating music from the banda de pífanos tradition to Cascabulho. A third new member was Alexandre Ferreira, on electric bass, saxophone, and pífano. Originally from southern Brazil, Ferreira had lived in Europe for several years and brought an affinity to jazz to the group. Percussionist Jorge Martins continued to be a primary force behind the group. A brief account of his life will illuminate how he has come to be intimately involved in Recife's local music scene.

Jorge Martins was born on March 5, 1965, and grew up in the Morro de Conceição neighborhood of Recife (located in Casa Amarela). There were plenty of community music and dance groups in the area representing local and national traditions (escola de samba, caboclinho, maracatu) and also Candomblé houses. Jorge told me:

I was afraid. But nonetheless, I would go to these places, and at times, I didn't even know why. Now, I understand that it was because the music was calling me. I always was going to these events but never participated. I wanted to, but I was ashamed. I was ashamed because my father was prejudiced, and I was ashamed to play. At times, I was going to participate, but then I was just too ashamed, embarrassed to ask. But I kept going, and then I began to construct percussion instruments out of cans.[25]

Martins wanted to participate in percussion bands, and he started forming groups with his own improvised instruments. He formed a samba school, but his father would not allow him to perform out in the streets. He persisted with his interests in percussion and became involved with capoeira. He identified with the berimbau (a one-stringed musical bow) and the percussion instruments. His interest in music remained an unfulfilled aspect of his life. He decided to try his hand at some formal training in music and entered a local music academy in 1989. After spending some three years, off and on, at the academy, he left in order to devote himself to performing and learning about the local culture of Recife. He became involved with a group of percussion students (some were university students) who, like himself, were interested in popular culture. What drew his attention most was the maracatu de baque virado. He had some contacts with Recife's oldest maracatu, Nação Elefante, so he took his group of percussionists there, hoping to establish an ongoing relationship whereby they could participate in and learn the maracatu tradition. Things did not work out with that maracatu, but Martins soon met another local maracatu, the Estrela Brilhante. During an outdoor celebration in which that group was performing, Martins took advantage of the situation to speak with the head of the group. He noted: "So, when they finished the celebration, I spoke with the president and told him that I gave percussion lessons to children and that I also participated in a group of young men and women who played percussion. And I asked if it might be possible for my group to learn how to play maracatu with them. He responded that that would be no problem."

Jorge Martins and the group of percussionists started attending rehearsals led by Estrela Brilhante's director of the percussion, Mestre Valter. Among the other percussionists participating was Éder Rocha of Mestre Ambrósio. There were also three female drummers, who were enrolled at the Federal University of Pernambuco: Cristina Barbosa, Virginia Barbosa, and Neide Alves. Estrela Brilhante became an active center for the cultural exchange among different socioeconomic sectors of the population. As Martins mentioned:

These movements were emerging, these things, in a way that was favorable for the traditional maracatus in the city, like the Estrela Brilhante. The mangue beat movement, people carrying the drums onto the stages, that was working on the consciousness of the people. Give importance to your own culture. The result, people today act, think, and have the need to learn to play the maracutu. All of these things. All of these rhythms. There were many things happening. It was a chain reaction that wound up with what's happening today. Today, even the Maracatu Nação Pernambuco is an export, like Estrela Brilhante too. The thing is crossing the border. I also want to cross borders. Not just with Cascabulho but as a professional [musician] too.

Jorge Martins began teaching percussion classes in Recife to middle-class children, teenagers, and adults. He also organized several projects funded through the city of Recife to teach percussion to underserved children in the area. In all of these activities, he specialized in transmitting the rhythm of maracatu de baque virado. Out of these pedagogical activities, he created a loose group of local amateur percussionists who interacted with several of Recife's traditional maracatus. Martins also frequently called on this group to enhance Cascabulho's live performances with maracatu parades that began on the stage and ended up in the audience. In a way, this was the reverse of Chico Science & Nação Zumbi's efforts to translate the power of the maracatu from their live format to the recorded format. Cascabulho attempted to reconnect the live audiences of Recife with the acoustic presence of the maracatu drums.

With the reformation of Cascabulho in 2000, Martins and the group rededicated themselves to traversing the borders of local musical traditions and international forms even further. They also maintained a strong sense of social commitment to their community. In 2000 and 2001, they began working on a new CD project, titled *Cacos de Vidro: Bom para o Corpo e a Alma* (Slivers of Pure Glass: Good for the Body and Soul). I was in Recife during the initial phase of this undertaking and helped the group translate into English their description of the project for a press packet they were putting together. The following is a transcript from part of that material:

> The reason that these people are so excited is found in the balancing act long sought after in the "Recife Scene," which Cascabulho has been able to master: a balance of the symbiotic relationship between rural culture—the music that, for their parents and during the childhood of most of its members, was like a sound track—and urban culture—the soundscape of the band's adolescent and adult ages. It is a delicate mix of these two poles, as well as the group's ease in manifesting influences from Charles Mingus to Jackson do Pandeiro, which has always been the strength of Cascabulho these last few years.
>
> More than anything else, and this is a promise, Cascabulho swears that it will not cut its roots. It will not forget the common artists who inspire the group who, at times, in the crazy whirlwind of show business, are left behind by other pop artists. Many times, the world of "popspace" is vacuous and without social comment, in contrast to the daily struggles confronted by communities. The help that Cascabulho has recently given to the Movimento Sem Terra (Homeless Movement) is part of the group's commitment to their community.

I was also in the studio when the group began working on one of the first pieces for the new CD, a piece that mixes the banda de pífanos tradition with forró, Afro-Pernambucan drumming from Jurema, and electronic sounds. The piece, titled "Perua do Egildo" ("Egildo's Turkey"), was written by Egildo do Pífano, and it exemplifies Cascabulho's innovative mixture of urban- and rural-associated sounds.

Final Comments: Mixture, Hybridity, and Brazilian Music

I began this book with scenes describing my own perceptions of three music and dance traditions of Recife's Carnival: the unrelenting driving pulse of the maracatu de baque virado, the nostalgic lyrics and melodies of the bloco carnavalesco, and the intricate feathered costuming and flute-and-drum music of the caboclinhos. In a certain sense, these traditions represent for me performance enactments of the African, the European, and the Amerindian heritages in Brazil. However, they also exemplify the hybrid nature of Brazilian cultural formation and artistic production, which extends from elite traditions to grassroots, community-level activities. Brazil's major sociological thinker of the twentieth century, Gilberto Freyre, championed the notion that Brazil was a hybrid mestizo society where culturally based racial differences should be celebrated as a cornerstone for nation building. In Freyre's view, this was Brazil's greatest asset. A northeasterner himself, he formulated his ideas largely through his own national and international activities, including formal training in anthropology at Columbia University in New York. With an internationally informed perspective, he brought into focus his new vision of a unified Brazilian society based on the idea of mixture. Rather than a modernity built along the lines of the "advanced" countries, Freyre envisioned a different sort of modernity for Brazil, one that could incorporate those Brazilian cultural elements that were then considered backward. Hermano Vianna noted that the entire history of Brazilian national consciousness can be related to the country's own perceived backwardness in relation to the so-called civilized countries of the world.[26] I believe that an equally important factor is the country's perceptions of the Northeast as a region of continued backwardness in relation to the modernized South. This is both the burden and the strength of the area. Though the focus of national activity in Brazil was certainly coordinated through Rio de Janeiro in the South, the Northeast must be credited for providing the necessary regional cultural background against which the nation took shape. As the samba ascended to national prominence as the country's primary expression of a unified hybrid society, the articulation of regional difference in Brazil through expressive popular culture was also occurring. The emergence and celebration of Luiz Gonzaga and the baião as a nationalized form of regional identity for the Northeast should be seen in this light. Like Brazil in relation to the industrialized countries of Europe and North America, the Northeast was conceptualized as a backward region in relation to the industrialized South of the country. Luiz Gonzaga came to celebrate the cultural markers of that supposed backwardness only after he moved to the South and experienced his region from a national perspective. Within that context, he put together a hybrid mix of cultural markers drawn from northeastern music (instruments, modal patterns, regional vocal accent, song themes) that distinguished his baião from the popular music of South.

The hybrid nature of the social and cultural life of Brazil—particularly in the Northeast—is long-standing. The folk traditions of the interior region of the Northeast have witnessed substantial interaction over time between urban and rural worlds and between different ethnic groups and social classes, and they have seen the expanding horizons of media communication thrust caboclo culture into the national consciousness. Linkages forged by intercultural mediators from the South with northeastern musicians should be also acknowledged as crucial for the establishment of Brazilian national culture and the idea of a distinctly regional sound associated with the Northeast.

Some 100 years ago, Pixinguinha, Catulo da Paixão Cearense, and João Pernambuco were major figures in this regard.

Although they exhibited new and creative ways of confronting the changing social and cultural landscape of Brazil, the new musical currents of Recife and Salvador reflected Brazilian processes that have been noted throughout this book. In the case of Salvador, the re-examination of African heritage and the valorization of all things "black" represented the continued search for a black place within the country's promised but never delivered racial democracy. By forging new and vibrant cultural components of blackness that were translocal in conception, a universal and inclusive aesthetic of blackness emerged, which in turn altered the national conception of blackness in Brazil. In contrast, the mangue beat movement centered in Recife focused not on a racial identity rooted in one of Brazil's three foundational races (Amerindian, African, and European) but rather on the condition of mixture itself. Echoing and updating the ideas of the main architect of Brazilian mestizo identity, Gilberto Freyre, Recife's new musical scene unmasked the complexity and interconnecteness of mixed racial identity, cultural belonging, and sense of locality. For Recife musicians, this was a return to the roots of their mixed identities and a discovery of their past in the present. The development of the mangue beat and the nova scena in Recife also highlighted how, from the point of inception, a complex array of social class affiliation, processes of hybridity, and global flows of information were at the core of the construction of new popular music forms. Likewise, in Salvador, the black cultural space that was carved out in the 1970s within the city's annual Carnival celebrating African heritage was initially stimulated by international black popular music forms that were conceptualized alongside local Afro-Bahian traditions. Intersecting networks of musicians, audiences, and media that cut across race, class, and geographic boundaries expanded the initial activity of the blocos afro into the national and transnational arenas of circulation known as world music.

As I have argued throughout this book, the Northeast has been on the cutting edge of the transnational conceptualization and circulation of music in Brazil from the initial encounters of the colony's earliest inhabitants to the present. From the influential *tropicália* of Bahian songsters Gilberto Gil and Caetano Veloso to the mangue beat of Chico Science & Nação Zumbi, northeastern-born popular musicians seem to have had a particular knack for linking themselves and their art to larger translocal communities. Along these lines, it is interesting to note that the initial point of departure for a recent book titled *Brazilian Popular Music and Globalization,* which deals with issues of internationalization in Brazilian music, is the song "Chiclete com Bananas," made famous by the northeastern singer Jackson do Pandeiro. In the introductory essay, the authors write: "One of the most flamboyant personalities in the history of Brazilian music, Jackson do Pandeiro was known, in fact, for crossing traditional material of the northeast with samba, in a kind of interregional act of hybridity within a diverse and enormous country."[27] Jackson do Pandeiro's music, like that of the Northeast, was also a kind of transnational act of hybridity within a diverse and enormous world. The last four lines of "Chiclete com Banana" reframe the common assumption that local forms of music around the world are being replaced by a homogenized version of Western pop: "I want to see a boogie-woogie / With a *pandeiro* and a guitar / I want to see Uncle Sam with a Brazilian frying pan / playing in a Brazilian percussion jam."

Appendix:
Musical Examples on the Compact Disc

Track 1: "Miçanga"
Performed by various members of Maracatu Nação Porto Rico de Oriente
Field Recording by Larry Crook, Recife, February 9, 1988
Duration: 4:42

I recorded this track in 1988, one week prior to Carnival. That year, the city of Recife sponsored nightly street performances of the various Carnival traditions in the large downtown area of the city. This was the night of maracatu nations, as groups from all over the city converged on the Praça do Diário to give their presentations. Each maracatu group performed for ten to fifteen minutes in the center of the plaza. In this example, Dona Elda of the maracatu Naçao Porto Rico de Oriente sings the song "Miçanga." The entire maracatu, with its large percussion group, was in the middle of the open square, with hundreds of onlookers crowded around in a large circle. In the middle of the track, the MC for the night can be heard acknowledging the group as they push through the crowd to leave the performance space.

Portuguese Lyrics
> Ê, vamos ver miçanga em Luanda
> Chegou, chegou
> Porto Rico, nação de Mina
> Nossa rainha já se corou

English Translation by Larry Crook
> Oh, let's see the beads in Luanda
> It arrived, it arrived

Porto Rico, nation of Mina [West Africa]
Our queen has been crowned.

Track 2: "Alegre Bando" / "Happy Band"

By Edgard Moraes
Performed by Coral Edgard Moraes
Arrangement by Marco César
From the CD *Coral Edgard Moraes—Frevos de Bloco.* LG Projetos e Produções 000.015.
Used by permission.
Duration: 3:36

This is a contemporary recording of the Carnival frevo de bloco song titled "Alegre Bando" by venerable Recife composer Edgard Moraes. The recording features the Coral Edgard Moraes, an all-women's chorus made up of the daughters and granddaughters of the composer. This group carries on the tradition of the *coro feminino* (female chorus) that was popularized in the 1920s among Recife's middle-class Carnival revelers. The accompaniment features the instrumental grouping referred to as the orquestra de pau e corda, or wood and string orchestra, that accompanies this kind of frevo song. The musical arrangement is by Marco César, one of Recife's most talented bandolim (mandolin) players.

Portuguese Lyrics

Abram alas, queridos foliões
Que vai passar o alegre bando,
Trazendo mil recordações,
Deixando o povo com prazer cantando
A canção que faz lembrar
Passados carnavais das fantasias tradicionais.
Pierrot, pierrete, e arlequim
Colombina e o dominó de veludo
Espalhavam alegria sem fim
No auge da festa do entrudo
Os foliões com emoção vibrando
Na frevolência louca do carnaval
Ouviam som de guizos anunciando
O bando de palhaços, colorido original

English Translation by Larry Crook

Open the wings, dear Carnival revelers
Because the lively group is passing by
Bringing thousands of memories
Leaving people joyful as they sing
The song that makes them remember
Past Carnivals of traditional costumes

Pierrot, Pierrete, and Arlequim [Carnival characters]
Colombina and the velvet domino
Spread happiness without end.
At the height of the entrudo,
The groups with their vibrant emotions
In the crazy frevolência of Carnival.
They heard the sound of bells announcing
The band of clowns, in original colors.

Track 3: "Pandeiro Solo"

Performed by Bernardo Aguiar (pandeiro)
Field recording by Larry Crook, Rio de Janeiro, July 9, 2006
Duration: 2:34

I recorded Bernardo Aguiar in a park on the grounds of the Palácio do Catete in Rio de Janeiro (you can hear children playing in the background). One of Brazil's top young pandeiro players and student of Marcos Suzano, Aguiar is known for his virtuosity and innovative use of ornamented strokes (flams) and multiple bass tones on the pandeiro. I placed the microphone (Audio Tecnica AT822) beneath the pandeiro on a small stand in order to highlight the bass range so important to the Suzano school of pandeiro playing. This example demonstrates the range of timbres and rhythms available on the pandeiro.

Track 4: "Freio à Óleo"

By José Menezes
Performed by the Orquestra do Maestro Duda
Arrangement by José Menezes
Drumset: Adelson
Surdo: Nildo
Pandciro: Adão
Saxophones: Duda, Spok, Gilberto, Rafael
Trumpets: Enok, Marquinhos, Alexandre Freitas, Bruno Dias
Trombones: Nilson, Nino, Barros
Electric bass: Mongol
From the CD *Frevos de Rua—Os Melhores do Século*. LG Projetos e Produções 000.010.
Peermusic GRA 6816164–0. Used by permission.
Duration: 2:13

This is a modern recording of José Menezes's classic frevo de rua, which was first recorded in 1950 in Recife. Like almost all frevos de rua, this piece is based on two musical sections that repeat several times and an arrangement that features the horn and wind instruments of the band playing interlocking syncopated melodies. This modern arrangement, by Menezes, features Recife's top frevo orchestra, led by bandleader and arranger Duda.

Track 5: "Frevo Rhythmic Cadence"

Performed by members of the Orquestra do Maestro José Menezes
Tarol: Adelson Pereira da Silva
Pandeiro: Evanildo Martins dos Santos
Surdo: Ivo José da Costa and Luiz Carlos Barbosa
Ganzá: unidentified
Field recording of Larry Crook, Recife, February 22, 2001
Duration: 1:11

I recorded this music in the downtown area of Recife during the Carnival of 2001. During parades, frevo drummers play cadences like this between frevo de rua pieces featuring the entire band. I was positioned in the middle of the percussion section of the frevo band as it marched behind the brass and wind instruments of the ensemble.

Track 6: "Poeta da Aurora" / "Poet of Aurora"

Music by Luiz Guimarães; words by Alvacir Raposo
Performed by Coral Edgard Moraes
Arrangement by Maestro Duda
From the CD *Coral Edgard Moraes—Frevos de Bloco.* LG Projetos e Produções 000.015.
Used by permission
Duration: 2:38

This is a contemporary frevo de bloco written in honor of the venerable Recife composer Edgard Moraes, a major figure in the city's Carnival. Luiz Guimarães, composer of the music, is also a local music producer and has been one of Recife's most active supporters of frevo since 1995. His efforts have resulted in numerous recordings, of which this is an excellent example.

Portuguese Lyrics

Acorda, poeta, acorda!
Vem ver a manhã
Vestida de azul.
Vem ver quantas flores novas
E a luz da estrela,
Que a noite esqueceu.
Acorda, vem ver as cores
Da aurora de amor,
Que o dia teceu,
São tantas canções
Que a lua nos deu,
Nos versos de um trovador.
Vem que a vida te espera:
Vem, o bloco te chama.
Sonhos, ilusões,

Lembranças e saudades,
São motivos pra viver e cantar.
Vem, vem, vem me falar
Vem, vem me dizer de paixão
Que um dia amanheceu,
Mas que se foi embora,
Para não voltar,
Nunca mais . . .

English Translation by Larry Crook

Awaken poet, awaken!
Come see the morning
All dressed in blue.
Come see how many new flowers
And the light of the star,
That the night forgot.
Awaken, come and see the colors
Of the aurora of love,
That the day wove together.
There are so many songs
That the moon left us,
In the verses of a troubadour.
Come, because life is waiting for you:
Come, the bloco calls you.
Dreams, illusions,
Memories and longings,
This is the reason for living and singing.
Come, come, come speak to me
Come, come tell me of passion
That one day dawned,
But then left,
Never to return,
Ever again.

Track 7: "Chorinho de Pífano"

Written by João do Pife
Performed by João do Pife (pífano) and Tavares da Gaita (reco-bamboo-som)
Field recording by Larry Crook, Caruaru, Pernambuco, November 11, 2001
Duration: 3:16

This recording was made one November afternoon in Caruaru, Pernambuco. I was visiting João do Pife and recording his group, Banda de Pífanos Dois Irmãos. The band had just finished several pieces when Tavares da Gaita showed up. Tavares is a well-known local musician who has had a long career playing harmonica and percussion. Now retired, he was about seventy-five years old when this recording was made. He is also renowned for the exquisite percussion instruments he invents and carves out of bamboo, coconut shells, gourds, and other materials. João and Tavares have known each other for many years and regularly sit around performing at Caruaru's famous market, where João sells his pífanos to tourists. João immediately asked Tavares to play a piece with him for me to record. The piece performed here is based on a semi-improvised genre from Rio de Janeiro called the choro. In the rhythm of a *sambinha* (little samba), João improvised variations of his own piece while Tavares played an instrument of his own invention that called the reco-bamboo-som (scraper made of bamboo). Using his thumb and the palm of his hand, Tavares extracted a wide range of timbres out of the instrument.

Track 8: "Bendita e Louvada Seja" (sung and played)
Novena de casa in Bezerros, Pernambuco
Various performers
Bandinha Nova Caruaru da Gente
Pífano: João Prosidono de Oliveira
Pífano: José Arruda de Oliveira
Tarol: José Benedito da Silva
Zabumba: José Manuel da Silva
Pratos: Cicero Severino da Silva
Surdo: Inácio José da Silva
Field recording by Larry Crook, Bezerros, Pernambuco, March 21, 1987
Duration: 3:45

This track was recorded at a novena de casa during the praying of the *terço* (one-third recitation of the rosary). There were approximately thirty people crammed inside the front room of a tiny house, where the statue of a saint was positioned. The track begins with group praying and then the singing of a devotional praise song: "Bendita e Louvada Seja" ("Blessed and Praised May You Be"). This is followed by an instrumental version of the tune from this song by the banda de pífanos Bandinha Nova Caruaru da Gente.

Portuguese Lyrics
Bendita e louvada seja
No céu a divina luz.
E nós também na terra
Louvemos a Santa Cruz.
E nós também na terra
Louvemos a Santa Cruz.

English Translation by Larry Crook
Blessed and praised may You be
In heaven the divine light.
And on earth we also
Praise the Holy Cross.

And on earth we also
Praise the Holy Cross.

Track 9: "Marcha de Novena"
By João do Pife
Performed by the Banda de Pífanos Dois Irmãos
Pífano: João do Pife
Pífano: Alfredo Marcos do Santos
Pratos: Severino dos Santos
Tarol: Larry Crook
Zabumba: Zeze dos Santos
Surdo: Cícero dos Santos
Field recording by Larry Crook in Riacho das Almas, Pernambuco, May 22, 1987
Duration: 2:39

This recording was made at the home of Severino dos Santos, brother of João do Pife, on the occasion of a family reunion between the two brothers and their father, Alfredo Marcos dos Santos. Alfredo, in his early seventies at the time of the recording, was no longer an active performer on the pífano. At this family affair, João's sons Cícero and Zeze also played. I was asked to accompany the piece on tarol, an instrument I had played many times during novenas and other occasions with João do Pife. This is one of the banda de pífano march pieces that João plays during the processions at novenas.

Track 10: "Arrancada da Bandeira"
Performed by Bandinha São João de Serra Velha
Pífano: Manoel Ribeiro Lima
Pífano: Pedro Joaquim de Paz
Tarol: Luiz da Silva
Zabumba: Ademar José da Silva
Pratos: Valdecir José da Silva
Surdo: Valdenir José da Silva
Field recording by Larry Crook in Pernambuco, February 2, 1987
Duration: 2:06

I recorded this piece during the procession of a novena de casa I attended as a guest of the Bandinha São João, from the rural hamlet of Serra Velha. The procession began in the late afternoon with the banda de pífanos playing several marches while women sang hymns. This piece accompanied the hoisting up of a banner.

Track 11: "A Dança do Araruna"
Performed by Banda de Pífanos Cultural de Caruaru
Pífano: Biu do Pife

Pífano: João Manuel da Silva
Tarol: Antônio do Nascimento
Zabumba: Manuel dos Santos
Pratos: João Alfredo dos Santos (João do Pife)
Surdo: Maurício Antônio da Silva
Field recording by Larry Crook in Caruaru, Pernambuco, September 3, 1987
Duration: 3:31

This recording took place during a rehearsal in 1987 with the Bandinha de Pífanos Cultural de Caruaru. The group was preparing its repertoire prior to going into a studio in Recife to record an album. Rehearsals consisted of the group members recording themselves and then listening to playbacks on a small, poor quality cassette deck. The track starts off with Biu do Pife playing the opening phrase of the tune and then talking with other members of the band regarding the best way to start the piece. One can hear Biu switching on the cassette recorder just before he announces the beginning of the take. This piece is representative of the secular repertoire of the bandas de pífanos and features the stylized imitation of the Araruna bird by the pífanos set to a xaxado rhythm.

Track 12: "Forró de Zabumba"
By João do Pife
Performed by the Banda de Pífanos Dois Irmãos
Pífano: João do Pife
Pífano: Severino do Santos
Tarol: Gelson Rodrigues de Moura
Zabumba: Sebastião Rodrigues
Pratos: José Feliciano Rodrigues Filho
Surdo: Cícero Alfredo dos Santos
Triangle: Marcos Antonio da Silva
Field recording by Larry Crook in Caruaru, Pernambuco, March 23, 2001
Duration: 4:04

This track was recorded at the interior courtyard of the Hotel Village in Caruaru. At the time, João do Pife's group Bandinha de Pífanos Dois Irmãos performed weekly at this hotel, playing for tourists. On this occasion, João's band was entertaining a group of German tourists. This track presents a forró piece performed to a baião rhythm that João do Pife wrote for his band.

Track 13: "A Família"
By Antônio Lisboa and Edmilson Ferreira
Viola and voice: Antônio Lisboa
Viola and voice: Edmilson Ferreira
From the independent CD *E Feito de Fato* (nd). Used by permission.
Duration: 5:50

This track comes from an independent CD recording by two cantoria de viola singers who live on the outskirts of Recife. The song is set in the sextilha format of six-line verses common to the desafilio song duel. In this song, Edmilson Ferreira and Antônio Lisboa alternate verses as they develop a poetic theme that critiques the confrontation of traditional family values and modernity.

Portuguese Lyrics

1. Edmilson Ferreira
A família foi a base
de toda sociedade
na disputa por espaço
na briga por liberdade
conquistando a abertura
e perdendo a autoridade

2. Antônio Lisboa
A responsabilidade
ficou em cima do muro
o jovem vive em conflito
o velho está inseguro
e um disequilibrio enorme
ameaçando o futuro

3. EF
Não tem mais casal maduro
orientando os guris (crianças)
a televisão confunde
a escola contradiz
e nessa torre de babel
não há quem seja feliz

4. AL
Nas famílias do país
as ordens não são cumpridas
os regimes muita abertos
as regras mal definidas
nem Freud nem Piaget
vão ajeitar essas vidas

5. EF
As filhas são deprimidas
os filhos sofrem jejum (fome)
passar a perna é normal
puxar tapete é comum
e perder a privacidade
não é problema nenhum

6. AL

Em nome do bem comum
multiplicaram as cobranças
neutralizaram os adultos
robotizaram as crianção
e a carga de informações
não acompanha as mudanças

7. EF

A confusão das finanças
gera transtorno no leito
a mãe se sente culpada
o pai fica insatisfeito
quem não aprendeu correto
é raro ensinar direito

8. AL

Todo casamento é feito
com duração vitalícia
termina com violência
juiz, divórcio, e polícia
todo mês atrasa a data
da pensão alimentícia

9. EF

Ainda temos notícia
que o comodismo vigora
machismo fora de época
chantagem depois da hora
não tem solução em casa
nem são resolvidos fora

10. AL

Tem padastro que deflora
mulher que planeja a morte
desespero no marido
desemprego na consorte
não tem cabeça que agüente
nem coração que suporte

11. EF

Existe um combate forte
a tudo o quanto é antigo
a droga é uma ameaça
o sexo é o inimigo

proibir é um problema
liberar é um perigo

12. AL

Trocaram irmão por amigo
deram casa por mobília
diminuíram o respeito
exageraram a vigília
transformaram o bem estar
num caos pra cada família

13. EF

Absorve-se a quizília
perdeu seu pudor fraterno
quebrou-se o tabu da honra
rompeu-se o valor materno
e o saldo disso é o preço
do dia-a-dia moderno

14. AL

Na lei do partido interno
do governo e do estado
é bom que a família fique
num ambiente-isolado
usando a mesma linguagem
votando do mesmo lado

15. EF

Para o empresariado
família é um quebra galho
tendo direitos e deveras
o amor pode ser falho
basta atender os apelos
do mercado de trabalho

16. AL

Contra qualquer ponto falho
e a depredação do lar
Pastor não move um palha
Padre não sai do lugar
vão ficar de camarote
vendo a família afundar

English Translation by Larry Crook

1. Edmilson Ferreira

 The family was the base
 for all society
 in the dispute for space
 in the fight for liberty
 conquering the opening
 and losing the authority

2. Antônio Lisboa

 The responsibility
 remained on top of the wall
 the young boy lives in conflict
 the old man is insecure
 it's a disequilibrium
 threatening the future

3. EF

 There are no more mature couples
 guiding their children
 the television confuses
 the school contradicts
 and in this tower of Babel
 no one is happy

4. AL

 In the families of the country
 orders are not fulfilled
 laws are very permissive
 rules are badly defined
 neither Freud nor Piaget
 are going to fix these lives

5. EF

 Daughters are weakened
 sons suffer hunger
 getting knocked down is normal
 dragging the carpet is common
 and losing privacy
 is no problem at all

6. AL

 In the name of the common good
 they increased the taxes
 they neutralized the adults

and made robots of the children
and the weight of information
did not accompany the changes

7. EF

The confusion of finances
causes problems in bed
the mother feels guilty
the father unsatisfied
whoever did not learn correctly
rarely teaches others rightly

8. AL

Every marriage that is made
for the duration of a lifetime
cnds in violence,
judgment, divorce, and police
every month the date gets later
to receive funds for nourishment

9. EF

Yet we hear the news
that egocentricism is stronger
out of place machismo
after-hours blackmail
there is no solution at home
nothing is resolved outside

10. AL

There are stepfathers who sexually abuse
wives who plan death
despair for a spouse
detachment from a partner
no one head can bear it
no heart can support it

11. EF

There exists a hard-fought battle
it's as old as anything
drugs are a threat
sex is the enemy
to prohibit is a problem
to turn loose is a danger

12. AL

They exchanged brother for friend
gave up their house for furniture
diminished respect
exaggerated restlessness
transformed wellbeing
into chaos for each family

13. EF

They were taken captive by this mess
the lost fraternal modesty
broke the taboo of honor
destroyed maternal virtue
and the result of this disorder
is the price of modern life

14. AL

The law of the party in power,
of the government and the state
is that the family remains
in an atmosphere of isolation
using the same language
voting on the same side

15. EF

For the businessmen
the family is not important
having duties and obligations
love can be a mistake
it's enough to pay attention to the needs
of the labor market

16. AL

Against whatever mistaken point
and the degradation of the home
the Pastor does nothing
the Priest doesn't budge
they remain in their lofty places
watching the family go down

Track 14: "Pé-de-Calçada"

Words and music by Sérgio Veloso (Siba)
Performed by Mestre Ambrósio
Rabeca and voice: Sérgio Veloso

Triangle and vocals: Mazinho Lima
Mineiros, reco-reco, and vocals: Hélder Vasconcelos
Pandeiro and vocals: Sérgio Cassiano
Agogô: Maurício Alves
Zabumba: Eder Rocha
"Pé-de-Calçada" by Siba (Sérgio Veloso) from the CD *Mestre Ambrósio*, Rec Beat 107.984, 1995. Used with permission of Trama Promoções Artisticas LTDA.
Duration: 2:45

This forró de rabeca (forró of the folk violin) appeared on Mestre Ambrósio's first CD, which was released in 1995. The music reflects Recife's new music scene and features the rabeca playing of Sérgio "Siba" Veloso, who is also the composer of the song. The recording reflects the ways in which Mestre Ambrósio has refined its acoustic-based sound to capture the idea of the Northeast as an area where the rural and the urban are closely intertwined.

Portuguese Lyrics

Mas eu fui num forró no pé duma serra
Nunca nessa terra vi uma coisa igual
Mas eu fui num forró no pé duma serra
Cumé quente, baiano sensacional
Rabeca véia do pinho de arvoredo
Espalhava baiano no salão
O pandeiro tremia a maquinada
Eu vi a poeira subir do chão
Hoje eu faço forró em pé-de-calçada
No meio da zuada pela contra-mão
Eu fui lá na mata e voltei prá cidade
De cabôco eu sei minha situação
Rabeca véia não me abandona
Zabumba treme-terra, come o chão
Na hora que o tempo desaparece
Transforma em pé-de-serra o calçada.

English Translation by Larry Crook

So I went to a forró at the foot of a hill
In this land, never have I ever seen something like that
So I went to a forró at the foot of a hill
How hot it was, a sensational baiano
An old rabeca of pine from the grove
Spread the baiano over the room
The pandeiro shook the secret scene
I saw a cloud of dust rise from the floor
Today I play forró in the city
In the midst of confusion going the wrong way

I went to the woods and returned to the city
From a caboclo I discovered my situation
Rabeca come and don't abandon me
Zabumba shake the earth, devour the ground
When time is gone
Transform the city into the country

Notes

Chapter 1: Brazil: A Country Divided

1   Copyright Edgard Moraes, reprinted with permission of the Moraes family.
2   Caetano Veloso, "Carmen Mirandada," in *Brazilian Popular Music and Globalization*, ed. Charles A. Perrone and Christopher Dunn (Gainesville: University Press of Florida, 2001), 39–45.
3   For an account of the rural social movement that led to the events at Canudos see Robert M. Levine, "'Mud-Hut Jerusalem': Canudos Revisited," *Hispanic American Historical Review* 68, 3 (August 1988): 525–72. For extended analysis of the Canudos event and the impact of urban elite responses see Robert M. Levine, *Vale of Tears: Revisiting the Canudos Massacre in Northeastern Brazil, 1893–1897* (Berkeley: University of California Press, 1992).
4   Ariano Suassuna, "Notas Sôbre a Música de Capiba," in *É de Tororó: Maracatu*, ed. Hermilo Borba Filho, Ascenço Ferreira, Ariano Suassuna, Capiba, Lula Cardoso Ayres, and Percy Lau (Rio de Janeiro, Brazil: Livraria-Editôra da Casa do Estudante do Brasil, 1951), 42.
5   Michael Hanchard, ed., *Racial Politics in Contemporary Brazil* (Durham, NC: Duke University Press, 1999).
6   Hanchard (1999).
7   George Reid Andrews, *Blacks and Whites in São Paulo, Brazil: 1888–1988* (Madison: University of Wisconsin Press, 1991).
8   Gerard Béhague, "Introduction," in *Music and Black Ethnicity: The Caribbean and South America*, ed. Gerard Béhague (Miami, FL: North-South Center Press at the University of Miami, 1994), V–XII.
9   Cited in Angela E. Lühning, "O Compositor Mozart Camargo Guarnieri e o 2° Congresso Afro-Brasileiro em Salvador, 1937 (Homanegem Póstuma)," in *Ritmos em Trânsito: Sócio-Antropologia da Música Baiana*, ed. Livio Sansone and Jocélio Teles dos Santos (São Paulo, Brazil: Dynamis Editorial; Salvador, Brazil: Programa A Cord a Bahia e Projeto S.A.M.BA., 1997), 69.
10 José Jorge de Carvalho, "Black Music of All Colors: The Construction of Black Ethnicity in Ritual and Popular Genres of Afro-Brazilian Music," in *Music and Black Ethnicity: The Caribbean and South America*, ed. Gerard Béhague (Miami, FL: North-South Center Press at the University of Miami, 1994), 187–206.
11 Gerard Béhague, *Music in Latin America: An Introduction* (Englewood Cliffs, NJ: Prentice-Hall, 1979), 71.
12 Serafim Leite, *História da Companhia de Jesus no Brasil*, Vol. 5 (Lisbon: Livraria Portugália, 1938), 421.
13 Daniel Mendoza de Arce, *Music in Ibero-America to 1850: A Historical Survey* (Lanham, MD: Scarecrow Press, 2001), 183.
14 Jaime C. Diniz, *Músicos Pernambucanos do Passado*, Vol. 3 (Recife, Brazil: Universidade Federal de Pernambuco, 1979), 197–208.
15 Jaime C. Diniz, *Músicos Pernambucanos do Passado*, Vol. 2 (Recife, Brazil: Universidade Federal de Pernambuco, 1971), 28.
16 Cited in José Ramos Tinhorão, *As Festas no Brasil Colonial* (São Paulo, Brazil: Editora 34, 2000), 88.

17 Diniz (1971), 29.

18 Marieta Alves, "Música de Barbeiros," *Revista Brasileira de Folclore* 7, 17 (1967): 5–14.

Chapter 2: Brazilian Music in Focus: A History of Hybridity

1 Interview with Marcos Suzano, Rio de Janeiro, July 6, 2006.

2 Tinhorão (2000), 88.

3 Suzel Reily, *Voices of the Magi: Enchanted Journeys in Southeast Brazil* (Chicago: University of Chicago Press, 2002).

4 Cited in Dicionário Cravo Albin da Música Popular Brasileira, http://www.dicionariompb.com.br/detalhe.asp?nome=Jo%E3o+da+Bahiana&tabela=T_FORM_A&qdetalhe=bio).

5 Cited in Sérgio Cabral, *As Escolas de Samba do Rio de Janeiro* (Rio de Janeiro: Lumiar Editora, 1996), 28.

6 Hermano Vianna, *The Mystery of Samba: Popular Music and National Identity in Brazil*, (Chapel Hill: University of North Carolina Press, 1999), 81.

7 For a discussion of Marcos Suzano, see Frederick Moehn, "Mixing MPB: Cannibals and Cosmopolitans in Brazilian Popular Music," PhD diss. New York University (2001).

8 Flávio Wilner, "Marcos Suzano: O Pandeiro Rouba o Lugar da Bateria," *Revista Backstage* 3, 24 (1997): 45.

9 Interview with Marcos Suzano, Rio de Janeiro, July 8, 2006.

10 Interview with Bernardo Aguiar, Rio de Janeiro, July 2, 2006.

11 For a discussion of the development of Carnival dancing in Rio de Janeiro prior to the development of samba see John Charles Chasteen, "The Prehistory of Samba: Carnival Dancing in Rio de Janeiro, 1840–1917," *Journal of Latin American Studies* 28, 1 (February 1966): 29–47.

12 Richard Graham, *Britain and the Onset of Modernization in Brazil, 1850–1914* (Cambridge: Cambridge University Press, 1968), 26.

13 Rita de Cássia Barbosa de Araújo, *Festas: Máscaras do Tempo—Entrudo, Mascarada e Frevo no Carnaval do Recife* (Recife, Brazil: Fundação de Cultura Cidade do Recife, 1996), 179.

14 Cited in Leonardo Dantas Silva, *Carnaval do Recife* (Recife, Brazil: Prefeitura da Cidade do Recife Fundação de Cultura Cidade do Recife, 2000), 22.

15 Cited in Silva (2000), 25.

16 For an analysis of the impact of radio broadcasts and the recording activities of Rio de Janeiro in spreading popular music including regional styles to domestic audiences throughout Brazil see Bryan McCann, *Hello, Hello, Brazil: Popular Music in the Making of Modern Brazil* (Durham, NC: Duke University Press, 2004).

17 An account of the development of música sertaneja and its impact on migrant communities in São Paulo is found in Suzel Ana Reily, "*Música Sertaneja* and Migrant Identity: The Stylistic Development of a Brazilian Genre," *Popular Music* 11, 3 (1992): 337–58. See also Rosa Nepomuceno, *Música Caipira: Da Roça ao Rodeio* (São Paulo, Brazil: Editora 34, 1999).

18 Reily (1992), 353.

19 Kazadi wa Mukuna, An Interdisciplinary Study of the Ox and the Slave (Bumba-meu-Boi): A Satirical Music Drama in Brazil (Lewiston, NY: E. Mellen Press, 2003).

20 Larry Crook, "Black Consciousness, Samba-Reggae, and the Re-Africanization of Bahian Carnival Music in Brazil," *World of Music* 35, 2 (1993): 90–108.

21 A thorough social history and musical analysis of the choro is given in Tamara Elena Livingston-Isenhour and Thomas George Caracas Garcia, *Choro: A Social History of a Brazilian Popular Music* (Bloomington and Indianapolis: Indiana University Press, 2005).

Chapter 3: Afro-Brazilian Musical Traditions: Candomblé, Afoxé, and Maracatu

1 Peter Fryer, *Rhythms of Resistance: African Musical Heritage in Brazil* (Middletown, CT: Wesleyan University Press and Hanover, NH: University Press of New England, 2000).

2 John Storm Roberts, The Black Music of Two Worlds: African, Caribbean, Latin, and African-American Traditions (New York: Schirmer Books, 1998).

3 Fryer (2000), 12.

4 Gerard Béhague, "Expressões Musicais do Pluralismo Religioso Afro-Baiano: A Negociação de Identidade," *Brasiliana* 1 (1999): 40–7.

5 Carvalho (1994).

6 Gerard Béhague, "Patterns of Candomblé Music Performance: An Afro-Brazilian Religious Setting," in *Performance Practice: Ethnomusicological Perspectives*, ed. Gerard Béhague (Westport, CT: Greenwood Press, 1984), 223.

7 José Jorge de Carvalho and Rita Laura Segato, *Shango Cult in Recife, Brazil* (Caracas: FUNDEF/CIDEF/OEA, 1992), 11.

8 Carvalho (1994), 188.

9   Carvalho and Segato (1992).

10 René, Ribeiro, *Cultos Afro-Brasileiros do Recife: Um Estudo de Ajustamento Social* (Recife, Brazil: Instituto Joaquim Nabuco de Pesquisas Sociais, 1978).

11 Roger Bastide, *The African Religions of Brazil: Toward a Sociology of the Interpenetration of Civilizations* (Baltimore, MD: Johns Hopkins University Press, 1978).

12 Carvalho and Segato (1992).

13 Field notes, October 28, 2000.

14 Interview with Guga Santos, Recife, November 8, 2000.

15 Oneyda Alvarenga, "A Influência Negra na Música Brasileira," *Boletín Latino-Americano de Música* 6 (1946): 357–407.

16 Nina Raymundo Rodrigues, *Os Africanos no Brasil* (São Paulo, Brazil: Companhia Editora Nacional, 1932), 270–1.

17 Cited in Rodrigues (1932), 236.

18 Peter Fry, Sérgio Carrara, and Ana Luiza Martins-Costa, "Negros e Brancos no Carnaval da Velha República," in *Escravidão e Invenção da Liberdade: Estudos sobre o Negro no Brasil*, organized by João José Reis (São Paulo, Brazil: Editora Brasiliense, co-edited with Conselho Nacional de Desenvolvimento Científico e Tecnológico, 1988), 263.

19 Cited in Fry, Carrara, and Martins-Costa (1998), 253.

20 Cited in Cid Teixeira, "Carnaval Entre as Duas Guerras," in *Carnaval da Bahia: Um Registro Estético*, ed. Nelson Cerqueira (Salvador, Brazil: Omar, 2002), 54.

21 Anísio Félix, "Batucadas e Escolas de Samba no Carnaval Baiano," in *Carnaval da Bahia: Um Registro Estético*, ed. Nelson Cerqueira (Salvador, Brazil: Omar, 2002), 62.

22 Donald Pierson, *Negroes in Brazil: A Study of Race Contact at Bahia* (Carbondale: Southern Illinois University Press, 1967), 201.

23 Edison Carneiro, *Religões Negras: Notas de Etnografia Religiosa* (Rio de Janeiro, Brazil: Civilização Brasileira, 1936), 112.

24 Edison Carneiro, *Folguedos Tradicionais* (Rio de Janeiro, Brazil: Conquista, 1974).

25 Carneiro (1974), 102.

26 Roger Bastide, *O Candomblé da Bahia: Rito Nagô*, trans. Maria Isaura Pereira de Queiroz (São Paulo, Brazil: Companhia das Letras, 2001), 99.

27 Sociedade Recreativa e Carnavalesca Filhos de Gandhy, http://geocities.yahoo.com.br/filhosdegandhy/index.htm (accessed June 4, 2004).

28 Anamaria Morales, "O Afoxé Filhos de Gandhi Pede Paz," in *Escravidão e Invenção da Liberdade: Estudos sobre o Negro no Brasil*, organized by João José Reis (São Paulo, Brazil: Editora Brasiliense, co-edited with Conselho Nacional de Desenvolvimento Científico e Tecnológico, 1988), 264–74.

29 Raul Giovanni da Motta Lody, *Afoxé* (Rio de Janeiro, Brazil: Ministério da Educação e Cultura Departamento de Assuntos Culturais Fundação Nacional de Arte Campanha de Defesa do Folclore Brasileiro, 1976), 18.

30 Juana Elbein dos Santos, "O Afoxé e o Africanismo Baiano," *Tribuna da Bahia* (March 23, 1974).

31 Cited in Antônio Risério, *Carnaval Ijexá* (Salvador, Brasil: Corrupio, 1981), 227–8.

32 Cited in Fred de Góes, *O País do Carnaval Elétrico* (Salvador, Brazil: Corrupio, 1982), 89.

33 Daniel J. Crowley, *African Myth and Black Reality in Bahian Carnaval* (Los Angeles, CA: Museum of Cultural History, UCLA, 1984), 23.

34 Risério (1981), 57.

35 Risério (1981), 65.

36 Risério (1981), 66.

37 Cited in Tinhorão (2000), 88; the original comes from Urbain Souchu de Rennefort, *Histoire des Indes Orientales* (Paris, France: Leide, Chez F. Harring, 1688).

38 Bastide (1978), 119.

39 Henry Koster and C. Harvey Gardiner, *Travels in Brazil* (Carbondale: Southern Illinois University Press, 1966), 135–7.

40 Cited in Leonardo Dantas Silva, "Quando Maracatu Era Caso de Polícia," *Suplemento Cultural, Diário Official, Estado de Pernambuco*, Ano X (February 1997): 5.

41 Cited in Leonardo Dantas Silva, "Elementos para a História Social do Carnaval do Recife," in *Antologia do Carnaval do Recife*, ed. Mário Souto Maior and Leonardo Dantas Silva (Recife, Brazil: Fundação Joaquim Nabuco/Editora Massangana, 1991a), xxxii–xxxiii.

42 Francisco Augusto Pereira da Costa, *Folk-Lore Pernambucano* (Rio de Janeiro, Brazil: Livraria, 1908), 207–8.

43 Cited in Albino Gonçalves Fernandes, *Xangôs do Nordeste: Investigações sobre os Cultos Negro-Fetichistas do Recife* (Rio de Janeiro, Brazil: Civilização Brasileira, 1937), 11–12.

44 Gonçalves Fernandes (1937), 68.

45 Costa (1908), 209.

46 Hermilo Borba Filho, ed., *Danças Pernambucanas* (Rio de Janeiro, Brazil: Casa do Estudante do Brasil, 1951).

47 Katarina Real, *O Folklore no Carnaval do Recife* (Recife, Brazil: Fundaçao Joaquim Nabuco/Editora Massangana, 1990), 59.

48   Real (1990), 60 citing Costa (1908), 207.
49   César Guerra-Peixe, *Maracatus do Recife* (São Paulo, Brazil: Irmãos Vitale, 1980).
50   Guerra-Peixe (1980), 33–7.
51   Interview with Dona Elda, Recife, July 3, 1998.

Chapter 4: Making Multiracial Carnival Music: The Frevo

1   José Ramos Tinhorão, *Os Sons dos Negros no Brasil: Cantos, Danças, Folguedos, Origens* (São Paulo, Brazil: Art Editora, 1988), 180.
2   Roberto da Matta, *Carnivals, Rogues, and Heroes: An Interpretation of the Brazilian Dilemma* (Notre Dame, IN: University of Notre Dame Press, 1991), 33.
3   José Ramos Tinhorão, *História Social da Música Popular Brasileira* (São Paulo, Brazil: Editora 34, 1998), 177. Tinhorão's account was drawn from the published writings of Padre Luís Gonçalves dos Santos, *Memórias para Servir à História do Brasil* (Rio de Janeiro, Brazil: Livraria Editora Zélio Valverde, 1943).
4   Leonardo Dantas Silva, "500 Anos de Fé: A Música das Procissões," in *Marchas de Procissão*, organized by Paulo Bruscky (Recife, Brazil: Companhia Editora de Pernambuco, 1998c), 17.
5   Leonardo Dantas Silva, *Bandas Musicais de Pernambuco, História Social* (Recife, Brazil: Governo do Estado de Pernambuco, 1998a), 20.
6   Diniz (1979).
7   Cited in Diniz (1979), 52.
8   Oliveira Lima, *Dom João VI no Brasil, 1808–1821*, Vol. 3 (Rio de Janeiro, Brazil: Livraria José Olympio Editora 1945), 1042.
9   José Pedro Damião Irmão, *Tradicionais Bandas de Música* (Recife, Brazil: Companhia Editora de Pernambuco, 1970), 127.
10   Irmão (1970), 72.
11   Gilberto Freyre, *The Mansions and the Shanties (Sobrados e Mucambos): The Making of Modern Brazil*, trans. from 1936 original by Harriet de Onís (New York: Alfred A. Knopf, 1968), 322.
12   Caio Prado Júnior, *The Colonial Background of Modern Brazil*, trans. Suzette Macedo (Berkeley: University of California Press, 1967), 331.
13   J. Lowell Lewis, *Ring of Liberation: Deceptive Discourse in Brazilian Capoeira* (Chicago and London: University of Chicago Press, 1992).
14   Freyre (1968), 261.
15   Valdemar de Oliveira, *Frevo, Capoeira e "Passo"* (Recife, Brazil: Companhia Editôra de Pernambuco, 1985), 82–3.
16   Oliveira (1985), 83, n. 47.
17   Costa (1908), 241–242.
18   Mário Sette, *Maxambombas e Maracatus*, 4th ed. (São Paulo, Brazil: Edições Cultura Brasileira, 1981), 129.
19   Leonardo Dantas Silva, "O Frevo Pernambucano," in *Antologia do Carnaval do Recife*, ed. Mário Souto Maior and Leonardo Dantas Silva (Recife, Brazil: Fundação Joaquim Nabuco/Editora Massangana, 1991b), 200.
20   Silva (2000), 83.
21   Silva (2000), 85.
22   Real (1990), 10.
23   Cited in Mário Souto Maior and Leonardo Dantas Silva, *Antologia do Carnaval do Recife* (Recife, Brazil: Fundação Joaquim Nabuco Editora Massangana, 1991), 256.
24   Melo cited in Souto Maior and Silva (1991), 256.
25   Mário Filho, *Se essa Rua Fosse Minha: Homenagem ao Valoroso Clube Carnavalesco Mixto Vassourinhas do Recife* (Recife, Brazil: Companhia Editora de Pernambuco, 1990), 22.
26   Raimundo Pereira Alencar Arrais, *Recife, Culturas e Confrontos: As Camadas Urbanas na Campanha Salvacionista de 1911* (Natal, Brazil: Editora da Universidada Federal do Rio Grande do Norte, 1998), 135.
27   Valdemar de Oliveira, "O Frevo e o Passo, de Pernambuco," *Boletín Latino-Americano de Música* 6 (1946): 159.
28   Interview with Luciano Ricardo Maciel da Silva, Olinda, June 2, 2001.
29   Filho (1990).
30   Evandro Rabello, "'Vassourinhas' Foi Compositada em 1909," *Diário de Pernambuco* (January 4, 1987): Section B, 1.
31   Filho (1990), 23.
32   Leonardo Dantas Silva, "Blocos Carnavalescos do Recife-História Social," in *Bocos Carnavalescos do Recife: Origins e Repertório*, ed. Leonardo Dantas Silva (Recife, Brazil: Governo do Estado de Pernambuco, 1998b), 26.
33   Real (1990), 36.
34   All "Marcha das Flores" lyrics printed with permission of the Moraes family.
35   Matta (1991), 34.

36 Henrique Cazes, *Choro: Do Quintal ao Municipal* (São Paulo, Brazil: Editora 34, 1999), 71.
37 Marilia T. Barboza and Arthur L. de Oliveira Filho, *Filho de Ogum Bexiguento* (Rio de Janeiro, Brazil: Edição FUNARTE, 1979), 152.
38 Oliveira (1946), 168–9.
39 Oliveira (1946), 169.
40 Guerra-Peixe (January 27, 1951).
41 Oliveira (1985), 41–42.
42 Vianna (1999), 11.
43 Silva (1991a), lxxiii.
44 Antônio Guilherme Rodrigues, "'Tá Sobrando Mulher,' Mas Está Faltando Frevo . . ." *Diário da Noite* (January 15, 1951).
45 José Teles, *Do Frevo ao Manguebeat* (São Paulo, Brazil: Editora 34, 2000), 44.
46 From the liner notes to SpokFrevo Orquestra, *Passo de Anjo* (CD. Viasom VS 200220, 2004).
47 SpokFrevo Orquestra, (2004).

Chapter 5: Inventing Northeastern Popular Music

1   Vianna (1999), 24–5.
2   Catulo da Paixão Cearense, *Modinhas* (São Paulo, Brazil: Editora Fermata do Brasil, 1972), 18.
3   José de Souza Leal and Artur Luiz Barbosa, *João Pernambuco: Arte de um Povo* (Rio de Janeiro, Brazil: Edição FUNARTE, 1982), 13.
4   Leal and Barbosa (1982), 37.
5   Jairo Severiano and Zuza Homem de Mello, *A Canção no Tempo: 85 Anos de Músicas Brasileiras* (São Paulo, Brazil: Editora 34, 1997), 38.
6   Sérgio Cabral, *Pixinguinha: Vida e Obra* (Rio de Janeiro, Brazil: Lumiar Editora, 1997), 40.
7   Vianna (1999), 82.
8   Leandro Carvalho, "A Música para Violão de Heitor Villa-Lobos e João Pernambuco," in *ANAIS: Primeiro Simpósio Latino-Americano de Musicologia*, ed. Elizabeth Seraphim Prosser and Paulo Castanho (Curitiba, Brazil: Fundação Cultural de Curitiba, 1997), 259. Carvalho cites the newspaper *Comércio de Campinas* (May 28–30, 1916) as the origin of this quote.
9   Cazes (1999), 49.
10 Cited in Barboza and Oliveira Filho (1979), 49.
11 Cazes (1999), 85.
12 Dominique Dreyfus, *Vida do Viajante: A Saga de Luiz Gonzaga* (São Paulo, Brazil: Editora 34, 1996), 81.
13 Dreyfus (1996), 92.
14 Cited in Sulamita Vieira, *O Sertão em Movimento: A Dinâmica da Produção Cultural* (São Paulo, Brazil: Annablume, 2000), 157.
15 Cited in Vieira (2000), 153.
16 Cited in Assis Angelo, *Eu Vou Contar pra Vocês* (São Paulo, Brazil: Icone, 1990), 53.
17 Adapted from John Patrick Murphy, "Performing a Moral Vision: An Ethnography of Cavalo-Marinho, a Brazilian Musical Drama" (PhD diss., Columbia University, 1994), 100.
18 "O Eterno Rci do Baião," *Vejaleia* 184 (1972), 82.
19 Murphy (1994), 100.
20 For further analysis of Luiz Gonzaga and his music, see Elba Braga Ramalho, "Luiz Gonzaga: His Life and His Music" (PhD diss., University of Liverpool, 1997) and Elba Braga Ramalho, *Luiz Gonzaga: A Sintese Poética e Musical do Sertão*, (São Paulo, Brazil: Terceira Margem, 2000).
21 Moura and Vicente (2001).

Chapter 6: Two Case Studies from the Northeast: Banda de Pífanos and Cantoria de Viola

1   Interview with João do Pife, Caruaru, February 20, 1987.
2   Diniz (1979).
3   Abelardo Duarte, *Folclore das Alagoas: Pesquisa e Interpretação* (Maceió, Brazil: Departamento de Assuntos Culturais/SENEC, 1974).
4   Interview with João do Pife, Caruaru, May 13, 1988.
5   Interview with João do Pife, Caruaru, August 28, 1987.
6   For a description of the oito baixos and its use in forró see John Patrick Murphy, *Music in Brazil: Experiencing Music, Expressing Culture* (New York: Oxford University Press, 2006), 100–7.
7   Larry Crook, "Brazil/Northeast Brazil," in *Music in Latin American Culture: Regional Traditions*, ed. John Schechter (New York: Schirmer Books, 1999), 202.

8   "A Família" (Antônio Lisboa and Edmilson Ferreira). From the independent CD *É Feito de Fato* (nd). Reprinted with permission.
9   This classic text has been reprinted in Luís da Câmara Cascudo, *Vaqueiros e Cantadores: Folclore Poética do Sertão do Ceará, Paraíba, Rio Grande do Norte e Pernambuco* (Rio de Janeiro, Brazil: Ediouro, 2000).
10   Interview with Antônio Lisboa, Recife, November 21, 2000. All of the following quotations from Lisboa are taken from my interview with him at his home in Pernambuco.
11   Interview with Edmilson Ferreira, November 22, 2000.
12   "A Família" (Antônio Lisboa and Edmilson Ferreira). From the independent CD *É Feito de Fato* (nd). Reprinted with permission.
13   Improvised oral poetry by Antonio Lisboa, from interview with author. Reprinted with permission.
14   Ralph Waddey, "Viola de Samba and Samba de Viola in the Recôncavo of Bahia (Brazil)," *Latin American Music Review* 1, 2 (1980): 196–212.

Chapter 7: Reinventing Africa and Remixing Hybridity: Blocos Afro and Mangue Beat

1   João Jorge Santos Rodrigues, "Olodum and the Black Struggle in Brazil," in *Black Brazil: Culture, Identity, and Social Mobilization*, ed. Larry Crook and Randal Johnson (Los Angeles: UCLA Latin American Center Publications, University of California, Los Angeles, 1999), 46.
2   Paul Gilroy, *The Black Atlantic: Modernity and Double Consciousness* (Cambridge, MA: Harvard University Press, 1993).
3   Interview with Antônio Carlos dos Santos (May 29, 1995), Salvador da Bahia.
4   Cited in Rosane Santana, "Entrevista Anônio dos Santos, Vovô, Presidente do Bloco Ilê Aiyê," in *Carnaval da Bahia: Um Registro Estético*, ed. Nelson Cerqueira (Salvador, Brazil: Omar, 2002), 117.
5   *A Tarde* (February 12, 1975); cited in Movimento Negro Unificado, *10 Anos de Luta Contra o Racismo* (São Paulo, Brazil: Confraria do Brasil, 1988), 10.
6   Risério (1981).
7   Crowley (1984).
8   Osmundo de Araújo Pinho, "'Fogo na Babilônia': Reggae, Black Culture, and Globalization in Brazil," in *Brazilian Popular Music and Globalization*, ed. Charles A. Perrone and Christopher Dunn (Gainesville: University Press of Florida, 2000), 192–206.
9   Perrone, Charles A, *Masters of Contemporary Brazilian Song: MPB 1965–1985* Austin: (University of Texas Press, 1989), 50.
10   Christopher Dunn, "Tropicália, Counterculture, and the Diasporic Imagination in Brazil," in *Brazilian Popular Music and Globalization*, ed. Charles A. Perrone and Christopher Dunn (Gainesville: University Press of Florida, 2000), 72–95.
11   Páginas do Mar, Publisher of *Canto da Cidade* (Daniela Mercury / Tote Gira), managed internationally by Universal MGB. Reprinted with permission.
12   Chris McGowan and Ricardo Pessanha, *The Brazilian Sound: Samba, Bossa Nova, and the Popular Music of Brazil* (Philadelphia: Temple University Press, 1998), 133.
13   Cited in Santana (2002), 119.
14   Rodrigues (1999), 47.
15   Portions of the material in this section derive from Larry Crook, "Turned-Around Beat: *Maracatu de Baque Virado* and Chico Science," in *Brazilian Popular Music and Globalization*, ed. Charles A. Perrone and Christopher Dunn (Gainesville: University of Florida Press, 2001), 233–44.
16   Philip Galinsky, *"Maracatu Atômico": Tradition, Modernity, and Postmodernity in the Mangue Movement of Recife*, Brazil (New York: Routledge, 2002), 33.
17   Teles (2000), 260.
18   Galinsky (2002), 34.
19   Timothy Dean Taylor, *Global Pop: World Music, World Markets* (New York: Routledge, 1997).
20   Cited in Teles (2000), 293–4.
21   This interview, titled "Chico Science: Do Mangue para o Pundo," is posted at the Brazilian Music UpToDate website, available at http://www2.uol.com.br/uptodate/. The English version can be found at http://www2.uol.com.br/uptodate/up3/interine.htm.
22   John Patrick Murphy, "Self-Discovery in Brazilian Popular Music: Mestre Ambrósio," in *Brazilian Popular Music and Globalization*, ed. Charles A. Perrone and Christopher Dunn (Gainesville: University of Florida Press, 2001), 245–57.
23   Cited in Murphy (2001), 252.
24   "Pé-de-Calçada" by Siba (Sergio Veloso). Reprinted with permission of Trama Promoções Artisticas LTDA.
25   Interview with Jorge Martins, September 18, 2000, Recife, Pernambuco; all subsequent quotes from Martins are from this interview.

26   Vianna (1999), 116.
27   Charles A. Perrone and Christopher Dunn, "'Chiclete com Banana': Internationalization in Brazilian Popular Music," in *Brazilian Popular Music and Globalization*, ed. Charles A. Perrone and Christopher Dunn (Gainesville: University Press of Florida, 2001), 3–4.

Glossary

Afoxé A Carnival group from Salvador and the music it plays derived from Candomblé

Agbe A beaded gourd rattle used in Candomblé in Recife

Agogô A double bell of African derivation used in samba, Candomblé, and other musics

Alfaia Large, double-headed bass drums played in the maracatu nations

Atabaque Conical-shaped, single-headed drums used in Candomblé, capoeira, and other Afro-Brazilian musical styles

Axé music A commercial term for Afro-Bahian pop music from Salvador popularized in the 1990s

Babalorixá A male priest in the Candomblé religion

Baianas Literally meaning "a female from Bahia"; in samba schools and maracatu nations during Carnival, the term is used to refer to female dancers dressed in Candomblé clothing

Baiano Literally meaning "a male or something from Bahia"; the term is used for a fast and syncopated rhythm in the Northeast that is related to the baião.

Baião Syncopated dance music from the Northeast first popularized by Luiz Gonzaga; the term also refers to the performance segments of cantoria de viola

Batucada Afro-Brazilian samba drumming on a variety percussion instruments of the samba schools that accompanies dance

Batuqueiros Afro-Brazilian drummers in the maracatu nations

Berimbau A one-stringed musical bow from Central Africa that is used in capoeira

Bloco afro Type of black Carnival group from Salvador da Bahia that emerged in the 1970s and celebrated African and black cultural heritages.

Bloco carnavalesco Type of Carnival group from Recife that performs songs in a march rhythm known as frevo de bloco.

Bloco de índio Type of Carnival group in Salvador da Bahia from the late 1960s that adopted the imagery of North American Hollywood Indians.

Caboclinho Type of Recife Carnival group that dresses in stylized Indian outfits and features music with a small flute, metal shakers, and a drum

Caboclo Mixed-race population (mestizo) comprising primarily European and Amerindian heritage, associated with the northeastern interior

Candomblé Afro-Brazilian religion found especially in Salvador da Bahia and in Recife, Pernambuco; the music of Candomblé uses three atabaque drums, agogô bells, and the agbe gourd shaker

Cantoria The singing of improvised poetry in the Northeast involving song duels between two singers.

Capoeira Afro-Brazilian martial-arts dance and music form popular in Bahia

Cavaquinho A small four-string guitar of Portuguese origin popular in samba, choro, and many other Brazilian music styles.

Choro Literally crying, an instrumental style of music featuring string and wind instruments that emerged in Rio de Janeiro in the second half of the nineteenth century

Clube pedestre Working-class pedestrian clubs in Recife that helped establish the frevo in the early years of the twentieth century

Coral feminine A female chorus that sings songs known as frevos de bloco in the blocos carnavalescos of Recife's Carnival

Cuíca A friction drum with a bamboo stick embedded in the skin that is rubbed to produce unusual squeaking sounds; this instrument is used in the samba schools

Embolada A tongue-twister song form with comical lyrics and a rapid-fire singing style, typically accompanied by a pandeiro or a shaker

Escolas de Samba Recreational Carnival associations in Rio de Janeiro and in other Brazilian cities that organize elaborate parades featuring percussive samba music and dancing

Fanfarra Brass, wind, and percussion bands that perform frevo music in the streets during Carnival in Recife

Forró Urban northeastern-style country dance music played by ensembles with accordion, triangle, and zabumba drum

Frevo Syncopated dance music from Recife's Carnival

Frevo de bloco Melodic and lyrical style of frevo sung by female choruses and accompanied by string and wind bands known as orquestra de pau e corda

Frevo de rua Fast instrumental frevo that is highly syncopated and played by brass, wind, and percussion bands

Frevo-canção A commercial, solo song frevo that was first popularized in the 1930s

Gonguê Large metal bell used in the maracatu de baque virado

Ialorixá A female priest in Candomblé

Mangue beat An eclectic popular music from Recife that emerged in the 1990s

Maracatu de baque virado African-related music and dance genre of the maracatu nations in Recife that perform in Carnival

Maracatu de orquestra A syncretic form of maracatu that uses brass and wind instruments, also called maracatu de baque solto (maracatu of the free beat)

Marcha carnavalesco Carnival song in a march rhythm

Marcha de bloco An alternative name for the frevo de bloco

Modinha A Brazilian sentimental song form that derives from Portuguese heritage

Orixá The generic term for Afro-Brazilian deities in Candomblé

Orquestra de frevo Professional bands that perform frevo in Recife

Orquestra de pau e corda Literally meaning "orchestra of wood and string," this is the type of ensemble that is used to accompany the frevo de bloco; it includes several guitar-type instruments and light winds such as the flute and clarinet in addition to the pandeiro and surdo

Pandeiro A Brazilian tambourine used in many different types of music

Polka-marcha A hybrid march rhythm of the early twentieth century in Recife that led to the frevo. Also called the marcha-polka

Rancho Type of Carnival group that sings slow march songs (marchas de rancho)

Repique (also **repinique**) A small, high-pitched drum that is played in samba schools and in the blocos afro Carnival groups

Requinta A small clarinet used in military bands and fanfarras in Recife

Samba-reggae A hybrid musical style and rhythm developed by the blocos afro in Salvador in the 1980s

Surdo A double-headed bass drum used in many styles of Brazilian music

Tango brasileiro A hybrid popular music in Brazil at the turn of the twentieth century that developed out of the Argentine tango; the term was often used synonymously with maxixe

Toque Literally meaning "a beat"; this term is used for the rhythmic patterns in the music of Candomblé and in other Afro-Brazian musics

Trios elétricos Electric guitar trios with percussion that perform atop sound trucks in Salvador's Carnival

Viola A ten-string guitar used throughout Brazil

Violão A Brazilian acoustic six-string guitar with nylon strings

Xangô Name of a powerful Orixá in the Candomblé religion; the term is also frequently used as a synonym for Candomblé in Recife

Xote Northeastern adaptation of the schottische

Zabumba A double-headed bass drum used in the banda de pífanos and the accordion trios that play forró and baião music. Also an alternate name for the ensemble known as banda de pífanos

Bibliography

Almeida, Renato. *História da Música Brasileira.* Rio de Janeiro, RJ, Brazil: F. Briguiet,1942.

Almirante (Henrique Foréis Domingues). *No Tempo de Noel Rosa.* Rio de Janeiro, RJ, Brazil: Livraria Francisco Alves Editora S.A., 1977.

Alvarenga, Oneyda. "A Influência Negra na Música Brasileira." *Boletín Latino-Americano de Música* 6 (1946): 357–407.

Alves, Marieta. "Música de Barbeiros." *Revista Brasileira de Folclore* 7, 17 (1967): 5–14.

Andrews, George Reid. *Blacks and Whites in São Paulo, Brazil: 1888–1988.* Madison: University of Wisconsin Press, 1991.

Angelo, Assis. *Eu Vou Contar pra Vocês.* São Paulo, Brazil: Icone, 1990.

Araújo, Rita de Cássia Barbosa de. *Festas: Máscaras do Tempo—Entrudo, Mascarada e Frevo no Carnaval do Recife.* Recife, Brazil: Fundação de Cultura Cidade do Recife, 1996.

Arrais, Raimundo Pereira Alencar. *Recife, Culturas e Confrontos: As Camadas Urbanas na Campanha Salvacionista de 1911.* Natal, Brazil: Editora da Universidada Federal do Rio Grande do Norte, 1998.

Bacelar, Jefferson. "Blacks in Salvador: Racial Paths." In *Black Brazil: Culture, Identity, and Social Mobilization,* edited by Larry Crook and Randal Johnson, 85–101. Los Angeles: UCLA Latin American Center Publications, University of California, Los Angeles, 1999.

Barboza, Marilia T., and Arthur L. de Oliveira Filho. *Filho de Ogum Bexiguento.* Rio de Janeiro, Brazil: Edição FUNARTE, 1979.

Bastide, Roger. *The African Religions of Brazil: Toward a Sociology of the Interpenetration of Civilizations.* Baltimore, MD: Johns Hopkins University Press, 1978.

———. *O Candomblé da Bahia: Rito Nagô.* Translated by Maria Isaura Pereira de Queiroz. São Paulo, Brazil: Companhia das Letras, 2001.

Béhague, Gerard. "Notes on Regional and National Trends in Afro-Brazilian Cult Music." In *Tradition and Renewal,* edited by Merlin H. Forester, 68–80. Urbana, Chicago, and London: University of Illinois Press, 1975.

———. *Music in Latin America: An Introduction.* Englewood Cliffs, NJ: Prentice-Hall, 1979.

———. "Patterns of Candomblé Music Performance: An Afro-Brazilian Religious Setting." In *Performance Practice: Ethnomusicological Perspectives,* edited by Gerard Béhague, 222–54. Westport, CT: Greenwood Press, 1984.

———. "Introduction." In *Music and Black Ethnicity: The Caribbean and South America,* edited by Gerard Béhague, v–xii. Miami, FL: North-South Center Press at the University of Miami, 1994.

———. "Expressões Musicais do Pluralismo. Religioso Afro-Baiano: A Negociação de Identidade." *Brasiliana* 1 (1999): 40–7.

Borba Filho, Hermilo, ed. *Danças Pernambucanas.* Rio de Janeiro, Brazil: Casa do Estudante do Brasil, 1951.

Braga, Júlio. "Candomblé in Bahia: Repression and Resistance." In *Black Brazil: Culture, Identity, and Social Mobilization,* edited by Larry Crook and Randal Johnson, 201–212. Los Angeles: UCLA Latin American Center Publications, University of California, Los Angeles, 1999.

Cabral, Sérgio. *As Escolas de Samba do Rio de Janeiro*. Rio de Janeiro: Lumiar Editora, 1996.
_____. *Pixinguinha: Vida e Obra*. Rio de Janeiro, RJ, Brazil: Lumiar Editora, 1997.
Carneiro, Edison. *Religões Negras: Notas de Etnografia Religiosa*. Rio de Janeiro, Brazil: Civilização Brasileira, 1936.
_____. *Folguedos Tradicionais*. Rio de Janeiro, Brazil: Conquista, 1974.
Carvalho, José Jorge de. "Black Music of All Colors: The Construction of Black Ethnicity in Ritual and Popular Genres of Afro-Brazilian Music." In *Music and Black Ethnicity: The Caribbean and South America*, edited by Gerard Béhague, 187–206. Miami, FL: North-South Center Press at the University of Miami, 1994.
Carvalho, José Jorge de, and Rita Laura Segato. *Shango Cult in Recife, Brazil*. Caracas: FUNDEF/CIDEF/OEA, 1992.
Carvalho, Leandro. "A Música para Violão de Heitor Villa-Lobos e João Pernambuco." In *ANAIS: Primeiro Simpósio Latino-Americano de Musicologia*, edited by Elizabeth Seraphim Prosser and Paulo Castanho, 255–64. Curitiba, Brazil: Fundação Cultural de Curitiba, 1997.
Cascudo, Luís da Câmara. *Vaqueiros e Cantadores: Folclore Poética do Sertão do Ceará, Paraíba, Rio Grande do Norte e Pernambuco*. 1939. Reprint, Rio de Janeiro, Brazil: Ediouro, 2000.
Cazes, Henrique. *Choro: Do Quintal ao Municipal*. São Paulo, Brazil: Editora 34, 1999.
Cearense, Catulo da Paixão. *Modinhas*. 1943. Reprint, São Paulo, Brazil: Editora Fermata do Brasil, 1972.
Cerqueira, Nelson. *Carnaval da Bahia: Um Registro Estético*. Salvador, BA, Brazil: Omar, 2002.
Chasteen, John Charles. "The Prehistory of Samba: Carnival Dancing in Rio de Janeiro, 1840–1917." *Journal of Latin American Studies* 28, 1 (1966): 29–47.
Costa, Francisco Augusto Pereira da. *Folk-Lore Pernambucano*. Rio de Janeiro, Brazil: Livraria, 1908.
Crook, Larry. "Zabumba Music from Caruaru, Pernambuco: Musical Style, Gender, and the Interpenetration of Rural and Urban Worlds." Ph.D. diss., University of Texas, 1991.
_____. "Black Consciousness, Samba-Reggae, and the Re-Africanization of Bahian Carnival Music in Brazil." *World of Music* 35, 2 (1993): 90–108.
_____. "Brazil/Northeast Brazil." In *Music in Latin American Culture: Regional Traditions*, edited by John Schechter, 192–235. New York: Schirmer Books, 1999.
_____. "Turned-Around Beat: *Maracatu de Baque Virado* and Chico Science." In *Brazilian Popular Music and Globalization*, edited by Charles A. Perrone and Christopher Dunn, 233–44. Gainesville: University of Florida Press, 2001.
Crook, Larry, and Randal Johnson, eds. *Black Brazil: Culture, Identity, and Social Mobilization*. Los Angeles: UCLA Latin American Center Publications, University of California, Los Angeles, 1999.
Crowley, Daniel J. *African Myth and Black Reality in Bahian Carnaval*. Los Angeles, CA: Museum of Cultural History, UCLA, 1984.
Dicionário Cravo Albin da Música Popular Brasileira. "João Bahiana." Website at http://www.dicionariompb.com.br/detalhe.asp?nome=Jo%E3o+da+Bahiana&tabela=T_FORM_A&qdetalhe=bio (accessed January 19, 2008).
Diniz, Jaime C. *Músicos Pernambucanos do Passado*. Vol. 2. Recife, Brazil: Universidade Federal de Pernambuco, 1971.
_____. *Músicos Pernambucanos do Passado*. Vol. 3. Recife, Brazil: Universidade Federal de Pernambuco, 1979.
Drewel, Henry John "Art History, Agency, and Identity: Yoruba Transcultural Currents in the Making of Black Brazil." In *Black Brazil: Culture, Identity, and Social Mobilization*, edited by Larry Crook and Randal Johnson, 143–174. Los Angeles: UCLA Latin American Center Publications, University of California, Los Angeles, 1999.
Dreyfus, Dominique. *Vida de Viajante: A Saga de Luiz Gonzaga*. São Paulo, Brazil: Editora 34, 1996.
Duarte, Abelardo. *Folclore das Alagoas: Pesquisa e Interpretação*. Maceió, Brazil: Departamento de Assuntos Culturais/SENEC, 1974.
Duarte, Ruy. *História Social do Frevo*. Rio de Janeiro, RJ, Brazil: Ed. Leitura, 1968.
Dunn, Christopher. "Tropicália, Counterculture, and the Diasporic Imagination in Brazil." In *Brazilian Popular Music and Globalization*, edited by Charles A. Perrone and Christopher Dunn, 72–95. Gainesville: University Press of Florida, 2000.
Félix, Anísio. "Batucadas e Escolas de Samba no Carnaval Baiano." In *Carnaval da Bahia: Um Registro Estético*, edited by Nelson Cerqueira, 60–7. Salvador, Brazil: Omar, 2002.
Filho, Mário. *Se essa Rua Fosse Minha: Homenagem ao Valoroso Clube Carnavalesco Mixto Vassourinhas do Recife*. Recife, Brazil: Companhia Editora de Pernambuco, 1990.
Freyre, Gilberto. *The Masters and the Slaves: A Study in the Development of Brazilian Civilization*. Translated from the 1933 original by Samuel Putnam. New York: Alfred A. Knopf, 1946.
_____. *The Mansions and the Shanties (Sobrados e Mucambos): The Making of Modern Brazil*. Translated from the 1936 original by Harriet de Onís. New York: Alfred A. Knopf, 1968.
Fry, Peter, Sérgio Carrara, and Ana Luiza Martins-Costa. "Negros e Brancos no Carnaval da Velha República." In *Escravidão e Invenção da Liberdade: Estudos sobre o Negro no Brasil*, organized by João José Reis, 232–63. São Paulo, Brazil: Editora Brasiliense, co-edited with Conselho Nacional de Desenvolvimento Científico e Tecnológico, 1988.
Fryer, Peter. *Rhythms of Resistance: African Musical Heritage in Brazil*. Middletown, CT: Wesleyan University Press and Hanover, NH: University Press of New England, 2000.

Galinsky, Philip. *"Maracatu Atômico": Tradition, Modernity, and Postmodernity in the Mangue Movement of Recife, Brazil*. New York: Routledge, 2002.

Gilroy, Paul. *The Black Atlantic: Modernity and Double Consciousness*. Cambridge, MA: Harvard University Press, 1993.

Godi, Antonio Jorge Victor dos Santos. "Presença Afro-Carnavalesca Soteropolitana." In *Carnaval da Bahia: Um Registro Estético*, edited by Nelson Cerqueira, 94–111. Salvador, BA, Brazil: Omar, 2002.

Góes, Fred de. *O País do Carnaval Elétrico*. Salvador, Brazil: Corrupio, 1982.

Gonçalves Fernandes, Albino. *Xangôs do Nordeste: Investigações sobre os Cultos Negro-Fetichistas do Recife*. Rio de Janeiro, Brazil: Civilização Brasileira, 1937.

Graham, Richard. *Britain and the Onset of Modernization in Brazil, 1850–1914*. Cambridge: Cambridge University Press, 1968.

Guerra-Peixe, César. "A Provável Próxima Decadência do Frêvo." In Diário da Noite. January 27. Recife, Brazil, 1951.

_____. *Maracatus do Recife*. 1955. Reprinted São Paulo, Brazil: Irmãos Vitale, 1980.

Hanchard, Michael, ed. *Racial Politics in Contemporary Brazil*. Durham, NC: Duke University Press, 1999.

Hasenbalg, Carlos "Perspectives on Race and Class in Brazil." In *Black Brazil: Culture, Identity, and Social Mobilization*, edited by Larry Crook and Randal Johnson, 61–84. Los Angeles: UCLA Latin American Center Publications, University of California, Los Angeles, 1999.

Irmão, José Pedro Damião. *Tradicionais Bandas de Música*. Recife, Brazil: Companhia Editora de Pernambuco, 1970.

Kazadi wa Mukuna. *An Interdisciplinary Study of the Ox and the Slave (Bumba-meu-Boi): A Satirical Music Drama in Brazil*. Lewiston, NY: E. Mellen Press, 2003.

Koster, Henry, and C. Harvey Gardiner. *Travels in Brazil*. Carbondale: Southern Illinois University Press, 1966.

Leal, José de Souza, and Artur Luiz Barbosa. *João Pernambuco: Arte de um Povo*. Rio de Janeiro, Brazil: Edição FUNARTE, 1982.

Leite, Serafim. *História da Companhia de Jesus no Brasil*. Vol. 5. Lisbon: Livraria Portugália, 1938.

Levine, Robert M. "'Mud-Hut Jerusalem': Canudos Revisited," *Hispanic American Historical Review* 68, 3 (1988), 525–72.

_____. *Vale of Tears: Revisiting the Canudos Massacre in Northeastern Brazil, 1893–1897*. Berkeley: University of California Press, 1992.

Lewis, J. Lowell. *Ring of Liberation: Deceptive Discourse in Brazilian Capoeira*. Chicago and London: University of Chicago Press, 1992.

Lima, Oliveira. *Dom João VI no Brasil, 1808–1821*. Vol. 3. Rio de Janeiro, Brazil: Livraria José Olympio Editora, 1945.

Livingston-Isenhour, Tamara Elena and Thomas George Caracas Garcia. *Choro: A Social History of a Brazilian Popular Music*. Bloomington and Indianapolis: Indiana University Press, 2005.

Lody, Raul Giovanni da Motta. *Afoxé*. Rio de Janeiro, Brazil: Ministério da Educação e Cultura Departamento de Assuntos Culturais Fundação Nacional de Arte Campanha de Defesa do Folclore Brasileiro, 1976.

Lühning, Angela E. "O Compositor Mozart Camargo Guarnieri e o 2º Congresso Afro-Brasileiro em Salvador, 1937 (Homenagem Póstuma)." In *Ritmos em Trânsito: Sócio-Antropologia da Música Baiana*, edited by Livio Sansone and Jocélio Teles dos Santos, 59–72. São Paulo, Brazil: Dynamis Editorial; Salvador, Brazil: Programa A Cord a Bahia e Projeto S.A.M.BA., 1997.

Matta, Roberto da. *Carnivals, Rogues, and Heroes: An Interpretation of the Brazilian Dilemma*. Notre Dame, IN: University of Notre Dame Press, 1991.

McCann, Bryan. *Hello, Hello, Brazil: Popular Music in the Making of Modern Brazil*. Durham, NC: Duke University Press, 2004.

McGowan, Chris, and Ricardo Pessanha. *The Brazilian Sound: Samba, Bossa Nova, and the Popular Music of Brazil*. Philadelphia: Temple University Press, 1998.

Mendoza de Arce, Daniel. *Music in Ibero-America to 1850: A Historical Survey*. Lanham, MD: Scarecrow Press, 2001.

Moehn, Frederick. "Mixing MPB: Cannibals and Cosmopolitans in Brazilian Popular Music." Ph.D. diss., New York University, 2001.

Morales, Anamaria. "O Afoxé Filhos de Gandhi Pede Paz." In *Escravidão e Invenção da Liberdade: Estudos sobre o Negro no Brasil*, organized by João José Reis, 264–74. São Paulo, Brazil: Editora Brasiliense, co-edited with Conselho Nacional de Desenvolvimento Científico e Tecnológico, 1988.

Moura, Fernando, and Antônio Vicente. *Jackson do Pandeiro: O Rei do Ritmo*. São Paulo, SP, Brazil: Grupo Pão de Açucar/Editora 34, 2001.

Moura, Milton Araújo. "World of Fantasy, Fantasy of the World: Geographic Space and Representation of Identity in the Carnival of Salvador, Bahia." In *Brazilian Popular Music and Globalization*, edited by Charles A. Perrone and Christopher Dunn, 161–176. Gainesville: University Press of Florida, 2001.

Movimento Negro Unificado. *10 Anos de Luta Contra o Racismo*. São Paulo, SP, Brazil: Confraria do Brasil, 1988.

Murphy, John Patrick. "Performing a Moral Vision: An Ethnography of Cavalo-Marinho, a Brazilian Musical Drama." Ph.D. diss., Columbia University, 1994.

_____. "Self-Discovery in Brazilian Popular Music: Mestre Ambrósio." In *Brazilian Popular Music and Globalization*, edited by Charles A. Perrone and Christopher Dunn, 245–57. Gainesville: University of Florida Press, 2001.

_____. *Music in Brazil: Experiencing Music, Expressing Culture*. New York: Oxford University Press, 2006.

Nepomuceno, Rosa. *Música Caipira: Da Roça ao Rodeio*. São Paulo, Brazil: Editora 34, 1999.

Nina Rodrigues, Raymundo. *Os Africanos no Brasil*. São Paulo, SP, Brazil: Companhia Editora Nacional, 1932.

"O Eterno Rei do Baião." *Veja e Leia* 184 (1972): 80–2.

Oliveira, Valdemar de. "O Frevo e o Passo, de Pernambuco." *Boletín Latino-Americano de Música* 6 (1946): 157–92.

_____. *Frevo, Capoeira e "Passo."* Recife, Brazil: Companhia Editôra de Pernambuco, 1985.

Oliveira, Walter de. *Nelson Ferreira*. Recife, PE, Brazil: Governo do Estado de Pernambuco/Secretaria de Turismo Cultra e Esportes, 1985.

Perrone, Charles A. *Masters of Contemporary Brazilian Song: MPB 1965–1985*. Austin: University of Texas Press, 1989.

Perrone, Charles A., and Christopher Dunn. "'Chiclete com Banana': Internationalization in Brazilian Popular Music." In *Brazilian Popular Music and Globalization*, edited by Charles A. Perrone and Christopher Dunn, 1–38. Gainesville: University Press of Florida, 2001.

Pierson, Donald. *Negroes in Brazil: A Study of Race Contact at Bahia*. Carbondale: Southern Illinois University Press, 1967.

Pinho, Osmundo de Araújo. "'Fogo na Babilônia': Reggae, Black Culture, and Globalization in Brazil." In *Brazilian Popular Music and Globalization*, edited by Charles A. Perrone and Christopher Dunn, 192–206. Gainesville: University Press of Florida, 2000.

Prado Junior, Caio. *The Colonial Background of Modern Brazil*. Translated by Suzette Macedo. Berkeley: University of California Press, 1967.

Rabello, Evandro. "'Vassourinhas' Foi Compositada em 1909." *Diário de Pernambuco* (January 4, 1987): Section B, 1.

_____. "A Aparecimento da Palavra Frevo." *Revista de História Municipal* 7 (1997): 93–99.

Ramalho, Elba Braga. "Luiz Gonzaga: His Life and His Music." Ph.D. diss., University of Liverpool, 1997.

_____. *Luiz Gonzaga: A Síntese Poética e Musical do Sertão*. São Paulo, SP, Brazil: Terceira Margem, 2000.

Real, Katarina. *O Folklore no Carnaval do Recife*. Recife, Brazil: Fundaçao Joaquim Nabuco/Editora Massangana, 1990.

Reily, Suzel Ana. "*Música Sertaneja* and Migrant Identity: The Stylistic Development of a Brazilian Genre." *Popular Music* 11, 3 (1992): 337–58.

_____. "Hybridity and Segregation in the Guitar Cultures of Brazil." In *Guitar Cultures*, edited by Andy Bennett and Kevin Dawe, 157–177. Oxford, New York: Berg Publishers, 2001.

_____. *Voices of the Magi: Enchanted Journeys in Southeast Brazil*. Chicago: University of Chicago Press, 2002.

Rennefort, Urbain Souchut de. *Histoire des Indes Orientales*. Paris, France: Leide, Chez F. Harring, 1688.

Ribeiro, René. *Cultos Afro-Brasileiros do Recife: Um Estudo de Ajustamento Social*. Recife, PE, Brazil: Instituto Joaquim Nabuco de Pesquisas Sociais, 1978.

Risério, Antônio. *Carnaval Ijexá*. Salvador, Brasil: Corrupio, 1981.

_____, ed. *Gilberto Gil: Expresso 2222*. Salvador, BA, Brazil: Corrupio, 1982.

Roberts, John Storm. *The Black Music of Two Worlds: African, Caribbean, Latin, and African-American Traditions*. New York: Schirmer Books, 1998.

Rodrigues, Antônio Guilherme. "'Tá Sobrando Mulher,' Mas Está Faltando Frevo . . ." *Diário da Noite* (January 15, 1951).

Rodrigues, Edson. "Abafo, Ventania e Coqueiro." In *Antologia do Carnaval do Recife*, edited by Mário Souto Maior and Leonardo Dantas Silva, 67–72. Recife, PE, Brazil: Fundação Joaquim Nabuco/Editora Massangana, 1991.

Rodrigues, João Jorge Santos. "Olodum and the Black Struggle in Brazil." In *Black Brazil: Culture, Identity, and Social Mobilization*, edited by Larry Crook and Randal Johnson, 43–52. Los Angeles: UCLA Latin American Center Publications, University of California, Los Angeles, 1999.

Rodrigues, Nina Raymundo. *Os Africanos no Brasil*. São Paulo, Brazil: Companhia Editora Nacional, 1932.

Sansone, Livio, and Jocélio Teles dos Santos, eds. 1997. *Ritmos em Trânsito: Sócio-Antropologia da Música Baiana*. São Paulo, SP, Brazil: Dynamis Editorial; Salvador, BA, Brazil: Programa A Cor da Bahia e Projeto S.A.M.BA., 1997

Santana, Rosane. "Entrevista Anônio dos Santos, Vovô, Presidente do Bloco Ilê Aiyê." In *Carnaval da Bahia: Um Registro Estético*, edited by Nelson Cerqueira, 112–23. Salvador, Brazil: Omar, 2002.

Santos, Juana Elbein dos. "O Afoxé e o Africanismo Baiano." *Tribuna da Bahia*, (March 23, 1974).

Santos, Luís Gonçalves dos. *Memórias para Servir à História do Brasil*. Rio de Janeiro, RJ, Brazil: Livraria Editora Zélio Valverde, 1943.

Segato, Rita Laura. *Santos e Diamantes: O Politeísmo Afro-Brasileiro e a Tradição Arquetipal*. Brasília: Editora Universidade de Brasília, 1995.

Sette, Mário. *Maxambombas e Maracatus*, 4th ed. São Paulo, Brazil: Edições Cultura Brasileira, 1981.

Severiano, Jairo, and Zuza Homem de Mello. *A Cançao no Tempo: 85 Anos de Músicas Brasileiras*. São Paulo, Brazil: Editora 34, 1997.

Silva, Leonardo Dantas. "Elementos para a História Social do Carnaval do Recife." In *Antologia do Carnaval do Recife*, edited by Mário Souto Maior and Leonardo Dantas Silva, XI–XCVIII. Recife, PE, Brazil: Fundação Joaquim Nabuco/Editora Massangana, 1991a.

_____. "O Frevo Pernambucano." In *Antologia do Carnaval do Recife*, edited by Mário Souto Maior and Leonardo Dantas Silva, 193–212. Recife, Brazil: Fundação Joaquim Nabuco/Editora Massangana, 1991b.

_____. "Quando Maracatu Era Caso de Polícia." *Suplemento Cultural. Diário Official, Estado de Pernambuco,* Ano X (February 1997): 5. Recife, Brazil: Companhia Editora de Pernambuco.

_____. *Bandas Musicais de Pernambuco, História Social.* Recife, PE, Brazil: Governo do Estado de Pernambuco, 1998a.

_____. "Blocos Carnavalescos do Recife-História Social." In *Bocos Carnavalescos do Recife: Origins e Repertório*, edited by Leonardo Dantas Silva, 11–58. Recife, Brazil: Governo do Estado de Pernambuco, 1998b.

_____. "500 Anos de Fé: A Música das Procissões." In *Marchas de Procissão*, organized by Paulo Bruscky, 11–22. Recife, Brazil: Companhia Editora de Pernambuco, 1998c.

_____. *Carnaval do Recife.* Recife, Brazil: Prefeitura da Cidade do Recife Fundação de Cultura Cidade do Recife, 2000.

Skidmore, Thomas E. *Black into White: Race and Nationality in Brazilian Thought, with a Preface to the 1993 Edition and Bibliography.* Durham, NC: Duke University Press, 1993.

Sociedade Recreativa e Carnavalesca Filhos de Gandhy. http://geocities.yahoo.com.br/filhosdegandhy/index.htm.

Souto Maior, Mário, and Leonardo Dantas Silva. *Antologia do Carnaval do Recife.* Recife, Brazil: Fundação Joaquim Nabuco Editora Massangana, 1991.

Souza, Marina de Mello e. *Reis Negros no Brasil Escravista: História da Festa de Coroação de Rei Congo.* Belo Horizonte, MG, Brazil: Editora UFMG, 2002.

Suassuna, Ariano. "Notas Sôbre a Música de Capiba." In *É de Tororó: Maracatu*, edited by Hermilo Borba Filho, Ascenço Ferreira, Ariano Suassuna, Capiba, Lula Cardoso Ayres, and Percy Lau, 33–65. Rio de Janeiro, Brazil: Livraria-Editôra da Casa do Estudante do Brasil, 1951.

Taylor, Timothy Dean. *Global Pop: World Music, World Markets.* New York: Routledge, 1997.

Teixeira, Cid. "Carnaval Entre as Duas Guerras." In *Carnaval da Bahia: Um Registro Estético*, edited by Nelson Cerqueira, 42–59. Salvador, Brazil: Omar, 2002.

Teles, José. *Do Frevo ao Manguebeat.* São Paulo, Brazil: Editora 34, 2000.

Tinhorão, José Ramos. *Pequena História da Música Popular: Da Modinha ao Tropicalismo.* São Paulo, Brazil: Art Editora, 1986.

_____. *Os Sons dos Negros no Brasil: Cantos, Danças, Folguedos, Origens.* São Paulo, Brazil: Art Editora, 1988.

_____. *História Social da Música Popular Brasileira.* São Paulo, SP, Brazil: Editora 34, 1998.

_____. *As Festas no Brasil Colonial.* São Paulo, Brazil: Editora 34, 2000.

Veloso, Caetano. "Carmen Mirandada." In *Brazilian Popular Music and Globalization*, edited by Charles A. Perrone and Christopher Dunn, 39–45. Gainesville: University Press of Florida, 2001.

Verger, Pierre. *Centro Histórico de Salvador: 1946 a 1952.* São Paulo, SP, Brazil: Corrupio, 1989.

Verger, Pierre, and Aparecida Nóbrega. *Retratos da Bahia, 1946 a 1952.* Salvador, BA, Brazil: Corrupio, 1980.

Vianna, Hermano. *The Mystery of Samba: Popular Music and National Identity in Brazil.* Chapel Hill: University of North Carolina Press, 1999.

Vieira, Sulamita. *O Sertão em Movimento: A Dinâmica da Produção Cultural.* São Paulo, Brazil: Annablume, 2000.

Vieira Filho, Raphael Rodrigues. "Folguedos Negros no Carnaval de Salvador (1880–1930)." In *Ritmos em Trânsito: Sócio-Antropologia da Música Baiana*, edited by Livio Sansone and Jocélio Teles dos Santos, 39–57. São Paulo, SP, Brazil: Dynamis Editorial and Salvador, BA, Brazil: Programa A Cor da Bahia e Projeto S.A.M.BA., 1998.

Waddey, Ralph. "Viola de Samba and Samba de Viola in the Recôncavo of Bahia (Brazil)." *Latin American Music Review* 1, 2 (1980): 196–212.

Wilner, Flávio. "Marcos Suzano: O Pandeiro Rouba o Lugar da Bateria." *Revista Backstage* 3, 24 (1997): 44–9.

Discography

A Arte da Cantoria: Regras da Cantoria. CD. FUNARTE ATR 32007, 1998.

Alegria, Alegria, Carnaval da Bahia '82. LP. Bacarrola 020.009, 1982.

Ara Ketu. *Ara Ketu*. LP. Continental LP 1–01–404–327, 1987.

Araújo, Manezinho. *Manezinho Araújo: Cuma É o Nome Dele?* CD. Revivendo RVCD-109, 2003.

Bahia Black: Ritual Beating System. CD. Axiom 314–510 856–2, 1992.

Banda de Frevo da Polícia Militar de Pernambuco. *O Têma é Frevo*, vol. 2. LP. Discos Rozenblit, Série Arquivo LP 90.015, 1982.

Banda Mel. *Força Interior*. LP. Continental LP 1–01–404–317, 1987.

Carlos Malta and Pife Muderno. *Carlos Malta e Pife Muderno*. CD. Rob Digital RD 017, 1999.

_____. *Paru*. CD. Delira Música LD 258, 2005.

Cascabulho. *Fome Dá Dor de Cabeça*. CD. Mangroove MR 0020, 1998.

_____. *É Caco de Vidro Puro*. CD. Via Som VS 200218/Atração Fonográfica ATR 31112, 2005.

Chico Science & Nação Zumbi. *Da Lama ao Caos*. CD. Chaos 850.224/2–464476, 1994.

_____. *Afrociberdelia*. CD. Sony Music CDZ-81996 2–479255, 1996.

Coral Edgard Moraes. *Coral Edgard Moraes—Frevos de Bloco*. CD. LG Projetos e Produções Artísticas LG 000.015, 1996.

Ferreira, Edmilson, and Antônio Lisboa. *É Feito de Fato*. CD. Independent, n.d.

Frevos de Rua: Os Melhores do Século, vol. 1. CD. LG Projetos e Produções. LG 000.010, 1998.

Gil, Gilberto. *Refavela*. LP. Philips 6349 329, 1977.

_____. *Um Banda Um*. LP. WEA BR 26 063, 1982.

_____. *As Canções de Eu, Tu, Eles*. CD. Warner Music Brazil WEA 857382768–2, 2000.

Gil, Gilberto, and Jorge Bem. *Gil e Jorge—Ogum Xangô*. LP. Verve 314 512 067, 1975.

Gonzaga, Luiz. *Luiz Gonzaga: 50 Anos de Chão*. CD (3 disc set). BMG/RCA 7432129416–2, 1996.

Ilê Aiyê. *Ilê Aiyê—Canto Negro*. LP. Odebrecht, 1984.

_____. *Ilê Aiyê, 25 Anos*. CD. Natasha Records 289.133, 1999.

Jackson do Pandeiro. *Sua Majestade—O Rei do Ritmo*. CD. EMI Copacabana 472644–2, 1998. Originally issued as LP in 1954.

_____. *Forró do Jackson*. CD. EMI Copabanana 472645–2, 1998. Originally issued as LP in 1958.

João do Pife and the Banda de Pífanos Dois Irmãos. *Flute and Drum Music from Northeastern Brazil*. CD. Nimbus Records NI 5635, 2001.

Lenine e Suzano. *Olho de Peixe*. CD. Independent CD-LS001, 1993.

Maracatu Nação Pernambuco. *Nação Pernambuco*. CD. Velas 11-V016, 1993.

_____. 2000. *Dez Anos de Baque Solto Virado*. CD. Independent, n.d.

Mendes, Sergio. *Brasileiro*. CD. Elektra 9 61315, 1992.

Mercury, Daniela. *O Canto da Cidade*. CD. Columbia CD 850.172/2–464348, 1992.

_____. *Feijão com Arroz*. CD. Sony Latin CDZ-82118 2–479390, 1997.

Mestre Ambrósio. *Mestre Ambrósio*. CD. Terreiro Discos TDCD 001, 2000. Originally issued in 1994.

Moreira, Moraes. *La Vem o Brasil Descendo a Ladeira*. LP. Sigla 403 6198, 1979.

_____. *Bazaar Brasileiro*. LP. Ariola 201609, 1980.

Musique du Nordeste, vol. 1: 1916–1945. CD. Buda Musique 82960–2, n.d.

Musique du Nordeste, vol. 2: 1928–1946. CD. Buda Musique 82969–2, n.d.

Muzenza. *Som Luxuoso*. LP. Continental LP 1–01–404–359, 1988a.

_____. *Muzenza do Reggae*. LP. Continental LP 1–01–404–332, 1988b.

Nascimento, Milton. *Yauaretê*. CD. CBS 231023, 1987.

Olodum. *Egito Madagáscar*. LP. BR Continental 1–01–404–325, 1987.

Reflexu's. *Da Mãe Africa*. LP. EMI Odeon LP 062–747544, 1987.

Simon, Paul. *Rhythm of the Saints*. CD. WB 26098, 1990.

SpokFrevo Orquestra. *Passo de Anjo*. CD. Viasom VS 200220, 2004.

Suzano, Marcus. *Sambatown*. CD. Warner Music Brazil MP, P 063016719–2, 1996.

Timbalada. *Timbalada*. CD. Philips 314–518–068, 1993.

_____. *Cada Cabeça É um Mundo*. PolyGram 522–813, 1994.

Veloso, Caetano. *Transa*. LP. Philips 6349 026, 1972.

Index

Note: *italic* page numbers denote references to Figures.